Shared Symbols,
Contested Meanings

SHARED SYMBOLS, CONTESTED MEANINGS

Gros Ventre Culture and History, 1778–1984

《 》

LORETTA FOWLER

CORNELL UNIVERSITY PRESS

Ithaca and London

First published 1987 by Cornell University Press.
First printing, Cornell Paperbacks, 1987.

International Standard Book Number (cloth) 0-8014-1878-X
International Standard Book Number (paper) 0-8014-9450-8
Library of Congress Catalog Card Number 86-47976

Printed in the United States of America

*Librarians: Library of Congress cataloging information
appears on the last page of the book.*

⊛The paper in this book meets the minimum requirements of the
American National Standard for Information Sciences—Permanence
of Paper for Printed Library Materials, ANSI Z39.48-1984.

paper: 9 8 7 6 5 4 3

To Regina Flannery Herzfeld

Contents

Contents

Maps and Illustrations

Maps

Illustrations

Illustrations

Acknowledgments

The Gros Ventre and Assiniboine people of northern Montana showed keen interest in my research and were unfailingly generous with their time, advice, and knowledge. During the six years I visited and, for several months at a time, lived on the reservation, I was extended every courtesy and formed friendships that I hope will last a lifetime. Rather than mention by name the sixty-some individuals who worked with me from 1979 to 1985, graciously instructing me in matters of etiquette, cultural perspective, and social relationships, I express my gratitude to the community as a whole.

I extend special thanks to a panel of tribal members who read and reviewed all or parts of the manuscript. Seven individuals—including Gros Ventres and Assiniboines, old and young, male and female—corrected errors and suggested ways to improve the analysis, and the Planning Department of the tribal government carefully checked factual material related to contemporary economics and demography. Some difference of opinion emerged among the members of the review panel. Some Assiniboines felt that their tribe was slighted by the expanded treatment of Gros Ventre history or by the presentation of Gros Ventre views that differed from their own. (And although most Gros Ventres were pleased with the analysis in Chapter 1, one felt that to discuss the Assiniboine perspective was to show bias against the Gros Ventres.) In response to the Assiniboine concern, I stress that I was led to focus on the Gros Ventres in large part by the fact that no other anthropologist was studying this group's lifeways, whereas three others were involved in Assiniboine ethnohistorical and ethnographic research.

The tribal review panel also thought that I should stress at the outset to the general reader (and the reader at Fort Belknap) that the numerous quotations throughout the book do not necessarily represent fact, but rather express the opinions of particular individuals. Thus, when a federal official makes a derogatory remark about one of the tribes or a tribal member compares the other tribe unfavorably with his own, their views do not represent my views, nor are they intended as factual characterizations. I have used these quotations to shed light on Indian–white relations or on attitudes that were held in some quarters at a particular point in time; quotations of this sort should not be construed as support for prejudice.

A third area of concern was the fact that the second half of the book deals with diversity in viewpoints at Fort Belknap. That such diversity exists is not questioned. But some (not all) reviewers worried that outsiders might be led to view Fort Belknap as conflict-ridden, that this material might present the people in a negative light. And some would be more pleased if their view of history were accepted as the correct one, rather than one of several views. I have to say, in all honesty, that the average reader at Fort Belknap probably will not see the value in my focus on how variations, contested meanings, stimulate creativity and adaptive change. But, in the last analysis, this book is written for a wide audience. Its goal is to encourage a more realistic view of contemporary Native Americans and a more sophisticated approach to the study of change. From this perspective, Fort Belknap is not inordinately conflict-ridden. Culture is not uniform throughout any society and contested meanings play a role in social change in all societies, not just Native American ones.

My approach to the study of culture and history is, then, not completely compatible with that of all Gros Ventres and Assiniboines. The tribes, however, have an excellent education department that to date has published two collections of oral history (*War Stories of the White Clay People* and *Recollections of Fort Belknap's Past*). I cannot, nor would I wish to, duplicate their noteworthy efforts. I hope that Gros Ventre and Assiniboine individuals, as well as the tribal office, will continue to write their history from their own perspective, and I would like this book to lend support to their efforts through its listing of archival and published sources. And, whether or not the people of Fort Belknap agree with all my interpretations of their culture and history, I hope that they see my affection and admiration for their community in the following pages.

Much of my research was done at archives: Special Collections, Montana State University; Montana Historical Society; Archives, Marquette University; Archives, Beinecke Rare Book and Manuscript

Library, Yale University; American Museum of Natural History, New York; Missouri Historical Society; Federal Archives and Record Center, Seattle; Oregon Province Archives of the Society of Jesus; National Archives; Hudson's Bay Company Archives, Provincial Archives of Manitoba. My work was facilitated by the expert assistance of the staffs of these institutions. And without access to the field notes of Regina Flannery Herzfeld, this work would not have been possible. Finally, I am grateful to the law offices of Wilkinson, Cragun & Barker, where I was permitted to consult the firm's files on Gros Ventre history.

I also thank several of my colleagues who read all or parts of the manuscript and made helpful suggestions: May Ebihara, Nancy Foner, Regina Flannery Herzfeld, Maria LaVigna. From his perspective as a Plains specialist, Raymond DeMallie made comments that were particularly useful. Much of the focus of the book emerged in discussions with Lawrence Rosen, and I am grateful to him for many stimulating conversations. And I owe an immense debt to Karen Blu, who painstakingly reviewed the manuscript and offered many insights that significantly improved the final draft. Finally, an abridged version of Chapter 3 was presented at a symposium, "Culturally Mixed Indian Villages and Communities," organized by Mary Druke at the 1983 Central States Anthropological Society meetings. I thank Mary Druke for including me in the program, for my participation helped the preparation of this chapter.

My stay on Fort Belknap was made particularly pleasant by hospitality extended to me by my friend Irma Gone, who was not involved in my research but helped make my visit there especially enjoyable. And I am grateful to the Dominican Sisters, School Sisters of Saint Francis, and Sienna House in Seattle for many kindnesses.

My field interviews were expertly transcribed and indexed by Ann Morris. John R. Fowler assisted with the research for the maps. Molly Ryan drew the maps. And much of the manuscript was typed by Maria Sanchez. All their efforts helped make this book possible.

The research was funded by grants held under the auspices of the Institute for the Study of Human Issues from the National Endowment for the Humanities (RO-20447-83; RO-20111-81) and the National Institute on Aging (RO1 AG02280), and by grants from the American Philosophical Society and the Research Foundation of the City University of New York.

LORETTA FOWLER

New York, New York

Shared Symbols,
Contested Meanings

Introduction

The road to Fort Belknap reservation goes by one ghost town after another. Small settlements with five or six businesses, now boarded up and deserted, line highway 2, running from east to west through northern Montana. As one draws near Fort Belknap, however, new homes dot the landscape, either occupied or in various stages of completion. The community exudes an air of energy and growth. For the last two decades Fort Belknap reservation has been in a period of resurgence, or, in the words of the Gros Ventre and Assiniboine Indians who live there, "cultural revival."

As one settles in and spends some time at Fort Belknap, other aspects of life there become noticeable, especially to an anthropologist like myself, who has worked on other Plains reservations. When I arrived in 1979, young men in their thirties were in the most prominent political positions and as a group were the most visible in rituals. It is more usual in Plains societies—according to my experience, at least—for elected leaders to be middle-aged and for elderly men to be orators at public gatherings or directors of ceremonies. Moreover, while Indians have tended in recent years to assume positions of authority within the federal bureaucracy that administers reservations, the extent of Indian control at Fort Belknap was striking. Positions that just a few years earlier had been occupied by non-Indians (reservation superintendent and realty officer are notable examples) now were held by Gros Ventres. The tribal attorney was a Gros Ventre, and most of the reservation programs formerly administered by non-Indians now were operated by the Gros Ventres and Assiniboines.

As I began to do archival research about Fort Belknap's history,

1

other intriguing questions came to light. Ever since this reservation was established in the late nineteenth century, federal officials have considered it exceptionally "civilized" and "progressive." From another perspective, several scholars have concluded that the Fort Belknap tribes "lost" their native culture some time ago. These initial findings led me to ask what "civilized" and "progressive" meant to federal officials and what they meant to the native peoples at Fort Belknap, for Gros Ventres and Assiniboines also described themselves in these terms. And I sought to learn what advantages, if any, derived to the Fort Belknap people from progressive behavior—did they fare better than other groups on the Plains in terms of economics or political independence? A related problem that emerged from the study of documents was how to define and trace changes in concepts of identity and how to relate cultural identity to a group's progressive reputation and to the obvious changes in their way of life since their settlement on the reservation. To pursue this point further, did progress, in the officials' sense, inevitably lead to culture loss?

Fort Belknap reservation society and its history present problems of interpretation not only for scholars but also for the Native Americans who live there, for the people themselves can disagree sharply about their culture and history. This is a small, face-to-face community with a population of about 2,000, where people not only know each other and interact regularly but are also kinsmen or in-laws. An array of symbols—political, ritual, sacred—have meaning and emotional impact for all, yet people disagree over the interpretation of these symbols. Often these disagreements are phrased in terms of what is "traditional" and what is not, and what is Gros Ventre tradition as opposed to Assiniboine tradition. Some Gros Ventre people say there are no more "real" Gros Ventres; others say Gros Ventre culture was "revived" several years ago and is now viable, even flourishing in some respects. But not even persons who feel that there are no real Gros Ventres accept the idea that Gros Ventre culture has been replaced by white culture. Moreover, I frequently heard that there are no longer two tribes at Fort Belknap but rather one "Indian community." Yet people are adamant at times that there are Gros Ventre and Assiniboine ways of doing things—of arriving at decisions, exchanging goods, dealing with kin, relating to the supernatural. I also found that narrators of Fort Belknap history have widely contrasting versions of events, relationships, and personalities. Interpretations of history vary not only by tribe but also according to age group. One of the central problems of my fieldwork, then, was how to understand disagreements among the insiders about culture and history. As I came to focus on the Gros

Ventres, I worked to construct a model of the dynamics of Gros Ventre culture and society that took account of and accounted for conflicting and different interpretations as well as cultural continuities.

This book is an account of selected aspects of Gros Ventre culture and history. No study of contemporary Gros Ventre or Fort Belknap society has been published before, despite the unusual and anthropologically interesting features of life there. And while two unpublished manuscripts on the reservation's history exist, neither discusses the culture and society of its people before they settled on the reservation or in the years since the mid-1950s. In this book I focus on Gros Ventre cultural identity and the ways it has been and is now symbolized to the Gros Ventres. I also examine the evolution of the Gros Ventres' culture within the context of their relations with white society and with other Indians. The Gros Ventres' ideas about their identity contribute to and are affected by a generation gap as well as a rivalry with the Assiniboines. This book accounts for the character of intertribal and age-group relations, as well as for the climate of political and ritual resurgence that makes Fort Belknap stand out.

Larger questions can be explored within the framework of Fort Belknap culture and history. Three interrelated issues are considered here. First, what role does a people's interpretation of events and relationships play in the evolution of their cultural identity, how do symbols of identity change, and how do they affect social relations and shape the course of change? Second, what role does intrasocietal variability—specifically, that based on age and tribe—play in culture change and adaptation? Fort Belknap is typical of Plains reservations, and of Native American communities in general, in being comprised of people with varied experiences, interests, and concerns. On the Plains, multitribal reservations are the rule rather than the exception.[1] A cultural gap between generations, often accompanied by social conflict, is commonly found as well. An understanding of Fort Belknap society in all its complexities requires us to discover what meanings are shared and what are not, and why interpretations vary between particular groups of people. In a broader sense, I consider why it is important to confront the fact that culture is not uniform and to explore the implications of that lack of uniformity for such societies as Fort Belknap's. Finally, this book suggests an approach, or rather a combination of approaches (ethnohistory, participant-observation fieldwork, the analysis of folk history, and cohort analysis), to explore the relationship between the past and the present. I ask how particular events over a long time span, and the ways they have been perceived and evaluated, have influenced Gros Ventre (and Fort Belknap) culture

3

and society today. I also examine the influence of contemporary perspectives and concerns on people's interpretations of history and the
social repercussions of those interpretations.

In this book I seek to discover how outside factors, such as contacts
with other peoples and their institutions, and internal variation in the
experience and interpretation of these factors precipitate particular
kinds of changes and differential kinds of adaptations. My approach to
the problems of internal variation and to understanding the dynamics
of change is different from that of many students of Plains culture and
history.

Plains Indian Culture and History: Other Approaches

Anthropologists who have done fieldwork on Plains reservations
recognize great cultural variability there and acknowledge that "there
are many different styles of Indian life" even within the same reservation community.[2] And most studies of contemporary reservation communities recognize that these societies are to a great extent products
of the way they were in the past and of what has happened to them
over time. However, the approaches that typically are used to understand variability and change have serious limitations.

Most anthropologists who have analyzed Plains Indian communities have dealt with the problem of variation and/or disagreement in
one of five ways or through a combination of two or more of these
approaches. Those who construct an idealized, composite abstraction
seek to find a common denominator, to determine what is more or
less uniform, or to build a model of cumulative cultural knowledge.
Others isolate for study one particular group or one group's views and
concerns—the perspective of one of the bands or one of the tribal
divisions, for example, or one age group's view, or the traditionals'
view. Third, variation has been described in terms of degrees of acculturation or assimilation. Those who take this approach assign segments of the population to positions along a continuum from least
white-oriented to most white-oriented. Often the most white-oriented
also are described as "mixed-blood" (having white ancestry) and the
least acculturated as "full-blood" Indian. Fourth, disagreements in
interpretation or point of view have been presented as factionalism—
as reflecting social conflict and schism. Finally, in multitribal communities, even while acknowledging that the tribes' members themselves
recognize cultural differences among the tribes, researchers have
sometimes concluded that tribal culture gave way to a merging or
blend, to "pan-Indian" culture. None of these traditional approaches

4

(which are common in areas other than Plains Indian communities as well) seemed appropriate for the situation at Fort Belknap.

It would have been inappropriate for me to try to build an idealized, composite cultural description, an abstraction of common features shared by all or most Fort Belknap people, or even by all or most Gros Ventres. Pronounced disagreement—often about the meaning of particular rituals in which all took part or about the interpretation of past events and circumstances in which everyone or everyone's ancestors participated—occurred primarily along tribal lines or according to age categories. To ignore these differences would be not only to oversimplify and overgeneralize Fort Belknap culture and/or Gros Ventre culture; it would also be to obscure the cultural dynamics of that society: people are aware of the contrasting ideas, and this awareness works to change people's perceptions, attitudes, and judgments in particular ways and to stimulate new social practices.[3]

If I had chosen to focus on only one group—one tribe or one age group—views would have been more uniform. But again the cultural and social dynamics of reservation or tribal society would have been less apparent. The Gros Ventres' sense of group identity (their ideas about their culture and history) takes shape in the context of their relations with and understandings about Assiniboines—what it means to be Gros Ventre cannot be understood apart from what it means to be Assiniboine. This is more than a matter of mutual borrowing of ideas or customs or technology. They adjust their notions of who they are and what their past has been as they react to perceptions of each other or as they struggle to influence each other. Among the Gros Ventres themselves, the contrasting experiences and understandings of different age groups similarly bring about readjustment, reexamination, innovation, and creativity in the way they are making sense of their past and present. A model of Gros Ventre life that did not include that dynamic exchange would be a distortion.[4]

Neither would an acculturation or assimilation model, so frequently used to explain differences and disagreements in Plains and other Native American societies, be very illuminating. One might, after reading what other researchers have said about Fort Belknap, be tempted to categorize differences between the two tribes as a reflection of the gap between "acculturated" Gros Ventres and "less acculturated" Assiniboines. Or differences between Gros Ventres who are college graduates and those who have less formal education could conceivably be described in this way. But this kind of categorization would be inappropriate. First, no such native categories exist—Gros Ventres at Fort Belknap do not attribute cultural variation to differences between "traditional" and "progressive" or "full-blood" and "mixed-blood" groups.

And there are other serious problems with the acculturation model. Degrees of acculturation (that is, the extent to which people have lost Indian culture and accepted a white-oriented way of life) generally are defined according to arbitrarily selected culture traits (that is, behavior patterns), such as participation in native religious ceremonies or success in the market economy. The meaning of particular behaviors may be interpreted from the ethnographer's perspective—he or she assigns the meaning, not native peoples themselves. Individuals also are assigned arbitrarily to a place on the acculturation continuum; for example, an individual's participation in a native ceremony may be ignored in favor of his participation in Christian rites, and, on this basis, the individual is assigned to a transitional or white-oriented category. These "traits" are taken outside of their cultural context; without an understanding of how these behaviors are interpreted by the actors themselves, the "culture" traits are inappropriate measures of change or of assimilation. Moreover, categories are assigned with no attention to cultural and social process, to the fact that people change their behavior and develop new interests and concerns in response to new opportunities and challenges. Does a man categorized as "acculturated" at one point in time become less acculturated if later in life he begins to participate extensively in Indian rituals, or is it rather that ritual leadership may be more culturally appropriate for elders than for youths? Culturally appropriate roles may in fact be related to a person's position in the life cycle. The acculturation framework often presents native peoples as essentially passive, or at best unsuccessful; change is viewed not as resulting from resourceful and creative acts or choices but as capitulation to pressures from the wider society. The underlying assumption is that eventually "natives" will assimilate or, if they do not, become hopelessly disorganized, marginal people. Ethnographers who take this approach tend also to overemphasize the shaping of Indian culture and history by social contacts with and adoption of ideas of non-Indians. They ignore the interactions among different Native American groups with varying lifestyles and the ways in which these peoples' ideas and actions are changed by such contacts. At Fort Belknap, culture and history have been very much the products of this kind of mutual influence, and not merely of exposure to white society. And the people at Fort Belknap have played a major role in the nature and direction of change there.[5]

The factionalism model, as it has been used in Plains studies, often assumes that conflict of ideas reflects social conflict and isolation. The people at Fort Belknap disagree on various issues. But to describe the society as factionalized would not be appropriate. Even though people disagree on such matters as the meaning of particular symbols, or on who is really a Gros Ventre, or on how best to organize an election, these disagreements do not necessarily inhibit cooperation in rituals, in politics, in household activities, and so on. Conflicts in the cultural realm do not necessarily result in overt social conflict. Moreover, use of a factionalism approach that overemphasizes the social isolation of various "factions" may suggest erroneously that the ideas or behavior of one group do not influence those of the others.[6]

Gros Ventres literally live side by side, interact intensively in all spheres of reservation life, and intermarry with the Assiniboines. The two groups have a long history of mutual borrowing, and, as I argued above, each group has influenced the way the other has changed. There are no rituals exclusively for members of one tribe; the reservation government is elected at large; English is used in most conversations. It might be proposed that Fort Belknap culture is a blend of Gros Ventre and Assiniboine, or is pan-Indian in general. Such a model has been used in similar reservation situations. But cultural identity at Fort Belknap is more complex than this model suggests. A person views himself as a member of both a tribe and a community, and both identities may be symbolized in the same social act. And borrowed ideas, objects, or customs are given new meanings that make it possible for the borrowers to accept innovations, even to view them as tribal tradition. Also, the assumption that the Gros Ventres and Assiniboines share the same culture because they occupy places in the same social system not only is erroneous; it obscures the fact that these groups' realizations of each other's contrasting interpretations of the same events, circumstances, or ceremonies influence the nature and direction of change in Fort Belknap society.[7]

Most studies of contemporary Native Americans fail to examine carefully the relationship between past and present. Often a brief, ethnographic-present description of precontact or early-contact lifeways or a sketch of major events in Indian–white relations is given, but how contemporary culture and society are affected by a particular history is ignored. To ignore the historical perspective can obscure the contexts or underlying causes that enable us to understand contemporary times. The few studies of the relationship between the past and the present on the Plains focus on explicating gradual "culture loss," documenting "persistence," or demonstrating the effects of increasing "powerlessness."[8]

Studies that focus on culture loss begin with a baseline so-cial/cultural system (usually lifeways at the time of contact with Europeans) and compare it with the contemporary culture. Gradual acculturation or assimilation is assumed to be the product of continued contact, with the degree of assimilation depending on the kinds of relations that existed between Indians and Europeans. But, as is the case with assimilation models of cultural variation within one society, there are problems with this approach. As time goes by, the members of the society reorganize and reinterpret the "traditional" baseline way of life from their own cultural perspective to reflect their new experiences. Unquestionably they did so before contact with non-Indians as well. Anthropologists have often predicted imminent assimilation after detecting nontraditional activity in a particular community, only to find years later a "resurgence" of Indian identity. The acculturation approach ignores the fact that a community may perceive innovations as expressions of their identity and as cultural continuities, as in fact the Gros Ventres do.[9]

Other studies have attributed cultural continuity to the "persistence" of certain ideas or customs, to native peoples' resistance to new ways of life and new ideas. Continuity does come about through the persistence of certain ideas or customs, through resistance to change. But identity also continues because of, not in spite of, the emergence of new concepts and values, because native groups adapt to a changing social world. Native American cultures today—distinct in many ways from non-Indian cultures—reflect *contemporary* concerns and ideals that are often quite different from or at odds with earlier ones. Studies that focus on persistence—that present only "traditional" life, for example—may, in the end, promote stereotypes about "real" Indians. This approach can also obscure the way earlier cultural and social forms are reinterpreted and reorganized by present-day communities. Moreover, to describe changes that led to improved health conditions or greater skill in dealing with federal officials, for example, as not "traditional" (as "un-Indian") is to characterize "real" Indians as unable to adapt in constructive ways to their changing circumstances. Success and survival become un-Indian.[10]

Several historical studies focus on Indian–white relations and on the detrimental influence of national policy on local affairs. Although these works generally are sympathetic to the plight of Native Americans, studies of this sort largely ignore Native Americans' interpretations, goals, and strategies and, in so doing, present a false picture of Indians as passive recipients or helpless victims of new cultural or social forms. Some authors have attributed culture change primarily to exploitation of Indians by the dominant society and have seen such exploitation as the most important factor in shaping Indians' contemporary circumstances. But native peoples' responses to world or national events are not simple reflex actions; their reactions, their new

8

behaviors depend also on their perceptions and interpretations of those events.[11]

These three approaches err in assigning a directive role to or focusing exclusively on either ideas ("traditional" concepts and values) or actions/events. In emphasizing the persistence of particular cultural forms, authors have ignored the ways in which new social events and contexts have shaped culture and, as a result, their works have, to some degree, misrepresented contemporary cultures. Acculturation models generally focus on the differences between contemporary social forms and earlier ones and ignore the meaning of those forms to Native Americans, thus finding loss of culture where there is continuity. An approach that emphasizes the powerlessness of Indian people—the political economy of Indian–white relations—and overlooks the way the exploited population interprets and reacts to those relations distorts the process by which Native American societies change. This book takes a different view of cultural and social processes; it focuses on their interplay.

Culture and History at Fort Belknap

Culture Reconstructed

My approach to the study of change is based on the work of Clifford Geertz, who argues that cultural and social processes are "independently variable yet mutually interdependent." "Culture" refers to a set of established meanings embodied in symbols. Through this model of social reality, people make sense of their society and evaluate their place in it. And the model, which people also use in reinterpreting and reevaluating social realities, thereby shapes attitudes and actions. It is in terms of these structures of meaning that behaviors are produced, perceived, and interpreted; thus meanings are socially established and we gain access to them by "inspecting events"—"what, in this time or that place, specific people say, what they do, what is done to them." Social processes, the forms that behavior takes, are not moved by ideational forces alone. Innovative social forms may be produced or initiated by events that originate outside a particular society and by new or unusual situations or relationships. We must look, then, at the interaction, the reciprocal interplay, between cultural and social forces if we are to come to terms with change over time: ideational factors (ideas, concepts, values) are independent but not self-sufficient forces—they act and have their impact "only within specific social contexts to which they adapt, by which they are stimulated, but upon which they have, to a greater or lesser degree, a determining influence."[12]

With this approach to the understanding of the relationship between culture and event, belief and practice, we can investigate the reciprocal interplay between the "evolving forms of human association" and the "no less changing vehicles of human thought." Meanings are altered in the light of new concerns and new aspirations drawn from new events, relationships, and circumstances. Thus symbols are invented, discarded, and reinterpreted as they are adapted to new social realities. A community's view of itself and its past is reconstructed and new symbols of identity emerge in the light of new social, ecological, and psychological conditions. No actual sequence of events can be predicted from cultural factors, yet no actual sequence of events can be explained without them.[13]

One kind of social reality that stimulates culture change is the social and cultural variation found in all societies. To a degree that varies from one point in time to another in a particular society or from society to society, individuals and groups occupy different social vantage points. They have varied experiences, interests, and perspectives. One result of social variation is that cultural forms can coexist yet differ or conflict. Thus, as Geertz points out, "the problem of cultural analysis is as much a matter of determining independencies as interconnections, gulfs as well as bridges." Cultural variation both emanates from and shapes social processes.[14]

This approach to the study of history has been used here to answer questions about Gros Ventre culture change. Why and in what ways have social and cultural forms continued or new ones appeared over time, and how has the meaning of Gros Ventre identity evolved? What accounts for the origin and character of the contemporary process of ritual revival at Fort Belknap and what do these rituals mean today to the people at Fort Belknap? How do Gros Ventres' accounts of past events express their ideas about their identity and motivate contemporary actions and attitudes, including the emphasis now on Indian control of Fort Belknap? To answer these questions we need to examine how meaning and event have mutually influenced each other. How have social processes provoked cultural reconstructions, and how has Gros Ventre culture and cultural variation shaped those social processes?

Many of the social forces that have initiated cultural reorganization were set in motion far from Gros Ventre country. The expansion of the fur trade wrought major social realignment and adjustment; the opportunities and problems it brought stimulated cultural formulations.

Similarly, the expansion of the American frontier and simultaneous destruction of the Gros Ventres' hunting-gathering way of life; the establishment of Indian reservations and the "civilization" policy, with its associated repression, exploitation, racism, and ethnocentrism; the decline of agriculture in Montana after World War II; the events of the 1960s and 1970s, including the Vietnam war, the civil rights movement, and poverty programs—all these developments in successive eras affected in fundamental ways the Gros Ventres' relations with each other, with non-Indians, and with other Indians (especially their neighbors, the Assiniboines), as well as their perceptions and evaluations of these relations. Cultural change is revealed in the changing patterns of symbolic action, including rituals; use of regalia, costume, and sacred objects; forms of exchange; political speeches. Through these forms, Gros Ventres said things to and sometimes challenged each other about, among other things, being Gros Ventre, defending group interests, earning respect and recognition from others, and influencing the supernatural. Such messages were exchanged between Gros Ventres and others as well. At particular points in time, these messages motivated and reinforced new kinds of behavior: the redefinition of Gros Ventre identity and the expression of it in new ways, the reevaluation and alteration of alliances and enmities, the search for new ways of attaining prestige and authority, and the conversion to new religions.

We can gain access to the symbolic action or socially established meanings characteristic of former eras, as well as the social events and circumstances of those times, by the ethnohistorical method. Here "ethnohistorical method" refers to the process of critically examining and evaluating the evidence provided by written records in light of the insights provided by anthropology. The kinds of documents that shed light on Gros Ventre attitudes, values, patterned social relations, and strategies include transcripts of meetings among Gros Ventres (or Assiniboines) or between Gros Ventres and others; letters or manuscripts written by Gros Ventres or Assiniboines; unpublished field observations and interviews by ethnologists; newspaper accounts; and reports, letters, and journals of non–Gros Ventres, including other Indians, missionaries, traders, and federal officials. Such documents often describe and comment on political acts, ceremonies, encounters, and sacred and other objects and their use. Many anthropological studies that attempt to incorporate historical perspective fail to make an exhaustive search for these kinds of documents (which for any one Native American group number in the tens of thousands). Instead, only the most easily available or published documents are used. This kind of omission can limit and distort findings as much as haphazard

or insufficient observation and interviewing can undermine participant-observation fieldwork.[15]

Folk history gives additional perspective on the present, for through
their stories about their past people at once reveal and influence their
culture and society. And the analysis of folk history in combination
with ethnohistory helps clarify events and relationships from the past.
My analysis of folk history at Fort Belknap departs in some ways from
other anthropologists' studies of oral tradition. Some authors have
drawn on oral traditions without attention to their social and historical contexts. Many have focused on determining the historical validity
of folk history, or the ways folk history can be used to evaluate or
elaborate on the documentary sources. Here I am interested primarily
in how folk traditions work in contemporary culture and society. As
William Sturtevant has pointed out, this is a "form of ethnography," as
ideas about the past form part of a cultural system that affects behavior in the present. My analysis differs in its direction from other work
of this sort in that studies of folk history often emphasize either its role
as a charter that orders behavior or its reflection of the social order. In
my view, folk history is not merely a charter for or a reflection of
society; rather, as part of cultural process it both affects and is affected
by social forces. I also am interested less in finding a common view of
the past than in sorting out how different and conflicting histories
have evolved in Fort Belknap society and how these stories have been
used to effect social ends. I am interested as well in how new and
different interpretations shape concepts of identity, not merely aspects of behavior. Thus, in the chapters that follow, I analyze folk
histories for the light they can throw on cultural differences and relations between Gros Ventres and Assiniboines, on the way Gros Ventre
identity is shaped both by these relations with Assiniboines and by
their understandings of those relations, and on the dynamics of
change in culture and society at Fort Belknap. I also study and compare folk histories of age cohorts to gain insight into contemporary
Gros Ventre culture and society and into the dynamics of change.[16]

Fort Belknap and Its People

Today, as in the past, there are cultural and social differences between people who consider themselves Gros Ventres and those who
consider themselves Assiniboines. They differ even though they have a
joint, elective tribal government, have intermarried, and speak English.
(English is spoken virtually all the time by Gros Ventres and by most
Assiniboines, although a minority of the latter at times converse in the

native language.) The Gros Ventre–Assiniboine association at Fort Belknap dates from the 1870s, but the two groups have been in contact with each other for almost three centuries. Their relationship is a product of the cultural and social differences between them, as well as of the experiences they have had with Euro-Americans.

The name Gros Ventres was given to them by traders; they called themselves *'aa'ááániinéñinah,* or White Clay People. They were the northernmost division of the Arapaho, spoke a dialect of Arapaho (an Algonkian language), and moved onto the Plains in the Saskatchewan area probably sometime before the eighteenth century. They were nomadic hunters of big game both before and after they acquired horses in the early eighteenth century. They spent most of the year separated into bands. When it was advantageous to unify the bands they were able to do so by means of an overarching political system based on men's societies and by supernatural sanctions associated with tribal rituals presided over by priests. For most of the eighteenth and early nineteenth centuries the Gros Ventres were intermittently at war with other native peoples, including the Assiniboine groups, who lived to the east and southeast.[17]

The Assiniboines and the Sioux separated sometime before 1640 and the former moved north to western Manitoba in the late seventeenth century. There were many divisions of Assiniboines (contemporary Assiniboines and Stoneys—who were also referred to as Assiniboines in the eighteenth and nineteenth centuries—live on nine reservations in Canada and the United States). They spoke a dialect of Dakota, a Siouan language, and considered themselves related, although some groups rarely came in contact with others. In the north they formed an alliance with the Crees and in the early eighteenth century became middlemen between the European fur traders on Hudson Bay and the more westerly tribes, expanding westward and southward. They did not become fully equestrian hunters until the late eighteenth century; even then, they never had horse herds as large as those of the Gros Ventres. The Assiniboine groups were organized into loosely allied bands led by headmen. By the end of the nineteenth century the Gros Ventres and some of the Assiniboine groups had formed an alliance and were hunting in north-central Montana, where they eventually settled on the Fort Belknap reservation.[18]

The Fort Belknap reservation is in north-central Montana, about thirty-five miles south of the Canadian border. Roughly rectangular, about forty miles in length from north to south and twenty-six miles in width, it is bounded on the north by the Milk River and on the south by the Little Rocky Mountains. The reservation's 652,594 acres contain alluvial bottomland along the Milk River valley, grassland from the river south to the mountains, and the Little Rockies (up to 4,000 feet in elevation) and break areas along the southern boundary.[19]

There are four population centers at Fort Belknap: along the northern boundary at the agency; in the Milk River valley; the Hays community, in the southwestern section of the reservation, in the foothills of the Little Rockies; and Lodgepole, in the foothills of the southeastern section (see map 1).

The Fort Belknap Agency, in the northwest corner of the reservation, is the headquarters for the Bureau of Indian Affairs (BIA), the Indian Health Service, and the tribal government. The agency has large new housing developments, where many government and tribal employees as well as other Fort Belknap Indians reside, and a recreational complex (including a powwow or dance area and an arbor). Some Assiniboines and Gros Ventres live in the nearby town of Harlem but work in and consider themselves part of the agency community. To the east, scattered throughout the river valley, are homes and farms, primarily of Assiniboines, although some Gros Ventre families live in the lower valley near the mouth of Peoples Creek. There are 858 Assiniboines living on the reservation and 60 percent reside in the agency and river areas. Fifty-two percent of the 1,082 on-reservation Gros Ventres live in the agency area or along the lower Milk River east and south of where the Assiniboines are settled.[20]

Hays, forty miles southeast of the agency, is populated largely by Gros Ventres, a few settled on family farms and ranches and most in two small housing developments. Hays has a small grocery store and gas pump, a public elementary and secondary school, St. Paul's Mission (a Catholic church and elementary school), a small evangelical Protestant mission, and a senior citizens' center. Forty-four percent of the on-reservation Gros Ventres live at Hays.

Lodgepole, an Assiniboine community about fifteen miles east of Hays, has a small grocery store and gas pump, Catholic church, and community hall. Families live in a fairly scattered settlement pattern. Twenty-eight percent of the on-reservation Assiniboines live in Lodgepole. In recent years, the populations of Hays and Lodgepole have been declining and the agency population increasing, because of the extensive housing projects there.

In 1982, 4,185 individuals were enrolled as Fort Belknap Indians. To be enrolled, one has to be of one-fourth Gros Ventre and/or Assiniboine ancestry. Forty-seven percent of these enrolled members were living on or near the reservation. Approximately one hundred non-Indians and French-Chippewas live on the reservation as spouses or employees. The French-Chippewas or métis are not legally entitled to

Ft. Belknap Res.

To Chinook and Havre

Harlem

Great Northern Railroad

Agency

Upper

Milk River

Three Mile Cr.

Milk R.

2

Lower

To Malta

Milk

River

White

Bear

Cr.

Fifteen Mile Cr.

66

Peoples Cr.

North Fork

South Fork

BLAINE

PHILLIPS

Peoples Cr.

Wild Horse Cr.

Lodgepole Cr.

Spring Cr.

Little

Peoples Cr.

Hays

Old Fairgrounds

Lodgepole

Big Warm

St. Paul's Mission

Little Rocky Mtns.

Lewis and Clark

National Forest

Beaver Cr.

○   Dance ground

☐   Community hall

▨   Dance hall (aban.)

⋯   Housing

0   5   10   15   20

Miles

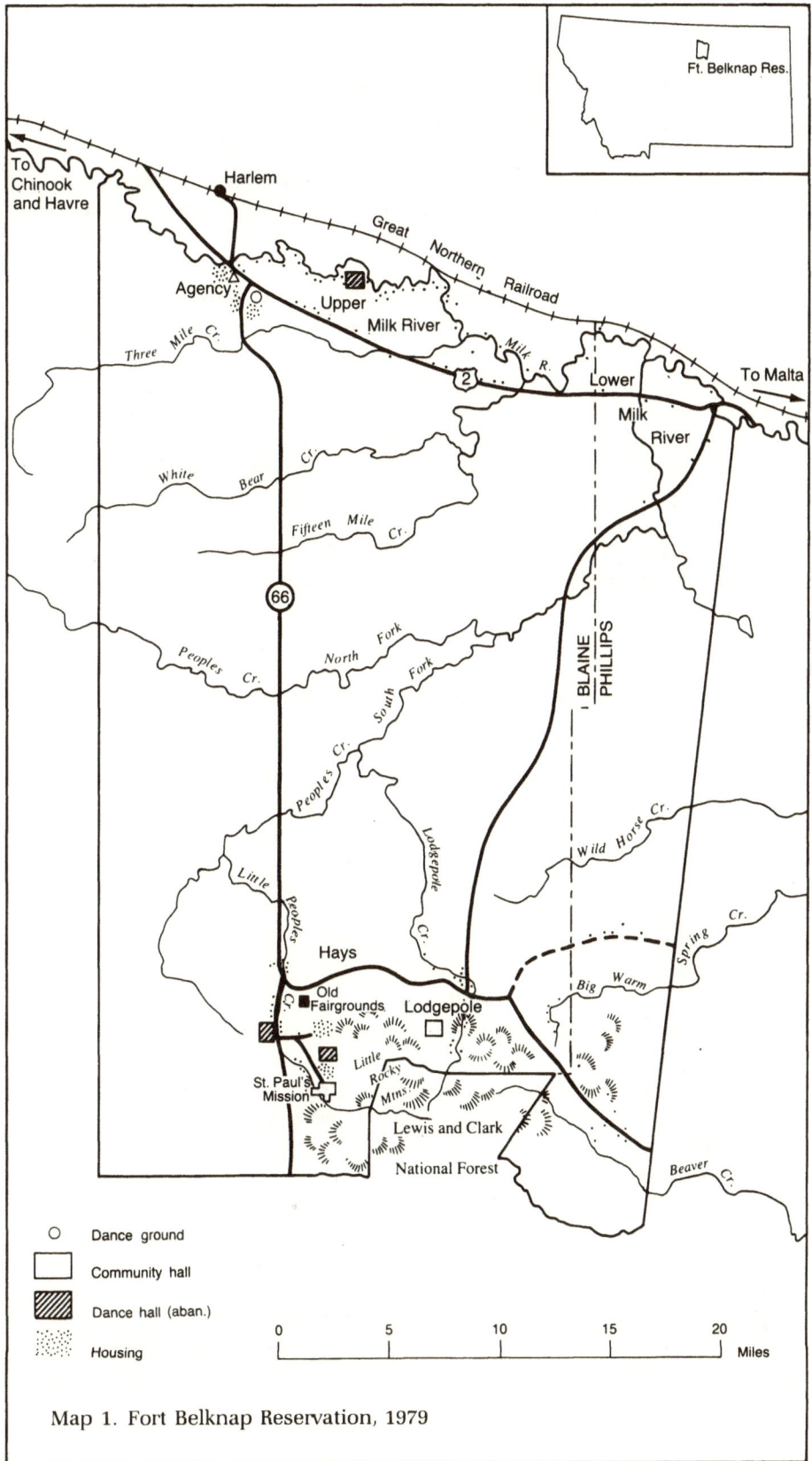

Map 1. Fort Belknap Reservation, 1979

the benefits and services of the tribal members, but if they are spouses of tribal members, they may in fact share in reservation resources.[21]

Most reservation residents do their shopping off the reservation, in Harlem, 5 miles west of the agency; in Chinook and Havre, 25 and 45 miles to the west of Harlem along highway 2; and in Malta, 45 miles to the east of Harlem. Small towns such as Harlem, Chinook, and Malta are struggling to survive, and the smaller settlements along highway 2 have become ghost towns, their homes and stores boarded up. As the small family farms and ranches fail and the people move away, the town merchants go out of business. Rural north-central Montana is an economically depressed area because the economy is based on agriculture. Agriculture is always risky because the weather is unpredictable. Moreover, costs of production are generally high, and prices for cattle and crops fluctuate but tend to be low. Furthermore, the increasing mechanization of labor has eliminated many jobs in agriculture. The economic decline began in the 1940s and stimulated a large out-migration to larger towns or rural nonfarming areas. Fort Belknap lies within Blaine and Phillips counties. The population of these counties has declined an average of 9.5 percent in each ten-year period from 1940 to 1960 and at a rate of 14.2 percent between 1960 and 1970. The Indian population, which comprises over 17 percent of the population in these counties, had been steadily declining until recent years. In 1970, 58 percent of Fort Belknap's enrolled members were living away from the reservation; this was the highest percentage among all the reservations in Montana and Wyoming. Because of the lack of economic opportunity during the last forty years, many Fort Belknap people worked off the reservation and have only recently returned, following the start of federal job and housing programs in the late 1960s and 1970s.[22]

The reservation community faces more severe economic problems than the wider north-central Montana area. Unemployment has been rising at the same time the birth rate has been increasing, and rates of unemployment and underemployment are high. In 1979 the median household income on the reservation was $6,486; in the state of Montana it was $15,420, considerably below the national figure. Reservation residents derive income from wages, transfer payments, leases, and agriculture. Most income is derived from wage work, and the largest source of income is salaries and wages from federal, state, and tribal government jobs. In 1981 the tribes employed 171 people; the Indian Health Service, 47; the BIA, 50; the public schools on the reservation, 40. Many of these jobs were created in the 1960s and 1970s through government-funded programs. This source of employment is undependable; with the federal budget cuts of the early 1980s, the number of such jobs began to decline. The rate of unemployment was 70 percent in 1981, considerably higher than the rate in Montana generally. Some Fort Belknap people receive transfer payments (social security, state-administered welfare, BIA general assistance, pensions). These payments also have been declining since 1980. Another, less important source of income is the leasing of individually owned land.[23]

The 112 enrolled reservation residents who operate farms and ranches have many problems: inadequate land base, cost-price squeeze, water shortage, inadequate capital. Seventy-seven percent of the reservation lands are used for pasture and grazing, 18 percent for crops. Livestock, hay production, and some small grain production are the primary activities. Sixty-five head is the mean herd size; 300 head are considered an economically viable unit. The trend is toward fewer, larger farms, and because of the high cost of technology and transportation and the cost-price squeeze, the number of Indian operators has been declining. Farming is a low-income operation in all of rural Montana, not only at Fort Belknap. In 1983 only 20 percent of the individually owned land on the reservation was used by the Indian owners; the remaining 80 percent was used by someone other than the owner under either a grazing permit or a farm pasture lease. Most Indian agriculturalists supplement their income from farming and/or ranching with wage work. Ninety-five percent of the reservation land is in trust status, that is, the U.S. government holds all title to Indian land so that the land cannot be sold or leased without the approval of the secretary of interior, and the land or income from it cannot be taxed. Thirty-two percent of lands in trust are tribally "owned" and 63 percent "owned" by Indian individuals. The tribes gradually have been purchasing individuals' land in order to enlarge the tribal land base, but only very limited funds are available to the tribal government.[24]

The employment problems are exacerbated by the fact that enrolled members have been returning and the birth rate on the reservation has been rising. The Indian birth-death ratio in 1983 was 6 : 1. In 1968 the resident Indian population was 1,572 and the available labor force was 514; by 1981 the population was 2,097 and the labor force 1,136.[25]

Responsibility for economic planning is largely in the hands of an elected Fort Belknap Community Council, comprised of six Gros Ventres and six Assiniboines. Six councilmen are elected every second year by all enrolled community (reservation) members and they serve four-year terms. Three officers—chairman, vice-chairman, secretary-treasurer—are elected by the councilmen from their own ranks. The council supervises tribal employees who direct programs in land management, economic planning, housing, health, and education. When jobs become available or a new program is funded, an employment committee comprised of councilmen interviews and selects job applicants and recipients. The council makes decisions about the purchase and exchange of tribal land and the leasing of tribal land to individual operators; although federal officials subsequently review the decisions, they rarely overrule the council. And the council also regulates elections and enrollment.

The reservation's economic problems are compounded by the fact that it lacks mineral resources or other sources of income that could generate capital or development. Hence tribal leaders must seek federal funding for development projects. Enrolled members have received no per capita payments from tribal income, as have Indians on many other reservations. This factor has contributed to out-migration. Pressure on the business council from constituents is unabating, and economic planning is extremely difficult, for the federal programs on which the reservation is dependent are uncertain.

Despite the economic problems, the increased activity—the building, the new programs, and the institutions introduced in many cases by people returning to the reservation—has led reservation residents to view their community as undergoing revitalization and recovery after years of decline. The economic and political realities of life at Fort Belknap have influenced and are influenced by contemporary Gros Ventre culture. And the present has been shaped by past events, and by people's perceptions of those events. The following chapters explore these and other aspects of Gros Ventre culture and history.

Chapter 1 uses the ethnohistorical method to focus on the interdependence between the Gros Ventres' cultural identity and their changing social world. I examine documents from 1778 to 1984 to show how the Gros Ventres' behavioral ideals, what they admired in each other, influenced the choices they made in coping with their changing circumstances and how these ideals and the way they have been expressed evolved over time in response to contemporary social forces. And I consider why the meaning of Gros Ventre identity has changed in some respects and not in others. I also show how the Gros Ventres' reputation for culture loss and their professed commitment to progress can be reconciled with the resilience of particular cultural orientations. For during this 200-year period, Gros Ventres were able to view themselves as a people culturally distinct from their neighbors—both Indian and white—although they found meaning in and shared a commitment to an extensive array of symbols and participated in many of the same social institutions as the other groups. This chapter also examines the conditions that have led to major political and ritual reorganization and resurgence at Fort Belknap since the late 1960s

18

and why the changes took the forms that they did. I examine how Gros Ventres can regard much of contemporary social and symbolic activities as "traditional," as having historical depth, even though these contemporary social forms and cultural orientations may differ from those of the past. An understanding of what particular kinds of actions meant to the Gros Ventres themselves exposes and helps correct misconceptions and misunderstandings about them in other published works. Finally, this chapter explores the roots of the divergent interpretations among Gros Ventres today, and of the evolution of the different folk histories of the Gros Ventres and Assiniboines—subjects pursued in Chapters 2 and 3.

Chapter 2 examines variations in concepts of Gros Ventre cultural identity and history among the generations. A generation is a cohort whose shared experiences significantly distinguish them from people in other age groups. Elders form one generation, but among youths there are two groups whose off-reservation experiences significantly differentiate them from each other. I examine how elders and the two groups of youths ascribe different meanings to the same symbols of identity, including sacred pipe bundles, powwows, naming ceremonies, and mortuary customs. And I explore the differences in their interpretations of the past. The origins and social repercussions of the generation gap also are discussed.

Chapter 3 analyzes the folk histories of the two tribes to show how their contrasting histories of reservation settlement—or "Who was here first, Gros Ventres or Assiniboines?"—express and reaffirm the distinct cultural identities of the two peoples. I examine how each tribe's knowledge of the other's interpretations influenced its own identity constructs and the way whites' characterizations of the tribes in relation to each other shaped group identities. Discussion of these folk histories as symbolic statements about identity and history leads also to an examination of how such histories are used to orient social action and motivate behavior.

In the concluding chapter I consider the implications of contested meanings at Fort Belknap—how these diverse understandings about Gros Ventre, Assiniboine, Fort Belknap, and Indian identity affect social relations and influence the nature and direction of change. Contrasted meanings work not only to bring conflicts into focus but also to stimulate individual flexibility, maneuverability, and creative reformulations. Moreover, contested meanings help foster a sense of cultural distinctiveness. Conflict over meaning is not merely a clash of interests but a struggle over the kind of Indians that Fort Belknap people are and will be; it is a struggle over the meaning of Indian and other identities in the contemporary world.

‹ 1 ›

Ways of Being Gros Ventre,
1778–1984

Over the past two centuries the Gros Ventre people's way of life has changed in very fundamental ways. Once they hunted big game on horseback; now they are doctors, lawyers, teachers, administrators, wage workers, and ranchers. They once organized political relations through an age-grade system in which men took on particular kinds of leadership statuses and roles according to their position in the life cycle, elders had considerable authority, and most decisions were made by consensus. Today Gros Ventre leaders are popularly elected and decisions are made by majority vote. When the Gros Ventres hunted bison and other large game, they sought supernatural assistance by prayers conveyed in pipe rituals and ceremonial dances. Religious activity for most Gros Ventres now centers on Catholicism. Though they took on new economic, political, and religious beliefs and customs and some new concepts about group identity, in many ways Gros Ventres saw, and still see, themselves as culturally distinct from other peoples, for there has been great continuity in the ethos that surrounds being Gros Ventre. Of particular importance was the fact that their definition of desirable behavior in certain contexts differed from other people's. Several of these ideals remained constant over time, while the ways in which such ideals were realized, the ways they were expressed, changed. This chapter traces through documentary sources the evolution of Gros Ventre behavioral ideals and the expression of those ideals over time, and it explores how Gros Ventres' characterizations of themselves as a people influenced and were influenced by contemporary social contexts.

21

Behavioral ideals and other ideas in regard to group identity are more difficult to decipher from documentary sources than from field interviews. Yet in letters and transcripts of meetings or interviews Gros Ventres made statements about what they strived for and admired in each other, and they characterized themselves to others. Economic, political, and religious activity reflect ethos, that is, the evaluative elements of a culture. Thus descriptive accounts of sacred and secular rituals, to give one example, reveal how individuals earned prestige and authority, and what they sought when they petitioned the supernatural.

One behavioral ideal, the pursuit of rank through generosity to others, has been especially consistent over time, yet has been expressed differently in successive eras. In the late eighteenth century, this quest to be *'eecáawúúúnén'i*, or "a prominent man," was realized through loans and gifts of horses. In early reservation days, Gros Ventres perceived the introduction of cattle as another opportunity to accumulate property that they could donate during moiety dances or hand games to earn rank. Today this ideal is realized in the distribution of property, primarily dress goods, at public "giveaway" ceremonies. Other behavioral ideals that have persisted for two centuries and that, to Gros Ventres, define group identity are unyielding tenacity in defense of group or sometimes personal interests (described as *'iníitaatéhk'i*, "he is fierce") and the fulfillment of a commitment to the Great Mystery, or Supreme Being, to take proper care of certain ritual objects. Being Gros Ventre was not dependent on a particular set of ritual symbols, ceremonial forms, or a pattern of structural alignments that ordered behavior. Rather, it emanated from the interpretations that made changes both meaningful and acceptable and enabled the Gros Ventres to make creative transformations of their world on their own terms.

The Gros Ventres' own interpretations must be taken into account, for otherwise misunderstandings arise about how and why Gros Ventre culture changed and about the nature of group identity. In his history of the Gros Ventres at Fort Belknap, Edward Barry concluded that a distinct Gros Ventre cultural identity had gradually eroded over time until the Gros Ventres became assimilated, that is, they accepted wholly and withou, reservation the cultural and organizational patterns of the white society. In another historical study of Fort Belknap, Michael Foley presented changes in Gros Ventre life as the products of a series of exploitive changes initiated by non-Indians and passively or begrudgingly accepted by the Gros Ventres because they felt themselves powerless to resist. The anthropologist David Rodnick presented the adaptations of Gros Ventres and Assiniboines, co-residents of

Fort Belknap, as independent of each other—that is, in Rodnick's analysis the decisions and actions of one group did not affect those of the other. As the reader will see from the following discussion, these interpretations distorted Fort Belknap history and culture.[1]

In examining how social context has influenced Gros Ventre identity I have identified five transitional periods that mark significant changes in the Gros Ventres' relations with others and in their general politico-economic circumstances. These changes stimulated such major adaptations that each following period may be seen as an era. From 1778 to 1877 the Gros Ventres forged an accommodation with white traders and United States government officials that reinforced older patterns of and ideas about rank, leadership, and ritual. And greater preoccupation with intertribal warfare was stimulated by relations with whites. Ideals of prominence and bravery were reinforced by trade relations. From 1878 to 1901, political and ritual life underwent major transformations precipitated by confinement along with Assiniboines within a reservation system in which government representatives both exerted repressive controls and offered new opportunities. Gros Ventres perpetuated ideals of prominence and tenacity but expressed these qualities in new ways that were still culturally distinct. They were able to realize personal ambitions that they carried over from prereservation times and yet maneuver for economic and political advantage in the reservation context because they accommodated certain aspects of their behavior to the agents' policies. In 1902 administrators at Fort Belknap helped set in motion some political and ritual revitalizations led by a generation of Gros Ventres born on the reservation and educated in reservation boarding schools. From 1902 to 1937, the quest for prominence and the tenacious pursuit of primacy in relation to the Assiniboines were goals realized through new ritual and political forms. By 1938 federal officials in Washington, D.C., had initiated new policies and programs that undermined the social and cultural innovations of the previous era. Economic decline and political domination made it increasingly difficult to attain prominence, meet ritual responsibilities, or compete for primacy. Intermarriages became more frequent, particularly marriages with French-Chippewas who moved into the area in response to federal programs. In the 1965–1984 era, War on Poverty funding and the Native American pride movement set the conditions for major political and ritual revival at Fort Belknap. Many people from urban areas were drawn back to the reservation community, the powwow ritual and its associated giveaway ceremony emerged to provide a means to acquire prominence, and the Gros Ventres began to focus again on establishing Gros Ventre primacy and fulfilling sacred ritual responsibilities.

Making a Career: Horse Owners and Traders, 1778–1877

From the late sixteenth through the early nineteenth century, Europeans and Americans could reap profits by trading with Indians for their furs. Furs brought good prices in the European market, while the Indians were paid for the furs with inexpensive manufactured goods. English and French trading companies pushed westward across Canada to tap new fur-rich territories. Late in the seventeenth century the English Hudson's Bay Company established York Factory on the bay in order to trade with the Crees and Assiniboines in that area. Some trade goods in the years that followed reached the Gros Ventres and Blackfeet groups (Siksika, Bloods, Piegans) in the upper Saskatchewan country through Cree and Assiniboine middlemen. By the 1740s French traders from Montreal established a fort on the Saskatchewan near the Gros Ventre and some Blackfeet groups. The English attempted to compete by encouraging the western tribes to visit the post on the bay, but without success. Eventually, then, Hudson's Bay Company established a post, Cumberland House, on the Saskatchewan in 1774 and another, Hudson House, near Gros Ventre country in 1778. In subsequent years posts were erected farther up the river, in the heart of Gros Ventre and Blackfeet country (see map 2). Although France had relinquished its interests in Canada to England in 1763, independent traders from Montreal (called "Canadians") continued to compete with Hudson's Bay Company. These men organized the Northwest Company in 1779. On the Saskatchewan, the traders obtained furs from the Crees and Assiniboines to the north and east; from the Blackfeet and Gros Ventres to the south they obtained primarily provisions and horses. From this time up until they settled on a reservation in 1878, the Gros Ventres became increasingly dependent on the guns, cloth, metal tools, and other goods brought by the traders.

By the 1830s there was a market for buffalo robes, and the Gros Ventres and Blackfeet groups became more heavily involved in trade, for they were expert at procuring hides and making robes. The traders in Canada could not purchase as many robes as the Americans along the Missouri. Steamboats carried large quantities of heavy robes for the American traders, but the Hudson's Bay Company had to rely on small canoes. By this time Gros Ventres had left Canada in response to attacks from Crees and Assiniboines. They and the southerly Blackfeet groups were now on the upper Missouri, where they were able to take good advantage of the upper Missouri forts, for they controlled this area and prevented other peoples from trading there until after mid-century. Their success in controlling this country was facilitated not only by the guns they acquired from the traders but also by their many

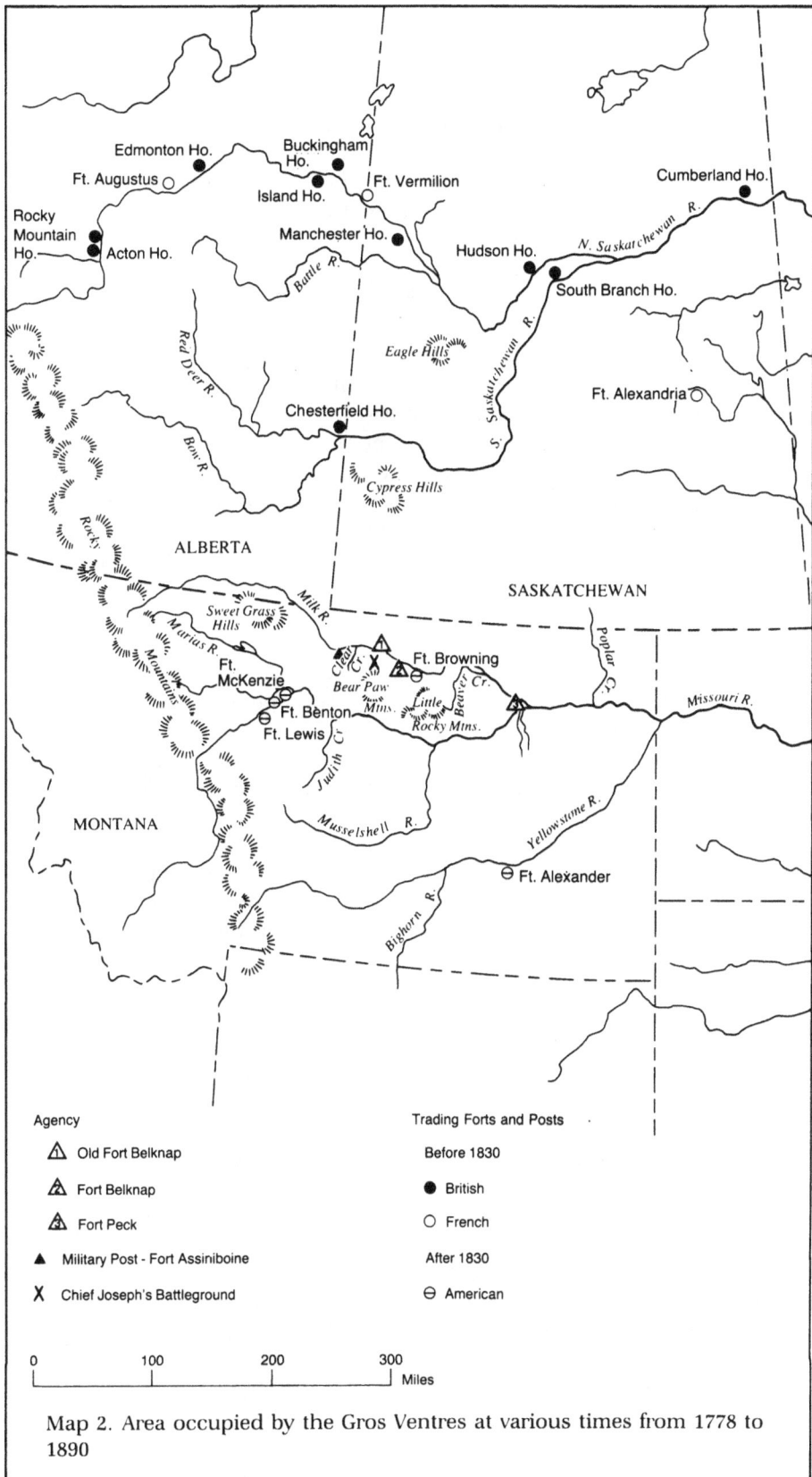

Map 2. Area occupied by the Gros Ventres at various times from 1778 to 1890

Agency

△ Old Fort Belknap

▲ Fort Belknap

△ Fort Peck

▲ Military Post - Fort Assiniboine

X Chief Joseph's Battleground

Trading Forts and Posts

Before 1830

● British

○ French

After 1830

⊖ American

0   100   200   300
|___|___|___|___| Miles

Edmonton Ho.
Ft. Augustus
Buckingham Ho.
Island Ho.
Ft. Vermilion
Cumberland Ho.
Rocky Mountain Ho.
Acton Ho.
Manchester Ho.
Hudson Ho.
South Branch Ho.
N. Saskatchewan R.
Battle R.
Red Deer R.
Eagle Hills
S. Saskatchewan R.
Ft. Alexandria
Chesterfield Ho.
Bow R.
Cypress Hills
Rocky
ALBERTA
SASKATCHEWAN
Milk R.
Sweet Grass Hills
Marias R.
Ft. McKenzie
Clear Cr.
Bear Paw Mtns.
X
Ft. Browning
Poplar Cr.
Missouri R.
Ft. Benton
Ft. Lewis
Little Rocky Mtns.
Beaver Cr.
Mountains
Judith Cr.
Musselshell R.
Yellowstone R.
MONTANA
Ft. Alexander
Bighorn R.

horses; they had more than most peoples that traded along the Missouri.[2]

When the English and French traders first made contact with them in the eighteenth century, the Gros Ventres were mounted. Probably peoples to the south furnished them with their first horses. The Gros Ventres became proficient in the use of horses to hunt, wage war, and transport their camps sometime between 1705 and 1754, before the second quarter of the century, according to John Ewers. Ewers has noted that the way of life of the Plains peoples when they were pedestrian hunters included some of the features present in horse and trading days. But he particularly stresses that society was fundamentally transformed by the acquisition of horses because some hunters owned many horses and others few. The acquisition of the horse undercut communal sharing, for those with horses had less need to depend on other hunters. Men with many horses were able to attract large numbers of horse-poor followers who depended on their bounty. Leadership and prestige became associated with the generous distribution of food from the hunt and loans or gifts of horses to the needy. Hunting technology became more efficient, too, so that the food supply was more reliable. These developments allowed time for a more elaborate ceremonial life and facilitated periodic gatherings of bands. Now when the people moved camp, horses could carry large quantities of possessions, including ritual regalia, clothing, and large tipi covers. And the ability to transport elderly people, children, and others unable to walk probably reduced mortality. But the frequency of raids against other tribes—for horses, primarily—also increased. And so did the rate of casualties. Warfare became a more prominent preoccupation. Trade relations with Europeans and Canadians, and later Americans, reinforced these trends. Trade buttressed Gros Ventre political and ceremonial organization. For with the goods they received from the traders, men continued to attract less well-off followers, and they made large ritual offerings and gift exchanges—all of which enhanced and validated rank. Trade further escalated warfare and reinforced Gros Ventre commitment to military vigilance and tenacity, because it increased intertribal rivalry.[3]

This social context, in which horse ownership and regular trade relations assumed such great importance, provided the conditions that led to the Gros Ventre behaviors that the traders described as preoccupation with a "career" and that Gros Ventres characterized as the ambition to "be somebody," that is, to attain prestige and influence in their society. The military struggles of the Gros Ventres in the fur-trade era contributed to their emphasis on tenacity and bravery and to their reputation among traders in the late eighteenth and early nineteenth centuries as an especially aggressive people and as the bravest in battle. For Gros Ventres, "position" or rank and "fierce" or tenacious behavior were ideals to strive for, and these motivations were intimately related to their politico-religious system.

"The Pipes Seemed to Hold the Tribe Together": The Politico-Religious System

The ethnographers A. L. Kroeber, John Cooper, and Regina Flannery interviewed elderly Gros Ventres in 1901, 1939, and 1940, respectively. These Gros Ventres, who were in the prime of life in the nineteenth century, considered their religion integral to their identity as a people. Religious beliefs and rituals both shaped and validated the group's political and military actions. Religion also motivated individuals to try to conform to Gros Ventre cultural ideals, including the pursuit of high rank and reputation for bravery. Contemporary documents written by traders and travelers supplement recollections recorded by ethnographers. From these data we can piece together what Gros Ventres meant when they told Cooper, "The Pipes seemed to hold the tribe together."[4]

Two tribal medicine bundles—pipes and other sacred objects wrapped in outer coverings—were symbols of creation and of the Gros Ventres' place in the universe. They represented the Gros Ventres' special relationship with the Supreme Being or Great Mystery Above, a relationship that was the basis for health and happiness. The most powerful and the oldest bundle was the Flat Pipe. According to Gros Ventre belief, that pipe bundle was given them when the world was created. The bundle represented their link with, obligation to, and blessing from the Mystery Above. The Flat Pipe's sacred objects, songs, and origin narratives represented the events of creation and the instructions and knowledge given the first Gros Ventre people about how to make their living, get along with one another, and obtain supernatural aid. Three seasonal Flat Pipe rites were essential to the people's prosperity. The rituals associated with the bundle both ensured and sanctioned success in the hunt, horse raid, and battle, and in the pursuit of wealth and a good life in general. The contents of the Feathered Pipe bundle also were important symbols of the Gros Ventres' relationship with the Great Mystery, and the rites associated with this bundle were important to their success.[5]

Priests, called "keepers," were trained to care for and perform the rituals of the two pipe bundles. A new keeper was chosen by ritual authorities every few years. Upon his selection as keeper, a man had to transfer horses and other property to his predecessor and instructors.

The keepers prophesied, cured, and obtained supernatural aid for the Gros Ventres in making war, hunting, and obtaining horses. These keepers, and former keepers as well, had responsibilities and duties beyond those associated with pipe-bundle rituals. They used their authority to generate consensus and cooperation among the people. They attended important meetings where decisions were made, and their consent was required before actions could be taken. They were able to resolve conflict, for they were regarded not only as holy but as capable of harming disrespectful or disruptive individuals by cursing them. When the Gros Ventres moved their camps, the people followed the Flat Pipe keeper (or split into two main divisions, each of which followed one of the two keepers). He and the pipe bundle led the procession, as he led the people in their relations with the Great Mystery.[6]

The Gros Ventres' concepts of authority were based on their ideas about proper relations with the supernatural, and authority roles were legitimized by acquisition of sacred knowledge attained in a series of age-grade ceremonies or "lodges." Men progressively earned greater ceremonial authority and took on new kinds of leadership responsibilities as they aged. The Gros Ventres organized their society largely in terms of this age-group system, the central symbol of which was the offered pipe. The offered pipe symbolized the pipe bundles.

When a young man joined the first ceremonial lodge of the graded series, he did so only after making a vow to the Great Mystery that he would join the lodge in return for supernatural assistance. After he made his vow, he took a pipe to an older man who had already become a member of the lodge and, if the older man accepted the pipe (he risked supernatural punishment if he did not), he became the novice's ceremonial "grandfather." The grandfather then represented the pipe-bundle keeper; the pipe represented the tribal pipe bundle. The offered pipe linked grandson and grandfather in the same way that the pipe bundle linked the Gros Ventre people and the keeper. The grandfather and the keeper supervised and assisted prayers to the Great Mystery. The grandfather instructed and assisted the novice, just as the keeper (representing the culture hero who first taught the Gros Ventres the pipe-bundle ritual) gave instruction and assistance during pipe-bundle rituals. As Cooper learned from elderly Gros Ventres in 1939, the offered pipe represented the Flat Pipe and/or Feathered Pipe, which had been given them "as the most powerful media to pray with, as the most assured means of getting a hearing." The grandson–grandfather relationship was an "implicit sacred pledge into which the Supreme Being himself entered." The bond between grandfather and grandson was symbolized by reciprocal gift giving during the ceremony. The two men were supposed to treat each other with the greatest respect. They were never to quarrel and were to do any favors each asked of the other. After the vower selected his grand-father, he also presented a pipe to the keepers and former keepers, who prayed for the success of his undertaking. Success at acquiring property or achieving battle exploits was viewed as the result of super-natural assistance. Proper attention to ritual responsibilities, then, was essential for success in life.[7]

The age-group system was based on membership in one age set and progressive initiation into the graded series of lodges. Male youths in late adolescence joined an age set, a group of peers who as youths were inducted into an age grade and moved together through a series of grades or ceremonial statuses as they aged. Members of an age set had a moral obligation to help and encourage one another in battle, disputes, and participation in the lodge ceremonies. The age grades were actually categories of persons who were in the same life stage, had acquired the ritual knowledge associated with the grade cere-mony, and had particular roles by virtue of their initiation into the grade. Participation in the first five rituals bestowed supernatural aid, particularly in war, and gave recognition to successful warriors by allowing them to wear special regalia. The six age grades were named Fly Lodge (for youths), Crazy Lodge, Kit-Fox Lodge, Dog Lodge, and Drum Lodge (all for more mature men), and Law Enforcers or Old Man's Lodge (for elders). Several age sets occupied each grade at the same time. The ceremonial knowledge and authority acquired in the lodges increased as a man advanced in the series. The highest ritual authorities were generally of the Law Enforcers' grade; these men had joined the first five lodges and had also completed the Sacrifice Lodge (often referred to as the Sun Dance), an annual ritual in which indi-viduals vowed to suffer physically in return for supernatural aid. The Old Man's ritual bestowed power to attract buffalo to the hunter. Moreover, persons of advanced age were considered to have been specially blessed by the Supreme Being; their prayers received a par-ticularly favorable hearing. Headmen and intermediary chiefs were from one of the grades whose members were in their late forties or fifties. The men selected for policing duties during group hunts or large gatherings were probably from the lower grades. The leaders of the lodges, in consultation with band headmen (who could also be leaders in a lodge), would confer with the group of keepers until a consensus was reached when decisions had to be made on behalf of the entire group. Decisions made in the councils were enforced by designated age sets, by force if necessary.[8]

In addition to progressing through the ceremonial lodges, the members of each age set, or "company," joined either the Star or the Wolf moiety at the time the company was formed. Ties between men of different moieties were promoted through the grandson–grandfather relationship, for a man chose someone from the rival moiety as his grandfather. The two moieties, composed of men from all levels in the series of ceremonial lodges, competed against each other in the acquisition of war honors and property, or for success generally, and in the display of generosity to others. The moiety competition was particularly effective in stimulating military vigilance. At moiety dances songs were composed and sung in praise of specific brave deeds of members. Moiety rivalry also encouraged wealth differentials and at the same time provided social insurance for those who were not well off. Each moiety had its own dance and associated songs, some of which were begging songs, in which the rival moiety would be encouraged to donate food and property to the people gathered for the dance. Individual Gros Ventre males also chose an "enemy-friend" from the rival moiety. The enemy-friend relationship began when one person gave property taken in war to another person; this act initiated a personal rivalry between the enemy-friends to see who could be more generous and more brave. A man could challenge his enemy-friend to acts of generosity at a moiety dance or to acts of bravery on any occasion.[9]

The age-group system enabled the Gros Ventres to unify and organize men (and their families) from different bands and from potentially antagonistic groups. This overarching political organization (buttressed by supernatural sanctions) facilitated their effort to defend themselves against more numerous enemies and to maintain social order. Age-grade ceremonies brought participants supernatural assistance and at the same time encouraged bravery and the acquisition of property. The ceremonies created bonds between ceremonial grandfathers and grandsons, as well as between the agemates who were initiated. Moiety competition, while it encouraged rivalry, also stimulated generosity and linked people in common enterprises.

The eyewitness accounts of traders and travelers who came in contact with the Gros Ventres in the nineteenth century give insight into how the age-group system functioned in actual situations. The observations, although sparse, are consistent in linking advanced age and authority, in indicating that the age-group system was basic to Gros Ventre social organization, and in noting that the system unified the Gros Ventres behind the age-group leadership. Gros Ventres are described as more unified than other northern Plains peoples, more willing to accept leaders' authority.

In 1800, traders at Edmonton House noted that the Gros Ventres were attempting to keep trappers out of their territory, for trappers interfered with their success in trade. A group of young warriors ambushed a party of trappers and, instead of killing or robbing them, took them to the main body of the tribe, where the "chiefs" and the elder men decided what to do. The older men returned them to the posts on the Saskatchewan but kept their arms and ammunition. A Hudson's Bay Company employee, D. MacKenzie, remarked in his journal on 30 January 1823 that all the quarrels his trading party had had with the natives originated with "the Chiefs and old men of the Fall Indians [Gros Ventres] and the young men of the Blood, and Blackfoot [Siksika]." The traders' observations make it clear that younger Gros Ventre men deferred to their seniors in the age-grade system on important political matters and that it was the elder men who had authority to articulate Gros Ventre sentiment in dealings of consequence. By virtue of their rank in the ceremonial grades, older men had more authority in political relations than young men.[10]

American traders also found that authority was associated with advanced age and with high ceremonial rank as well. When Prince Alexander Maximilian, traveling up the Missouri in 1833 with American Fur Company employees, met a band of about sixty Gros Ventres, he noted that they had two leaders: an "old man" by the name of Sun and another man called Iron That Moves, who wore his hair in the style of a high-ranking priest (that is, in a large pompadour or knot above the forehead; this style was adopted by pipe-bundle keepers, according to Cooper's informants). On another occasion that year, Maximilian wrote that the "chief of the Gros Ventres" was Niatohsa (Little Frenchman or French Child), a "medicine man" who wore his hair tied in a bunch over his forehead.[11]

In 1846, Father Nicolas Point, who lived in Gros Ventre and Piegan camps in his attempts to convert the Indians, noted the importance of Gros Ventre elders in political life. In the camp he visited, he wrote, "the principal personality" was The General, the eldest of the group, whose name had been given him by the traders because of his "courage and prudence." This "wise old man," respected by all the Gros Ventres, was appointed to listen to Point's requests. Point described several "venerable" elderly men; his painting of one shows a man whose hair is worn in the fashion of a keeper. Of all the native peoples he met, he wrote, the Gros Ventres were notable for the large number of men who were devoted to prayer. It may have been the Gros Ventres' keepers and former keepers who made such an impression on him. When several bands of Gros Ventres, numbering 200 tipis, approached Fort Lewis to trade, Point described them thus: the men were on foot in several rows, chiefs and calumet (pipe) bearers in the

1. Karl Bodmer, *Niätóhsä (Little Frenchman or French Child), Atsina [Gros Ventre] Chief.*
1833. Watercolor and pencil on paper. 10 × 12½ in. Bodmer accompanied Prince Maximilian on his journey to the Upper Missouri country, where Maximilian identified
Niätóhsä as "Chief of the Gros Ventres," a "medicine man." Niätóhsä wears his hair in
the style of a high-ranking priest. Courtesy of Enron Art Foundation, Joslyn Art Museum,
Omaha, Nebraska.

front line, older warriors and great men in the second row, and the
"soldiers proper"—"young men commissioned to maintain order"—
in the third line. Traders admitted the highest ranking individuals into
their forts first; Point's description of the order of procession reflects
the Gros Ventres' age-group system. The Flatheads (who had no age-
group system), he wrote, advanced in several lines with one of their
"bravest chiefs" circling about ahead of them.[12]

Ferdinand Hayden met the Gros Ventres in 1855 when the United
States was attempting to effect a treaty with the tribes in Montana. The
government hoped to persuade the Indians to guarantee non-Indians
safe travel in this area. Hayden remarked that the Gros Ventres were
"social and united in their undertakings, and easily influenced and
guided by their chiefs." The Blackfeet groups, in contrast, had difficulty reaching consensus and enforcing council decisions. In 1864, the
federal government's Indian agent for the Montana Superintendency,
G. Upson, noted that in contrast to the Blackfeet chiefs, Gros Ventre

headmen could control the young warriors: "I consider this the best governed tribe in the Blackfeet nation [confederacy]; their head chief appears to have complete control over them." In April 1877, near the Fort Belknap trading post, Lemuel Burke observed one (or more) of the age sets policing a large Gros Ventre camp. The camp was moving out on the plains to hunt. Some in the group wanted to cross the Milk River and go north from the fort. Others wished to go down the river some distance before crossing. Several families began to cross over at the fort. Burke noted that the Soldier Lodge (the age set or possibly some members of a moiety designated to maintain order) held a council and determined that the camp should cross on the south side of the river five or six miles downstream. The "Soldier Band" ordered the people to stop crossing and to return. When the people did not obey, they began to throw the disobedient households' goods out of the boats and tried to set the boats loose on the river. Burke described what happened to those who continued to move their horses and effects across the river by fording at the wagon crossing: "The Soldier Band soon paid their respects to them, and brought the whole party back with the exception of one or two lodges [families] who had crossed the river and gone. The Soldiers however had to kill some of the dogs to prevent them from persisting in crossing, but that soon brought the refractory party to obedience and the whole camp joined in the march down the south side of the river."[13] The age-group system must have been an important factor in the ability of the Gros Ventres to unify behind their intermediary chiefs (the leaders who articulated consensus in dealings with outsiders) and in the leadership's success at making people conform or cooperate.

It is difficult to know exactly how relations with traders or with other peoples on the Plains affected the Gros Ventres' politico-religious system, for no documentary sources exist that would shed light on the origin of the pipe bundles or the age-group system. Tribes borrowed ritual symbols and ceremonies as well as technology from each other (nomads borrowed ideas and techniques from horticultural villagers, for example) before the days of horses and trade relations with Europeans. Yet it must have been the horse that made possible a political system headed by men of advanced years, for the use of horses to transport the aged while the people followed buffalo herds probably lengthened the life span. And since older men no longer able to hunt or go to war could lend their horses to younger men, they were able to retain authority and prestige. Horses allowed transportation of the elaborate dance regalia, and the use of the horse in hunting resulted in more leisure time for ceremonies and larger food supplies to support big camps and public feasting. Probably the transfer of wealth became associated with ritual authority after the Gros Ventres obtained horses. Pipe keepers were prosperous, generous men (who had support from well-to-do relatives). Although property offerings as an aspect of prayer predate the introduction of horses, offerings must have become more important and elaborate afterward. The horse also seems to have increased the Gros Ventres' preoccupation with warfare, and the advantages of a more structured military organization may have favored the development of an age-group system.[14]

Trade relations served to reinforce both the Gros Ventres' quest for prominence through the generous distribution of wealth and their emphasis on bravery and tenacity. Trade goods supplemented horses in property transfers and in generosity to others. The escalation of warfare during the trade era would have strengthened the need for an already existing age-group organization that bolstered military vigilance and vigor. It is possible, however, that some of the theocratic aspects of the Gros Ventre age-group system were stimulated by the effects of the fur trade. Since trade relations resulted in drastic population losses and dislocation through both epidemics and increased warfare (as discussed below), the pipe keepership, which, according to Gros Ventre oral tradition, was once hereditary in one band, became an office that was frequently transferred. In this way, a group of elderly ritual authorities (former keepers) from several bands could have developed over time. But about this we can only speculate.[15]

To "Acquire a Little Wealth and Position in Life": A Man's Career

The French-Canadian and the Hudson's Bay Company traders needed to enlist the aid of native leaders to succeed in the fur trade on the Saskatchewan. As David Thompson has noted in his narrative about his trading days in that region in the 1780s, traders attempted to get a "respectable chief" (a warrior with a record of bravery and social responsibility) to associate himself with them and assist them in trading with his people. After the smallpox epidemic of 1780–81 devastated the traders' reliable allies, the Assiniboines and Crees, the Gros Ventres and Blackfeet groups that had been trading with these Indian middlemen were recruited with zeal. The Gros Ventres and allied Blackfeet groups—Siksikas, Bloods, and Piegans—were living to the southwest of the Assiniboines and Crees. They, too, were hard hit by the epidemic, but Hudson's Bay Company men deliberately courted their chiefs in order to compensate for the loss of so many of their former clients and employees. William Walker, a trader for Hudson's

Bay Company at Hudson House, wrote on 12 August 1782 that many of the Crees and Assiniboines he used to trade with were dead but that the "Yachathinues" (the Gros Ventres and their allies) were numerous. He noted in his journal on 14 July of that year that the Indians he was used to trading with were fewer than before the epidemic, so there was intense competition between the Canadian traders and the Hudson's Bay people. Thus William Tomison at Hudson House wrote on 1 March 1783 that he did his best to encourage the Gros Ventres to trade. Encouragement came in the form of "rigging," or outfitting, and otherwise bestowing gifts and recognition on leading chiefs.[16]

When Gros Ventre men came to the French-Canadian and English posts (see map 2), the traders' attentions helped them establish, reinforce, or maintain prominence and high rank in their society. When a well-known chief approached a fort, he sent unproven youths to the trader for presents, always including tobacco; the gift of tobacco represented the traders' acknowledgment of the chief as intermediary for his trading party and at the same time symbolically demonstrated his high rank and authority within the party. The chief then entered the fort and was "rigged" in a special costume of European cloth and decorative notions. Peter Fidler gives us an indication of how a chief used the outfit to enhance his prestige and set himself apart from others when he attempted to persuade his people to act in a certain way. The Piegan chief of the group Fidler wintered with in 1793 tried to discourage young men from borrowing Fidler's horses: the chief "rigged himself out in our clothes & . . . made a long speech." A chief was also sometimes given a company flag as an emblem of the regard in which he was held by the post and the influence he had with the company.[17]

American Fur Company traders at the upper Missouri River posts continued the practice of rigging in the early nineteenth century. Prominent chiefs were given special clothing and flags. When Gros Ventres attacked George Nidever's party of trappers in 1832, the leader was wearing a bright scarlet coat, a "chief's coat." Maximilian noted in 1833 that the principal chief of the Gros Ventres had an American flag on a pole in front of his tipi. Chiefs wore their "uniforms" (chief's coat trimmed with lace and hat with feathers) given them by traders when they entered a fort to trade. In 1846 Father Point noted that Eagle, the Gros Ventres' head intermediary chief, wore a chief's coat, as did other "great" men. The General, who so impressed Father Point, wore a laced coat given him by the traders, "as sometimes happened in the case of chiefs considered to be above the others." Rigging was symbolic of the chief's influence with the trader and also of his ability to provide trade goods to his people.[18]

2. *The Travellers Meeting with Minatarre [Hidatsa] Indians [in 1833] near Fort Clark* (on the Missouri near present-day Bismarck, North Dakota). Engraving with aquatint, hand-colored, after Karl Bodmer. 11¼ × 13¾ in. First published in *Travels in the Interior of North America*, 1839. In their travels, Maximilian, on the left, and Bodmer encountered parties of Gros Ventres, whose leaders (like the Hidatsa leader shown here) wore "chief's hats" presented to them by traders. Courtesy of Enron Art Foundation, Joslyn Art Museum, Omaha, Nebraska.

Men with many horses had an advantage in trade, for they could provide more meat to the traders and could trade their horses as well. The trade goods they received served to reinforce the gap between those wealthy and those poor in horses. Traders, such as Canadian Daniel Harmon and Hudson's Bay man Thomas Heron, pointed to clear-cut, wide disparity in horse ownership in the late eighteenth and early nineteenth centuries. And Father Point observed that hunters with no or few horses had a more difficult time getting game and obtained smaller quantities than those with horses. He wrote, "There are more poor Indians than rich ones"; for every prosperous family, ten others were poor. Without enough horses to transport poles and heavy tipis, poor men had small tipi lodges; prosperous men had very large ones. In 1856 Indian Agent E. Hatch reported that while the average household had ten horses, some individuals had more than 200.[19]

An abundance of horses enabled a man to obtain large quantities of trade goods as well as meat, and Gros Ventres were ambitious for both kinds of luxury. Gros Ventres told Regina Flannery that a man used to want a lot of horses because he " 'knew from experience that if a man had a lot of horses he could acquire a little wealth [particularly from hides and provisions sold after the hunt to traders] and position in life.' " But some men would have only one horse and consequently " 'Wouldn't amount to much; they would be by-passed all the time and couldn't get anywhere.' " Position in life was extremely important to women as well. One elderly woman explained, "If a woman was a good worker she would have lots of things [from the sale of her tanned robes and dried meat, half of which she kept for herself after dividing them with her husband]. . . . The men used to like a woman who had all these things and was a good worker. They used to like a woman who was a good worker because she came up [in status, because she had more property, such as cloth, beads, and metal utensils] if she was a good worker." The man and woman would go half and half when they traded. Gros Ventres told Flannerý that the "aristocratic" families were the ones with the best clothes (which were lavishly decorated with trade goods) and the most horses (which were needed to obtain and transport surpluses of the hides or meat sold to the traders). Poverty—defined as the lack of property, not scarcity of food, for food was freely shared—was dreaded, as is shown in this account of what happened when a young man was initiated into the Kit-Fox lodge, probably in the 1860s: At the end of the dance, the dancers gave gifts, including horses, to their ceremonial grandfathers. One young man " 'did not have anything to give, and it just so happened that all his relatives were poor and did not come to his rescue. Therefore he did not pay his grandfather anything, and he was terribly embarrassed and ashamed.' " Sometime after the ceremony ended, the man deliberately rode into enemy ranks and died in battle because he felt disgraced. The man's disgrace was in not being able to be conspicuously generous, rather than merely being without property. For to be truly prominent, to have position in life, one had to distribute one's property generously to others.[20]

People who obtained horses or property through war or trade were expected to share or redistribute them. And keepers gave away goods brought as offerings, as well. One woman, whose uncle was a Flat Pipe keeper in the 1860s and a Feathered Pipe keeper later, explained that he would distribute robes (the offerings made by petitioners) used to cover the Pipe to the "poor and needy old folks." Keepers entertained anyone who came to pray with a sacred pipe bundle. A prominent man was expected to entertain guests at meals every day, and he provided tobacco to elderly men. His wives invited women from needy families to help prepare the meals in return for part of the food. Men with many horses were expected to lend them to those without. Women who were able to trade their robes used their earnings to give away property and feed guests to honor their relatives. Moreover, each moiety sang begging songs to the prominent men of the opposite moiety during tribal gatherings, or a man would sing in front of an enemy-friend. If the recipient of the song wished to enhance his reputation, he gave food and property to persons at the gathering. Later the donor's moiety would retaliate by singing their own begging songs. As one of Flannery's informants insisted, " 'Those who are stingy don't come up [in status]; they just go back, back, back.' "[21]

Chiefs were presented with a quantity of trade goods as gifts in addition to what they received in the actual trading transaction. In the early nineteenth century, Alexander Henry described how a chief, bearing a flag as he entered a French-Canadian post, presented the flag to the trader; when he left, the trader returned the flag with tobacco and cloth on it. Such items as European tobacco and liquor were sought-after luxuries to the Gros Ventres and other tribes, and since a prominent Gros Ventre validated his rank by extending hospitality to others, the traders' gifts enhanced a man's reputation. People's expectations had risen as the posts penetrated westward to the upper Saskatchewan from York Factory on Hudson Bay in the 1770s. George Sutherland, at Edmonton House in 1796, wrote that when the Gros Ventres wanted to get back in the good graces of the Hudson's Bay Company traders after a period of hostilities, some of the chiefs gave them three horses and some furs "to make peace" and to compensate them for any damages they had incurred on account of the Gros Ventres. It was the wealthy, prominent men who assumed the responsibility of paying indemnity to the traders. And Henry noted that the principal chiefs routinely assumed responsibility for presenting the traders with gifts—a horse with furs or skins on it, or a robe and cap.[22]

At the American posts, only prominent chiefs were allowed to enter the fort, where they were given gifts and entertained before trading began. Maximilian noted in 1833 that the chiefs gave the trader horses with beaver skins on their backs. James Kipp complained of the expense of presents made to the Indians: "They are troublesome and expensive. I had to clothe fourteen chiefs independent of liquor, tobacco, and ammunition I gave. . . . They are . . . in the habit of getting too many free gifts from us." When Point visited a Gros Ventre camp in 1846, he found that the "greatest man" next to the chief was the best trader, the man who sold the most robes to the post and therefore could maintain a "good lodge [tipi]"—that is, could entertain lavishly. Point gave tobacco to chiefs he courted, in order to enable them to "play the generous host," he said. The Fort Benton journal during the mid-1850s contains the names of the most prominent Gros Ventre traders, occasionally described as wealthy; these are the individuals who signed the treaty of 1855 on behalf of the Gros Ventres. When they visited the post to trade, they did everything they could to wrest gifts from the trader. In 1856 the Fort Benton trader described up-and-coming Sits Like a Woman, soon to be head intermediary chief, as "having begged us all tired of him." The Fort Benton journal in 1856 also records that prominent Gros Ventre chiefs took responsibility for giving robes as presents to the trader there.[23]

Traders also furnished the tribes in the Saskatchewan area, and later on the Missouri, with guns and ammunition. Arms aided group defense; in fact, without arms a group was at a distinct disadvantage if guns were available to their enemies. At first, firepower also signified something of a supernatural nature to the Saskatchewan peoples. Thus a man who owned a gun could influence others to follow his lead or consider his counsel. Renowned Gros Ventre chiefs exchanged provisions and wolf pelts for guns and ammunition and had their guns repaired by the traders. Fidler, in the Piegan camp in 1792, described how the chief, as buffalo pound master, had to kill the first buffalo with his gun, then the young men killed the rest with arrows. Chiefs would lend guns to other men, as well. The loan helped ensure the beneficiary's loyalty.[24]

The traders also could help a man begin a "career"; that is, by supplying a young or poor man with a horse or arms and ammunition, they provided a means of social mobility. By helping create new chiefs, they probably contributed to increased rivalry and competition among the Gros Ventres. William Tomison, at Manchester House in 1791, noted that he traded with a small group of Gros Ventres and gave presents to their headman, "as he was very Poor." In 1794, Duncan M'Gillivray of the Northwest Company wrote that when a young man desired to begin his career as chief, he would hunt for the traders in return for rigging and gifts. At Chesterfield House on 6 October 1800, Fidler gave tobacco for five chiefs among twenty-three tents, and on 1 March 1801 "rigged nine Fall [Gros Ventre] Indian men, two of which are the heads of all the Fall Indians." In 1822, MacKenzie complained that the Gros Ventres were expert in manipulating the traders: "These scamps try by every means when they are put in requisition to be supplied with all the necessaries" needed for such a journey. He points out that young men claimed to need to be furnished a horse and arms before they could assist the Hudson's Bay Company traders. Father Point noted in 1846 that a young man, the son of the principal intermediary chief, Eagle, asked him for a "letter of recommendation" to present to the traders at Fort Alexander, in Crow country: he was leading a war party and he wanted to "gain entry into the fort" in the capacity of a "brave," as his father had done. In other words, to become prominent a youth had to be both a successful warrior and a successful trader.[25]

In accordance with the treaty signed by the Gros Ventres and their Blackfeet allies with the United States in 1855, the government distributed trade goods annually for ten years. The chiefs received special clothing, and at treaty councils they were given horses, silver medals, and other presents symbolic of their status. Sometimes the federal agents, appointed as liaisons between the government and the tribes, were also given horses by prominent Gros Ventres. Even after the 1855 treaty expired, agents gave prominent chiefs extra provisions and gifts.[26]

The pursuit of prominence was a major preoccupation in Gros Ventre life in the trade era. Yet the basing of social status on property ownership—the association of generosity (in the distribution of food and property) with leadership and rank—must have resulted from the adoption of an equestrian life. Although we have no first-hand observations of the Gros Ventres as pedestrian bison hunters, John Ewers argues convincingly that we can infer certain social repercussions as a result of the adoption of the horse. Contact with traders would have reinforced this pattern, adding trade goods to the horses and other forms of property that were shared or given away. The traders' introduction of liquor and tobacco, for example, expanded but did not create the obligations of a well-off man to his supporters. Food—which the Gros Ventres did not obtain from traders—was still a crucially important item to share with the needy or with followers. Traders' documents show that the important intermediary chiefs were assisted but not created by the traders. In their daily journal entries the traders in Canada recorded the important chiefs and gave no indication that they favored one chief over another. On the other hand, the Gros Ventres' preoccupation with rivalry and competition—in moiety relations or the enemy-friendship relation, for example—could have been stimulated by the traders' distribution of gifts and chief's coats to lesser chiefs and the influx of new luxury goods. Perhaps more individuals had more means to try to achieve recognition for generosity. Still, to trade, a man generally needed a surplus of horses. Horse ownership and trade relations buttressed each other. It seems to be no coincidence that, among the northern Plains peoples, Gros Ventres and the Blackfeet groups—with at once large numbers of horses and the most favored position in the robe trade from the 1830s on—have been characterized as having the most developed association of rank with wealth and generosity.[27]

"An Audacious, Turbulent Race": The Struggle to Survive

During the late eighteenth and nineteenth centuries, warfare was a preoccupation of the Gros Ventres, at first out of a desire to raid or protect horse herds, later out of the need to defend themselves against efforts to dispossess them of their territory. "Fierceness" or stalwartness in battle was especially valued, and this ideal was given expression in such institutions as moiety competition and the enemy-friend relationship.

The traders' expansion westward on the Saskatchewan put such pressure on the Gros Ventres that eventually they had to try to displace other peoples from the new territories where they were forced to move. These conditions worked to strengthen the Gros Ventre commitment to fierceness. Traders' attitudes toward the Gros Ventres underwent considerable change from the 1770s to 1830, by which time the Gros Ventres had all migrated south across the international boundary into Montana. In the 1770s, the traders spoke admiringly of the Gros Ventres, portraying them as more "European-like" and as wealthier and more independent than the Crees and Assiniboines with whom the traders were used to dealing. Increasingly, however, the traders came to characterize the Gros Ventres as particularly hostile, aggressive, and warlike toward Europeans, as an "audacious" and "turbulent" people, more "dangerous" than the other peoples with whom the traders dealt. The change in the Europeans' perception reflected the changes in Gros Ventre behavior that marked their adjustments to the repercussions of trade relations in the 1790s.

When Matthew Cocking traveled to the Forks area in the winter of 1772–73, he met a group of Gros Ventres ("Water-fall Indians"), probably two bands, near Eagle Hills. Cocking's companions obviously regarded this as the Falls' homeland: the Cree and Assiniboine guides pointed to the buffalo pounds, tobacco plantings, "tent places," broken pots, and "several stone heaps on the tops of the high hills" that were put there and used by "Archithinue" natives (that is, Gros Ventres and possibly Blackfeet groups). Cocking points out that the Crees and Assiniboines were on friendly terms with the Gros Ventres and that the Crees served as middlemen in the trade with Hudson's Bay posts farther east, downriver. The Gros Ventres and other Archithinues came to trade with the Crees and Assiniboines in the spring: Gros Ventres were used to trading "horses and buffalo skin garments for winter apparel; also wolfskins and other furs" were exchanged for trade goods. The Gros Ventres at that time were fighting the Snakes (Shoshones) to the south; Gros Ventre and Blackfeet groups had driven

41

the Snakes from the region several years earlier after acquiring horses and some guns, but Snakes still raided into the area of the South Saskatchewan. Cocking considered the Gros Ventres superior to the Crees and Assiniboines in that they had many good riding and pack horses, they were more expert in the hunt, and they were more independent and technologically proficient. The Gros Ventres themselves must have felt superior to the horse-poor Crees and Assiniboines. In 1776 the Gros Ventres were still trading peacefully with the middlemen. But by 1777, things had changed.[28]

French-Canadian and English companies, competing for the Indians' furs, began to build inland from the bay. Hudson's Bay Company established Cumberland House in 1774 and Hudson House (near Gros Ventre country) in 1778. The Cumberland House journal for 1777 records that the Crees and Assiniboines were warring against the Archithinues. The inland posts eroded the middlemen's position, motivating them to try to prevent Archithinues from coming to the posts. Gros Ventres nonetheless brought provisions and skins regularly to Hudson House in 1779. By 1785 the trader complained that they had become so experienced and shrewd about the trade that they were "hard to deal with." The hostilities between the Gros Ventres and the Crees and Assiniboines continued to escalate, for the homelands of the latter had been hunted out to meet the traders' demands for furs and provisions, and the Indians had become dependent on trade goods. The more numerous Crees and Assiniboines set out to dispossess the Gros Ventres and their westerly neighbors and allies of their lands. By 1787 warfare was so intense that trade suffered. Between 1788 and 1795, the Gros Ventres were particularly hard hit by the Crees. The trader at Manchester House reported in 1788 that Crees ambushed a party of Gros Ventres at Battle River, killed the headman, and robbed the group: they "killed the leading man, . . . cut off his arms, head, Private Parts and took out his bowels," and then took the furs. Duncan M'Gillivray wrote in 1795 that the Crees had been "involved in frequent quarrels with the Gros Ventres for many years past, but as they mutually feared each other their hostilities amounted only to the death of a few of either party." He noted, however, that in the summer of 1793 Crees murdered the occupants of sixteen Gros Ventre tipis asleep near South Branch House. They killed all but a few children, whom they kept as slaves. In the traders' accounts of these years, none of the other tribes suffered any comparable losses. Gros Ventres suffered inordinately in relation to their more westerly neighbors, the Siksikas, Bloods, and Piegans, because they bordered the west flank of the Crees and Assiniboines, who were moving west into the Forks.[29]

In summer and fall 1793 and summer 1794 the Gros Ventres began for the first time to attack the traders, an unheard-of act in the Saskatchewan area. Tomison wrote to James Bird that these were "a peaceable People til now." They must have done it "out of spite" because "they could not be avenged on the Southward [Cree] and Stone [Assiniboine] Indians" for killing so many of them last summer. Bird expressed surprise at "hearing of a House plundered by a People I thought the most rational and inoffensive in this part of the country." The Gros Ventres were aware that the arms and other supplies their enemies used against them in their own territory came from the traders' posts. Gros Ventres robbed and killed the employees at Island House, robbed Manchester House, and robbed and killed employees at South Branch House. M'Gillivray noted that because they saw the traders as Cree allies, the Gros Ventres attacked the Hudson's Bay Island House and, less successfully, the nearby Canadian post. Forty Gros Ventres entered Manchester House on the pretense of trading, then stole horses and other goods. The trader at Buckingham House reported that the attack was in retaliation for Cree and Assiniboine attacks; in particular, two of their "Old Men" were killed and many women and children captured. These elders were probably important ritual leaders; their deaths would have been particularly traumatic to the Gros Ventres.[30]

The attacks on traders made life more difficult for the Gros Ventres, for subsequently the traders were reluctant to allow them in the posts to trade for guns and ammunition. And the devastating attacks on them did not stop. After 1795, Gros Ventre relations with the traders in Canada were uneasy; they attempted to stay on good terms in order to have access to trade goods, especially arms and ammunition, but sporadically they attacked or were abusive (in the traders' view). Their position in Canada was increasingly precarious. Alexander Henry, employed at Fort Vermilion in 1809, commented that the Gros Ventres were south of the Siksikas, Bloods, and Piegans, between the South Saskatchewan and the Missouri, whereas formerly they had been between the North and South Branches eastward to the Fork. And "formerly they were very numerous and much dreaded by neighboring nations," but smallpox in 1781 and 1801 and attacks by other tribes had reduced their numbers.[31]

The Gros Ventres blamed their troubles, and the fact that they were pushed out of their lands between the North and South Saskatchewan, on the traders. Daniel Harmon, Northwest Company trader at Fort Alexandria in 1801, noted that the Gros Ventres "say that we furnish the Crees and Assiniboines with what firearms they want, while they get but few." Fidler wrote that Akaskin, the head chief in 1801–2, was particularly hostile to the Europeans and was "generally stirring his countrymen up against them" because his brother was shot at South Branch. In spring 1800 and winter 1802, parties of Canadians and their Iroquois employees were attacked by Gros Ventre warriors, who killed some of them and robbed them of their guns and ammunition. They told the Hudson's Bay men that they would have killed them also if they had had the chance. The Gros Ventres were particularly angry at these parties of trappers in their country. As James Bird at Edmonton House noted, their steel traps were destroying too many beaver and endangering the Indians' trade. In the summer of 1807 some Gros Ventres, with the aid of Siksikas and Bloods, robbed Fort Augustus of guns and ammunition, according to David Thompson. Henry, who was on the North Saskatchewan between 1809 and 1811, observed that the Gros Ventres would trade nothing and that they blamed their unhappy situation on the traders at Fort Augustus, who gave better terms for provisions and skins to other tribes and refused to sell guns and ammunition to Gros Ventres: this "made their hearts bad toward the whites." Ambivalent relations continued into the 1820s. MacKenzie encountered many problems in his efforts to travel through country occupied by the Gros Ventres in 1822, for they suspected him of trading with their enemies. Even though he met with the "chiefs and old men" to try to facilitate his work, in October a large hostile camp forced him to return to Chesterfield House and abandon his travels. One chief would not accept his tobacco. MacKenzie never "met with greater insult" than was shown him by the Gros Ventres; they were "the most indolent and turbolent of the Slave [Archithinue] Tribes."[32]

When they were not hostile to the traders they tried to encourage trade in various ways. At Chesterfield House, Fidler noted in 1800 that the Gros Ventres "killed more skins than the Blackfeet man for man" and that they prepared their skins well—better than the Blackfeet groups. Militarily at a disadvantage compared to the Blackfeet (because they bore the brunt of the attacks from the east and were fewer in number than the Blackfeet groups), the Gros Ventres were attempting to get better prices for their skins and to obtain a larger share of the trade. The Gros Ventres brought good trade, Henry said—provisions, skins, and robes. "In dressing these robes they are far superior to the Slaves [Blackfeet groups] and fully equal to the Mandans." He noted that they dressed the skins in a particular method of their own, "far superior" to that of other Plains tribes, and that they were more "industrious" than others. Henry also thought that they were particularly ambitious in providing women as consorts and wives to the traders, doubtless in an effort to gain a trade advantage.[33]

The Gros Ventres were not always successful in their efforts to increase their profits, for the traders were mistrustful and took advantage of their precarious position. Henry wrote, "They take whatever we offer them in exchange for their produce, without demanding a higher price." He indicated that the cause of their "docility" was their knowledge that they had a "bad reputation" with the traders—as an "audacious, turbulent race"—because of the past hostilities. For the most part they traded horses and did not ask high prices. They still had many horses, and with their Piegan allies kept the traders away from one of their main sources of supply, the Kutenai, west of the Rockies. It was during the first decade of the nineteenth century that the Gros Ventres—"the easiest people to trade with," accepting what was offered and not "dunning" the traders like the Piegans—became known as the "most lavish . . . in offering their women."[34]

Another repercussion of the Gros Ventres' worsening circumstances was that in Canada they allied themselves more closely to the Blackfeet groups. Without their assistance the Gros Ventres could not have hoped to defend themselves against the Crees and Assiniboines. Bird asserted in 1806 that the Blackfeet groups were "master of the Plains" from South Branch to Acton. Some Gros Ventres came into Edmonton House, Fort Vermilion, Chesterfield House, and Rocky Mountain House between 1806 and 1829, but always in the company of these allies. Some obviously had made the trip north from Montana. These were bands of Gros Ventres that had left Canada and moved south after the troubles of the 1790s. Henry estimated the Gros Ventres who regularly traded on the upper Saskatchewan to number eighty tipis in 1809. In 1823, 450 tipis of Gros Ventres reportedly traded at Edmonton, some of whom must have come up from Montana to sell the furs that they stole from American trappers. That year Thomas Heron reported that about 600 tipis (seven people per tipi) had traded at Chesterfield House, and that the Gros Ventres were most closely allied to the Piegans, in control between the Bow River and the northern branches of the Missouri east to the junction of Red Deer and Bow. The traders in 1822 observed, however, that the Gros Ventres were "the most independent [from Hudson's Bay Company] of the Slave tribes"; many avoided visits to the Hudson's Bay posts for years.[35]

The Gros Ventres apparently stayed generally in two north–south groups, a fact reflected in Lewis and Clark's statement in 1806 that the "Fall Indians" (Canadian or northern group) of 260 tipis (2,500 population) traded with the Northwest Company on the upper Saskatchewan and roamed between the Missouri and Bow Rivers. And the "Staetan tribe" (southern group) of 40 tipis (400 population) were with the Arapahoe (ca-ne-na-vich) and roamed the headwaters of the Loup branch of the North Platte River. The Gros Ventres apparently maintained two divisions in later years, for Point told Father De Smet that the Gros Ventres were in "two camps" in 1847. And the Fort Browning

45

trader James Stuart noted that in 1872 a group of thirty tipis under the leadership of White Eagle ranged with the Crows near the Missouri, while the remainder were under Young Man Bear north near the Cypress Mountains.[36]

Peter Fidler probably knew the Gros Ventres best during the early nineteenth century, for he served at Chesterfield House, where large numbers of Gros Ventres regularly traded. He called them a "desperate sort of Indians." He summed up their situation thus: unlike other tribes in the region, they had had smallpox (which they contracted from Arapahoes to the south) in the summer of 1801 and lost more than a hundred of their young people (born after the epidemic in 1781), and "on account of the war and disease this summer cutting off such numbers of them, appear desperate, and [are] nearly ready to fall on anyone they can." He also added that after losing many horses in the severe winter of 1801–2, they are "ill off" and "in a sour mood." Hostilities continued with the Crees and Assiniboines. In 1800–1801 the latter killed 150 Gros Ventres, mostly women and children, and stole 114 horses. Fidler stressed how terribly "downcast" the Gros Ventres were. That same year two young Gros Ventre men were out killing foxes when some Blackfeet murdered them and stole their 170 skins. The ensuing hostilities between the two peoples lasted at least two years and further undercut the Gros Ventres' position, as they needed an alliance with the Blackfeet groups. By 1811, Henry wrote, "destruction stared them in the face."[37]

Many Gros Ventres responded to their predicament by boldly setting off for new territories. Beginning in 1794 bands began to move to the upper waters of the Missouri and farther south. This was apparently an alternative strategy in the aftermath of their weakened position in the Saskatchewan area. M'Gillivray reported in 1794 and 1795 that, according to Blackfeet groups and Assiniboines, after the Gros Ventres attacked the traders, they separated into two large segments and one went south to the Rocky Mountains to try to ally themselves with the Snakes, intending to abandon the Saskatchewan area. The other, about ninety tipis, remained and sought to renew peaceful relations with traders. The alliance with the Snakes, if it materialized, must have been very brief, for during the next three decades Gros Ventre bands continued to separate and move south, and joined in alliances with a closely related people, the Arapahoes, and with the Blackfeet groups. They also attempted to ally themselves with Crows. In 1801 Fidler observed that Tattooed Indians (Arapahoes) came to Chesterfield House in the company of the Gros Ventres: "This is a part of a nation that never saw Europeans before. They inhabit on the eastern borders of the mountain far to the south of this, they have been forty-four days in coming, they speak nearly the same language as the Fall [Gros Ventre] Indians and are at peace with them, who have escorted them here. . . . They are a pretty numerous tribe amounting to about 90 or 100 tents. Their manners are different from the Fall Indians, but [they] are nearly of the same size and features." He noted that these Gros Ventres had been living south (in Wyoming and Colorado) with the Arapahoes for at least two years. In 1802 some of the Blackfeet told the traders that all the Gros Ventres went to the Missouri River to meet and ally with the Arapahoes and Mountain Crows. A group of Gros Ventres, about 300 tipis, found the Crows on the Bighorn River in September 1805, and attempted to make peace and trade for horses, according to François Larocque. Some Gros Ventre bands resided with Arapahoes up until the 1830s, when most rejoined their people in Montana.[38]

In Montana the Gros Ventres and Blackfeet groups, especially the Piegans, were closely allied throughout the early nineteenth century. They were strong enough to dominate the upper Missouri east to the Yellowstone. Warfare with the Crows was mentioned by Thompson in 1807 and by Henry in 1811, and this fighting continued through the first half of the century. By effectively keeping the Crows out of the upper Missouri area, and by making that area too dangerous for American trappers, the Gros Ventres and Blackfeet groups prospered. Here they obtained provisions, robes, and skins (often stolen from Americans daring enough to travel in this country), which they traded in Canada or to the south in the company of Arapahoes. By 1830, Hudson's Bay Company traders reported that all the Gros Ventres had gone south to Montana: John Rowand wrote from Rocky Mountain House that "no less than 400 tents of Fall Indians—all there were of them—have left us . . . to the southwest upon American ground."[39]

In 1831 a change in the American Fur Company's trade policy made Montana a particularly favored location for Indian hunters. In 1831 the American Fur Company built Fort Piegan at the mouth of the Marias and began to buy skins, robes, and provisions from the Gros Ventres and their allies, rather than employing their own hunters. Officials of the company had decided to "confine ourselves to trade and give up hunting in the upper Missouri—Indians are now too well aware of the value of furs to let us hunt them in peace." Access to the traders helped the Gros Ventres improve their circumstances and better arm themselves. Maximilian noted, "These Indians were formerly very poor . . . ; they have, however, recovered of late, and supplied their wants." The traders were initially generous with gifts in order to promote amicable relations. Maximilian observed that the Gros Ventres camped along the river, waiting for the traders' boats to pass, for the traders gave them presents. He described the Gros Ventres as invete-rate beggars, worse than the Blackfeet groups. Father Point, on a visit to Fort Lewis in 1846, also described the Gros Ventres as "terrible demanders."[40]

Although in 1832 a band of Gros Ventres traveling north from Ara-pahoe country to rejoin the main body of the tribe had gotten in a battle with George Nidever's party of trappers at the edge of the Rock-ies in Wyoming, by 1833 their reputation with the traders had begun to improve. David Mitchell, in charge of Fort McKenzie, which was built six miles above the mouth of the Marias in 1832, reported that he "transacted business with them with pleasure and had never had any proofs of the treachery imputed to them." When Prince Maximilian visited Fort McKenzie in 1833 he described how a trading party of several Blackfeet and Gros Ventre bands "delivered up their colors"—the flag they had been given by the English in Canada—to symbolize their wish to establish good relations with the American traders. The Gros Ventres' need for friendly relations with the traders was so great, according to James Bradley, a soldier at Fort Benton in the 1870s, that they overlooked occasional killings of Gros Ventres at the forts. And when a Gros Ventre shot an employee at Fort McKenzie in 1839, his own tribesmen killed him.[41]

Hostilities with traders came to an end for the Gros Ventres, but fighting with Crows, Assiniboines, and Crees continued unabated. The Gros Ventres bore an inordinate proportion of the fighting, compared to the Blackfeet groups, for they ranged to the east of the Blackfeet, between them and the enemy. Assiniboine attacks had been particu-larly deadly in the 1830s. Trader Edwin Denig reported that Gauche's band massacred thirty tipis of Gros Ventres. Bradley noted that Assini-boines and Crees killed 400 Gros Ventres at Sweetgrass Hills in 1835.[42]

Traders not only supplied Gros Ventres with the trade goods they needed; occasionally the traders gave them military assistance against their enemies. Bradley describes a successful Gros Ventre raid against Crows in 1855 with the aid of a party of traders. In the 1870s Gros Ventres sometimes traveled with traders for greater safety. And Gros Ventres told Kroeber how well-armed traders aided their warriors. Black Wolf gave this account of what happened when Sioux surprised him in the 1850s or early 1860s: "The entire party was all about me, all of them shooting. Bullets struck the ground all about me, and there was no noise but that of shooting. . . . Suddenly the attacking party split. A white man was running from the store [trading post on Milk River] with a gun to help me. I ran to him, and reached him almost exhausted. He took my hand and we ran back to the house. . . . My father had sent word to the trader to keep me there if I should come, so I stayed there some time."[43]

By the mid-nineteenth century, the expansion of the American frontier had driven the Sioux west into Montana. The Gros Ventres and other groups there were forced to defend themselves against Sioux incursions for most of the remainder of the century. To fight the Sioux, who greatly outnumbered them, the Gros Ventres needed help. Thus in the 1850s and beyond they tried to establish peaceful relations with peoples they formerly fought. The Gros Ventres' wealth in horses enabled them to form an alliance with the Assiniboines, for the Assiniboines had relatively few horses. Edwin Denig, a trader among the Assiniboines, wrote that in 1851 the Gros Ventres made overtures to the Assiniboines, and gave them between 400 and 500 horses to cement an alliance. Denig wrote, "The Gros Ventres show great anxiety to preserve peace, have never been to war against the others [Assiniboines] since their friendly connection commenced, but the Assiniboines were not united enough among themselves for this end." By 1869 the Upper Assiniboines had been weakened by attacks from the Sioux and by disease; they eagerly promoted the tenuous alliance with the Gros Ventres and sought to report to the same agency on Milk River to obtain annuities and benefit from the combined forces of the two peoples. Agent A. S. Reed reported in 1870 that the Upper Assiniboines gave 100 women as wives to the Gros Ventres, presumably to cement their alliance. By 1873 Long Hair's band of Assiniboines were regular visitors to the newly established Fort Belknap agency on Milk River and maintained an uneasy alliance with the Gros Ventres against the Sioux. Agent W. Fanton wrote in December 1873, "The Gros Ventres are few in number and have a larger proportion of horses than most tribes to protect from enemies"; consolidation with the Assiniboines would be good for mutual protection.[44]

An alliance with the Crows was formed in the wake of an outbreak of hostilities with the Gros Ventres' former allies, the Piegans. Bradley noted that in 1861 the Gros Ventres attacked a party of Piegans whom they mistakenly blamed for stealing some of their horses. The result was intertribal raiding between the Gros Ventres and the Piegans and their Blackfeet allies until the early 1880s. The Blackfeet groups prevented the Gros Ventres from trading at Fort Benton, so they initiated an alliance with the Crows, trading and hunting farther down on the Missouri during the 1860s. The Crows had been driven closer to the Gros Ventre territory by the Sioux. By 1866 the Indian Office's representative in Montana recommended that an agency be established for the Gros Ventres and Crows together. The agent reported at the Gros

Ventre and River Crow Agency, established in 1869, that the Assiniboines were regular visitors and that they received rations there. The
Crows' hostility to the Assiniboines, coupled with their desire to avoid
smallpox when the Gros Ventres contracted it in the winter of 1869, led
most of the Crows at the agency to move south to rejoin the remainder
of their people. As late as the 1870s, however, White Eagle's band of
Gros Ventres often camped with the Crows, and Crows visited Fort
Belknap Agency.[45]

By the 1850s it was clear to the Gros Ventres that they could not hold
their place in Montana (along the Milk River northwest to the Cypress
Mountains and southwest to the Marias) without white allies. They
sought them not only among traders, but also among the United States
government representatives who were in contact with the Gros Ventres after the treaty of 1855. Although members of Bull Lodge's band
did not hesitate to waylay Father Joseph Giorda in 1862 and attempted
to hold the missionary hostage for several weeks until white settlers
returned some stolen horses, Gros Ventres were generally friendly to
whites. Federal officials welcomed their help against hostile Indians in
Montana. While the Sioux were constantly harassing boats going up
the Missouri and hindering westward migration and settlement in the
late 1850s and 1860s, Indian agents for the Blackfeet and Gros Ventres
were able to secure their consent in 1855 to passage and posts in their
country. Agents stressed that from 1856 through the 1870s the Gros
Ventres remained friendly to the United States. In 1860 Agent Vaughan
reported that the army informed him that there were no "better behaved" Indians than the Gros Ventres. When some of the Blackfeet
groups engaged in fighting with whites between 1866 and 1869, the
Gros Ventres remained peaceful. During this time the Gros Ventres
were able to subsist by hunting and were not dependent for food on
the federal government (as were many of the tribes on the central and
southern Plains). They did not view whites as the main source of their
problems, and their lands were not being appropriated by miners and
settlers, who were concentrated to the southwest of the Gros Ventres,
around Fort Benton. Thus the Gros Ventres perceived the whites to be
their allies, and this perception influenced the choices they made in
reservation times and the strategies they developed later to cope with
their changing circumstances.[46]

The Gros Ventres were in more precarious circumstances than
other groups up to 1878 because of their geographical position and the
size of their population—which was considerably smaller than that of
the combined Blackfeet groups or the numerous bands of allied peoples known as the Cree, the Assiniboine, and the Sioux. The despera-
tion that fed Gros Ventre fierceness was in great part a reaction to

conditions that accompanied trade relations and, after 1855, the expansion of the American frontier. Warfare was encouraged by the frequent small raiding parties that became more prevalent after the acquisition of horses, and raiding was reinforced by the market for horses and provisions provided by the Canadian and American posts. Casualty rates went up, and epidemics introduced by traders resulted in severe population losses that threatened the Gros Ventres' ability to defend themselves. Intertribal fighting was escalated in Canada by the westward movement of the Crees and Assiniboines and in Montana because there were still buffalo herds there in the late nineteenth century. Plains Indians flocked to Montana to hunt after the game in their own territory was exterminated as a result of frontier settlement. According to Bradley, Alexander Culbertson reported that in 1835 there were about 500 tipis of Gros Ventres (probably a population of 3,500–4,000). Smallpox killed almost 200 in 1837. By 1855, officials at the treaty council reported that there were 2,970 (360 tipis). In 1865, 160 died of measles. Then in 1867 the Piegans massacred 300 Gros Ventres at Cypress Hills, and in 1869 smallpox killed another 741. By 1870 A. Sully, superintendent for Montana Indians, observed that there were only 1,300, and when Fort Belknap Agency was temporarily established during 1874–76, Agent Fanton reported that the Gros Ventres who came there numbered 960.[47]

Some traders and travelers singled out the Gros Ventres as the bravest among the northern Plains peoples. Emphasis on bravery and fortitude was not unique to the Gros Ventres during these times, for these were ideals shared by Plains peoples in general. But some institutions that gave special emphasis or encouragement to "fierceness," such as the competition between moieties to gain prestige for their members by exploits in war, do seem to be unique to the Gros Ventres. Group goals would have been reinforced by the age-group system, of which the moieties were part, particularly because the system was supernaturally sanctioned. The enemy-friend relationship was also unique to the Gros Ventres. Flannery noted that an ambitious man "selected his enemy-friends with care so as to ensure opponents worthy of his efforts." And Gros Ventres told her that "everyone watched with interest the contest between well-matched enemy-friends," who held bragging contests about their war deeds. Two famous enemy-friends, Sits Like a Woman and Bull Lodge, were mentioned by Flannery's informants as exemplifying the way the relationship encouraged tenacious, unyielding, aggressive behavior in battle. Bull Lodge insulted Sits Like a Woman's record as a leader of war parties. Shortly afterward, Sits Like a Woman returned from a successful expedition and insulted Bull Lodge, then challenged him:

" 'If you choose to pay me back in the way I have treated you, go ahead. But first lead a successful war party. If you then do to me what I have done to you, I won't be mad. But I'll lead still another war party and do far worse to you that second time than I have done this time.' "[48]

Descriptions of behavior on war parties suggest that sanctions against "lazy" or unassertive behavior were particularly harsh. Gros Ventre men were described as being afraid of particular leaders because they would humiliate those who fell short of the ideal in an especially degrading fashion. One leader would dance, imitating a wolf, circling around until he came to a young man he thought "lazy." Then, in front of the man, he would raise his leg in imitation of a urinating dog.[49]

Kroeber observed that the Gros Ventres' Sun Dance ritual, in contrast to the Arapahoes', emphasized "ceremonies relating to war." It may very well be that their age-group system and related ceremonies once differed little from those of their relatives the Arapahoes, and that the Gros Ventres developed the moiety system, enemy-friend relationship, and Sun Dance modifications to cope with their desperate need to defend themselves during a period when war escalated and survival was uncertain.[50]

Throughout the 1778–1877 era, the Gros Ventres emphasized to each other the importance of being tenacious, unyielding, and aggressive—or, as they often expressed it, "fierce." As Cooper pointed out, among the foremost of the nineteenth-century Gros Ventre character ideals were "strongheartedness" and the ability to "bear and forgo." Tenacity and strongheartedness were encouraged in all areas of life, including the acquisition of prestige and rank. One of Flannery's elderly informants characterized her grandmother, who made her work very hard to learn all the skills that a woman needed to attain prominence, as "fierce." That they survived disaster after disaster, rebuilding their fortunes and improving their circumstances, must have validated those ideals to the Gros Ventres themselves. That whites aided them in their efforts to retain their territory along the Milk River encouraged a strategy to convince officials that they were "civilized" in the reservation era.[51]

"I Call Myself a White Man": 1878–1901

Beginning in the middle of the nineteenth century, federal government policy was to concentrate Plains Indians on reservations removed from areas settled or heavily traveled by whites. It was not until the 1860s, however, that non-Indian political and business interests in

Montana began to exert pressure on the government to confine the Indians in Montana Territory to designated reservations and then gradually to reduce the size of those reservations. For Indians, settlement on reservations became more necessary as the last of the buffalo herds began to disappear. On the reservations the government's Indian agents distributed food and supplies—at first to attract Indians to the agencies on the reservations, later to prevent starvation. Federal policy also was to "civilize" the Indians once they were confined. Indian agents were directed to use military force if necessary to suppress native customs and educate the Indians to an agricultural way of life that approximated that of neighboring non-Indian settlers. Any activity government officials deemed uncivilized—polygyny, native religious rituals, horse raiding—was banned.

Fort Belknap was reopened in 1878, and Gros Ventres and Assiniboines began to be subjected to the civilization policy after Agent Wyman Lincoln took up permanent residence there in June. Shortly afterward, they began to be pressured to cede most of the territory recognized as theirs by treaty and executive order. After 1883 they were no longer able to subsist by hunting and were dependent on the federal government as never before. So in 1887 they ceded land in return for regular rations and supplies. Reservation conditions presented many challenges to the Gros Ventres. How were they to live up to ideals of bravery against their enemies when raids were banned? How were they to continue to fulfill ritual responsibilities when their ceremonies were prohibited? And how was one to accumulate food and property in order to be generous to others when the basis of one's economy, the buffalo, was gone?

After 1878 some Gros Ventres began to settle in the vicinity of the agency, at least for part of the year. Bands or groups of families camped along the creeks, where they could get firewood and water. Gradually all the Gros Ventre bands came to the reservation. Alongside their tipis many built log cabins to live in during the winter. The agency buildings were several miles northeast of the Gros Ventre camps. The Assiniboine camps generally were east of the agency. Most of the Indian agent's time was spent handling the weekly issue of rations. He and his staff had to care for the agency's cattle herd, butcher the beef, and issue meat, flour, and other foodstuffs to family heads. The Indians supplemented the ration by hunting small game and by buying food from the trader's store at the agency. For their subsistence needs, Gros Ventres relied on the trader, missionaries, and a few white men married to Gros Ventre women as much as they relied on the agent. The agent had far-reaching powers: he could withhold rations or imprison uncooperative individuals, if he chose. He selected several Gros

Ventre and Assiniboine men as Indian police, and they were charged with executing his policies. The agent also could call on troops at Fort Assiniboine to assist with his civilization program, but this was never necessary. The fort was built in 1879 about twenty-five miles from the agency. Little actual agricultural instruction was provided the Indians by the small agency staff, for they had all they could do to herd cattle, grow feed, and repair agency buildings. Indian adults generally had only brief, weekly contact with the agent and his staff. But, at the agent's direction, children were placed in a government-operated boarding school, established in 1891 at the agency, or at St. Paul's boarding school, opened by Catholics in 1887, sixty-five miles south-east of the agency. Despite the fact that the agents did not have daily contact with the Indians, their actions affected all Gros Ventres and Assiniboines. They controlled the money and resources of both tribes, and when they and their superiors in Washington, D.C., failed to stop non-Indians from trespassing on reservation lands to graze cattle or from stealing supplies or minerals such as coal and gold, they contributed to the tribes' deprivation. Most agents, in collaboration with Montana businessmen and politicians, also embezzled or otherwise misappropriated tribal money and property. The fortunes of individual Indians were greatly influenced by the agents' actions, as well.[52]

Gros Ventre ambition to be "prominent"—that is, to have enough property to be able to give generously to others—persisted even in these trying circumstances. Those with the means began to recognize new ways to be generous, such as donating cattle to tribal gatherings or lending tools needed for agriculture. And horses continued to be valued highly, for they could still be sold to traders and others despite the end of the hunting way of life. Although the age-grade ceremonies, at which gifts were once exchanged, were no longer performed, opportunities for public generosity were provided by the pipe bundle rituals that were still held and by the moiety dances, as well as by new ceremonies that seemed harmless to officials and that became popular after reservation settlement. Intertribal wars ended, but the Gros Ventres continued to feel threatened by the tribes around them. They especially viewed their co-residents at Fort Belknap, the Assiniboines, as rivals for political influence with federal officials and for limited resources. A quest for primacy on the reservation began to preoccupy Gros Ventre leaders to the same extent that ambition for success in battle once had done. "Fierceness" came to describe not military vigilance, but tenacious, adversarial behavior toward other groups perceived as threatening. Because the Gros Ventres needed the aid of their civilizing agents, the route to both prominence and primacy came to be behavior that was symbolic of civilization to federal officials. The Gros Ventres themselves interpreted these behaviors as expressions of ideals that predated reservation settlement. In their view, prominence and tenacity still were attainable goals. But the people's ability to unify and cooperate was undermined by reservation conditions.

"The Indians Are Talking All Different": The Decline of Cooperative Altruism

In the early years of reservation settlement the pipe bundles and their rituals were still central to Gros Ventre life. A few years before the Gros Ventres settled at Fort Belknap, Crow Bull became official keeper of the Flat Pipe and received the necessary training from a former keeper, Under Bull. While the three seasonal rites were apparently discontinued, several other pipe ceremonies were held. One was the face-painting rite, in which children and many adults had their faces painted with sacred red paint in a design that symbolized creation and the Gros Ventres' relationship with the Great Mystery. Some individuals vowed to "cover the pipe" in return for the Supreme Being's aid or blessing. When a number of "coverings" (offerings) accumulated, the keeper held a sweat-lodge rite and smudged them (held them over a sacred smoke that symbolically carried the prayers associated with the offerings to the Great Mystery). Then the keeper left some of the offerings in the mountains or on buttes and gave the remainder to the poor and needy. After Crow Bull died in 1887, the Flat Pipe was without a keeper at first, then White Bird was chosen, and he was followed by Bird Sits High, who died soon after. Then, from around the turn of the century, without having received instruction, Bird Sits High's father, Otter Robe, kept the pipe until about the time of his death in 1911. Apparently the Flat Pipe rituals were rarely if ever held after the death of Crow Bull in 1887 until the pipe was again formally transferred to a new keeper sometime between 1909 and 1911. Sitting High was officially installed as keeper of the Feathered Pipe by the former keeper Bull Lodge at about the time the Gros Ventres settled at Fort Belknap. Sitting High conducted the spring rite, during which he painted the bundle, conducted a sweat lodge, and supervised the offerings to the pipe. The keeper had various powers in the area of weather control, as well as in protecting the people from illness or danger. During Sitting High's tenure, Gros Ventre individuals covered the pipe, were painted, and danced and prayed with objects in the bundle, all in fulfillment of vows. Sitting High's tenure lasted until his death in 1905.[53]

During the early reservation years, the Catholic mission made few inroads among the adult Gros Ventres, who continued to follow their native religion or, in the 1890s, became followers of a revitalization movement, the Ghost Dance complex. In 1888 the priest in charge at St. Paul's Mission, established among the Gros Ventres at the foot of the Little Rockies in 1887, admitted that there were no Catholics among the adults. The fact that a number of Gros Ventre children died of measles that year did much to hinder the missionary work, for the Gros Ventres believed that baptism was the cause of the deaths. In 1891 the priest wrote to the commissioner of Indian Affairs that they were "rather adverse than inclined to get religious instruction." According to Father Charles Mackin, also at the mission in the 1890s, some young people did become converted when they experienced a vision. A dying youth dreamed of a dead relative "in hell," who advised him to convert; a dying girl dreamed that the Blessed Virgin appeared to her and told her to convert. At the mission boarding school, Indian Office officials charged, children were terrorized by descriptions and threats of hell, and the school's policy, strictly enforced, was to repress the expression of Indian culture and language.[54]

While the Gros Ventres continued to try to fulfill their ritual responsibilities toward the pipe bundles, they stopped holding the age-grade ceremonies. In view of the agents' efforts to prevent such gatherings, it probably would have been difficult to hold them, especially since the lodge rituals took several days and required everyone's presence. Such gatherings took people away from their work, the agents thought. Besides, after the severe population losses before they settled on the reservation, there probably were not enough ritual authorities still living to supervise the ceremonies. Ordinarily a man would join successively the Fly Lodge, Crazy Lodge, Kit-Fox Lodge, Dog Lodge, and (as the Drum Lodge had not been held since the 1830s) the Old Men's or Law Enforcers Lodge. But only the Crazy and Dog lodges were held in the 1870s (a Kit-Fox Lodge had been held about 1870) and the Crazy Lodge again in 1884. Thus young men who had not been old enough to join an age set and the first age grade by about 1870 were not part of the age-group organization. When the Old Men who were alive at the time of reservation settlement died, they were apparently not replaced as ritual leaders. In 1901 Kroeber found only one elderly man who had completed the series of grades. In 1886 the Gros Ventres abandoned their annual Sun Dance, or Sacrifice Lodge, as well. Agent Lincoln had threatened to suppress the ceremony with military force, if necessary, and the Gros Ventres (for reasons explored below) were eager to persuade the agent of their commitment to civilization.[55]

There are indications that although the Gros Ventres recognized the importance of tribal unity and sought to effect it, they had difficulty reaching consensus after their settlement on the reservation. Possibly the disunity reflected the loss of the lodge organization with its supernatural underpinnings. In the winter of 1884 Agent Lincoln reported that the Gros Ventres had called in all their people to their camp on Clear Creek for a council. Lincoln observed that they were trying to mobilize consensus to "stick together" in formulating their strategy for dealing with whites in upcoming land-cession negotiations. But a few bands refused to agree with the majority and left the meeting. Later, in 1895, they again were unable to reach unanimous agreement on the question of the cession of the Little Rockies area on the southern border of the reservation.[56]

Despite the end of the age sets and age-grade ceremonies, the Gros Ventres continued the moiety organization and its associated rituals. Kroeber observed that in 1901 there was "a division of the young men of the tribe into two groups" (moieties called Stars and Wolves). He added that until "recently" (probably in the late 1890s) one group practiced the Star Dance, the other the Grass or War Dance. About the time of reservation settlement, many youths joined one of the moieties. They were instructed by older men in the moiety's songs, dances, and responsibilities. When a moiety held its dance, they sang their begging songs (for example, "Harden your hearts, Wolfmen, be prepared to give") before men of the rival moiety, who then donated food for those attending the dance and distributed property, particularly to rivals in the opposite moiety. At a later time, the other moiety held their dance and their rivals could then try to outdo them in generosity. The Gros Ventres apparently were able to deceive or otherwise dissuade the agent so that no attempts were made to suppress these dances. Unlike the lodge rites, moiety gatherings did not require the presence of all the Gros Ventres and could be of only a few hours' duration. When Assistant Commissioner of Indian Affairs R. V. Belt was visiting the reservation in 1892, he came upon a small gathering of people watching a Grass Dance. The Gros Ventres told Belt and Agent A. Simons that they were dancing to express their pleasure at having brought their children to the mission school.[57]

Gros Ventres still sought supernatural aid with the help of individuals who had personal medicine power. Medicine power—that is, aid from spirit helpers who were manifestations of the Great Mystery—was sought by a vision quest: an individual fasted alone and otherwise inflicted suffering on himself in order to gain pity, and therefore assistance, from the supernatural. Medicine power could also be obtained through apprenticeship or dreams. Actually, Gros Ventres felt that power obtained in this way ultimately was harmful to its owner; they stressed to their children that prayer through the pipe bundles and lodges was preferable. Men with medicine power to help or harm individuals not only continued to be among the prominent, but perhaps increased their influence in the wake of the demise of the Old Men or age-grade leaders and the keepers. Medicine men received payment for their services. The activities of the medicine man were difficult for the agent to control, particularly since some of his Indian police were themselves powerful medicine men. Some of the medicine men, who once used their powers against the Gros Ventres' enemies, now used their powers primarily to harm rivals or force people to do things against their will. Or so the Gros Ventres thought. One such individual who had power in war and curing, a Gros Ventre told Flannery, was "a good doctor but was treacherous with it." These men noted for their medicine power were often among the dissidents when the Gros Ventres failed to reach consensus in important councils. People were afraid to criticize them publicly. Before reservation settlement such a man could leave the main group with his followers; now he stayed in the community and might work against group goals or side with the agent.[58]

In the 1890s the Ghost Dance and the associated hand game ceremony were introduced to the Gros Ventres. The Ghost Dance, a new religion that promised a return to prosperity in return for performance of the rites, developed in response to the deprivation and despair on Plains reservations. Practitioners danced until they lost consciousness or fell into trance, at which time they had a vision experience. The Gros Ventres learned about the Ghost Dance revitalization movement through their contacts with the Arapahoes in Wyoming. The two peoples visited each other regularly. The agent notes, for example, that Otter Robe, active in the Ghost Dance complex, went to Wyoming in 1887 and 1901. And groups of Arapahoes visited the Gros Ventres in 1894, 1898, and 1901. In 1890 Returns to War, a man with one Gros Ventre parent and one Arapahoe parent, came to Fort Belknap from Wyoming and started the Ghost Dance religion ("little round dance") among the Gros Ventres. Agent Simons thought it to be "not violent or dangerous." Subsequently, a form of the hand game was introduced in conjunction with the Ghost Dance.[59]

The hand game was a guessing game in which one team attempted with supernatural aid to use a guessing stick to determine which player on the opposite team was holding a bone button. Correct guesses were rewarded with counter sticks. The first team to win all the sticks won the game. The game was sponsored by someone as an offering to accompany a prayer for supernatural aid. If the ritual was conducted properly, the sponsor's team won. Gros Ventres born in the early and mid-nineteenth century believed that the Supreme Being created and controlled everything through thought. This Being endowed humans with the ability to think and thereby to cause things to happen. This idea was the basis for prayer in all Gros Ventre rituals. Prayer before the hand game was an important part of an individual's attempt to get supernatural aid. It may be that in their prayers the mission-educated generation equated the Supreme Being with the Christian God; thus a Catholic might vow to God to sponsor a hand game, generously providing for others, in return for a relative's recovery from illness. Officials generally viewed the hand games as harmless entertainment, although if the agent thought that the games interfered with work, he might try to prevent them.

Several Gros Ventre men, including Otter Robe, had hand game bundles they obtained from the Arapahoes. The Ghost Dance, which according to Flannery incorporated aspects of Flat Pipe and Christian religion, was abandoned after two or three years, apparently because its leaders were discovered committing fraud and soliciting exorbitant fees, but the hand games were frequently held during the 1890s and early years of the twentieth century. Individuals with problems (illness or trouble of some sort in the family) would vow that in return for supernatural aid they would sponsor (pay the expenses of) a hand game. The bundle keeper would pray for them at the time of the ceremony and would direct the ritual to make sure everything was done correctly. One Gros Ventre woman explained to Flannery that when her husband was very ill she promised the Supreme Being, "If you spare his life I will make a hand game." He recovered and she bought the food for a hand game to which the whole tribe was invited. The women sat on the east side during the game, the men on the west side. The two sides competed with each other in guessing who had the buttons.[60]

The Gros Ventres' accounts of their life in the early reservation days indicated that there were two kinds of ritual leadership: that which expressed cooperative altruism and that which expressed competitive egoism. The pipe and moiety rituals required cooperative altruism. The ceremonies worked only if people cooperated and thought or prayed in harmony. Leaders were supposed to think only good thoughts about people. But there were also ritual leaders who acted in the capacity of shamans (that is, their power came from personal contact with the supernatural, not from training in ritual formulas), who were accountable to no one, and who often competed with other leaders. They could use their powers to harm others and destroy rivals; of course, they risked supernatural punishment if they did so. Those with shamanistic roles were medicine men, Ghost Dance "bosses," and to some extent owners of hand game bundles. After reservation settlement, shamanistic prominence gradually took precedence over the priesthood. Individualism or egoism overshadowed cooperative altruism as the age-set/age-grade system ceased to function and medicine men expanded their role in ritual life by dominating activities associated first with the Ghost Dance, then with the hand game. The federal government's civilization program helped to undermine the role of the priests (keepers and former keepers). The formation of the Indian Police by Agent Lincoln served particularly to undercut the authority of elderly ritual authorities. The agent helped the middle-aged police attain the wealth that led to prominence (as will be discussed below), and in turn the armed police used force to carry out the agent's policies. The Gros Ventre police, many of whom were medicine men, and their followers were not reluctant to oppose former keepers and moiety leaders. The dissenter or the individualist, medicine man or not, could attain prominence by acquiring wealth and redistributing it. He was not necessarily viewed as a "good" man, that is, one who cooperated with and respected others. But such a man was a role model for some young men. Formerly he would not have risen to great heights in Gros Ventre society; now, with the agent's help, he might.[61]

The growing problem of individuals who were divisive or disruptive próbably was related to the whiskey trade. In the latter nineteenth century liquor was sold to Indians in unlimited quantities despite regulations to the contrary. In 1878, 1879, and 1883 the agent reported "drunken quarrels" that ended in violence. The leading chiefs and elders even asked the agent to intervene, for they admitted they could not control the problem.[62]

Federal officials pressured the tribes to cede more land in 1895. At the cession council, quarreling among the Gros Ventres was probably an outgrowth of a rivalry between the most prominent Indian police and their followers and the old-guard moiety leadership and its followers. Jerry Running Fisher was the leader of the Indian police; Under Bull (also known as Lame Bull) was the leader of the Star moiety and the most influential of the former keepers. Thirty-seven Gros Ventres voted to cede the portion of the Little Rockies where gold had been found in return for $360,000 to be expended for the Indians over a four-year period. The majority of 153, led by Under Bull, refused. One Gros Ventre identified the assenting minority: "I say the same thing as those headmen, those policemen." Both Jerry Running Fisher, captain in the Indian Police, and Otter Robe, lieutenant, had medicine power. Under Bull appealed to the men to join him in resisting the sale, saying, "Look at my hair, it is gray." Gray hair suggested advanced age and symbolized his authority and his status as a high-ranking ritual leader in the age-group system. At the council it was noted that the "young men" followed him. Actually, a few men in their thirties followed Running Fisher and Otter Robe, but they must have been marginal to the moiety organization at this time. Running Fisher and Otter Robe cast aspersions on Under Bull and his followers, portraying them as "like children playing, they don't know what they are talking about." This council was deeply disturbing to the Gros Ventres. As Sleeping Bear put it, "The Indians are talking all different and I don't know what to do."[63]

Otter Robe, a prominent man of means, a renowned warrior, and a powerful medicine man, has the kind of personal history that exemplifies the role of individualists and their impact on Gros Ventre society at this time. In the 1880s, when he was in his thirties, he was the ultimate fierce warrior. He led the successful fight of 1886 when a Gros Ventre war party killed six Bloods—this was virtually the last of the war parties, and it took place against the wishes of the federal officials. In 1883 he got drunk at Fort Assiniboine, fought with other Gros Ventres, and defied the military commander, to the dismay of the chiefs and elders. He used his medicine power, Gros Ventres told Flannery, to coerce others to give him property; according to one account, he intimidated a man into giving him his wife and child. In 1896 an agency official reported that the Gros Ventres were "bitter against" him because of his defiance of their wishes. He and High Bird (presumably his son, Bird Sits High) fought with a policeman (appointed in 1896 by a new agent who removed such older men as Otter Robe from the ranks of the Indian Police) who was attempting to arrest him for illegally butchering stock. Representatives of the young men of the moieties appealed to the agent to control Otter Robe and others like him. But it was not until a decade later that, in the view of Gros Ventres, Otter Robe received his just due—death by supernatural means in retribution for his failure to meet his ritual responsibilities.[64]

"We Like to Become Rich Cattlemen": Achieving Prominence

After reservation settlement men with horse herds concentrated on building and caring for their stock so that they could sell their horses to obtain trade goods and food, as well as give them away. With the end of intertribal raiding, their herds increased. But young men, born too late to have acquired horses before United States and Canadian authorities suppressed horse raids among the Indians of the Northern Plains, had a more difficult time achieving prominence. After 1883 the buffalo were so scarce in the area that the robe trade, an important source of wealth, collapsed. By the late 1880s young men, and to a considerable extent even older, prominent men, began to depend on the resources of the agent, missionaries, or other whites to acquire the means to be generous and therefore to be somebody. All of the agents (Wyman Lincoln, 1878–1887; Edwin Fields, 1887–1889; A. O. Simons, 1889–1892; William McAnaney and Charles Robe, 1893; J. M. Kelley, 1893–1895; Luke Hays, 1895–1900; M. L. Bridgeman, 1900–1902) helped individuals' quests for prominence in several ways.[65]

By convincing an Indian agent that they were "deserving"—that is, that they cooperated with the agent's civilization effort—individuals received various kinds of property or favors that they could use to achieve prominence. Seven Gros Ventre and seven Assiniboine Indian policemen (appointed by the agent) received salaries and extra rations, which they shared with others; guns, which facilitated hunting and defense of horse herds and also intimidated rivals; and cow hides from the agency herd, for which the trader would exchange trade goods. The police also had authority to arbitrate property disputes, seize stolen horses, and use force against those engaged in uncivilized pursuits. For the "deserving" prominent, middle-aged men, the agent plowed a large section of land (about 600 acres). Each man's followers were assigned small sections within the large field, where they planted and harvested vegetables. They gave a portion of the crop to their headman, who could then generously feast others or sell or trade the produce. All of the agents made it a practice to issue cow hides to "industrious and deserving Indians"—individuals who did not oppose the agents' programs. If he chose, the agent could buy wood, crops, and horses from individuals. Gros Ventres also sold surplus produce at Fort Assiniboine. The agent lent farm machinery to deserving headmen, who organized their followers into work groups, and sometimes hired out to neighboring white ranchers, collecting food and trade goods in payment. Wagons, harness, and other items were issued, but, as there were not enough to go around, deserving men were favored. The agent also had been given authority by the commissioner of Indian Affairs, specifically in the land cession agreement of 1887 (ratified in 1888) and in the 1895 land-cession agreement, to issue to deserving individuals the cattle that were bought for the Gros Ventres and Assiniboines in return for the cessions. Individuals could acquire herds of cattle and then sell or butcher them for the benefit of others. Prominent Gros Ventres were well aware of the advantage to be had from the ownership of cattle as well as horses, for they routinely pressed the government to issue cattle to them. They stressed in 1886, just a year before the land-cession council, that they wished to become "rich cattlemen."[66]

Contemporary documents illustrate how prominent Gros Ventres used military and agency resources to acquire wealth and maintain reputations for generosity. Chief Jerry Running Fisher became a scout for Fort Assiniboine in 1881. His camp of followers stayed close to the troops when they patrolled, so they hunted undisturbed by enemy tribes. The scouts were given extra rations (which they shared), as well as arms and ammunition (which were difficult to get). Traders at the fort gave the scouts presents to distribute to their people to encourage their trade. After Running Fisher was appointed captain of the Indian Police by Agent Lincoln in 1883, his influence and wealth increased until some whites began to refer to him as head chief and many young men, particularly police, followed his lead—although most Gros Ventres recognized Under Bull as their spokesman. As police captain, Fisher requested and apparently received supplies that enabled him to feast the people once a week. The agent purchased sizable quantities of potatoes and onions from him ($150 worth in 1886). When he went to Washington to meet with the commissioner as a member of the Gros Ventre and Assiniboine delegation of 1894, he remarked, "I want to be a white man and to be treated like a white man." He urged officials to increase the pay of Indian employees (like himself), who hitherto had received less pay than whites for the same work, and to continue to issue cattle to deserving individuals.[67]

Sleeping Bear was a prominent chief with a large herd of horses and eventually of cattle. Lincoln thought so much of Sleeping Bear's efforts to become civilized (he had fifty-two acres under plow in 1885) that when fifty of his horses were stolen by whites from Canada, Lincoln not only financed Sleeping Bear's expedition to Canada to retrieve the animals but also arranged to furnish him with a few horses to help replace the ones he had lost. In later years, when his agricultural endeavors had become even more impressive and he opened a trading post (in competition with white traders) where his young mission-educated daughter served as bookkeeper, the Indian Office supported the project. Under Bull and other prominent chiefs received pay for freighting and selling produce and wood. Young men, who had been children when the Gros Ventres arrived at the agency, were particularly dependent on help from the agent. Agent Hays championed them in 1896 when he appointed younger men to the police force in place of the middle-aged "old barnacles" who had been police for many years.[68]

Gros Ventre men also turned for aid to the Catholic missionaries. By sending their children to the mission boarding school, chiefs obtained loans, wage work, and a ready market for wood, grain, and other crops. Younger men who supported the mission programs could obtain not only employment from the priests but sometimes even wives from

3. Gros Ventre and Assiniboine delegates to Washington, D.C., 1894. *Standing, left to right:* Sleeping Bear (Gros Ventre), Sitting High (Gros Ventre), Charles Perry (Assiniboine, interpreter), Jim Matt (Gros Ventre, interpreter); *seated, left to right:* The Male (Assiniboine), Wetan (Island) (Assiniboine), Jerry Running Fisher (Gros Ventre), Eyes in the Water (Assiniboine), Otter Robe (Gros Ventre); *seated in front,* Little Chief (Assiniboine). At their meeting with the commissioner of Indian Affairs, the delegates attempted to dissuade the government from insisting on the cession of the Little Rockies and argued for more economic assistance, including the distribution of cattle to the Indians at Fort Belknap. At this time the Gros Ventres were emphasizing their accomplishments in "civilization." Running Fisher remarked to the commissioner that he had cut his hair to indicate his commitment to civilization. Both he and Otter Robe—also with short hair—wear their Indian Police uniforms. The Assiniboine leaders, all of whom had short hair, stated that they had their hair cut in order to indicate their interest in taking up the white way of life. Today Assiniboine folk history attributes their short hair to the government's reprisals for the death of Agent A. O. Simons. Identification of delegates from the photograph collection of the National Anthropological Archives, Smithsonian Institution. Photo courtesy of Blaine County Museum, Chinook, Montana.

among the young female pupils under the priests' supervision. Obtaining a wife this way spared a man the expense of a gift (usually in horses) to the bride's family. Running Fisher's support of the mission—he even brought children to the school by force—won him considerable aid in his quest for prominence. He built his ranch and farm next to the mission, thereby benefiting from the adjoining irrigation system built by the priests. In correspondence with government and church officials in Washington, the priests represented Fisher as head chief of both the Gros Ventres and Assiniboines.[69]

Gros Ventre men obtained the assistance of white traders, stockmen, and agency employees to whom they married their female relations. These whites, in addition to advising the Gros Ventres on how to deal with government officials and often serving as interpreters, helped their Gros Ventre in-laws with farming, gave them stock and trade goods, employed them, and offered hospitality in general.[70]

Wealth differentials, largely in stock ownership, were as characteristic of early reservation days as of the prereservation era. Although the level of deprivation on the reservation was severe at times, the percentage of prominent people may have increased under reservation conditions. The size of the horse herds certainly did. But the sector of the population that was poor in property probably also increased. Without horse raids that ensured mobility—upward or downward—the older men with herds increased their stock by breeding, while younger men had to seek other paths to prominence. With the suppression of polygyny, the agents generally allowed a man to keep wives that he had but forbade him additional ones. Many widowed women were left husbandless, and they and their children had a difficult time making a living. Orphans, however, sometimes were able to get a start in life, even a start at careers as prominent men, for they often spent their early years at the mission and there secured the assistance of the priests.[71]

As prominence had to be validated by publicly recognized generosity, the giveaways persisted, despite the agents' efforts to suppress them. As the trader Thomas O'Hanlon acknowledged in 1881, when a man gave gifts, "it looks [*sic*] as if he was the 'chief.'" Some of the rituals in which Gros Ventres gave away property—such as the transfer ceremony of a sacred pipe bundle—eventually were abandoned, but others continued. The men's moiety dances and the begging songs continued almost until the turn of the century. A prominent man was expected to give many horses to the family of the bride when he married, "for the honor," explained Kroeber. It was customary for well-to-do parents to designate one or more of their children as a "beloved child" (*niiheeníOaa'*), and they then were obligated to give away property to persons who either honored or had conflict with that child. The new hand game rites were another outlet for generosity, but perhaps more important were "tea" or "house" dances. The agents noted in 1885 and 1890 the popularity of individually sponsored dances and feasts (where tea was routinely served) at which the host gave away property. The agents do not indicate if the tea dance was a custom of both the Assiniboines and the Gros Ventres or how it originated, but by the early twentieth century tea dances were frequently held among both tribes. Perhaps the custom began in the late nineteenth century among both. An elderly Gros Ventre told Flannery that her tribe had been introduced to the tea dance by the Assiniboines.[72]

The importance of being somebody is clearly a major theme in Flannery's interviews with Gros Ventres. The Boy, speaking of his boyhood, tells through an interpreter how he began his career (probably about 1880) as a prominent person by helping a poor boy:

> He remembers one occasion which made a lasting impression which was the starting point of his career of being sympathetic and having consideration for other people besides himself. That was when the Gros Ventres moved towards these mountains from the lower reaches of Beaver Creek. . . . [The little boys] were all on horseback, a big group on this occasion, . . . and as they were going along they saw someone on foot. When they got up to him it was a little boy walking and crying and completely nude. Everybody passed him by, all the other boys did, but The Boy pulled up his horse and rode to this little boy. . . . So The Boy put him on his horse . . . ; he rode to where his folks were starting to make camp. . . . So they took him in and fed him and made clothes for him. . . .[73]

"My Country . . . It Belongs to Me": Prominence and Primacy

At the same time that Gros Ventres competed among each other for prominence, they competed with people of other tribes for primacy. In fact, there was a fit between pursuit of individual prominence and the pursuit of primacy in relation to other tribes: evidence of civilization brought an individual wealth, and it also (or so the Gros Ventres believed) might bring good, even preferential treatment of the Gros Ventre people by the dominant whites. Thus the Gros Ventres' strategy for dealing with whites and for coping with the problems brought by white settlement in Montana and the increasingly exploitive policies in Washington was to convince whites that Gros Ventres were civilized. They were remarkably successful.

As early as 1885 an inspector distinguished the Indians at Fort Belknap from the Piegans, settled on a reservation to the west: The Gros Ventres and Assiniboines "are doing better than their neighbors . . . ; they evince a desire to become civilized . . . and are making some progress in that direction." In 1898 an inspector from Washington wrote specifically of the Gros Ventre community: "The 'tepee' is a thing that has passed and in its stead there is the little log cabin, neat in its appearance and surroundings, the barn, the corral, the grain stacks, the fenced fields. . . . The valley of 'Peoples Creek' presents a picture that is pleasant to contemplate, and it is difficult to believe that one is looking upon a community of savages."[74]

Their seeming embrace of civilization was an outgrowth of their friendly strategy in earlier years. As friendlies before reservation settlement, for example, they had benefited from issues of ammunition when some other tribes got none. When the army asked a band of them to provide scouts in 1882, they talked it over among themselves and agreed. Then in 1887, when Gros Ventres were insisting on a new agent in an effort to improve reservation conditions, they attempted unsuccessfully to have the commander at Fort Assiniboine appointed. They and their scouts were on good terms with the commander, who had "distinguished himself against their enemies the Sioux." They had hoped to obtain an agent sympathetic to them. They also needed to appear friendly and cooperative, for by themselves they could not keep the flood of tribes from Canada and the Northern Plains out of their hunting territory; they needed the federal troops to do this during 1878–1882. The troops also returned horses that had been stolen from them. With this history of alliance with whites and in the absence of a history of warfare with the United States (like the Plains tribes farther south), the Gros Ventres developed a strategy of behaving like civilized people to try to fend off the pressure of white Montanans for land cession.[75]

Despite the 1855 treaty agreement with the United States which led to their settlement in the vicinity of Fort Belknap, the Gros Ventres subsequently were threatened with the loss of their homeland. The white settlers and their representatives put pressure on the federal government to evict the Gros Ventres (as well as other tribes) from the lands assigned to them in Montana. Between 1878 and 1887 efforts were made to remove the Gros Ventres to reservations already occupied by other groups, including the Teton Sioux, Lower Assiniboines, Crows, Mandans, and Hidatsas, and also to the Indian Territory in Oklahoma. By 1883 the Gros Ventres were resigned to cession, but when a group of Gros Ventre leaders met with congressional agents who were negotiating with the Montana tribes, they made it clear that they wanted to retain as their reservation a strip of land between the Milk and Missouri rivers, approximately 150 miles east to west and 50 miles north to south. They were more civilized than other tribes, they pointed out; they should be permitted to retain most of their land because they would make productive use of it as agriculturalists.[76]

When the Gros Ventres met with Inspector C. Dickson in February 1886, their spokesman, Under Bull, insisted that the inspector tell the president that "we are now capable of taking care of our cattle. . . . You have seen our houses that were built by ourselves. . . . You have seen our fields and our fences. We have raised many potatoes, vegetables, and some grain. . . . If we had a boarding school we would send our children." And Running Fisher added, "I am preparing to put in large crops this year; so are my people." Later that year, greatly alarmed by reports that they would not be allowed to retain their lands, they enlisted the aid of Father F. Eberschweiler (and the influential Bureau of Catholic Indian Missions in Washington, D.C.) to prepare a petition to the president. The priest had promised to help them obtain their reservation and a subsidy from the government; in return they agreed to support his efforts to build St. Paul's Mission at the foot of the Little Rockies. In the petition they stressed that they were already very civilized, and that if their petition was granted, they would become a model of civilization, as successful as the Flatheads. "There we and our descendants can once possess large and good farms and become in course of time as rich as the white farmers." They reminded the president of their history as friendlies: "We never caused troubles to the whites; we always proved our faithful friendship to them, especially in their difficulties with hostile Indians. Their enemies were our enemies." The Gros Ventres (and their Assiniboine allies) got their reservation, but they retained much less land than they had wanted when the cession agreement, signed on January 21, 1887, was approved by Congress on May 1, 1888. The reduced reservation was approximately twenty-five miles from west to east and forty miles from north to south. The Gros Ventres (who were settled outside the boundaries of the reduced reservation) moved, a few bands at a time, until eventually by 1890 they had all resettled on the reduced lands, most in the Little Rockies area (see map 3).[77]

The Gros Ventres then turned their attention to obtaining the best possible treatment from the government. They persisted in their strategy of evincing civilization. In a council held to make peace between the Indians of Fort Belknap Reservation and the Bloods of Canada on June 9, 1887, the Gros Ventres were described as more cooperative than the Assiniboines. Under Bull is quoted thus: "I call myself a white man and look upon the white men as my brothers." Running Fisher remarked, "I call myself a white man." These remarks are English translations, but Father Eberschweiler makes clear that "calling oneself a white man" meant to the Gros Ventres a willingness to engage in civilized activities. He describes Running Fisher thus: "He likes to be like a white man in farming, educating children." In other words, being like a white man did not mean abandoning Gros Ventre values and viewpoints; it meant being given a fair chance to succeed in the reservation context.[78]

1855

1874

a) 1888
b) 1895

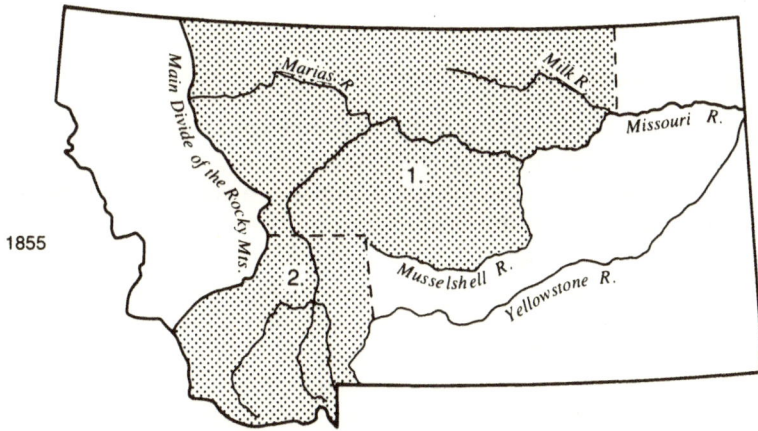

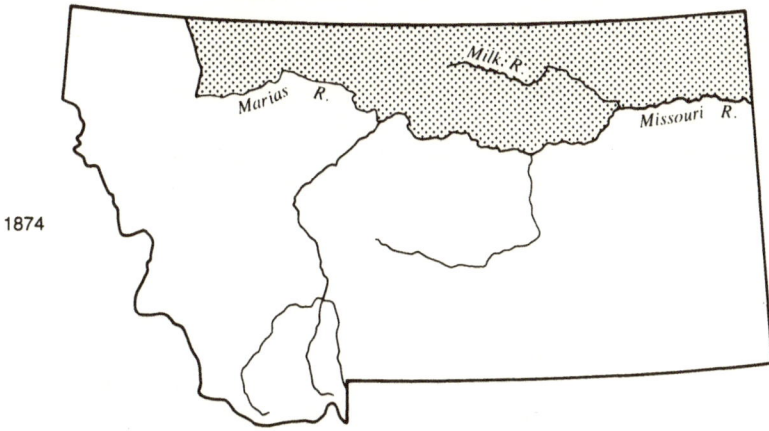

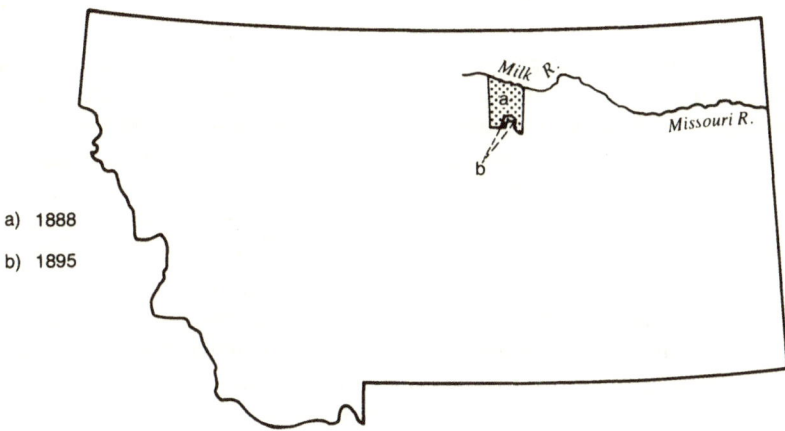

1855	1. Lands reserved to Blackfeet and Gros Ventre, Treaty of 1855
	2. Common hunting ground for Blackfeet, Gros Ventre and other tribes, Treaty of 1855
1874	Lands set aside for Blackfeet and Gros Ventre by Executive Order, April 15, 1874
1888	Lands Reserved to Gros Ventre and Assiniboine, Agreement of May 1, 1888
1895	Land ceded, September 19, 1895

Map 3. Reduction of reservation lands assigned to the Gros Ventres, 1855–95

At first the Gros Ventres viewed their alliance with the Assiniboines as a means of fending off intrusions from other Indians and, during the uneasiness over the cession negotiations, as a way to strengthen their claim to their lands. By claiming to be "one people" with the Assiniboines, they increased their numbers and made it more difficult for the government to move them. But when they began to view the Assiniboines as a threat to their political position, as well as to their ability to subsist at Fort Belknap, their strategy was to try to outdo the Assiniboines in exhibiting civilized behavior.[79]

Initially, the Gros Ventres were clearly more numerous than the Assiniboines and more influential in political relations with whites. In 1878 the Gros Ventres reportedly numbered 956 and their Assiniboine allies 737; ten years later, they outnumbered the Assiniboines enrolled at Fort Belknap 964 to 830. When white cattlemen wanted permission to graze their stock on the reservation in 1878, they consulted only the Gros Ventres. But as early as 1883, the Gros Ventres began to show anxiety over the Assiniboine presence, apparently recognizing that it threatened Gros Ventre primacy at Fort Belknap. Running Fisher insisted to a congressional delegation, "My country does not belong to the Assiniboines; it belongs to me. I want to have the Assiniboines with me, but I want to mark out my own lands." The Assiniboine leader Little Chief responded: "If the Gros Ventres are dissatisfied with us, we would like a reservation down the Missouri River with the Lower Assiniboines." The Gros Ventres' anxiety was due partly to the fact that the Upper Assiniboines were encouraging Lower and Northern Assiniboines, and some Crees and French-Chippewas, to settle among them as "Assiniboines," thus swelling their ranks. By 1890 the agent reported that the Assiniboines at Fort Belknap numbered 952, the Gros Ventres 770. The Gros Ventres were also alarmed because the Assiniboines initially impressed federal officials as more inclined to civilization than the Gros Ventres. The Assiniboines were far more willing than the Gros Ventres to leave the large camps and settle on small family farms. Agent Lincoln remarked in 1882, "The Assiniboines show greater adaptability for farming and for work of any kind than the Gros Ventres; they do more farm work, and work more for hire. . . ." The first to join the Indian Police were Assiniboines. The Assiniboines were more agreeable to putting their children in school. Father Eberschweiler initially devoted his attentions and the resources of the church to the Assiniboines, who were settled nearer to the agency headquarters than the Gros Ventres.[80]

By 1884 (at the height of their anxiety over land cession) the agent noted that the Gros Ventres had undergone an "entire change": they showed more interest in "labor." In 1889 more Gros Ventre than Assiniboine children were attending school. In 1886 they stopped holding their Sacrifice Lodge, which the agent regarded as a savage custom. By 1896 federal officials agreed that, in the words of Inspector C. C. Duncan, the Gros Ventres were exceptional and that they were "doing much better than the Assiniboines." Agent Hays concurred: "The Gros Ventres are in much better condition than the Assiniboines. . . . They have been more successful in farming" and "more successful with their stock." About this time, too, the fathers expressed a preference for Gros Ventres as pupils at the mission. By 1900 Agent Bridgeman reported that the Gros Ventres produced more wheat and oats than the Assiniboines and had 5,000 horses and 2,000 cows to the Assiniboines' 2,000 horses and 1,200 cows. By the late 1890s Gros Ventres saw themselves as materially better off (though not so well off as they wished) and more capable than other peoples in the reservation context. They viewed themselves as successfully competing with whites, as well. They were aware that local whites thought so much of their houses and fields in the ceded area that they purchased or appropriated them. So Gros Ventres held their achievements in civilization in high regard.[81]

When in 1895, in response to pressure from white Montanans, the federal government began formal negotiations to persuade them to cede the southern section of the reservation where gold had been found by trespassing miners, the Gros Ventres again relied on their strategy as civilized people. They were aware of the potential value of the gold deposits there, and they had a plan to mine the region themselves and to send their children for the necessary training to do it. With income from mining, the Gros Ventres could expect to prosper in years to come. As White Weasel said, "The whites say that there isn't much money in that mountain [Little Rockies], but I don't believe it." Federal officials, angry at the Gros Ventres' opposition, portrayed them as foolish and unprogressive. When the vote was taken, the votes of the more numerous Assiniboines to cede the land destroyed the Gros Ventres' hopes. The Assiniboines were more destitute and more eager to please officials, as one of their number had killed Agent Simons three years earlier.[82]

Leaders of the 1878–1901 era—the men of the moieties, the warriors, the medicine men—were frustrated and bitter by the end of the century. The Little Rockies cession had turned many Gros Ventres against the Assiniboines. In the last decade of the century, the people of Fort Belknap experienced particularly severe deprivation as a result of graft on an unusually large scale on the part of Agents Hays and Bridgeman. Rations were sold before they reached the Indians; money that Congress appropriated for rations and supplies was pocketed by

71

the agents and their accomplices. Gros Ventres still sought to be somebody through public generosity, and the pursuit of primacy at Fort Belknap still was an important goal. The possibility of realizing these personal and group goals must have seemed remote. But in the early twentieth century, new means to these goals emerged.[83]

"We Progressive Stockraisers": 1902–1937

In the early twentieth century, federal Indian policy continued to be geared to assimilation of Indians. Without consulting or involving them, federal officials developed programs to make Plains Indians agriculturalists, fluent and literate in English, and Christian. Rations were drastically reduced in order to "encourage" the Indians to become self-supporting. And allotment of reservation land in severalty (authorized by Congress in 1887) was pursued with vigor. This policy was designed to promote individualism and private ownership by severing individuals' ties to the tribe or group. But in actuality it worked to erode self-sufficiency and to deplete resources, because "surplus" reservation land (land not allotted to individuals) was sold to non-Indians, and hard times forced most Indians to lease or eventually sell their allotments. One new policy that accompanied leasing was the establishment of an advisory body, a business council of Indian leaders, whom the agent was supposed to consult on land matters. The agent was in no way obligated to follow the council's advice. However, Indian leaders showed increasing sophistication in their dealings with officials, for they had learned to use contacts with various Indian rights groups and to pursue their goals in the courts. During Franklin Roosevelt's administration there was a major shift in Indian policy. John Collier, who became commissioner of Indian Affairs in 1934, was instrumental in getting Congress to pass the Indian Reorganization Act that year. This legislation ostensibly provided for greater self-determination and economic development in Indian communities, and Collier's administration defended religious freedom for Indians. Throughout this era, the government, acting as trustee, had control over Indian resources. Federal officials were supposed to protect Indian resources and help Indians use them to become self-supporting. But policies vacillated from one approach to another, and graft and mismanagement were characteristic of local administrations. In retrospect, the federal government failed to fulfill its responsibilities as trustee.

The agents at Fort Belknap encouraged "progressive" behavior, that is, agriculture (farming and/or ranching) and boarding school education. One agent stressed cattle ranching and withdrew support for farming; another stressed farming and discouraged the raising of cattle. And some tried to develop horse ranching, while others tried to destroy it. A high turnover in agents made policy quite inconsistent. And the Fort Belknap people continued to be victimized by stock trespass on their grazing lands, cattle rustling, diversion of their water, and the leasing of land to outsiders at very low rates, as well as outright graft on the part of their agents. In addition, agriculture suffered from periods of drought and a depressed national economy. Tribal income (from leases, primarily) was controlled and expended by government officials, and tribal members were denied a role in deciding how the money was to be used. In support of agriculture, expensive irrigation projects of dubious value were undertaken with tribal funds; then Indian agriculturalists were charged water fees whether they used the water or not. If they could not pay the charges, their lands were leased to non-Indians. Over the objections of Indian ranchers, in 1913 agents decided to lease most of the reservation grazing land to non-Indian cattlemen. A cattle herd was purchased with tribal funds without the Indians' consent, and this herd took remaining grazing land that Indian ranchers could have used; eventually the government sold the herd at a loss instead of using the stock to help Indians rebuild their herds. These and similar developments fostered a determination on the part of the Indians, and of the Gros Ventres especially, to take control of their own affairs. Gros Ventre business council leaders fought successfully to allot the entire reservation, with no setting aside of surplus land that could be sold, and to recover damages from the government for treaty violations. They persisted in trying to have incompetent or dishonest agents removed and to convince the government that Gros Ventres themselves could administer reservation programs. The allotment and other government policies also escalated Gros Ventre–Assiniboine competition. This, and the influx of French-Chippewas who frequented St. Paul's Mission, spurred the Gros Ventres to seek self-determination during the twentieth century.[84]

Remarkably, the conditions that Gros Ventres encountered in the early twentieth century stimulated their political and ritual revitalization at Fort Belknap. Tribal unity, fostered by a consensus-oriented decision-making process, ultimately was the result of the institutionalization of a business council in 1904 and by several new, secular rituals that were developed in the early twentieth century by Gros Ventres who grew up on the reservation. These political and ritual innovations were oriented toward reinforcing the pursuit of prominence and primacy and toward a commitment to self-determination. "Progressive" activities—such as a ranching economy, an agricultural fair, allotment of reservation lands, fluency in English—suggested a commitment to assimilation in the agents' view. But to the Gros Ventres, such activities offered the means to perpetuate cultural traditions and behavioral ideals. In difficult times, Gros Ventres pooled their money and property and, as groups—specifically, residence-based moieties organized at the turn of the century—participated in celebrations that provided outlets for public generosity. To the Gros Ventres, self-determination was a means to prominence and primacy and to continued tribal unity. The Indian Reorganization Act, then, was viewed as the realization of their aims, the culmination of their efforts. And Gros Ventre leaders enthusiastically supported the act. Gros Ventre leadership of the early twentieth century was bilingual and boarding school–educated. They were perceived as progressive by federal officials. Among the Gros Ventres, they were known as prominent men active in ritual life and tenacious advocates of primacy and self-determination.

"Big Crowd of People Spellbound": Reestablishing Social Solidarity

The establishment of a business council in 1904 encouraged the development of a tradition of intermediary leadership that revived consensus decision making. In addition, the agent in charge of the reservation from 1902 to 1910 was very tolerant of Indian ceremonies. Tribal unity was encouraged through new, secular rituals that became part of Gros Ventre life during this era. Gros Ventres found that the political and ritual institutions of earlier years no longer met their needs. A general process of revitalization unfolded, a conscious effort to create new, more appropriate and satisfying institutions.

In the early part of the century the Gros Ventres made attempts to continue their pipe-bundle traditions, motivated, it seems, by elderly tribal members. When John Carter visited Fort Belknap in 1909 he reported that Otter Robe, who had the Flat Pipe in his possession, reportedly knew only fragments of the pipe ritual and would not perform it in its entirety. Gros Ventres believed that his illness—he had become blind, and the agent had reported him insane—was due to the fact that he had violated one of the rules for the keeper. Shortly before or just after his death in 1911 the Flat Pipe was formally transferred, apparently with the ritual knowledge that the keeper would need, to Horse Capture, age fifty-three. Horse Capture conducted ceremonies, although most participants were apparently elderly. When Horse Capture died in 1924, the pipe was left alone and virtually abandoned, according to Gros Ventres whom Flannery interviewed.[85]

After Sitting High, the keeper of the Feathered Pipe, died in 1905, sixty-six-year-old Sleeping Bear was asked to take charge of it, although he was not made official keeper. Sitting High had presided over several rites—one in 1903 in which a man vowed to dance with the pipe and was cured of blindness. About 1904, during a Fourth of July celebration when the Assiniboines and Gros Ventres camped together to dance, Sitting High and other old men sang all night to stop rains from ruining the gathering, and the weather cleared up. In 1910 the Feathered Pipe was formally transferred to a fifty-two-year-old medicine man, Curly Head. He kept it until his death in 1938, and he conducted successful ceremonies. But Gros Ventres were distressed by his keepership, as well as by the neglect of the Flat Pipe. Flannery was told that Sitting High warned the people, when he knew that he was going to die, "not to pass it back to Bull Lodge's line [Bull Lodge was a former keeper and the father of Curly Head] because, if they did, something terrible was going to happen. But Curly Head got it anyway. . . . A lot of things happened that year, too—drought, earthquake, and a fellow killed himself at the Fourth of July celebration. . . . Curly Head made lots of mistakes. They don't tell him that he is wrong but

4. Curly Head with the Feathered Pipe bundle, at his home, 1925. Courtesy of Bureau of Catholic Indian Mission Records, Department of Special Collections and University Archives, Marquette University.

they know it and tell one another . . . ; just because he was raised with it he acted like he didn't give a darn whether he was right or wrong." Another person told Flannery, "Curly Head was crazy. He has no respect for anything and everybody knew that it would be no good when he got hold of the Feathered Pipe." And another Gros Ventre remarked, "Curly Head used to get mad and lick his wife"—but "the medicine men [keepers]" are "not supposed to talk about their neighbors or get cross."[86]

A few Gros Ventres continued to participate in pipe bundle rituals or leave offerings with the pipes, and occasionally a Gros Ventre man would participate in the Assiniboines' Sun Dance, which had been held fairly regularly, if sometimes surreptitiously, since reservation settlement. Hand games were held, but when the bundle owners died, one by one, they did not transfer their bundles. As discussed in Chapter 2, for most Gros Ventres, particularly those born in the 1890s or later, ritual participation (other than attendance at Catholic mass) revolved around the secular rituals—the Grass Dance, the Christmas dance, the moiety organization, and the fair.

About the turn of the century, the Grass Dance of the Wolf moiety was transformed into a ceremony in which all Gros Ventres participated. How the transformation occurred—perhaps by formal transfer of the ceremony by some individual or individuals—is unknown. But thereafter new regalia and other elements were added to the dance. The Grass Dance drew together elderly, middle-aged, and young people in a ritual that was at once an engrossing spectacle and a vehicle for the expression of cultural identity. The high point of the Grass Dance was the dog ritual (also central to the dance as performed by the Wolfmen). In this ceremony, the two men authorized to wear crow belts danced; then, together with the fork or "spear" keeper and spoon keeper, they positioned themselves west of the kettle containing cooked pup meat, while the two whip men and their two assistants were on the opposite side. The eight men danced four times around the kettle, then one of the crow feather bustles was put on by the fork man, who danced around the kettle four times and, on the last circuit, speared the pup with the fork. The bustle was then put on the spoon keeper, who, after dancing four times around the pot, served the meat

5. A giveaway at the Assiniboine Sun Dance, Fort Belknap Reservation, July 1906. A dancer is in the foreground; women in the background are probably presenting the gifts on behalf of a relative; the older man to the right, Horse Boy, is the director of this aspect of the ceremony. At this time Agent William Logan tolerated, sometimes even encouraged, Indian ceremonies. The Sun Dance or Medicine Lodge ("without the torture features") was held July 6–9 under The Male's direction during the weeklong Fourth of July celebration. Sumner Matteson observed 200 camps of Gros Ventres and Assiniboines in the vicinity of the agency, where the event occurred, and

counted twenty-one men dancing and four women fasting in the lodge. Hand games, Grass Dances, sham battles, and horse races were also held. Courtesy of National Anthropological Archives, Smithsonian Institution, Washington, D.C. Photo by Sumner W. Matteson.

to four warriors from among the spectators. After the meat was eaten, the regalia wearers danced, followed by the warriors, then the warriors recounted their war exploits. Each phase of the dancing had its series of special songs. During the dancing, the whistle keeper could call for a "punishing song," and the dancers would have to dance to exhaustion. There was also a war bonnet dance in which warriors removed the bonnets from the two female keepers, danced with the headdresses four times in a circle, then passed them to two other women, who danced with the bonnets and passed them on to two other women, and so on, until all had danced. In addition to watching the dog ritual and war bonnet dance, the spectators were prodded by the whip men to dance during the owl and ringtail round dances; couples put their arms around each other and danced clockwise in a circle in the ringtail dance and follow-the-leader style in the owl dance.

The Grass Dance was particularly important for young Gros Ventres. They seem to have played an important role in the innovations in the ceremony. The Boy, born in 1870, was an active participant in and composer of songs for the Grass Dance when he was a young man in his thirties and forties. His interpreter relayed his feelings about the Grass Dance to Flannery:

> The Boy composed those words in there [in a Grass Dance song] and he did it at a time when the old-time Indian dances were showing signs of dying out. The younger generation didn't know how to take it [what to do]. They figured out some way to keep on dancing, modified dances. . . . They sang this song and it kind of bridged that gap that existed at that time [between old and young]. . . . The song might seem simple and unimportant but it seemed to be the missing link that provided [helped them] to keep on having their social affairs. When they sang this song everybody got pepped up and got up and danced and yelled . . . ; they kept on doing something, in some way, and that was the way [to perpetuate Indian dancing].[87]

The Grass Dance allowed both sexes and all age groups to assume important roles in Hays ceremonial life. Old people supervised the "old-time Indian dances," such as phases of the Grass Dance that were survivals from the old moiety dance. And young people looked after the dance hall in which the ceremonies were held. Old men received public acknowledgment when they recited their war exploits during the dog ritual or were otherwise singled out. Young men could win acclaim by their skill in dancing and singing. One, a noted singer, was described to Flannery thus: " 'He could hold a big crowd of people spellbound. . . . He would sit up at the drum as straight as a lord and never attempted to be inconspicuous.' " Old warriors recounting exploits, young men exhibiting their flair for dance, prominent men leading horses into the hall to give away—the spectacle of the Grass Dance and the dances at Christmas or the fair, which later included the Grass Dance in abbreviated form (without the dog ritual)—helped motivate Gros Ventres to pool resources, cooperate, and redistribute property. The two men's moieties were replaced by a moiety organization that was based on a north–south division of the area where the Gros Ventres were settled. These new moieties (Black Lodge and Mountain Crow) cooperated to sponsor celebrations. The dance hall served for Gros Ventres as a symbol of their solidarity and of the merging of the old and the new. Under the charge of young men, it was built of logs but was circular, like the lodges or camp circles in which ceremonies were formerly held. One elder described it to me in 1984: "They all pitched in and built a hall. . . . Mountain Crow cut so many logs and then the Black Lodge cut so many logs. . . . It's a circle as much as logs would make a circle."[88]

A renewed sense of tribalism and a channeling of individual ambition into the pursuit of group goals characterized political life as well as ceremonial activity during the early twentieth century. In the summer of 1902, Agent Bridgeman was replaced by William Logan (1902–1910). In an effort to introduce reforms in the aftermath of scandal, in

6. Old dance hall at Hays, 1933. Note the entranceway; it was built large enough to accommodate the horses brought into the hall to be given away during the dances. Courtesy of Federal Archives and Records Center, Seattle, Washington.

1904 Logan started a business council of Gros Ventre and Assiniboine leaders, with whom he discussed reservation affairs.[89]

The business council organized by Logan was encouraged by the Indian Office in Washington, which wanted the agent to secure the Indians' formal consent to the leasing of reservation lands. Logan convened the council twice a year. In the beginning he apparently invited the prominent older men of both tribes to serve as councilmen. By 1908 he was directing the Gros Ventres at Hays and the Assiniboines at Lodgepole and in the Milk River valley to select young councilmen in group meetings—six from Hays, three from Lodgepole, three from the river area—and he appointed two others; he also invited the three Indian judges who had been appointed to preside over trials on the reservation to join the council. By then he was attempting to manipulate or pressure the tribes into choosing young, "educated" men, rather than the old men, because by 1907 these older councilmen were disillusioned with Logan and were complaining about him to the Indian Office. Sleeping Bear and other prominent Gros Ventres requested a formal investigation of reservation conditions and more authority in reservation affairs, maintaining that Logan was rustling Indian cattle for his own ranch and that he ignored the people's wishes. "We want to have something to say ourselves," insisted Sleeping Bear.[90]

At first, from 1904 to about 1908, the councilmen selected by Logan were prominent, elderly warriors and headmen, including Running Fisher, Under Bull, Sleeping Bear, and Otter Robe. Then gradually young bilingual men were selected in group meetings. At first the elders resisted the young men's role in politics, particularly as they saw the heavy hand of the agent in their selection. The elderly Powderface complained to Logan in 1909, "I didn't like these young boys for the chiefs [the 1909 councilmen's ages ranged from twenty-five to forty-three]—it is alright after they are about forty. . . . If those old chiefs would pick out six men it would be alright." In January 1910,

---

7. Jerry Running Fisher, 1908. In 1908 Running Fisher was retired from the Indian Police. Wearing his hair long once again, he posed with a warrior's staff. Decorated with eagle feathers, this kind of staff often was carried by qualified warriors to symbolize their exploits. Edward Curtis wrote of Running Fisher, whom he interviewed at length, "He has a fine war-record, having counted seven first [there appear to be seven feathers on the staff, but I do not know if it belonged to Running Fisher] and seven secondary coups, captured four guns and one bow, taken one tethered horse, which he captured in broad daylight with the whole Sioux camp shooting at him, and taken three scalps. He has killed twelve men with a gun, two with a knife in hand-to-hand conflicts, and two with a bow—sixteen men in all. He has led fourteen successful war-parties, and on one occasion his warriors brought back three hundred horses." In fasting for a vision experience, he obtained power in war, symbolized by a single downy feather of an eagle. Courtesy of Smithsonian Institution, Washington, D.C. Photo by Edward Curtis.

when Logan's representative was encouraging young men to dominate the selection of new councilmen, elders left the meeting in dis-
gust and complained to Logan. In 1914, Powderface wrote to Superintendent Miller that the council should include "Indians" (elders) as
well as "schoolboys": "The Indians know more about that treaty" and
"schoolboys have been to Washington twice [as delegates to a con-
ference] and they haven't done any good to the Indians." Gradually the
young men came to view their role as that of expressing and imple-
menting group consensus. Elders withdrew from council positions
and instead became advisers who served the young councilmen as
experts on past treaties or agreements between the Gros Ventres and
the federal government, for one of the Gros Ventres' political goals at
this time was to sue the government for the violation of the 1855 treaty.
Young men served as advocates and intermediaries in dealings with
federal officials. Eventually, as these young men aged, their influence
increased.[91]

As part of their selection of councilmen, the Gros Ventres instituted
an initiation ceremony modeled on older rituals in which individuals
were selected for positions of leadership. From the Gros Ventre point
of view there were six councilmen, regardless of what Logan or later
superintendents reported. In fact, they called the business council
néicaafaních, the "six-bunch." One elderly Gros Ventre described the
selection ceremony this way: The old-timers "got on one side [of the
camp circle or hall] and said, 'All of you people that want these people
on, get up!' Some guys remained sitting; they didn't quite understand
it. So they got these influential people [to announce], 'What are you
sitting down here for? Get up! Get up there; get up there!' And they got
up and they voted for it." After the men were chosen, they danced in
the center of the circle: "They had an honor song where they'd make
them dance later on during the night there. 'Well, we want these six to
get up here and dance.'" After the honor song, the councilmen and
their families gave away property to the crowd. The honor—that is,
the recognition of a man's prestige and acknowledgment of his authority—had to be validated by a public display of generosity. This
same procedure had been followed in the transfer of offices in the
Wolfmen's Grass Dance, as well as in the twentieth-century Grass
Dance.[92]

Gradually the councilmen gained the respect of their constituents
so that there was great continuity in membership over time. The superintendents who came after Logan—H. H. Miller (1911–1914), J. Martin (1915–1916), Charles Rastall (1916–1917), Charles Munro (1917–
1918), A. Symons (1918–1920), J. T. Marshall (1921–1929), M. B. Clark
(1929–1930), L. W. Shotwell (1930–1934), and J. W. Elliott (1934–1936)—

consulted the council (although they often ignored their wishes) and sometimes asked them to serve as arbitrators in disputes among the Indians. Gros Ventres attributed some successes to the business council. As early as 1901 Gros Ventres had been petitioning the Indian Office to build a fence on the reservation border so that the Indian cattle would not be stolen by white ranchers and so that trespassing cattle owned by whites could be kept off the Indians' grazing land. Logan had the fence built, and this success enhanced the office of councilman. Councilmen succeeded also in persuading the Indian Office to continue to issue cattle and farming implements on the reimbursable plan after Logan's removal—although they eventually became disillusioned with the program. And the councilmen finally succeeded in having the reservation lands allotted and in winning their claim against the government for treaty violations—two issues that were of immense concern to the Gros Ventre people, as discussed below.[93]

The success of the councilmen in legitimizing their authority to act as spokesmen for the tribe also was due in large part to their success at behaving like prominent men, providing for others, and in part to their ability and willingness to articulate group consensus rather than pursue their own individual goals and inclinations. The young men did not have medicine power, nor did they have war records with which to impress or intimidate others. They were more willing to conform to the general sentiment and to accept advice from the old warriors and headmen still living. The records of the council meetings and the correspondence between councilmen and the Indian Office between 1911 and 1937 show unanimity among the six Gros Ventre councilmen and also a pattern of referral of important decisions to the tribe as a whole.

"They Made Them Shell Out": Achieving Prominence

The means to prominence was facilitated by the Indian agent, or superintendent, as he was called in the twentieth century. Old as well as young men sought wealth by the "progressive" activities of raising horses and cattle, growing hay and grain, and working at their sawmill in the Little Rockies. Gros Ventre councilmen, old and young, were generally men of wealth by Gros Ventre standards. When Running Fisher, known to the agents as "one of the best farmers of his tribe," died in 1909 at the age of sixty-seven, he had forty acres plowed and hay stacked. In addition to work horses he left his two widows a wagon, mower, plow, and cultivator. When Under Bull died in his eighties in 1908, he left his two wives, three children, and one grandchild two houses, a ranch, twenty-six head of cattle, fifteen horses, two wagons, and two plows. When Otter Robe died in 1911 he left "a bunch of horses and other property," according to his brother, Curly Head. Such prominent and progressive headmen as Running Fisher, Under Bull, Otter Robe, and Bushy Head were invited to be councilmen during Logan's term. Logan assisted them at times in their efforts to remain prominent. John Carter, who visited Fort Belknap in 1909, remarked that when Bushy Head killed his third wife ("she visited around too much and wouldn't work"), Logan paid her father "to wipe tears away" and spare Bushy Head expense or retaliation. At his discretion, Logan issued stock, seed, and tools to individuals.[94]

Toward the end of his term Logan promoted younger councilmen who had attended boarding schools such as Carlisle or Fort Shaw, for by then the older men were complaining to the Indian Office about his performance as agent. Logan described one such young councilman, Belknap Fox, as "making a name for himself and accumulating considerable property": he owned "quite a herd of horses" and "a nice bunch of cattle" and farmed a "considerable tract of land." His horse herd amounted to 125 head in 1912. He and two other prominent young men attempted (with encouragement from St. Paul's Mission) to start a "Loan Trust company" with capital of $400. Another young councilman, Peter Capture, is described as a capable farmer who grew forty to eighty acres of grain, cut 100 to 150 tons of hay, and had a small bunch of cattle and a number of very good horses. The Boy (Under Bull's son) owned a store and grew 320 acres of alfalfa and hay, much of which he sold to whites. It is clear that now Gros Ventres regarded commitment to progressive agricultural pursuits in the same way that in former times they had viewed tenacity in raiding for horses—as a means to prominence. Flannery recorded one of the songs sung at the community dances; it says the life of a warrior is like the life of a cowboy—"you have to be tough." And one of the elderly men she interviewed commented that in the old days "they would do desperate things to acquire horses. It seems to be that way today, not with horses but with other things."[95]

Although all sought to be somebody, only a few men achieved prominence. Logan had reported in 1902 that only twenty-seven Indian men were able to sell hay that year and fifty sold cattle. He wrote in 1910 that adult males had from one to twenty-five horses, some as many as 200. The size of Indian cattle herds decreased during his term, according to the Indians, because he took Indian cattle into his own herd. After Logan was transferred, Gros Ventres tried to rebuild their herds of cattle by obtaining "reimbursable loans" from the Indian Office: men who the agent determined were progressive received a few head of cattle that they were expected eventually to repay in kind. Only a few individuals actually benefited from the program. Many of the cattle went to white men married to Indian women. By 1919 Superintendent Symons reported that Fort Belknap Indians owned 8,000 to 10,000 horses; eight individuals owned 1,400 and some owned few. As for cattle, after Logan's term the majority of the Indians had none.[96]

The horse industry then was threatened by the Indian Office's decision to begin killing Indian-owned horses that showed evidence of a disease called dourine. Gros Ventre horse owners, referring to themselves as "progressive stock raisers," wrote to Superintendent H. H. Miller on 25 March 1914 that they wanted the dourine testing stopped: "The horses we own are our last and only hope." The Gros Ventres were particularly active in raising horses, not only for exchange among themselves but also for sale. Although the stock of white horse owners trespassed on reservation range and mingled with Indian stock, their horses were not killed.[97]

Efforts to raise cattle also were undermined by the federal government's decision to lease most of the reservation grazing land to the Matador Cattle Company of Texas between 1913 and 1927. The Gros Ventres complained that the lease hurt Indian stockowners and that the fees paid were unfairly low. The Indian Office ignored the wishes of the business council when it allocated the money collected from Matador. The Gros Ventres had hoped to use the money to upgrade their farming equipment and tools. Father B. Feusi of St. Paul's wrote in 1917 that the Indians "were poorer now than when I left twenty-three years ago," partly because of stealing on the part of the agency employees. Increasingly, individuals had to make joint purchases of farming equipment in order to survive economically.[98]

In their quest for prominence, Gros Ventres pooled their wealth and distributed it on ceremonial occasions. Several Gros Ventre leaders organized the Hays community into two moieties: people who lived north of the round dance hall were called Black Lodges, those to the south Mountain Crows. The two divisions competed against each other at Grass Dances, at dances and celebrations during Christmas week, and in various events at the Gros Ventres' fair, "so that it would give some picture of what it used to be here in the [ceremonial] lodges," an elderly Gros Ventre told Flannery. Prominent men were expected to make generous donations. One Gros Ventre told Flannery, "These people just kind of share everything and it kind of holds back the ones that are prosperous."[99]

In the twentieth century any individual, male or female, could be somebody by holding a Grass Dance office or by generosity on behalf of relatives who held such an office. The performance of the dance required twenty-two male officers: four chiefs who made the rules and paid the expenses, two crow belt keepers, two whip men and their two errand runners, a spear or forked stick keeper, four singers, a drum-keeper, a spoon keeper, an announcer for the men and one for the women, two war bonnet keepers, and a whistle keeper. There were two women chiefs (black dress owners), two war bonnet keepers, and two whip women with their two assistants. The regalia—feathered belts or bustles, whips or quirts, drum and four drumsticks, spear, whistle, and black dresses—were treated with deep respect, and great importance was placed on correct form and order. Individuals facing a personal crisis could vow that in return for supernatural aid they would request a Grass Dance. The request would entail some sort of contribution. But the main financial burden for the Grass Dances was borne by the officers.[100]

Those who received offices had to pay. A transferring song was sung, and the person giving up the office arose and danced toward the intended recipient of the office, making a motion as though helping him up three times and on the fourth actually doing so. The officeholder danced back and forth in front of the recipient and around him. During this time the recipient's relatives gave away property in his honor. The recipient also paid a fee (as big a gift as he could afford) to the former officeholder. Flannery was told, "The new officer would kind of show off and let people know he was worthy of this office and he or she would make a dance involving lots of meat and food." And if the "chiefs" happened to be in a good financial condition at the time, "they made them 'shell out' that way." The whip men could make people dance and could take property from people before a dance; to redeem it they would have to come to the dance or donate something. With this authority went the obligation to pay for it by generous donations. A person could lock the door of the dance hall and prevent people from leaving; he would pay for the right by sponsoring the next dance. The Boy paid over $100 dollars for the right to allow children to dance during the celebration. The Boy also served as a whip man, drum keeper, and crow belt keeper. According to Flannery's interviews, quite a bit of food and property was exchanged between the prominent and the needy: "In the old days when they had the Grass Dances in the round log house, they used to eat one and a half or two beefs every night plus thirty-five dollars' worth of white man's food. Extensive money changed hands—1000 dollars a night not unusual—tie money on sticks, give away horses, cow, blankets, overcoats, harness, saddle." Thus a Grass Dance office at once honored a person, bestowed authority on him, and enforced sharing. As Flannery concluded, the public display of generosity in giving away property was a marked feature of the Grass Dance and "carried on and accentuated the method most common in older Gros Ventre culture for the gaining of individual prestige."[101]

Probably by the 1920s the Grass Dance ceremony had become incorporated in abbreviated form into the annual Christmas-week dances and the Hays Fair. The Christmas celebration became a part of Gros Ventre ritual life about the turn of the century, according to elderly Gros Ventres today. At that time the Gros Ventres also built their round log dance hall at Hays. Contemporary agency correspondence shows a Christmas dance held at the "dance house" on Peoples Creek (Hays) in 1902, and the Christmas celebration is mentioned in subsequent years as well. The celebration included a Christmas tree with gifts and sacks of fruit and candy for children. Agent Logan furnished a beef and crackers for the occasion. But generally the expenses were borne by Gros Ventres, who also determined the nature of the celebration. Groups of Gros Ventre men periodically volunteered to make repairs on the dance hall. In 1911, for example, several wrote the agent, "The people have put us in charge of rebuilding the hall." Father H. Post at St. Paul's Mission noted that in December 1913 the Gros Ventres repaired the hall and danced eight consecutive days and nights "at their old dances." Prominent men raised money for the expenses of the dance by donating personally and by holding tea dances where other Gros Ventres came to dance, socialize, and contribute. In February 1912 Frog asked the superintendent for a "permit for giving tea dances once a week for three weeks." The government farmer at Hays, W. D. Cochran, wrote in March 1913 that there were dances all winter—presumably tea dances—two or more times a week.[102]

It was during Christmas week that the Black Lodge–Mountain Crow moiety organization was most important. The moieties took turns accumulating food and firewood and organizing the entertainment, each usually being responsible for three days of celebration. Finally on New Year's Eve the two moieties joined together to sponsor a dance. One moiety gave gifts to the other, and they competed with each other to provide the best entertainment and to outdo each other in generosity. According to Gros Ventres, the moiety names referred to bands or settlements on the Crow Reservation, for at the turn of the century several Gros Ventres visited the Crows and observed their fair. The Crow Fair then served as a model for the Hays Fair.[103]

The suggestion for the fair came from Logan, in 1906: "I held a council with the Gros Ventres, who are good farmers, looking toward holding a fair upon the reservation next fall where they could exhibit cattle, horses, and farm products." Logan planned to have Indian judges and to award prizes. The fair was held in the fall of 1906, and

Logan said they "imitated a white man's fair as nearly as they could." But while the Gros Ventres cooperated with Logan and attended fairs in neighboring towns, it appears that they had their own ideas about the kind of fair they wanted, ideas that evolved after their visit to the Crows and to the Northern Arapahoes (who had horse races and other games, although not a fair on the Crow scale). Gros Ventres credit the elderly Stiffarm, a medicine man and councilman, with organizing the first fair. In 1909 the Gros Ventres' fair became an annual event. That year, The Boy wrote to Logan, "We had a meeting over the Reservation Fair which was postponed by you the other day. Everyone is glad of it, but for the visitors [from other tribes]. They [Gros Ventres] don't know what to do with them. We are expecting in more this week so I wish you would give us permission to dance sometime next week." It is clear that at the fairs Indian dances were of primary concern to the Gros Ventres, although they showed keen interest in the prizes as well. Logan's successor, H. H. Miller, reported that too much money was spent on entertainment. He noted that the Gros Ventres had set aside land at Hays for their fairground and that the fair was financed by "private subscription." While the idea of the fair was borrowed, the Gros Ventres transformed the fair into an event that was of cultural relevance and meaning to them.[104]

Prominent Gros Ventres pooled their resources or donated individually to obtain the prizes that were awarded at the fairs. In later years they also solicited contributions from local white businessmen. Miller noted that a "committee of four Gros Ventre men" managed the Hays Fair in the fall of 1913. They charged admission, held races and contests for Indian dress, beadwork, dancing, and games, and awarded prizes for exhibits. There was also a tug of war between the Black Lodges and Mountain Crows. According to Charles Rastall, superintendent in 1916, the Gros Ventres also had pooled their money to buy two large circus tents that were used for exhibits and dancing. The fair's leaders "bought this big tent from selling hay, each one of them put in so much," one elderly Gros Ventre explained to me. "It hurt their pocketbook but they enjoyed it." The Boy's letter to Logan indicated that he had promised to "give a dance" at the 1909 fair.[105]

The program of events at the fair not only appealed to traditional interests (Indian dancing, lodge-pitching contests, foot races, horse races) and the stock-raising background of the Gros Ventres (rodeo events), but also boasted a carnival, airplane rides, baseball games, and boxing matches. People brought their produce, stock, and handiwork to the fair to be judged; after the judging, they earned additional recognition or prominence by giving away their produce and craft entries to the people attending the fair.[106]

The giveaway was an ever-present feature of the fair and the Christmas celebration in the dance hall. Giveaways were held during the transfer of a political or ceremonial office, the naming of a child, or the honoring of a deceased relative, as well as during the Grass Dance. And individuals who were particularly well off invited people to their homes for a gathering. Such a gathering was described to me by an elderly Gros Ventre:

> [In 1921] my dad had butchered a bunch of beefs there and he'd had a real successful year in raising crops there. He raised, which was a lot of grain at that time, about 2,600 bushels of grain. They had it in the papers there—where this reservation Indian [and two other Gros Ventres] had grown more wheat than the whole entire reservation. . . . So my dad put on a big party for all of the old-timers. . . . My dad told me, "Go up there and get Red Whip and bring him over and set him down over here. He's one of our most famous warriors here and we'd like to treat him good." So I brought him over there, set him down over there and took a pipe over to him and give it to him there. . . . So he told my grandmother, "I want to give my grandson my name." . . . My dad gave each one that participated in there a beef and it cost him a lot of money. My grandfather left me eleven cows and so I used some of that, too.[107]

The prominent Gros Ventres of this era often served as councilmen, and always were expected to be leaders in ceremonial life. One of the most important moiety leaders, active in the Christmas celebration, was Henry Dwarf, one of Belknap Fox's partners in the apparently short-lived Loan Trust Company. He raised wheat, potatoes, and vegetables, and owned fifty-four horses. Leaders of the Hays Fair included Councilmen George Cochran, Stiffarm, Rufus Warrior, Ben Horseman, and Clarence Brockie. All were well off by Gros Ventre standards.[108]

"They Want Some Control of Their Land": Pursuing Primacy

The Gros Ventres watched the mismanagement and exploitation of their resources and concluded that they could do better. As Councilman George Cochran expressed it in 1931 when he argued that the superintendent's powers in leasing should be curbed, "They want some control of their land. . . . They asked the council to bring this up." During Logan's term the business council was so critical of the agent and so persistent in its attempts to expand its own role in reservation affairs that Logan, once an enthusiastic supporter of the council, recommended that it be dissolved. In their efforts to convince federal officials that they were qualified to make decisions about their reservation—much more qualified than the Assiniboines—the Gros

Ventres persisted in their commitment to agriculture and to education. As they gained confidence in their abilities and became increasingly assertive and tenacious in their demands, they impressed agency personnel not only as progressive but also, in the words of the agency physician, D. A. Richardson, as more "haughty," "aggressive," and "arrogant" than the Assiniboines.[109]

Throughout the 1902–1937 era the Gros Ventres were remarkably successful in convincing whites that they were progressive, certainly more progressive than other Plains tribes. Logan noted that the Gros Ventres were "better workers than the Assiniboine, and therefore, more thrifty." Superintendent Miller felt that the Gros Ventre councilmen, unlike the Assiniboine, were "quite active in seeking some method or plan for the improvement of the Indians. Their influence is helpful to the administration." Superintendent Martin commented, "The Gros Ventres are much the more progressive and their council is composed of influential men, capable of exerting quite an influence for good." Martin described the Gros Ventres as "the more intelligent" of the Fort Belknap Indians, and he wrote Frances Densmore that "the Gros Ventres on this reservation are the most noble and manly band of Indians it has yet been my opportunity to meet." Even the assistant commissioner of Indian Affairs, E. B. Meritt, was impressed: the Gros Ventres at Hays, he commented, had better houses and were generally more prosperous than the Indians on other parts of the reservation. Superintendent C. W. Rastall noted that the Gros Ventres were the "most progressive," "the best class of Indians on the reservation." Rastall's successor, Charles Munro, was so impressed by the Gros Ventres that he recommended that the commissioner consider giving them their share of the proceeds from grazing leases in per capita payments; he did not so recommend in the case of the Assiniboines. (Commissioner Cato Sells nevertheless rejected Munro's recommendation.)[110]

The Gros Ventres' eagerness for the allotment of their lands in severalty struck federal officials as particularly progressive. The cession agreement of 1895 had explicitly exempted the reservation from allotment until two-thirds of the adult males so requested. To the Gros Ventres of the early twentieth century, allotment meant greater self-determination, relief from poverty, protection from the surrounding white community, and a chance to reestablish primacy in relation to the Assiniboines. They began to press for allotment in 1911, against the opposition of many Assiniboine leaders. In 1912 Inspector Fred Baker characterized the supporters of allotment as young progressives and their opponents as old conservatives, but the names on the petitions make it clear that support for allotment was virtually unanimous among the Gros Ventres, old and young. The Gros Ventres sent delegations (and sometimes Assiniboine delegations went with them) to lobby in Washington in 1912, 1913, 1920, and 1921, at times by raising money through donations and at times by obtaining permission to use tribal funds. In 1912 the delegation was gratified that the commissioner favored the allotment of Fort Belknap, but spent the next few years trying to influence federal officials to allot to each individual sufficiently large acreage, specifically 360 acres of grazing land, so that no surplus land would remain.[111]

The Gros Ventres' support for allotment stemmed from their awareness of pressure from whites for further cessions of Fort Belknap lands. Although Logan had succeeded in pressuring the federal government to obtain a federal court ruling guaranteeing the Fort Belknap tribes' rights to the waters of the Milk River, surrounding whites renewed their efforts to control the water and also to obtain land in the valley, newly in demand for beet growing at the turn of the century. In 1906 the white citizens of Harlem pressed their congressman to "open up" the lands along the river, and the Fifty-ninth Congress considered such a bill. In 1909 John Buckman, Gros Ventre councilman, wrote the agent that the Gros Ventres wanted to send a delegation to Washington out of "fear that we will be dispossessed of our present land holdings" and so would be "in second place" in relation to whites.[112]

The Gros Ventres' awareness that their resources had been mismanaged was another motive for seeking allotment. They reasoned that if they had control over their lands individually, the government could intervene less in their lives. They made it clear to a representative of the Indian Rights Association in 1917 that they sought allotment so they could "be relieved of the supervision of the government over their affairs." And allotment offered relief for impoverished Gros Ventres, for an allotment could be leased by its owner.[113]

Tribal rolls had to be prepared, listing individuals qualified to receive allotments. The delegation of 1913 attempted, without success, to convince the Indian Office that the Assiniboines should be allotted land with the other Assiniboine bands at Fort Peck reservation rather than at Fort Belknap because they were not party to the 1855 treaty, which set aside lands, including those of Fort Belknap, for Gros Ventres and Blackfeet groups. Congress passed the Allotment Act in 1921, and an enrollment commission was formed at Fort Belknap: one Gros Ventre, one Assiniboine, and Superintendent Marshall. The Gros Ventres had sufficient influence over the superintendent, and perhaps over the Assiniboines, to obtain the rejection of several individuals who they felt were not entitled to be allotted land at Fort Belknap: several Northern or Canadian Assiniboines, Cree–French Chippewas, and a few individuals who were biological descendants of Gros Ventres but lived elsewhere and had no association with the tribe. Subsequently, some Assiniboines objected to the Gros Ventres' "ruling the Commission" and asked the commissioner of Indian Affairs to oppose them on the enrollment issue, so that all the Assiniboines (not only the Upper bands) would be enrolled.[114]

The secretary of the interior approved the commission's roll on 9 January 1922, then rescinded his approval on 19 June, in response to a rash of complaints from persons denied enrollment. Superintendent Marshall was instructed to hold a meeting of both tribes and have them vote on the enrollment of the individuals rejected by the commission. At the meeting, held in Hays, George Cochran and an Assiniboine, Russell Young, were both nominated as chairman. The Assiniboines slightly outnumbered the Gros Ventres, and Young received 165 votes to Cochran's 150. The Gros Ventres' main spokesman was Councilman The Boy, then fifty-two years old. He argued that when they settled at the agency, the Gros Ventres had "adopted" some (Upper) Assiniboines, and they had no objection to enrolling those people and their descendants. The Assiniboines to whom they objected were those who had come later. Assiniboine speakers insisted that they had outnumbered the Gros Ventres from the beginning, so they could not have been "adopted" by the minority. Cochran suggested that the histories of the individuals in question be discussed, but the people were informed (presumably by the chairman) that the discussion time had expired. A vote was taken, and 206 voted to enroll the Assiniboines and Cree–French Chippewas who had been rejected by the commission. The nay vote was 161. The vote on several individuals of white and Gros Ventre ancestry, rejected by the commission because they had not been in association with the Gros Ventre people, was 203 for enrollment and 158 opposed. Later the Gros Ventre councilmen protested the enrollment of these individuals and enclosed a petition for their removal signed by virtually all adult Gros Ventres, but to no avail.[115]

In their protests to the Indian Office, the Gros Ventres stressed that the presence of the "Canadian Assiniboines" undermined their "progress," that as the hosts at Fort Belknap, they had offered hospitality and then been taken advantage of by their guests. Progress was associated with primacy, and loss of primacy with the undermining of Gros Ventre progress. Thus the enrollment of the individuals rejected by the commission was extremely disturbing to the Gros Ventres. One man remarked, "We, the Gros Ventre Indians, have become poorer and poorer because we have shared our property with the Northern Assiniboines, and now they are even getting our land." Gros Ventre councilmen wrote that the Northern Assiniboines "succeeded to sponge on our kindness for some years and . . . seem to just make this a pretext of their claim."[116]

The Gros Ventres were angry and discouraged by the decision on enrollment, but undaunted in their pursuit of primacy at Fort Belknap. In their struggle to win a judgment in the Court of Claims against the United States, they hoped to obtain federal recognition that the Assiniboines did not have treaty rights to be at Fort Belknap. The Gros Ventre delegation in 1913 raised the issue of a claim against the United States for the violation of the 1855 treaty. The councilmen worked to obtain legal counsel for the tribe. By 1926 attorneys were interviewing elderly Gros Ventres about the treaty and Gros Ventre history. In brief, the Gros Ventres sued the federal government for appropriating some of the territory recognized in 1855 as belonging to the Blackfeet confederacy. When the tribe won their claim in 1935, Gros Ventres considered their treaty rights confirmed and their quest for primacy bolstered. The Gros Ventre councilmen also responded to their defeat on the enrollment issue by a successful effort to exert control over business council offices so that Gros Ventres dominated council proceedings. In fact, in 1923 all the council offices were held by Gros Ventres. The six Gros Ventres had voted for Gros Ventres, while the six Assiniboines split their vote. Usually, by gentlemen's agreement, offices were divided between the tribes. Apparently the Gros Ventres convinced some Assiniboines that Gros Ventres had primacy at Fort Belknap. At the time of the enrollment for allotment, several Assiniboines with Gros Ventre–Assiniboine ancestry switched tribal affiliation. In 1921, 1,229 people were enrolled: 46.9 percent Gros Ventres and 53.1 percent Assiniboines. Later the percentage of Assiniboines began to decline. Rodnick pointed out in 1935 that "many of the mixed Assiniboine and Gros Ventre [are] calling themselves Gros Ventre, although their fathers were Assiniboine." By 1938 both tribes' numbers had steadily increased, but of the 1,540 enrolled, 54.8 percent were now identified as Gros Ventre and 45.2 percent as Assiniboine.[117]

Requests for allotment supported the Gros Ventres' reputation for progressiveness, for federal officials saw those requests as a clear indication of a desire for individual rather than communal enterprise and of willingness to "detribalize." Even the obviously communal celebrations, such as the dances and particularly the fair, were viewed as indications of the Gros Ventres' progressiveness. Logan reported that he encouraged the Gros Ventres to have a fair in 1906 because an agricultural fair seemed particularly appropriate for such progressive people. The emphasis on giveaways at the fairs and dances certainly encouraged stock and crop production. A successful Indian-managed fair also brought the tribe recognition from the surrounding white community. The fair committee sought and got Montana's U.S. senators and congressional representatives to attend. A local newspaper quoted a committee member: "'Come and see what the lazy Indians can raise'; but he smiles as he says it." The Gros Ventres even sought to compete directly with whites at the fair, in tug-of-war contests and boxing matches. And like the county fairs, it boasted airplane rides and a carnival. The *Phillips County News* had to admit that the Hays Fair was the most popular Indian fair in northern Montana and that it drew huge crowds.[118]

The superintendents at Fort Belknap attempted to pressure the Gros Ventres into joining forces with the Assiniboines to have one reservation-wide fair. But the Gros Ventres, who saw their fair as an opportunity to demonstrate that they were more business-minded and better organizers than the Assiniboines, steadfastly refused. The Grass Dance and Christmas-week celebration were also opportunities to express tribal pride. While the Assiniboines had their own distinctive all-tribal ceremonies, the most important of which were the Medicine Lodge or Sun Dance and the Fools Dance, the Hays celebrations were public expressions of Gros Ventre identity. Well into the 1920s the two tribes engaged in contests and sham battles during these events.[119]

To a considerable extent the Gros Ventres' commitment to St. Paul's Mission can be understood in the light of their quest for primacy. It appears that they understood that apparent conversion favorably impressed federal officials. One of the most influential medicine men told Logan in 1908, "We have the same religion as you, Major, and wish all to be Catholics." The mission was helpful in agricultural pursuits and was influential, through the Bureau of Catholic Indian Missions, in Washington. Conversion to Catholicism also was probably related to the Gros Ventres' realization that at the mission school the French-Chippewa students, whom they scorned and resented, were taunting the Gros Ventre children as "savage" and "pagan." The métis were the descendants of Canadian Indians and French traders. Since the establishment of Fort Belknap Agency, French-Chippewas (called half-breeds or métis) had been taking timber, stock, and game from the reservation. Gros Ventres bitterly protested then and continued to do so in later years when métis families came on the reservation and used its resources. St. Paul's Mission received operating funds from the government; they had contracted for a certain number of students. Not enough Fort Belknap students attended, so the mission enrolled the métis children. The métis were often able to make a more favorable impression on the missionaries than the Gros Ventre children because they were Catholic, spoke French or English, and dressed more like whites. In this context, then, parents apparently began to urge their children to embrace Catholicism wholeheartedly. Elderly and many middle-aged Gros Ventres were ambivalent about their own conversion. Some ceased participation in native rituals and put aside their personal medicine rather than pass it on; others continued to practice native religion while urging others to convert and perhaps attending mass themselves. Being a "good Catholic" began to be a means of acquiring prestige. Youths especially committed themselves to Catholicism. Even Sitting High's grandson refused power from his father, because "the Catholics did not want you to do such things."[120]

The self-determination that the Gros Ventres sought in the 1930s would give them an opportunity to reestablish primacy as well. In this context, the Gros Ventres enthusiastically accepted the program for self-determination set forth in the Indian Reorganization Act (IRA) of 1934.

In March 1934, Commissioner John Collier organized a conference of Plains tribes at Rapid City. Here representatives of the Plains reservations heard Bureau of Indian Affairs personnel extol the advantages of reorganization. One of the delegates from Fort Belknap, The Boy, expressed a favorable attitude toward the IRA because he believed it would enable Indians to fight "one-sided rules and regulations and laws that he [the white man] compels the Indians to live under because they are hopelessly in the minority." He equated the IRA council with the 1855 treaty council. In the fall of 1934 the councilmen asked for assurance that acceptance of the act would not undermine *tribal* integrity and independence. They were particularly anxious to obtain a guarantee that they could determine their own membership if they accepted reorganization. The bureau reassured the Gros Ventres. When the 210 eligible voters at Hays voted on the IRA on 27 October 1934, 152 voted to accept reorganization and only 20 voted against it. Reservation-wide, the vote was 371 for, 50 against, with 183 not voting. Fort Belknap, the first Plains reservation community to accept the act, became a "reorganized" reservation.[121]

Felix Cohen arrived in June 1935 to assist the council in preparing a constitution and by-laws, which would be submitted to the people for a vote. During their deliberations, Cohen came to realize that they believed they had been promised extensive financial aid in return for their acceptance of the IRA. Aid was desperately needed at Fort Belknap at this time: in 1933, 200 families (almost half) were on relief. The councilmen argued that they understood Collier to say in Rapid City that they would get funds for economic development. Cohen replied that they had misunderstood him. A draft of a constitution was

prepared and sent to Washington for approval. There officials eliminated a provision that guaranteed districts (in other words, tribes) a
measure of independence. But the revised constitution did provide
that six Gros Ventre councilmen would be elected by Gros Ventres and
six Assiniboine councilmen by Assiniboines. The people voted on the
constitution and by-laws on 20 October 1935. At Hays, 118 of 186 eligible voters approved the constitution, with 7 opposed. Reservation-
wide, the vote was 316 in favor and 28 opposed, with 260 not voting.
There are no minutes of the meetings at which the constitution was
discussed, but apparently people felt that they could hope for financial help only if they accepted the document, as the bureau urged.[122]

The bureau insisted on the acceptance of a charter before any financial aid or land purchase was begun. But in 1936 firm resistance to the
proposed charter was building among the Gros Ventres. They viewed
it as an attempt to ensure the loss of tribal identity. They now perceived the reorganization process that created Fort Belknap Community and the Community Council as the means by which the two tribes
would be fused, to the disadvantage of both, but especially of the Gros
Ventres, who were still insisting that they should be compensated for
the Assiniboines' settlement at Fort Belknap. The Gros Ventres also
insisted on federal recognition that there were two tribes at Fort
Belknap, not one "community." But on 10 August 1936, Assistant Commissioner William Zimmerman argued, "Since the Gros Ventre and
Assiniboine Indians have been living together on the reservation for
many years, the fact that there are many intermarriages between the
members of the two tribes, that they have already organized under the
approved constitution as one tribe, that they have had a joint or community council for years, . . . we are at a loss to know why [they are]
opposed to incorporation." The Gros Ventres viewed this position as a
betrayal, given the assurances they had received at the time of the vote
on the IRA. As for intermarriages, in 1933 only 40 of 604 persons of
voting age were of mixed Gros Ventre and Assiniboine heritage. In late
1936 and 1937 the Gros Ventre councilmen struggled to convince the
bureau that some tribal business should be transacted only by Gros
Ventre councilmen and that each tribe should have a separate charter
because they often had different perspectives on issues. As one councilman put it, "Politically, our friends here [the Assiniboines] have
been always a handicap to us." But the Assiniboines favored one
charter, primarily because they thought the Gros Ventres' opposition
threatened the promised economic aid. Federal officials took the position that the tribe was not an appropriate organization to manage the
affairs of a modern-day reservation.[123]

By the spring of 1937 the Gros Ventres were bitter and disillusioned with reorganization. They opposed the charter and, in fact, attempted to rescind their acceptance of the IRA itself. Even Felix Cohen, sent to Fort Belknap in the summer to persuade the Gros Ventres to accept the charter, had to conclude that their disillusionment was justified. He found that for them reorganization consisted of paper promises, that federal officials ignored or violated the new constitution, and that the IRA was viewed as one more broken treaty. Specifically, the tribes were not consulted on matters that they were entitled to be consulted on, and the promised economic aid had not been forthcoming. One Gros Ventre councilman summed up Gros Ventre feeling thus: "The people are so touchy now over things in this Reorganization and all of that, they believe that false policies have been made to them." Despite Gros Ventre opposition, on 25 August 1937 the charter was accepted, primarily because of heavy Assiniboine support: the vote was 277 for, 158 against, with 116 not voting.[124]

"All Kinds of Bad Luck"

By the end of the 1902–1937 era, several events were at work that would fundamentally affect Gros Ventre society in the future. The perceived failure of the IRA, which had raised such high hopes, hardened the Gros Ventres' resolve for self-determination and primacy at the same time that it aroused cynicism about reservation government and leadership. The problems and reversals suffered by the Gros Ventres were increasingly laid at the doorstep of the Assiniboines and the métis, who became more and more conspicuous in Hays as the years passed. This interpretation of their history as a people put upon by others was being advanced among Gros Ventres to account for contemporary problems. In addition, they were anxious about their responsibility to the pipe bundles.

In July 1936, Curly Head held a Feathered Pipe ceremony in which he apparently unwrapped the pipe. He reportedly charged admission and permitted whites to be present. In August two forest fires devastated the Little Rockies, destroying the livestock and the timber industries and creating conditions for severe erosion and flooding. At this time the Flat Pipe was in an "abandoned state," according to Gros Ventres who talked to Flannery. Thick's wife claimed that she could hear the pipe in distress: "It bothers her to think it is alone, and in her sleep it calls her." Another elder stated that neglect of the pipe was causing the Gros Ventres to die off: "We have all kinds of bad luck." In June 1938, Thick and The Boy held a Flat Pipe ceremony to help a Gros Ventre fulfill a vow. Gros Ventres told Flannery, "He [the sponsor] didn't bring any feed or put anything down for the Pipe but of course they are supposed to. . . . They had a sort of flood soon after that and the reason was that somebody didn't do right with that Pipe. . . . There wasn't anybody [a keeper] to attend to it right." Another Gros Ventre told Flannery, "They should have followed the rules when Thick wanted to open this Pipe. . . . And right after the doings they were almost all drowned out. Rocks came down from the canyon and they just lived in a lake here at Hays. . . . " The seating arrangement was wrong: "all of which just shows they don't know what they are doing anymore." Many Gros Ventres agreed that the disaster of the Little Rockies fire and the subsequent erosion and flooding could be traced to neglect and abuse of the pipes. All in all, the Gros Ventres' circumstances in 1937 were deeply disturbing to them and provoked changes in their way of life in the years to come.[125]

"There Is a Revolution Taking Place Here": 1938–1964

The repercussions of the Fort Belknap people's acceptance of the IRA were many, and not what they had expected. Congress failed to appropriate adequate funding for Collier's aims of land purchase and revolving credit programs, and many Bureau of Indian Affairs personnel worked against Indian self-determination despite the Collier policies. By 1945, Collier's opponents in Congress had the upper hand. Collier's successor advocated termination as the best form of self-determination. Congress's new approach to Indian affairs was designed to end federal wardship and services. There were to be no more loans for economic development, and tribal assets were to be divided among individual members of the tribe. Special services to Indians were to be curtailed, and states or local governments would serve Indians just as they did other citizens. Also, a large-scale relocation effort was begun. Indians were to be encouraged and given aid to leave their reservations and migrate to urban areas to work. The termination policy prevailed through the 1950s and early 1960s.

In the years following their acceptance of the IRA the Gros Ventres and Assiniboines were consistently disappointed in their efforts to attain self-determination. And federal officials, bent on detribalization, frustrated the Gros Ventres' goals of preserving tribal independence and reestablishing primacy in relation to the Assiniboines and a small population of métis. Rather than economic recovery, Fort Belknap reservation entered a period of steady decline. As in earlier eras, policies changed as frequently as the superintendents. Superintendent F.

W. Boyd (1936–1939) stubbornly resisted the Fort Belknap tribes' efforts to take on responsibility and make decisions for themselves. He was replaced, and his successor, H. N. Clark (a man of Winnebago Indian descent), wholeheartedly embraced the ideals of Collier's New Deal for American Indians. He worked to encourage and aid the business council to take on responsibilities formerly held by committees or families. He also promoted business council leadership by instituting business enterprises jointly owned by the Fort Belknap tribes. In 1947 Clark was succeeded by J. W. Wellington (1947–1954), and shortly thereafter the Collier policies gave way to a new policy of termination, with its efforts to withdraw protection and assistance from the Fort Belknap tribes. Community-owned enterprises were dissolved, loans curtailed, and individuals encouraged to relocate in towns and cities off the reservation. As Wellington admitted, despite all their earlier surveys and plans for economic development, in the 1950s the Bureau of Indian Affairs did not want to spend time and money improving economic conditions at Fort Belknap. Now a reputation for progress was used as justification for termination. Ironically, Wellington insisted that the Fort Belknap business council was competent to manage reservation affairs without the bureau's help, that they were the most competent Plains group in Montana.[126]

Economic decline and the continued interference of the federal government in reservation political and social life had major repercussions for the Gros Ventres. Their orientation toward the pursuit of prominence and their quest for primacy and self-determination were undermined. Community-wide ceremonial activities and communal cooperation waned. Increasingly, Gros Ventres committed themselves to strive for individual family prosperity, and the size of the groups with whom they shared or toward whom they were generous became more constricted. There was a gradual ebb of the communal sharing and large-scale public redistribution that had characterized Gros Ventre society before the 1940s. As the Gros Ventre business councilmen experienced one setback after another in their efforts to improve reservation conditions, their constituency became disillusioned. Leadership status and recognition for prominence in the 1940s and 1950s were elusive. With the difficulty of living up to the behavioral ideals that were meaningful and realistic in earlier eras, Gros Ventre "blood" increasingly was recognized as symbolic of Gros Ventre identity. Blood degree—percentage of Gros Ventre ancestry—was not lost when one moved away from the reservation to try to better one's lot, as many Gros Ventres did. One did not have to participate in community rituals to have Gros Ventre blood.

"We Can't Do Anything; We Tried": The Pursuit of Prominence and Primacy Undermined

During these times, the people at Fort Belknap had growing aspirations. A subsistence-level standard of living was no longer enough for many; young people, especially, wanted purchasing power. Wage work became more difficult to get after World War II brought an end to work relief programs. Federal regulations and, ultimately, the government's withdrawal from the reservation's economic problems increased the people's poverty. Agriculturalists had a very difficult time making a living. In 1934 the government had distributed cattle in poor condition—drought victims—to the Indian ranchers, and then required them to pay prime prices in installments for these sickly, underweight animals. Also, the government loan program was insufficiently funded to help stockraisers expand to the point where they could make a living. Agriculture was becoming so mechanized that without adequate capital an individual could not hope to succeed. Mechanization reduced the number of jobs available locally. Many individuals leased some or all of their allotted land in order to obtain cash income. But the Bureau of Indian Affairs sometimes refused to pay individuals directly the income earned from leases. Instead, local officials acting in their capacity as trustees decided how the money should be used. In this way, the government could force Indians to pay grazing fees on lands they leased and water charges whether they used the lands or not. But these same officials often failed to require non-Indians to pay for the Indian lands that they used. The bureau also did not curtail the rustling of Indian stock. Individuals fell deeper and deeper in debt as the years wore on. Eventually the government used the indebtedness as a rationale for curtailing the loan program altogether.[127]

While conditions during Clark's term were not good, the termination era produced outright despair, for in the Gros Ventre view it actually reversed most of the gains they had made. In 1941, 159 Indians owned stock; by 1951, stockowners totaled 123. The agriculturalists at Fort Belknap needed an adequate land base in order to graze stock and grow feed. Since lands were allotted only to Gros Ventres and Assiniboines alive in 1922, most persons born after 1922 had only inherited shares in several allotments. There could be scores of heirs to an allotment. In fact, in 1952 one-third of the land was in multiple heirship. In such situations, 51 percent of the landowners had to agree before any of the allotted land could be used or leased. Individuals owned a percentage of the land but not actual acreage; before acreage could be assigned, all heirs had to agree to partition.

Government funds had been used in 1937 to purchase almost 30,000 acres along the southwest border of the reservation for the tribes, but the land was of poor quality. In 1953 Wellington reported that less than 2 percent of the Indian stockmen had an adequate land base. Despite the urgent need at Fort Belknap, the government stopped lending money to the tribes to buy land from heirs so that stockmen could lease tribal acreage. Moreover, the bureau, which made appraisals on allotted lands that the tribes wanted to buy, rejected those offers the business council was able to make on behalf of the tribes. The government also required lessees to be bonded, an expense that further discouraged the Indians. At first the business council was able to administer a small credit program, but because of government regulations and small appropriations from Congress, they could make only very small loans to agriculturalists. In 1956 the council complained that they had not been able to make any small loans for a year and any larger loans for three years. Government regulations and rigid repayment schedules discouraged loan clients, as well. One elderly prominent rancher explained:

> These Indians had cattle here when they took the upper end of the reservation, and the cattle were given to them and were bought from the proceeds from the sale of the land up west here [1888 cession]. These cattle were given outright to the Indians, and they took care of them themselves. They were very successful, and nothing was held over their heads. . . . If you give more responsibility to the Indian, he could do much better than if you lay down the laws and regulations, and they are so strict. It seems to knock them over. . . . A loan client came in to pay his bill and figured he would have three to four hundred dollars left. He paid up his loan and then they made him pay for the next year. When they got through with him, he had one dollar and seventy-five cents left. *They dug into him until they took all the sap out of him* [italics mine].[128]

One by one the tribal enterprises established during Clark's term were liquidated: bull pool, hay farm, cattle herd, timber operation. Eventually the business council had only one hope to generate tribal income that could be used to help individuals make a living on the reservation: the payment of royalties and fees from the production of oil on the reservation. But the federal government delayed approval of leases with oil companies and in the 1950s successfully worked to see that oil royalties went to individual members of the community rather than to the reservation as a whole. The Allotment Act of 1921 had provided that mineral rights on all land would be secured to the two tribes jointly, but, apparently because of a government error, the deeds issued to allottees did not always so specify. The Department of Justice instituted a suit on behalf of the allottees against the tribes, arguing that any oil money should go to individuals. All oil money that accumulated was held in escrow during the controversy. In 1958 the U.S. District Court ruled in favor of the allottees. At that time, 7,201 acres were leased by the tribe and 39,628 acres by allottees; in June the latter received $217,131 in payments that varied from $51 to $7,900. The business council and its hopes for a future source of tribal income received a major blow.[129]

Work relief programs were gradually curtailed, and with the mechanization of agriculture, wage work was difficult for Indians to find in the reservation vicinity. The result of the unemployment and agriculture problems was increasing poverty. These problems were compounded by population growth—the average net increase at Fort Belknap from 1950 to 1955 was 38.4 percent per year. By 1964 the Gros Ventres numbered 1,873 and the Assiniboines 1,282. Public (state) welfare assistance increased from $40,000 in 1947–48 to $156,000 in 1952–53. Aid to Dependent Children cases increased over 50 percent between 1949 and 1954.[130]

For many Indians, like neighboring whites, the best solution was to migrate to towns and cities to look for work. During the 1940s and 1950s, 20 percent of the enrolled Fort Belknap members lived off the reservation: in 1951 (the only year for which data on migration are available), two-thirds of those who lived off the reservation were Gros Ventre and one-third Assiniboine.[131]

For those Gros Ventres who remained, there were obstacles to public displays of generosity, even if a family had the means. Stockmen were held accountable for losses so that a donation to a celebration would adversely affect a stock grower's ability to obtain loans. Moreover, as is discussed below, during Clark's term the bureau encouraged the financing of celebrations from tribal funds and oversaw the planning of activities. These and other factors contributed to a decline in tribal celebrations at Hays. Elderly and middle-aged people recognized and objected to the potential repercussions of Clark's programs. Entrepreneurship was at the heart of the Gros Ventres' pursuit of prominence, of competitive relations with others. One prominent elder chided younger men for cooperating with agency personnel who closely supervised family farms and ranches:

> In my time we did not have to be told or coaxed or offered prizes to plant a garden and store away vegetables for winter; we knew that winter was coming on, so we hanked up and dabbed our houses and piled up a load of wood, had enough hay for our stock. You can still see horse and cow trails all over this reservation because we owned enough horses and cattle to fill the entire reservation. We did not have to have a lot of

102

government employees come out here to tell us when and how to plant or when and how to handle our stock. We took care of all these things without being told. *That is the life, self-supporting and self-government* [italics mine]. I am wondering what the present generation of Gros Ventres is coming to.[132]

Given the difficulties of an agricultural way of life, young people were encouraged by their elders to acquire higher education so that the youths would have better options than they had had. David Rodnick observed that two Gros Ventres had been elected to the three-member local school board in the late 1930s. Part of the termination effort was to close boarding schools and place Indian students in public schools. The Gros Ventres welcomed the challenge—they struggled to influence school policies and programs. Higher education was perceived as the best way to make a successful life for oneself, to compete successfully with whites and others on the reservation and elsewhere. Elders sacrificed for and encouraged youths, urging the business council to give priority to the needs of young people. Statistics for 1955 show a trend toward increasingly high educational levels: the average level of education for persons born between 1911 and 1930 was the eighth grade, but for those born between 1931 and 1939, the twelfth grade. By 1956 several individuals had college or vocational education beyond high school.[133]

Many young people who were hard-working and ambitious were employed elsewhere or were uninterested in council or other leadership positions. Gradually the association of the generous distribution of wealth with leadership waned. One of the young Gros Ventres elected in 1952 explained why Gros Ventre elders had to turn to a young Assiniboine man, as well as himself, when they tried to instruct and influence young men to replace them on the council: "At that time the Gros Ventre people that had served in various branches of the service my age [born 1911] had gone out and looked for employment away from the reservation so there was hardly any interest in getting into this political part."[134]

The pursuit of prominence, then, was gradually abandoned. Individuals and families sought to better their lot by migrating, or, if they stayed at Fort Belknap, left the sponsorship of community celebrations to the business council.

The business councilmen had a difficult time satisfying their constituents on a number of fronts. The fact that the councilmen began to receive pay during this era—to profit personally, in the Gros Ventres' view—alienated the constituents. Councilmen received $3 per meeting day plus per diem in 1952, and by 1956 were receiving $6.50. The Gros Ventres expected advances in self-determination and gains in the pursuit of primacy, but the business councilmen could do nothing to help.[135]

The Gros Ventre councilmen had hoped to revive the agricultural industry on the reservation and obtain more income for the tribe by taking more responsibility for decision making. They demanded that they be allowed to decide if and for how much they would lease their grazing lands. The superintendent had been making these decisions, and the Gros Ventres were convinced that they could be more successful at managing reservation resources. They wanted higher fees than the Bureau of Indian Affairs advocated; the Assiniboines did not wish to oppose the bureau on the matter. But Boyd and his employees denied the Fort Belknap people greater authority in general, and thwarted the Gros Ventres' effort. Tom Main, Gros Ventre councilman during Boyd's era, said, "We have no voice whatever and almost all of our recommendations and suggestions have been ignored or rejected. . . . The Interior Department goes on with its arbitrary rule the same as ever." The Gros Ventres were more optimistic about self-determination after Clark replaced Boyd. Bureau officials noted that of all Montana reservations, only at Fort Belknap did the tribal representatives consistently attend staff meetings to participate in planning. But even in Clark's term the Gros Ventres' views were often ignored. They were not allowed serious input in the agency budget or the selection of the next reservation superintendent, as they had expected. The Gros Ventres in Hays were particularly angered by the bureau's failure to respond to their request to prevent "non-ward" (métis) Indians in and near the Hays community from hunting and cutting wood on reservation lands. One Hays resident complained, "They [métis] are bold and bullheaded . . . ; it is not right that they have no respect for us at all." The métis' illegal use of scarce reservation resources created more hardship on the Fort Belknap tribes. The events of the 1950s further demoralized the business council. One councilman said in 1955, "They are detribalizing you as fast as they can." Another added, "They got your land, oil, and now the bulls [one of the tribal enterprises liquidated by the federal government]." Another despaired in 1957, "We can't do anything; we tried; there is no chance in the world."[136]

The Indian Reorganization Act had the effect of undermining tribal independence. For federal officials, the Gros Ventres and Assiniboines were no longer two tribes, but rather one Indian community, and therefore could not adopt distinct policies. On these grounds they had rejected the Gros Ventres' efforts to raise grazing fees above the amount that the bureau recommended and that the Assiniboines agreed to. It is clear that primacy was still an important goal of Gros

Ventres during the 1940s and 1950s. Flannery's informants constantly compared the Gros Ventres favorably with the Assiniboines. Despite bureau policy, by gentlemen's agreement council offices were equally divided between the two tribes and each had its own credit and relief committee. By custom a Gros Ventre was usually elected president and the president appointed three Gros Ventres and two Assiniboines to the important joint committees. The loan programs processed more applications by Gros Ventres than by Assiniboines. And Gros Ventres received more cattle (56 percent) and more of the available funds (59 percent). Gros Ventres credited their councilmen with obtaining Boyd's removal. Finally, the Gros Ventres filed (in 1951) and pursued a claim against the government, arguing that they were underpaid for the 1888 cession, and insisting that the Assiniboines should not share in the award.[137]

However, the bureau pressed the tribes to apportion representation by the population in each settlement area or district. Before 1943 nearly all Gros Ventre councilmen were selected from Hays. Assiniboines elected three from Lodgepole and three from the agency and Milk River area. In 1943 the council agreed that Gros Ventres living in the agency area (most of whom were agency employees) would have one delegate and Hays would have five. In 1953 the Gros Ventre agency district was allowed two seats and Lodgepole Gros Ventres (living on land allotted to the families of their Assiniboine spouses) one seat on the council, while Hays retained three seats. Finally, pressure built to elect all twelve councilmen at large. At Wellington's urging the council had decided in 1953 to hold a referendum on this issue, but it was not actually held until 1964. There was considerable opposition among the Hays Gros Ventres, who saw such a change as an attack on tribal independence and Gros Ventre primacy. But reservation-wide, the referendum passed 138 to 86. Of the 664 eligible voters, only 224 voted: Hays, 60 for, 50 against; Upper Milk River, 26 for, 15 against; Lower Milk River (a Gros Ventre settlement area), 14 for, 2 against; Lodgepole, 38 for, 19 against. Since 1964, the six Gros Ventre and six Assiniboine councilmen have been elected by all enrolled members of the Fort Belknap Indian community.[138]

"I Do Not Like Group Activities": Communal Solidarity Undermined

The 1940s and 1950s were difficult times for the Gros Ventres, for old ideals still existed, but the means of realizing them were no longer at hand. One elder told Flannery, "The Gros Ventres think quite a lot of themselves and don't bow down very easily." This emphasis on being somebody and on tenacious pursuit of goals began to find expression through competition for individual or family gain. Ethnologist Rodnick described the beginnings of this new trend in the mid-1930s: "An attitude that has been growing on the reservation has been that of 'individualism.'" When the Gros Ventres had a community meeting in 1942 to discuss solutions to their economic problems, some advocated a continuation of the old strategy of pooling labor and equipment. But the group could not reach agreement, for some took the position of this young man: "I do not like group activities. I have been trying to get away from that. I don't like to have anybody come on to my place and tell me what to do. If I lend my team or machinery to anyone it would be broken. I worked hard for my things and I get along all right. If anybody is a fool enough not to put in a garden, let him starve to death." The erosion of consensus and communal sharing was the result of several factors in addition to economic hardship and higher aspirations: gradual acceptance of the concept of individual owner-ship of lands and per capita distribution of tribal assets; the disillu-sionment with business council leadership and the inability of those leaders to motivate consensus; the changing social composition of the Hays community; and the end of Hays secular rituals and the associ-ated moiety system.[139]

The trend toward individualism was in large part a product of the allotment of land, a concept initially introduced by federal officials. By the 1940s many allottees had grown to rely on the money they re-ceived from leasing their lands. Some regularly got considerably more income than others. Thus differentials were relatively more fixed than in the earlier days, when people lived off their fields and stock and were subject to more or less the same vagaries of weather, rustling, and graft. Individualism was further encouraged by the distribution of the 1935 claim money in 1937 in per capita shares. People began to consider tribal income and property to be assets in which they should have a per capita share, not (as Under Bull's followers had thought in 1895) primarily as a resource for future generations or a buffer against further exploitation by non-Indian society. The trend toward indi-vidualism helped to undercut the ability of the business council to mobilize consensus.

The business council's prestige declined and its constituents gradu-ally lost faith in it. With the gradual decline in tribal income the coun-cil could provide little financial aid and few jobs to compensate for the federal cutbacks and unfulfilled promises. The demoralization of the councilmen shows in their remarks as early as 1946. Gros Ventre coun-cilman Clarence Brockie said, "The job of chairman is getting to be quite rough, and we are catching hell all the time." Another Gros

Ventre councilman, Tom Main, added, "I have heard things, that the rising generation of highly educated boys and girls make remarks of their primitive council—a debating society they called it." Ten years later, Gros Ventre councilman Rufus Warrior said, "In my experience as a member of this council, we were unable to do justice to our people due to the fact that we were working with short money and could not take care of their business properly. . . . Under these policies such as liquidation [termination] of the Indians of Montana, [they] have been too busy defending themselves; they have done very little toward helping our tribes." The hard times in 1946 and later motivated councilmen's constituents to press (albeit unsuccessfully) for a reduction in council membership in order to reduce expenses.[140]

In the 1952 election there was a high turnover of Gros Ventre councilmen; several young World War II veterans replaced older councilmen who had served for decades. Older ex-councilmen began to concentrate on pressing the tribe's 1951 claim against the federal government by acting as a "treaty committee." The entry of younger men did not improve the council's image, however. Dissension over the anticipated oil money escalated. Rumors circulated that the council was secretly spending the money. Councilman Warrior complained, "These Indians are clamoring for oil leases, as they are hearing about other reservations [that have oil money]." The council's predicament was made worse by the growing perception of the proud Gros Ventres that "the Fort Belknap reservation is rated as the poorest reservation in Montana," according to one Gros Ventre in 1958. Adding to their embarrassment was the fact that they could not afford to pay their share of the expenses of the claim filed in 1951, and the co-plaintiff, the Blackfeet tribe, paid the Gros Ventres' share.[141]

The mineral rights controversy that emerged in the 1950s effectively destroyed the political authority of the council and the ability of the councilmen and other leaders to generate consensus. Tom Main said in talking of the oil issue in 1952, "There is a revolution taking place here. This generation is waking up—you can see by the membership of this council. They are raising a lot of questions—that is, the people are, about their standard of living. . . . The allottee will say, 'that [oil money] is mine.'" From 1955 to 1958 the council had tried unsuccessfully to persuade the allottees not to oppose the effort to reserve mineral rights for the tribes.[142]

In 1957 two Gros Ventres (married to non–Gros Ventres and living off the reservation) led most of the allottees in a struggle to subvert the council's efforts. One, before he was elected to the council in 1958, told the councilmen: "The people want their money and could use it. Why keep it tied up the way it is [in escrow] . . . ? I don't know why you folks are so selfish about it, and you want it to go tribal. . . . I think you folks should just let it go and let the people have it, because you are going to have enemies for the rest of your lives." The new sentiment put the individual before the tribe, the few over the many. This particular speaker quit the council as soon as the U.S. District Court ruled in favor of the allottees in 1958. This new breed of councilman viewed himself as an advocate for special interest groups rather than for the Gros Ventres as a whole. The other councilman who spearheaded the movement to permit mineral rights to allottees expressed this new sentiment thus: "A referendum would not be fair. The number of people who don't own land outnumbers the allottees." Under pressure from these two councilmen and other individuals, the business council did not appeal the ruling.[143]

The Hays community gradually began to lose its homogeneity, as well as some of its members. In 1942, 35 percent of the Hays Gros Ventres were residing off the reservation, many in war industries or in uniform, and many subsequently raised their children off the reservation. Migration away from Hays continued during the 1950s. Life in Hays was also disrupted by the establishment of a town site there in the mid-1920s, which was provided for in the Allotment Act. Rodnick described the town site in 1935 as having three trading stores, two pool halls, two restaurants, and two rooming houses. By the 1940s many non–Gros Ventres were living there. Work programs initiated by the federal government (to repair roads, for example) had brought outsiders to the reservation. In 1942 there were thirteen non-ward métis in the township and five families in the wider Hays community with a métis spouse. The council believed in 1958 that "Hays is just full of [métis]." In any case, the council believed that the township was a trouble spot in which youths ran amok, a problem compounded by state and federal authorities, who could not agree on who should police the township area, and elders were not able to control young people. Wellington's successor, Superintendent Darrell Fleming, commented in 1954, "All we are doing is raising a bunch of Miles City boys."[144] Miles City was a rough town, by contemporary Montana standards.

During the 1940s, intermarriage between Gros Ventres and Assiniboines increased, and several Gros Ventres married métis. One Gros Ventre councilman remarked in 1951, "We, both tribes, all do everything together nowadays. They have intermarried and a lot of the younger generation does not know whether they are Gros Ventre or Assiniboine anymore." According to Gros Ventres, some of the métis men who by the late 1940s and 1950s had married Gros Ventres did not permit or help their families to participate in Indian activities. Gros Ventres felt that Hays community ceremonies were undermined because they no longer had full participation of all Gros Ventres. In fact, in the late 1950s the few dances held were joint Gros Ventre–Assiniboine ventures rather than events sponsored and primarily attended by one tribe.[145]

The Gros Ventre Christmas dances and fairs, which had provided a means for attaining or reaffirming prominence and expressing primacy, gradually ceased to be held, in large part because the responsibility for these ceremonies was transferred from the prominent families and from the moieties to the business council. Superintendent L. W. Shotwell reported that the Black Lodge–Mountain Crow organization was thriving in 1933, but in 1942 Superintendent Clark noted that the moiety organization was a thing of the past. In fact, Clark had discouraged "committees" (moieties) from sponsoring dances and fairs, preferring to promote community reliance on the business council. The business council, pleased by Clark's effort to obtain funds for loans and land purchase, cooperated. But as the council's funds were reduced there was little money for dances. In 1934 the WPA work crews built a rectangular community hall (with basketball courts) in Hays, and the Gros Ventres were persuaded to dance there instead of in the old round hall, a few miles to the northwest. The Boy said, "They [halls] should be round. Everything they did was in a circle. People don't like this hall, oblong, so well as the round one." The dance committee applied to the council for tribal funds to organize the Christmas and other celebrations. The council donated beef from the tribal herd and even paid the light bills for the hall. But after the new hall burned down in 1956, the community dances were phased out. Those who were committed to Indian dances joined with the Assiniboines, who sometimes had dances in the Milk River area or at Lodgepole. People in Hays appealed to the councilmen to get them a new dance hall in 1956, 1957, and 1958, but nothing happened. The increasingly rare community activities came to be held at the mission, under the supervision of the mission staff. The council also took over management of the fair, using agency funds for prizes, but it ended in the 1940s.[146]

The ceremonial life and associated patterns of generosity of the pre-1940s era now were perceived as irrelevant or detrimental to prosperity and to competition with whites for jobs. Elders criticized youths at times for their disregard of old ways, but even the elders were ambivalent about these customs and values, and they encouraged youths to live a different life. One middle-aged Gros Ventre told Flannery in 1945 that he and his wife had grown up with the ideal of generosity to others but that, for his children, it was a new age, and new values were appropriate. Flannery summarized this man's remarks: "While he hands out, he tells his children they must be different from him." Flannery was told by a respected elder in 1948, "It isn't like it used to be years ago like somebody stayed with you and you didn't mind it; you acquired things easily. Everything is now expense, expense." Another remarked, "They are not as generous as they used to be because they would be entirely out." Times were hard, most food had to be purchased, and credit was difficult to come by. Hospitality and generosity were a noticeable drain on family resources. Young people, one middle-aged man complained, "would rather pick up a white man's book and give it all their attention, rather than sit and listen to [Gros Ventre oral tradition] the very facts of which they should hold dearest to their hearts." Yet elders urged youths to seek higher education. In 1935 Rodnick suggested that young Gros Ventres had begun to avoid traditional Indian activities because such things suggested inferiority in the eyes of whites. At the Gros Ventre fair that year, a few young men attempted to start an owl dance (a social dance done by couples), but gave up because few young people would join them. In the late 1930s and 1940s, white-style dancing became popular with young people. In the 1950s electrical power lines were extended to Hays, and exposure to the national media increased. In many ways, youths' expectations began increasingly to parallel those of their non-Indian contemporaries.[147]

"They Believe in It But Don't Follow the Do's and Don'ts": The Sacred Pipes

The elders also were worried about the Gros Ventres' responsibility to the pipe bundles. In the mid-1940s, The Boy had taken custody of the Flat Pipe to prevent neglect; Gros Ventres in distress told Flannery that the bundle was infested with mice. And Iron Man began caring for the Feathered Pipe in 1937, after Curly Head's death. Neither pipe was formally transferred. The Boy made a vow to open the Flat Pipe bundle to ensure the safe return of Gros Ventre soldiers from the war, and the ceremony was held in 1946. Apparently The Boy and other Gros Ventre relatives and friends of the soldiers and some white friends of The Boy bore the expense. The safe return of the soldiers did not spark renewed commitment to the pipes, for The Boy noted that year that "the rising generation of Gros Ventres would not go back to this form of worship. . . . They are too far gone into religion of the white man."[148]

The Boy and other elders who retained some commitment to the Flat Pipe broke with tradition and agreed in 1951 to open the bundle in Superintendent Wellington's presence and allow him to photograph its contents. Wellington was interested in and appreciative of Indian

8. Praying with the hand game sticks before the hand game at a tea dance at Takes the Bow's home, Hays, Montana, August 1937. Fred White, the bundle owner, prays, holding a bag containing the bone buttons, the counter sticks (made of willow, with two crow feathers and bells), and the two guessing sticks, one for each team (also with feathers attached, but more elaborately decorated; the stick was held by the guesser and was thought to assist him in finding the bones). Seated on the ground, the second man from the left, a singer, holds a hand drum. By 1937 the hand game apparently had begun to become more secularized and was held as part of the entertainment at the tea dance rather than in fulfillment of a vow. Photo courtesy of Richard A. Pohrt.

traditions. Iron Man also agreed to Wellington's request to watch and photograph the unwrapping of the Feathered Pipe bundle in 1952. A few elderly people left cloth offerings for sick relatives on these occasions. The Boy recognized that people were no longer following the rules. He told Flannery through an interpreter, "It is a sure sign how Gros Ventre culture has deteriorated when these men [prominent elderly men] suggest that [opening the Flat Pipe to show Flannery], because it is known that only when someone vowed could . . . the bundle be unwrapped." The pipes came to be viewed to a considerable extent as a business council responsibility. When the elders attempted to have the pipe ceremonies in 1951 and 1952, they succeeded in getting the council to donate beef from the tribal herd. This was apparently the first time that anyone other than an individual petitioning the Supreme Being had borne the expenses of a pipe ceremony.[149]

A few years before, The Boy had helped design for St. Paul's Mission a banner showing the two sacred pipes in a subordinate or supplicatory position in relation to the cross. In fact, he stated that the Supreme Being may well have willed the Gros Ventres to convert to Catholicism. The Boy's attitude toward the Flat Pipe was probably typical of the elders of that time. He told Flannery in 1948 that Gros Ventres "still have the pipe and everything it means to the Gros Ventres even though most are Catholics or Protestants today." The pipes symbolized the chosen status of the Gros Ventres spiritually, as well as their proud history.[150]

By 1956 the elderly Gros Ventres, with the involvement of the coun-

9. Gros Ventre children's choir, St. Paul's Mission, Hays, Montana, 1938. The banner represents the two sacred pipes giving way to the Christian cross and at the same time honors the pipes. The banner was made for the St. Paul's delegation to the Eucharistic Congress in Great Falls, Montana, in 1937 by Sister M. Giswalda Kramer of the School Sisters of St. Francis under the direction of Tom Main and other Gros Ventres. Photo courtesy of Bureau of Catholic Indian Mission Records, Department of Special Collections and University Archives, Marquette University.

112

cil, were communicating with the Montana Historical Society about helping to preserve and safeguard the pipe bundles. The council suggested also that they collect donations and erect a building for the pipes on the reservation. Nothing was accomplished, however. The two men taking care of the pipes died, The Boy in 1957 and Iron Man in 1959.[151]

By the time the ethnologist Verne Dusenberry visited Fort Belknap in March 1958, Rufus Warrior had moved the Flat Pipe, at The Boy's dying request, to his home to protect it. Dusenberry said of the five old men—born between 1874 and 1886—who were apparently considered the leading authorities: "They feel that they are the only ones who really care about the fate of the two Sacred Pipes." He quoted one man thus: "We realize that the power is gone from these Pipes, but they have always been with the Gros Ventre people. We don't want to give them to a museum. They belong here. The priests have been kind and offered us a place on their land where we can build a kind of a shrine and put them in. But we are poor, and we have no money to buy the material to build anything. And our young men don't care. Maybe we should . . . take them up in the hills and let them lay there and go back to dust." These old people believed that the strength of the Feathered Pipe had left the bundle according to prophecy—it was prophesied long ago that the pipe's usefulness would end after it was transferred from Curly Head. Dusenberry does not discuss why the powers of the Flat Pipe seemingly were thought to have ended. Probably disrespectful treatment of the pipes was potentially dangerous, for he noted a "sense of urgency" among the elderly Gros Ventres about what should be done with the pipes. It is also clear that older people were unwilling or unable to motivate younger Gros Ventres to help erect a shrine. In 1958, then, apparently not all Gros Ventres shared the concern of those born in the late nineteenth century that the problem of the pipes should be resolved. In 1961 elders expressed their dismay about the pipes. Although a few people still left offerings, even the elders were neglectful. One old man said, "They believe in it but don't follow the do's and don'ts." They were sure that no one "would know [about] or want it." There was still talk of building a house for the pipes, but the old people feared that "young fellows would destroy or break in a house or sell it [the pipes]."[152]

"We Are Deteriorating":
Blood Degree and Gros Ventre Identity

The new circumstances of this era precipitated one further change in the way that Gros Ventres defined themselves as a people. Whereas

Gros Ventre identity had basically been defined culturally before this era, now "blood degree" began to be a component. When federal officials prepared a constitution and by-laws at the time the IRA was adopted, provisions were included defining "community" (reservation) membership in terms of degree of Indian blood. By 1958 there was some sentiment among the tribes for defining identity as Indian rather than as Gros Ventre or Assiniboine. But although one councilman (married to a member of a non–Fort Belknap tribe) supported the IRA constitution's provision that a person had only to be "one-fourth Indian" to be enrolled at Fort Belknap, the majority objected to it. In fact, in 1958 the council held a referendum to change the constitution. Voters determined that to be enrolled a person needed one-fourth Assiniboine blood or one-fourth Gros Ventre blood or one-fourth Assiniboine and Gros Ventre blood combined. A majority (178 to 52 out of 542 eligible voters) also voted in favor of no residency requirement, a reflection of their feeling that leaving the reservation was not a rejection of one's people or heritage, but rather a necessity.[153]

The concern with blood degree reflected the feeling of many older people that the Gros Ventres were losing their cultural heritage by intermarriage with other Indians (particularly métis and non-Plains peoples), but that interaction (or intermarriage) with whites was not similarly a cause of "deterioration." Speaking through an interpreter, one elderly man put it this way in 1945:

> When the Indians of the several tribes were living in different areas of the country and living their lives in their own way, they each had customs and practices and different cultural aspects from each other and rarely intermarried. But in recent times and especially right now, they are intermarrying very rapidly. They quit fighting and are living stationary lives, but they visit and learn from each other something new and that is contributing to the fact that we are [losing cultural heritage]. They are mixing the bloodstreams and instead of producing good results, it is producing the opposite. They influence each other in habits and customs that don't fit in another area and all of that seems to be contributing to [the fact that we are deteriorating] and losing track of the systematic way they used to live. . . . Sooner or later the Indian race is going to assimilate; . . . even though that will happen, they [Gros Ventres] want to keep up the good stock of Indian people so when they marry with whites they will be presentable and apart from . . . unworthy people. . . . If only they had retained the Gros Ventre language even down to children, how much nicer it would have been for him and others of his age to pass on and try to give advice and to infuse that system the Gros Ventres had *where the Indian boy had a lot of determination and self-direction early in age* [italics mine].

114

"Gros Ventre blood," then, came to symbolize for Gros Ventres their way of life before 1938, including their ceremonial organization and the values it expressed, such as prominence and pursuit of primacy. They may have thought that this way of life had ended, but in just a few years their circumstances changed again.[154]

"The New Indian Awareness": 1965–1984

During the 1960s, the United States was undergoing tremendous conflict and change. The War on Poverty and other new social legislation helped to transform American society. Indian communities also were greatly affected by legislation in civil rights, aid to education, housing, manpower training, and economic development. The commissioner of Indian Affairs during the John Kennedy and Lyndon Johnson administrations, Philleo Nash (1961–1966), worked to ensure that the new legislation benefited Indians by persuading Congress to approve the eligibility of Indian reservations for War on Poverty funds. The provisions of the Manpower Development and Training Act were applied to Indian communities, and the Office of Economic Opportunity established a Community Action Program for Indian reservations. Nash encouraged tribal leaders to apply for and use federal grants. Agencies with funds for Indians often dealt directly with the tribal governments, thus expanding the tribes' responsibilities and powers. Before 1960 the Bureau of Indian Affairs had no housing program. After the establishment of the Department of Housing and Urban Development (HUD) in 1965, an extensive housing program was begun in Indian communities, and with the aid of funds from the Indian Health Service (IHS), water and sanitation improvements were initiated as well. The provisions of the Elementary and Secondary Education Act, as amended, funded special programs, such as Native American studies, for Indian students at public and Indian schools. The Indian Self-Determination and Education Assistance Act of 1975 gave additional impetus to the new policy, as articulated by President Richard Nixon, of self-determination without termination, for it transferred partial responsibility for administration of programs for Indians, along with federal funding, to tribal governments. Programs formerly run by the bureau were contracted for by the tribes, and sometimes the level of funding was increased to cover tribal overhead in administering the program. The changes in public attitude and government policy toward minorities in this era both encouraged and reflected

115

Native American pride and the formation of groups that vigorously pressed for Indian rights.[155]

At Fort Belknap the War on Poverty programs, which largely were begun in 1964 and 1965, resulted in hundreds of jobs, both unskilled and skilled, and offered administrative positions to tribal members with a college education. The tribes applied for and received funds authorized by the Comprehensive Employment and Training Act (CETA) of 1978. This money, as well as other funds from the Department of Labor and Department of Agriculture food and nutrition programs, was used to employ people. Grants awarded to the reservation by the Economic Development Administration also helped to create jobs. Another source of employment was an extensive home-building program implemented in 1964.

With money from HUD, the Indian Housing Authority at Fort Belknap constructed 423 rental and mutual help units in all parts of the reservation, although the largest concentrations of homes were in the agency area and in Hays. The Fort Belknap community got additional grants for housing rehabilitation and senior citizen and recreational buildings, as well as water and sewerage improvements. The new, improved housing attracted tribal members back to the reservation, the community centers encouraged and facilitated public gatherings, and a new tribal government complex (occupied jointly with the Bureau of Indian Affairs) contributed to the expansion and prestige of the business council's role in reservation affairs.

After the passage of the Indian Self-Determination and Educational Assistance Act, the tribal government negotiated contracts for the operation of the reservation's health programs, law-enforcement services, and education department. This move increased the authority of councilmen as well as employment opportunities. Federal funds permitted salaries for council officers and higher per diem payments, which helped to draw more people, particularly young, college-educated tribal members, into tribal politics.

Federal funds for Indian education were used to employ Indians and to provide college scholarships and special Indian studies programs at the elementary, secondary, and college levels. In addition, many Indian veterans of the Vietnam conflict used their veterans' benefits to attend college. In this era of affirmative action and ethnic pride, young people were exposed to the presentation of Indian culture and history in a positive light and to activist and confrontational approaches to Indian affairs. One young college graduate remarked, "All of a sudden Indian people were of value on the outside. They meant something. Before, it seemed like something you had to live with."

In sum, the new programs not only invigorated the reservation economy and expanded the role of the business council but also drew back to the reservation tribal members who had moved away, including people of retirement age and young people with college education who had trained for managerial and professional jobs. Not only did young men find employment opportunities on the reservation, but women now began to be employed on a large scale in the new programs. And many of the programs generated and encouraged interest in native traditions. The new legislation and new attitudes toward Indians—as one young Gros Ventre put it, "the new Indian awareness"—helped revitalize the Gros Ventres' ideals of prominence and primacy and gave them new means of realizing those ideals.

"To Make Enough to Give Out": Renewing the Quest for Prominence

In the late 1960s, the Gros Ventres at Fort Belknap had new opportunities to become sufficiently well off to begin once again to pursue prominence through public generosity. This ideal, probably alive in family oral tradition, combined with the new sources of income, spurred the revival of ritual life and raised the status of business council leaders.

It is clear from the observations Gros Ventres make about themselves as a people today that material success is highly valued and that success is not complete without recognition for prominence. Their success, they feel, is based largely on their competitive and assertive or tenacious nature.[156]

One young man expressed the ideal of success thus: "A person doesn't have to be somebody else's worry." Another remarked, "A Gros Ventre wants to improve." Elderly and middle-aged people agree. One elder commented, "People respect one who makes a good living and is independent." While not all succeed in making a good living (and in being somebody), generally they try. Gros Ventres living off the reservation have written letters to the Fort Belknap newspaper in an effort to influence community decisions—about how the 1951 claim money, settled in 1967, should be disbursed, for example. Most attempted to convince readers that their views should be considered by calling attention to their material success. One writer argued, "We are away from our birthplace only because we have to make a living for our families." Another maintained that he and other off-reservation Gros Ventres held "responsible positions in business and industry." Gros Ventres note that they were successful because they were competitive. In the words of one elderly man, "Gros Ventres are known for not taking a back seat to anyone." One woman commented, "They have to have the best." An elderly man spoke of the "pure simple joy" of finding out "who's best." One elderly man stressed that Gros Ventres could and should "compete with whites." To Gros Ventres, education indicates success in competition with whites. A young man put it this way: "We feel it is important to live up to white standards as to succeed—not to believe or act like them, but achieve like them." He is pointing out that making a good living is important to Gros Ventres, but not an end in itself; material things are not valuable in themselves, but only as items to be given away or used to help others. Assertiveness or tenacity is another quality to which Gros Ventres attribute their success. Some still refer to it as "fierceness." One young man explained that "it paid off" for Gros Ventres to be assertive because they were particularly successful at what they did. Another commented, "It is good to like a challenge; you can do anything you want and succeed at anything." And one remarked, "Gros Ventres want everything done three days ago." An elderly man characterized a man he considered a good Gros Ventre councilman as "a scrapper." An elderly woman described one of the most outstanding councilmen in earlier years as one who "made a good impression on the Indians" because they thought he "couldn't be overrun by whites." She also insisted that Gros Ventres did well only when they did not let others "walk over us." This characteristic of fierce tenacity is described as having great historical depth. One youth said, "The Blackfeet were anxious to ally with the Gros Ventres because they were so savage," that is, relentless. An elderly Gros Ventre stressed, "Gros Ventres are fierce and competitive—probably because they were always having to fight off groups, being pushed here and there. . . . These tipi rings around here, the big ones are Shoshone and Cheyenne. They were kind of peaceful. But the little ones are Gros Ventre—they were always on the run."[157]

In fact, Gros Ventres have been remarkably successful in taking advantage of educational and other new opportunities. Education levels have been rising during the last twenty years. The number of college graduates and those with some college training has grown considerably. In 1980, over 53 percent of the Indian people over the age of twenty-five were high school graduates, and 6.3 percent were college graduates. Eighteen percent of the residents were attending college in 1981, compared to 2 percent in 1966. Among the reservations of the Northern Plains, Fort Belknap had the highest percentage of college graduates in 1980, a majority of them Gros Ventres. Out of about 300 young people in the Gros Ventre tribe, there are 2 physicians and 4 attorneys; 3 have doctorates, and more than 20 have master's degrees—a startlingly high number compared to other Northern Plains communities of the same or even larger size.[158]

Competitiveness and assertiveness contribute to the success Gros Ventres have had in getting managerial positions and employment locally. In the early 1980s, the reservation superintendent was a Gros Ventre, as were the tribal attorney and most of the occupants of high-level tribal and BIA positions. Applicants for jobs are interviewed and asked to submit résumés. The experiences that Gros Ventres have had away at college or in urban areas contributed to their ability to compete for jobs and to write the grant proposals that help get funding for reservation programs. Tenacity was encouraged by off-reservation experiences as well as by family oral tradition. One youth explained that in urban areas he had to be "very bold, forward, in order to get along." The competition with other reservations for grants requires great tenacity. The Gros Ventres feel they must be particularly resolute because Fort Belknap reservation is without the clout of many others—they have little mineral wealth and no close ties to congressional leaders (as do some other tribes with leaders who have thirty and forty years' tenure on their councils).

People with well-paying jobs are expected to be generous; if they are not, they risk gossip and disapproval. But social pressure is not the primary motive for generosity. As one young man put it, "Gros Ventres must be somebody, do something. Gros Ventre people have to be somebody, have to produce and be responsible and make enough to give out." Without generous display one is not really somebody. Generosity is valued in Plains Indian societies in general, and the Gros Ventres are no exception. Visitors, those in need, and, to a considerable extent, relatives are recipients of gifts of cash and property in nonpublic contexts. But individuals (and their families) with the ability to make large distributions generally do so publicly as well, and it is these public giveaways, often held at powwows (intertribal dances) at the agency, that particularly serve to validate status. In the giveaway ceremony, a family—usually represented by the senior women—come before a crowd and, speaking through an announcer, tell the people the reason for their distribution of gifts—they want to honor a deceased relative, perhaps, or celebrate a relative's accomplishment, or show their appreciation for an honor bestowed on a relative. The family then dance clockwise around the arena or dance floor while an honor song brings to the people's attention the accomplishments of the family or one of its members. Afterward the announcer calls the names of individuals or groups whom the family has chosen to receive gifts, and one by one these individuals come forward to receive from the women of the family cash, blankets, shawls, dress goods, utensils, and occasionally handmade quilts. Sometimes the family members also serve the crowd a meal.

A young Gros Ventre woman commented that it was "Gros Ventre nature" to invest a great deal of time and money in public giveaways and to do so in a very conspicuous way. One youth, a frequent sponsor of giveaways, explained, "Gros Ventres are committed to getting respect; people will respect you if you give." An elderly woman, asked how she would translate the Gros Ventre word for "giveaway" into English, said, "Being a chief for a little while." Another woman, when asked to translate the Gros Ventre word for "chief" into English, said, "Providing man." This association of generosity and leadership is common on the Plains in general. But besting one another (or not being bested) in generous display also is important to many Gros Ventres, particularly to those who seek prominence: "Gros Ventres say, 'If one gives away, I will give more.'" Comparative studies of the Plains giveaway do not exist, so it is impossible to know if competition is typical of Plains giveaways. My impression is that it is not typical. Crow giveaways are competitive, but the competitive element does not seem characteristic of Assiniboine giveaways, nor did I find it among Northern Arapahoes.[159]

The public arena for Gros Ventre giveaway ceremonies is now primarily at the dance ground in the agency area, although some families in Hays have recently held public giveaways on their own land. Competition has so far been an individual matter. In 1985 a committee in Hays organized a powwow there, but it is too early to know if competition between agency and Hays Gros Ventres will develop. There is the potential, however, for a reemergence of a moiety organization.

Prominence is sought not only through the giveaway ritual but also by the political route, and recognition for prominence can enhance one's political influence. Leaders today—business councilmen, particularly—are expected to be conspicuously generous in dealings with constituents. "A real leader helps people, not himself," remarked one elderly woman. As councilmen, individuals have dependable resources with which to be generous. Young councilmen with college credits or degrees stress to constituents that their education made possible a reduction in unemployment on the reservation. Unemployment is a major problem on the reservation. The educated councilmen have stressed that largely through their efforts to write grants and obtain contracts for reservation services, unemployment dramatically decreased: from 63 percent in March 1968, when jobs were available through the War on Poverty programs, to 44 percent in April 1979. Before the poverty programs, in March 1965, unemployment had stood at 77 percent. (Cutbacks during Ronald Reagan's administration raised unemployment back to 70 percent in April 1981.)[160]

The Gros Ventre Treaty Committee, which began to assume its modern form with the election of committee members, was given the authority by Congress to administer a percentage of the funds from claims paid the tribe in 1972 and 1983. In 1983 80 percent of the money was disbursed in per capita shares. Treaty Committee meetings are occasions for Gros Ventres in need to petition committee members for aid. The committee has given grants to people with health or other problems and to community organizations or groups to assist local activities or celebrations. The business council, which obtains federal grants for social service programs, often refers constituents to the program staff rather than disburse tribal funds to individuals. Because constituents perceive that grants more often come to individuals through the Treaty Committee than through the business council, they sometimes comment that "real" or "traditional" leaders are Treaty Committee members rather than councilmen. One man remarked, "People come to the Treaty Committee for personal needs; the Treaty Committee is more respected than the council." Opponents of educated leaders may charge that such leaders "don't want to be bothered with people's problems"—that they discourage the council from routinely making small grants or loans.

"If They Do Good, We Do Twice as Good": Primacy and the New Tribalism

Today many Gros Ventres are commited to an effort to reestablish Gros Ventre primacy at Fort Belknap. This effort is viewed as a revival of a cultural tradition, a tradition that Gros Ventres' views should prevail over Assiniboines' because Gros Ventres have more legitimate right to the lands along the Upper Milk. The quest for primacy through competition with Assiniboines and métis began to appear overtly in the political and ritual context in the late 1960s and 1970s. Competition was encouraged by a great (though still inadequate) increase in new jobs, by renewed interest in serving on the business council, and by the payment of two claim settlements.

Gros Ventres often assert that they are by nature more competitive than Assiniboines and that they are especially high achievers. A young man remarked, "There is a fierce competition between the tribes. If they do good, we do twice as good." Another youth said, "Gros Ventres always had to be superior here. They had to be in control. Assiniboines didn't object. They could sit back and get what they wanted." In other words, the Gros Ventres did not deprive them. One young Gros Ventre woman said, "Gros Ventres work harder." Elderly Gros Ventres share the same sentiments. One man remarked, "Gros Ventres were several jumps ahead of Assiniboines." Another said, "Assiniboines tag along after the Gros Ventres." And another commented, "There is a kind of class system here. The Assiniboines accepted it in some things. We always tried to be fair, divide things up." (Of course, as we shall see, the Assiniboines do not entirely share the Gros Ventres' interpretations of intertribal relations.) Recently there has been increased interest in running for the business council. For the first time, both primary and run-off elections were held in 1983. The interest has been sparked by the fact that the position pays $100 per diem, the council now has the power to act independently of the BIA in several areas, and interest in tribal government was generated among young people on campuses and by the Indian rights movement. Some Gros Ventre councilmen and candidates for office gain support by pointing out to their constituents that they are pursuing advantages for their tribe in relation to Assiniboines and métis (or descendants of métis). When the councilmen recently elected an Assiniboine as chairman, some Gros Ventres attempted to mobilize intertribal opposition to the election on the grounds that by tradition the position alternated between tribes; because an Assiniboine had previously held the position, it was a Gros Ventre's turn. Yet the election of Gros Ventres to the chair for two consecutive terms elicited no complaints from them. On another occasion, Gros Ventres attempted to challenge the political authority of a rival who had some Assiniboine ancestry on the basis of his tribal identity. When Gros Ventres were meeting to decide how to allocate funds from a claim settlement, one Gros Ventre wrote that the Seattle-area Gros Ventres "won't stand for Assiniboine council members participating in the programming of Gros Ventre treaty money." In vying for participation in the decision-making process, he presented his group as proponents of primacy. The claim discussions provided a forum for the expression of old resentments against the Assiniboines, as well as a platform for would-be leaders. The summer powwow has recently become an opportunity for some Gros Ventres to attain primacy by displaying their exceptional skills in managing the event, and to compete in this way with the Assiniboine members of the committee.[161]

Attempts to revive the Flat Pipe ceremony are in some respects part of the Gros Ventres' quest for primacy. Their sacred responsibility for the pipes, in the Gros Ventres' view, makes them unique among peoples. The most important distinction between Gros Ventres and Assiniboines, who have no tribally owned medicine bundles, one elderly woman explained, is simply that "we have two pipes." One elderly man felt strongly that spiritual leaders of other tribes should not be allowed to participate in pipe bundle matters: "Only a Gros Ventre can do pipe ceremonies because they are Gros Ventre ceremonies." A young man, speaking of another youth's reputed vision while fasting, characterized the spirit's message thus: "There was only bad medicine left to get—all of it non–Gros Ventre. Gros Ventres should only use their pipes," for power from any other source would lead a person to harm others. Many Gros Ventres—young and old—have attributed their problems to neglect of the pipes. The Flat Pipe is now in the care of Rufus Warrior's widow. The Feathered Pipe is being watched over by the son of Iron Man. People sometimes leave an offering with the Flat Pipe, but rituals have not been performed regularly with either pipe bundle. In public meetings held to discuss the Gros Ventre claim or treaty money, the topic of the pipes frequently arose. In fact, at one meeting tribal members voted to allot thousands of dollars out of the 20 percent reserve fund to provide for the pipes in whatever way the tribe eventually determined. There is tremendous pride that the traditions of these pipes are unique to the Gros Ventres. Individuals who attempt to "do things for" the pipes achieve the respect of many Gros Ventres and can often sway others to side with them in political struggles by mentioning their efforts or sacrifices on behalf of one of the pipes.

There is controversy over the pipes—whether or not to build a house for them, whether or not to try to revive pipe ceremonies. But the controversy is also in part an expression of Gros Ventre anxiety about their identity today and their position in relation to others, to whites and Assiniboines in particular. Many Gros Ventres view the fact that the formal ceremonies are currently no longer performed as a shortcoming in the eyes of other Indians. This perception is a challenge to Gros Ventre ideals of competitiveness and primacy. The emphasis on Native American pride and Native American studies has regenerated interest in native religion among Indians everywhere. At Fort Belknap, the young seek out the old for their knowledge of Gros Ventre religion, and the old are aware of the youths' desire to practice native religion. In the 1970s and 1980s, perhaps in part because the media treated Native American culture more positively than in previous eras, and because many federal and other officials affirmed its right to exist, Gros Ventres have become concerned that other Plains peoples—in fact, the Assiniboines—have retained some religious ritual that the Gros Ventres have not. One young Gros Ventre had felt at a disadvantage in college when he met other Indians who practiced their native religion: "It was almost like they were more Indian than I was." This experience motivated him to try to participate in native rituals at Fort Belknap. A general commitment to reviving cultural tradition and a desire to see Gros Ventre religion hold as prominent a place as other native religions among Plains peoples are both motivating factors in the movement to revive the pipe ceremonies.

Other Gros Ventres, as well as some Assiniboines, consider it more appropriate to seek self-determination and a better life for the Fort Belknap community as a whole, rather than for their tribe. In fact, these individuals refer to the multitribal Fort Belknap community as "the tribe." Others commit themselves politically to the community in its entirety, yet pursue Gros Ventre primacy in the ritual sphere.

Many young Gros Ventres in their thirties and forties are commited to strengthening the authority of reservation (they may say "tribal") government in relation to federal and state governments. Their ideas about tribal sovereignty developed to a great extent on campuses and in urban areas in the 1960s and 1970s, when intertribal organizations secured Indian rights to greater participation in national and state political and economic institutions. This background in intertribal politics has fostered a commitment to the Fort Belknap multitribal community—to the "new tribalism"—rather than to one tribe. At the University of Montana, for example, the Indian Club (Kyi-Yo), many of whose members were Gros Ventres, successfully lobbied the state government for free tuition for Indians at state universities and were instrumental in the establishment of an Indian studies department at the university. The club also organized several workshops with guest speakers active in the Native American rights movement nationally, and club members registered for courses in tribal government taught from this perspective. Several of these youths, as well as others from other campuses and urban organizations, subsequently became involved in tribal government at Fort Belknap.

In the ritual sphere, youths who stress the new tribalism view pow-wow committee work as a way to strengthen ties with Assiniboines. At colleges, Indian students met, exchanged ideas, and formed friendships with other Indians at intertribal powwows.

Some proponents of intertribal alliance argue that the business council should act as a treaty committee for both tribes. And the strengthening of the reservation government's jurisdiction in legal matters and resource development in relation to federal and state governments also is an important goal. For example, in the 1980s they set out to develop and consistently implement policy for water use. One of the problems faced by agriculturalists at Fort Belknap is water shortage, which is made more serious by state-supported efforts of non-Indians upstream to use water from the Milk without regard for tribal rights. The tribal government asked agricultural operators to file a water use plan so that the tribe could attempt to prevent the state of Montana from taking jurisdiction over water use within reservation boundaries.

The new tribalism tends to conflict not only with efforts to establish Gros Ventre political primacy but also with the heritage left from twenty-five years of the politics of individualism. Thus some Gros Ventres do not favor the strengthening of the tribal government at the expense of individuals' control over their own affairs. Some oppose purchases or control of land by the tribal government and favor per capita distribution of tribal income. As one man explained, "Some will say, 'This is *mine* because I'm a Gros Ventre.' "

Differences in viewpoints also have crystallized around the criteria that should determine membership in the Gros Ventre tribe. "Blood degree" is important symbolically, as well as legally, in determining who is Gros Ventre.

"I Am Three-Eighths Gros Ventre in Blood, One-Hundred Percent Indian in Heart": Blood Degree and Cultural Identity

Cultural identity and legal enrollment in the community and tribe, which is determined by blood percentage, are not the same. Symbols of cultural identity influence people's actions and sometimes generate social conflict through the understandings of Gros Ventre culture and history they convey and the emotions they raise. "Gros Ventre blood" is such a symbol. Controversy over legal membership is encouraged by the fact that to qualify for money and services that have become available in recent years, one must be legally enrolled.

Gros Ventres today speak of four categories of Gros Ventres: full bloods, Dodson Gros Ventres, Creeventres, and River Gros Ventres. These labels are not merely descriptive of individuals' ancestry but symbolic of ideas about group identity—that real or traditional Gros Ventre life is linked to Gros Ventre blood, and the dilution of that blood through intermarriage with other peoples resulted in the dilution of Gros Ventre culture. These ideas about Gros Ventre blood shape political behavior and social interaction in general.

"Full blood" is a cultural category that does not necessarily accord with enrollment status. One can be "full blood" and enrolled as three-fourths or one-half Gros Ventre. Only a handful of Gros Ventres are enrolled as full bloods, and many or most of them actually have some white ancestry. Gros Ventres generally use the term to refer to elderly people (all allottees) who lived in Hays during its heyday in the 1930s and earlier and often to their children, particularly if the children live

125

in Hays and are not Creeventres. Today some full bloods live in Hays, others in the agency area.

The Dodson or "blue-eyed" Gros Ventres live or once lived in the northeast corner of the reservation near the small settlement of Dodson. Their ancestors were white men (thus "blue-eyed") and their Gros Ventre wives, who regularly associated with the Gros Ventres in Hays. At the time of reservation settlement, about six white men were settled in the northeastern section of Fort Belknap. Many of the children of these men and their Gros Ventre wives intermarried, so that these men's surnames are widespread among the Dodson Gros Ventres. Some Gros Ventres with white ancestors also lived in Hays, but the leading men there were full-blood Gros Ventres, and whites played minor roles in Hays society. Today most Dodson Gros Ventres live near Dodson or in the agency vicinity. Their identity as Gros Ventres is not in question.

Such is not the case for Creeventres. These people are descendants of Gros Ventres who married non-ward métis (called Crees by the Gros Ventres, and usually French-Chippewas by the Creeventres) in the 1940s and later. Most live in Hays. One elderly full-blood Gros Ventre man remarked, "They [métis] contributed nothing to blood degree but decreased it. They did not fully participate in Gros Ventre life." A middle-aged man said, "Crees are thinning out our blood." And a young man remarked, "The Gros Ventres feel they were wronged. They dispute that Creeventres are Gros Ventres. They are somewhat marginal. They have ties to the Gros Ventre [tribe] but are not really part of it." This feeling is especially strong toward those with métis surnames. Although several Creeventres have participated enthusiastically in contemporary ritual life, other Gros Ventres insist that Gros Ventre culture and ritual life "petered out," as one man put it, when Gros Ventres began to marry métis. One young full-blood man at Hays remarked, "There aren't too many Indians now [at Hays]; intermarriage makes people forget all their own ways." Gros Ventres often speak of Creeventres as "the one-eighths"; these people are not, in other words, legitimately Gros Ventre, even though some actually have more than one-eighth Gros Ventre ancestry and in fact are enrolled. Rejection of claims for payments submitted by Creeventres with less than one-fourth Gros Ventre blood is a kind of symbolic retaliation against the métis, toward whom the tribe has long been antagonistic.

River Gros Ventres or agency Gros Ventres live in the vicinity of the agency, most in the new housing projects there. Although once only a few Gros Ventre families lived at the agency and the Milk River area was populated largely by Assiniboines, now there are more Gros Ventres in the agency area than in Hays. Some are descendants of the Gros

126

Ventres who originally lived at the agency; others moved there recently to obtain housing. Income and employment levels here are higher than at Hays. There is rivalry between Gros Ventres at Hays and at the agency over jobs, housing, and other programs and benefits. Most of the Gros Ventre support for young, college-educated council leaders comes from the River Gros Ventres (and River Assiniboines). Gros Ventres from Hays sometimes describe River Gros Ventres as "mixed Gros Ventre and Assiniboine." Many Hays people feel that these people are hurting their district; tagging them with Assiniboine blood (although they generally have no more Assiniboine ancestry than those at Hays) links present-day resentment of the agency population to the historical resentment of the Assiniboines. Since the center of most ritual life today is at the agency, River Gros Ventres, on the other hand, see the agency area as the new locus of Gros Ventre culture and of a new heyday for the Gros Ventres.[162]

Interpretations of the past, then, affect evaluations of cultural identity today. Gros Ventre blood symbolizes primacy in relation to Assiniboines and métis. To many, Gros Ventre blood also means Gros Ventre culture in its heyday—thus individuals who were part of that florescence are full bloods, despite physical evidence of white ancestry. Less than one-fourth blood, particularly one-eighth blood, symbolizes culture loss, for culture loss is generally attributed to thinning or diluting of their blood through marriage with non–Gros Ventres. Such dilution, all agree, is what has torn apart the social fabric of Gros Ventre life, as people remember it or have heard about it; it is this that has ultimately led to quarreling and divisiveness.

Gros Ventres manipulate symbols of identity, including blood, to motivate and influence others and on occasion to challenge others for power, authority, and resources. In fact, obtaining recognition as a Gros Ventre probably consumes as much energy today as the pursuit of prominence did in earlier eras. The Treaty Committee is often referred to as more "traditional" than the business council; its members are the "real" Gros Ventres, for one must be enrolled in one of the two tribes to belong to it, whereas members of the business council need only to be enrolled at Fort Belknap as "community members." It was the Treaty Committee that mobilized a majority of the people who attended treaty claim meetings to deny payment to people of less than one-fourth Gros Ventre ancestry. They won support by stressing the theme of Gros Ventre primacy, symbolized as "strengthening Gros Ventre blood." On the one hand, this appeal served to unify Gros Ventres and give expression to cultural identity. On the other hand, their actions created dissension. It was especially in the context of the treaty payment discussions that "blood degree" gained power as a symbol of Gros Ventre identity. Individuals who professed to promote primacy won election to the six-member Treaty Committee and worked to solidify support for reviewing the qualifications of individuals for enrollment in the Gros Ventre tribe. By challenging blood degrees publicly, the "real" Gros Ventres undermined their opponents. Individuals with the right political connections appealed successfully to have their blood degree changed. The meetings became occasions for public arguing among the Gros Ventres. This outspokenness frequently resulted in political success, if only because some opponents withdrew to avoid unpleasantness. People deemed to be ineligible, many of them descendants of métis and Gros Ventres, were referred to as "one-eighths." Sometimes "one-eighths" and "Creeventres" were used interchangeably. The one-eighths fought against their exclusion. Committee members had to take sides publicly. Opponents of individual committee members would accuse them, particularly those with Creeventre relatives, of being "for the one-eighths." The individuals who successfully fought to exclude the one-eighths were perceived as advocates of primacy and gained political influence.

Conflict over legal enrollment has been encouraged by the fact that the criteria for enrollment have been inconsistent over time. Thus some people feel unfairly treated. When the reservation was allotted in 1922, the two tribes prepared lists of Gros Ventres and Assiniboines who were considered "enrolled" and entitled to land at Fort Belknap. The rolls were based in large part on cultural definition, for although in some cases BIA officials intervened, the tribes themselves attempted to determine membership on the basis of "association," on participation in community life. Many persons on the roll as full bloods had considerable white or other Indian ancestry, and persons were listed as full, one-half, or one-fourth Gros Ventre quite arbitrarily. Basically, any person who was part of community life was Gros Ventre, and actual percentage or degree of Gros Ventre ancestry was not particularly important. When the tribes accepted the IRA, the federal government began to keep a roll of community members. No one already enrolled was removed from the roll, and by federal standards, persons who were one-fourth ("one-fourth degree") or more Indian were considered members or "enrolled" at Fort Belknap. Thus some people who were officially less than one-fourth Gros Ventre or Assiniboine were enrolled. This was not satisfactory to the tribes, and finally in 1959 they held a referendum and changed the IRA constitution to read that enrollment required one-fourth Gros Ventre and/or Assiniboine blood. As a result, some people who had been born before 1959 were enrolled while their brothers and sisters born after 1959 were excluded.

The wish for enrollment and the controversy over requirements for enrollment escalated with the competition for new jobs, services, and money, for which enrollment as a member of the tribe or of the Fort Belknap community was required. The incidence of intermarriage with people not enrolled at Fort Belknap has been increasing since the 1940s, so that many young people today barely qualify for tribal enrollment and their children are able or will be able to qualify in even smaller numbers. If a person who has less than one-half degree tribal blood marries outside the tribe, their children cannot qualify with one-fourth degree tribal blood. Elderly people—those born between 1889 and 1929—are by and large one-half degree or more Gros Ventre or Assiniboine. This is the case for 64 percent of the Gros Ventres and 52 percent of the Assiniboines. Of the people born between 1930 and 1955, about 49 percent are one-half degree or more Gros Ventre or Assiniboine. Among people born after 1955, only about 17 percent of Gros Ventres and 26 percent of Assiniboines have one-half degree or more. Without enrolled status an individual is at a disadvantage in the reservation community.[163]

When by the 1960s the Gros Ventre (and Assiniboine) court claims against the United States had progressed to the point where people expected a payment, the tribe held meetings to decide who would be entitled to receive a share of the impending judgment. By majority vote those in attendance voted that to receive money from the Gros Ventre claim a person would have to be one-fourth or more Gros Ventre. This requirement would exclude some persons who considered themselves Gros Ventre, and were so considered by others, but who were on the roll as less than one-fourth Gros Ventre. The issue continued to be controversial, and when the eventual award was distributed in 1972, Congress decided that those who were less than one-fourth but who had received a payment in 1937 from the 1855 claim (allottees and their children, for the most part) would be paid in 1972 for the 1888 claim. In 1972 there were more than 400 individuals who had more Assiniboine than Gros Ventre blood, though they considered themselves Gros Ventres; the Gros Ventres voted them ineligible, and subsequently they received their 1888 claim money from the Assiniboines' share.

There was a great deal of bitterness among Gros Ventres over the payment of the claim money in 1972 (for lands ceded by Gros Ventres and Assiniboines for an unconscionable amount in 1888) and again in 1983 (a claim for interest from 1874 to 1981 on lands taken by the government from the Gros Ventre and Blackfeet groups in 1874 without compensation until 1935). Many people thought of themselves as culturally Gros Ventre even though they did not live on the reservation and resented not being part of the decision-making process when eligibility for receipt of the claim money was determined. One man wrote to the reservation newspaper, "I don't live on the reservation now but intend to move back some day. . . . I am three-eighths Gros Ventre in blood, one-hundred percent Indian in heart. Why haven't I been consulted . . . ?" Individuals on or off the reservation who were less than one-half and whose spouses were not Gros Ventre were bitter that their children were ineligible. Many were angry that their relatives were entitled to the payment and they were not; some who also had Assiniboine ancestry were eventually paid from the Assiniboine share of the money, but were bitter that people of whom they had considered themselves a part had rejected them. Others felt that because they participated in Fort Belknap community life they should be entitled to the payment regardless of blood degree. One woman spoke for these last when she wrote:

> I who always claimed my Indian [identity] am not entitled. People who have for years have [sic] been ashamed of their Indian [heritage] now claim their Indian blood. Now that it be profitable to be Indian. . . . True, I have lived in the White society and not the reservation since a young child. But I have been treated as an Indian by this White society so I have suffered some of the prejudice that I would not have had to go through if my parents stayed on the reservation. The White people treated me as an Indian; there is no difference in the degree of blood—an Indian is an Indian.

In 1984, 2,236 Gros Ventres and 1,437 Assiniboines qualified for their respective tribal rolls. In addition, 421 individuals who had one-fourth degree combined Gros Ventre–Assiniboine blood were paid claim money at the direction of Congress, and 91 persons with one-fourth degree Indian blood qualified as community but not tribal members— if they were one-eighth Gros Ventre and one-eighth Cree, for example.[164]

Conflict over cultural identity does not merely reflect the controversy over legal enrollment. That is, people whose children or grandchildren cannot be enrolled still may be among the strongest proponents of the one-fourth degree cutoff rule. Moreover, the antagonism shown toward those whose Assiniboine or (especially) métis ancestry prevents their enrollment as Gros Ventres is stronger than toward those whose white ancestry prevents enrollment.

The coming together of people with different backgrounds and viewpoints at Fort Belknap between the late 1960s and the early 1980s resulted in conflicting notions about the relationship of blood to Gros Ventre identity, about tribalism, and (as we shall see in Chapter 2)

about ritual life. College-educated segments of the population sometimes view the Gros Ventres' circumstances and opportunities differently than other tribal members do. The return to the reservation of
many Gros Ventres who had been living elsewhere and the visits of
Gros Ventres who have permanently settled in distant cities and towns
have introduced new ideas about and ways of getting along with others. These people have not necessarily lived their lives in a small
community where tact and cooperation are useful strategies. The Fort
Belknap community has more access to the wider society now than in
previous eras, for most families have automobiles and television. There
is less feeling of estrangement from the world outside the reservation
community. Gros Ventres describe themselves as outspoken by nature.
Elderly Gros Ventres stress that being outspoken against adversaries of
the tribe was and is a good thing. One man commented, "Gros Ventres
were more outspoken [to whites] than other Montana tribes." Another
man, speaking of Gros Ventre characteristics that have historical
depth, noted, "The Gros Ventre personality is belligerent." But Gros
Ventres observe that in recent years this outspokenness has been directed toward each other rather than outside adversaries. One elder
remarked, "Now the Gros Ventres can't agree on anything. People were
different in the 1930s and before—they helped each other out—they
were not jealous." A young man observed, "There is not that bond
between Gros Ventres. . . . When there are conflicts, they aren't together." Another said that Gros Ventres were "outspoken and judg-
mental . . . , not serene, tactful."

The social diversity and lack of uniformity in outlook do result at
times in social conflicts. But, to a great extent, the interplay between
contrasting ideas over the past twenty years has led to accommodation, compromise, and creativity in the ways Gros Ventres view themselves and their society. New ideas about tribalism are emerging. Advocates of primacy, confronted by their Creeventre grandchildren, may
eventually reconsider their ideas about Creeventre participation in
tribal affairs. Since the late 1960s, despite differences, the Gros Ventres
have been caught up in the revival of tradition, as they see it, in perpetuating their culture.

Cultural Continuity and Innovation:
Conclusions and Controversies

There has been much cultural continuity in Gros Ventre life over the
past two centuries. Two behavioral ideals that have remained central
to the ethos of the Gros Ventres are the quest for prominence and the

tenacious defense of group interests. These ideals have been expressed symbolically in different ways during the various eras through which the group has passed. But despite the changes in symbolic forms, their meanings remained the same, and this continuity helped to perpetuate the Gros Ventres' sense of group identity. Cultural ideals were expressed in emotionally compelling ways in Gros Ventre ritual life. Gros Ventres shaped the way their society changed by the interpretations they put on ritual acts, as well as on other behavior, events, and relationships. The social circumstances in which they found themselves influenced their concepts of group identity and the ways cultural ideals were expressed.

In the 1778–1877 era, property in the form of horses and also in trade goods made an individual "wealthy," that is, better off in property than others in his society. The Gros Ventres associated the generous distribution of wealth with leadership and rank, and virtually all sought to be prominent in this way. Gros Ventres also attempted to earn prestige and rank by fierce, tenacious attacks on the enemies that increasingly threatened them after the expansion of the trading posts into the Plains. These ideals were reinforced and expressed through the symbolism of a series of age-grade and moiety rituals and the enemy-friend relationship—all particular to the Gros Ventres. These ceremonies involved the distribution of property by prominent persons or groups. In their ritual life Gros Ventres competed among themselves for public recognition of generosity and bravery.

Between 1878 and 1901, the Gros Ventres' circumstances changed drastically. Warfare and age-grade rituals did not survive reservation settlement. There were no robes to exchange for trade goods, for the buffalo were gone. But Gros Ventres continued to pursue recognition for prominence and tenacity. Horses (now bred rather than stolen), cattle, and trade goods purchased with cow hides were wealth, and individuals obtained them with the assistance of the agent in return for apparent cooperation in the civilization program. Moiety rituals continued to be a means for Gros Ventres to compete for prominence through generous distribution. The newly introduced hand game ceremony and house dance offered two other routes to prominence, for individuals who bore the expenses of these ceremonies earned prestige. Generosity in the new rites symbolized the association of leadership and status with the distribution of wealth. Assiniboines were perceived as threatening to Gros Ventre interests, and Gros Ventre leaders were expected to be fierce in trying to gain political advantage over Assiniboines in reservation affairs. Tenacity came to be expressed in the pursuit of primacy over the Assiniboines rather than in war. In the reservation context, Gros Ventres sought to outdo the Assiniboines in civilized pursuits.

From 1902 to 1937, stock continued to represent wealth, and leaders were expected to donate generously to Gros Ventre ceremonies. The men's moieties were replaced by community-wide moieties, and these two groups competed with one another in the display of generosity, just as individuals did. The symbolism in moiety begging songs gave way to the symbolism of songs for the transfer of Grass Dance offices. The newly organized Grass Dance ceremony, the seven-day Christmas celebration, and the Hays Fair were the rituals in which participants donated to earn public recognition. Changes in federal policy led to the establishment of a business council. Despite the officials' plans, Gros Ventres expected leaders to pursue primacy in relation to the Assiniboines. They did so not only in competition in "progressive" pursuits but also through work on treaty claims that involved the construction of a history of how they were wronged by Assiniboines as well as by whites. The Gros Ventres sought also to pursue primacy through the Hays Fair, through endeavors that symbolized progress to whites, and in contests of skill and strength. Leaders began to be expected to attain more control over reservation affairs. They backed their aggressive efforts to obtain more authority by demonstrations of their progressive bent. Allotment of land symbolized progress to whites and Indian control to Gros Ventres. Their enthusiastic acceptance of the Indian Reorganization Act was an expression of both these strategies.

In the era from 1938 to 1964, prominence was an ideal for elders and the middle-aged, but one they gradually gave up hope of realizing. Ritual life waned as the commitment to agriculture gave way to the desire to obtain higher education or an occupation that would provide more means to prosper than the reservation's agricultural economy offered. Leaders were still expected to pursue primacy, and they attempted to do so within the business council. In the wake of the expectations aroused by the IRA, they were increasingly expected to obtain self-determination. As leaders fell short of their goals, constituents became alienated. Many Gros Ventres began to associate the loss of ritual life and the erosion of support for the business council with the end of Gros Ventre tradition. Thus the old round dance hall—not the new rectangular one—was viewed as the real Gros Ventre or traditional hall. And Hays (before out-migration and intermarriage with métis changed its social composition) came to symbolize traditional or real community life.

Between 1965 and 1984, wide-reaching social change in American society affected Fort Belknap reservation, reviving ritual (at the agency rather than Hays) and renewing interest in the business council. Large numbers of people returned to the reservation from towns and cities. War on Poverty funds and an emphasis on ethnic pride revitalized ritual life. The Gros Ventres renewed their commitment to the association of authority and prestige with the generous distribution of wealth. The intertribal powwow held at the agency became the most important ritual in which people gave away property to validate position or honor a relative. And a renewed interest in intrasocietal competition in the sponsorship of ritual began to emerge in the 1980s. As a person had to have cash to purchase manufactured goods to distribute, advanced education or a skilled trade came to be associated with prominence. The Gros Ventres' struggle for primacy was given new impetus by the influx of funding, by the increased authority of tribal leaders that accompanied contracting and the administration of War on Poverty programs, and by the payment of two claims won against the federal government.

Throughout the past two centuries Gros Ventres have associated their responsibility to the sacred pipe bundles with group identity and with their ability to pursue prominence and to succeed at life generally. The pipes, then, were important symbols for the Gros Ventres, but the precise meaning of pipe symbolism changed from one era to the next. Before 1878 the sacred pipes symbolized the Gros Ventre concept of creation and their place in it, including a view of themselves as a chosen people. Pipe rituals reinforced generosity and bravery. And they supported the association of authority and rank with generosity and old age. Fulfillment of one's ritual responsibilities would facilitate success in one's pursuits. In the 1878–1901 era, the pipes continued to symbolize the Gros Ventre world view. They symbolically validated and motivated success, now in the reservation context rather than in battles. But an increasing number of boarding school children became alienated from the pipe tradition. For elders in the 1902–1937 era, the pipes still were a means to pray to the Great Mystery. But for many younger Gros Ventres the pipes came to symbolize supernatural power that was too dangerous to tap. Toward the end of the era the Flat Pipe was described by Gros Ventres as mice-infested, a ruin of its former self. Pipe rituals came to represent an idealized past, a symbol of the tribe's former greatness and cohesiveness. As the rituals gradually came to be viewed as unsuccessful, the condition of the pipes also symbolized the Gros Ventres' breach of their covenant with the Supreme Being. During the period from 1938 to 1964, for most Gros Ventres the pipes symbolized a bygone era, yet also dangerous supernatural power. A banner designed for the Gros Ventre community by a respected elder portrayed the two pipes giving way to the cross of Catholicism. At the same time it paid homage to the past pipe tradition. Pride mingled with a feeling that much of the past way of life had become irrelevant to contemporary concerns. In the 1970s and 1980s (as we shall see in Chapter 2) the pipes still stood for pride in the past and power that was dangerous, but also for Indian religion (as opposed to a uniquely Gros Ventre world view, according to some people, and in opposition to the dominant white society's values, in the view of others). Pipe responsibilities that were fulfilled indicated rejection of white society; those responsibilities unfulfilled stimulated Gros Ventre anxiety over cultural identity and political and social status or primacy.

Their changing circumstances also precipitated new ideas about cultural identity. The idea that Gros Ventre blood or degree of Gros Ventre ancestry defined cultural identity was a concept foreign to Gros Ventres before the 1930s. They routinely incorporated people from other groups or their descendants into their society as Gros Ventres. The emergence of blood as a symbol of cultural identity came about in response to a particular set of social circumstances. The influx of métis into Hays as a result of the establishment of a town site in the 1920s and federal jobs in the 1930s, as well as the subsequent marriages of Gros Ventres and métis and the settlement of métis in Hays, aroused great resentment among the Gros Ventres. In the Gros Ventre view, Gros Ventre blood links a person with an idealized past, with Hays before intermarriage undercut community life there. Gros Ventre blood represents traditional culture; a diminishing of blood degree through intermarriage (particularly with métis) represents loss of Gros Ventre culture. Non–Gros Ventre blood also symbolized what Gros Ventres viewed as the exploitive nature of others' relations with them. They felt that they were especially put upon by Assiniboines and métis; thus rejection of Assiniboine and métis blood in enrollment policy represented their effort to act on this historical resentment, to retaliate for it. Receipt of claim money and federal funds from the 1960s through the 1980s depended on one's enrollment as a member of the tribe and of the community, respectively. Thus disputes over blood escalated as people struggled to be enrolled or to have their children or grandchildren enrolled, often by gaining approval from the Treaty Committee or business council to change blood degree. The new money brought the blood symbolism to the fore and highlighted it so that it figures importantly in political interaction. Today cultural identity is changed or reclaimed in part by a change of blood degree.

My findings suggest that other studies of the Gros Ventres at Fort Belknap need to be reexamined. Three scholars—Edward Barry,

135

Michael Foley, and David Rodnick—conducted studies of Fort Belknap history and came to conclusions about culture change there. Their interpretations contrast significantly with mine, in large part because my focus, although based on many of the same sets of documents as theirs, included the perspective of the Gros Ventres themselves, while theirs did not. And my approach, unlike theirs, considered how the perspectives and actions of Gros Ventres and Assiniboines influenced each other and shaped each other's choices over time. Barry, Foley, and Rodnick all view the change in Indian ideas and behavior that took place at Fort Belknap as loss of native or traditional culture, though their interpretations of Fort Belknap history vary.

Barry used an assimilation model to explain how and why the Fort Belknap peoples changed. Foley was more sympathetic to the Indians than Barry, but he too viewed them as failures. To Foley, the Indians were passive victims of exploitation by whites. Paralyzed by poverty and defeat, they could not resist the changes imposed on them. Rodnick quoted opinions of his informants in 1935 on past agents, events, and circumstances. But he accepted the assimilation model, viewing adoption of white values and patterns of interaction as the inevitable response to contact with whites. He viewed intermarriage with whites as a major factor in assimilation, correlating social and culture change with a decrease in the number of full-blood Indians. And he discussed Assiniboine actions outside the context of their relations with their Gros Ventre neighbors. A look at some of these three studies' specific interpretations of occurrences at Fort Belknap will reveal how these interpretations differ from mine and why an approach that considers the meaning of social acts to the people at Fort Belknap is essential.

Barry misunderstood much of what went on at Fort Belknap because he did not consider the Indians' perspective. He saw the people of Fort Belknap steadily assimilating through time, dragging their feet all the while. He portrayed the Gros Ventres as more assimilated than the Assiniboines at every turn. Barry concluded that any change signified an abandonment of Indian culture. For example, he concluded that only "progressives" (the most assimilated) raised potatoes and oats in the 1878–1901 era. Yet the successful gardeners he mentioned by name were outstanding warriors and medicine men, prominent in Gros Ventre terms. Barry argued that short hair, living on a "small ranch," and infrequent dancing indicated that an individual was assimilating. But Gros Ventres did not tend cattle and cut hay with the same goals in mind as did their white neighbors.[165]

Barry also interpreted lack of change—the continuation of social dances, for example—as an indication of incomplete assimilation, as stubborn resistance to acceptance of a new way of life. He did not see that reorganized secular rituals (such as the Grass Dance or Christmas dance or house dance) expressed authority relations and values about generosity that were part of early-nineteenth-century Gros Ventre culture and at the same time adaptive responses to reservation conditions. He described the Hays Fair as different from the whites' fairs because Gros Ventres failed in their efforts to copy whites; he did not recognize its role in strategies of pursuit of primacy and self-determination.[166]

Barry interpreted change purely as a response to white pressure or initiative; thus Gros Ventres abandoned the Sun Dance because whites forbade it. But discontinuance of the Sun Dance was also part of a larger strategy of pursuing primacy in relation to the Assiniboines. He did not recognize that a great many of the changes in Gros Ventre life were accomplished on their own terms, not those of whites. Thus, when he discussed the early twentieth century, he characterized the generation born on the reservation as assimilated, as having a "decimated" quality of life, increased depression and despair, mental and physical deterioration. Yet it was precisely this generation that took major responsibility for revitalizing political and ceremonial life—reorganizing the moiety system, expanding community participation in the Grass Dance and associated giveaways, and starting the Hays Fair, which was one of the biggest and most famous on the Northern Plains. And leaders of this generation successfully lobbied for allotment on their own terms and pursued a multimillion-dollar claim against the federal government for treaty violation. Barry was correct in drawing attention to the problems of poverty but mistaken in assuming that Gros Ventres simply accepted their lot. Barry seemed to accept the agent's evaluation of situations and to ignore documents written by Gros Ventres or transcripts of their remarks. For example, he dismissed Gros Ventre complaints about Assiniboines as expressions of personal pique. He missed the struggle for primacy that was so important in Gros Ventre life—how and why it developed, how it was expressed, and how it influenced the choices and strategies of both tribes. It figured importantly in the Gros Ventres' response to the introduction of Catholicism, agriculture, and allotment, for example. Other events that, relying on the agents' descriptions, he misunderstood are the Ghost Dance complex and the hand game revitalization movement that accompanied it. He portrayed the Gros Ventres' interpretation of the Ghost Dance rituals as "war-like." And the killing of Agent Simons, he mistakenly observed, "caused no excitement among the Indians."[167]

Ignorance of Gros Ventre culture and society led Barry to other errors. He accepted government reports that allotment was favored by

Gros Ventre mixed-blood progressives, while opponents were Assiniboine full-bloods (whom he described as "stand-patters"). In actuality, the petitions for allotment carried the names of virtually all Gros Ventre males. And the Assiniboines were no more full blood than the Gros Ventres. When he discussed the business council in the 1920s, he accepted the agent's claim that the councilmen were young progressives who took over from elderly, presumably more conservative or traditional men. But among the Gros Ventres the leadership of the council did not change appreciably in the 1920s—the same men had been on the council in earlier years. And their views on the issues did not differ from those of their constituents. Barry's conclusion that the Indians at Fort Belknap "had adopted white ways . . . but lacked the tools, animals, and education needed to be successful" appears extremely ethnocentric once the Indians' perspectives on their world are considered.[168]

Foley argued that the Indians' lack of success was due not to their lack of education but to the federal government's mismanagement, neglect, and paternalism. He concluded that the Fort Belknap people exhibited "passive submission to the years of exploitation," when in point of fact they devised political strategies to improve their circumstances and they reorganized their social institutions in an effort to deal with change on their own terms. Whether entirely successful or not, they indefatigably pursued their own goals. Nowhere did he recognize the Gros Ventres' efforts to reorganize their ritual life and the relationship of these changes to new forms of political and economic organization. To demonstrate that the Gros Ventres were unsuccessful in their struggle to adapt to reservation life, Foley maintained that reports of success in agriculture were unfounded, given that several of the agents made fraudulent purchases, that they claimed to have bought hay or oats that had not really been grown. But the fact that the majority were not well off does not minimize the importance of those few individuals who were prosperous by Gros Ventre standards. The apparent possibility of prominence reinforced people's ideals and gave direction to their behavior. The desire to donate, even if one had only a shawl or some bread, contributed to the success of ceremonies. Foley also misunderstood the import of the Gros Ventres' debate at the 1895 cession council. He ignored the tribe's stated plan to teach their young people to mine the gold on these lands themselves. Uncritically accepting the commissioners' views on the council, he dismissed Under Bull's group's dissent as a protest of only a few "younger men" and portrayed as consensus Running Fisher's statements that Gros Ventres would cede the land because they were totally dependent on the government. Yet the great majority of the Gros Ventres of all ages opposed the cession. When one of the commissioners threatened that if they did not agree to the cession, they would "have to starve," one Gros Ventre remarked, "I like these mountains and I can't sell them. If all my hide falls off my face [from starvation], it would be all right; even if my fingernails drop off, it would be all right." Another said, "If I starve to death it will be all right. . . . I can't very well sell. . . . " Foley was certainly correct in pointing out that the tribes at Fort Belknap were exploited, but he distorted the nature of the relationship between Indians and whites and misrepresented Gros Ventre and Assiniboine culture by suggesting that the tribes' views were essentially the same and that they were passive, without goals and values of their own.[169]

Rodnick, too, described the Indians at Fort Belknap as passive. His 1935 study focused on the Assiniboines, but some of his conclusions were general enough to refer to the Gros Ventres as well. He argued, for example, that boarding school discipline produced a population that feared new things and had a "submissive attitude." His analysis of the allotment era was flawed by this view. First, he presented allotment as something the Indians "received," and failed to acknowledge their role in the legislation and its subsequent implementation. He also does not see that Assiniboine actions then were in large part a reaction to the Gros Ventres' quest for primacy. Rodnick mistakenly reported that Assiniboines from Canada and Fort Peck and Crees and Chippewas who moved on the reservation after 1888 were not enrolled. He did not recognize that the Assiniboine strategy of claiming these people as kinsmen can be better understood in the context of the Gros Ventre effort to expel not only Fort Peck and Canadian Assiniboines but also those Upper Assiniboines whose direct ancestors were not part of the late-nineteenth-century alliance. Rodnick saw the history of culture change at Fort Belknap as one of steady assimilation; he divided the Assiniboines into four groups, distinguished by blood and age, whose assimilation of white values and behavior differed by degree. He associated degree of assimilation with ancestry. He defined mixed bloods biologically, as persons with some white ancestry. As the population became more mixed blood over time, culture was progressively lost, in Rodnick's view. He presented people under the age of forty (the elderly of today) as accepting the supremacy of white culture and rejecting Assiniboine culture. He predicted complete assimilation in two generations, sooner for the Gros Ventres, whom he viewed as more assimilated than the Assiniboines in 1935.[170]

Rodnick erred in linking biological and cultural identity. Persons on the rolls as mixed bloods often were culturally indistinguishable from full bloods. Moreover, his portrayal of people under forty lacked cultural perspective, for this age group was not expected to assume leadership positions or even to participate regularly in community ceremonies. As youths they were expected to sow wild oats. His own data showed that all age groups participated in some way in the expression of Assiniboine culture ("culture," as Rodnick understood it, apparently meant customs as well as beliefs), whether they were mixed or full bloods. In fact, it is from this group of youths—today's elders—that young people today have sought knowledge and instruction in the cultural revival that began in the late 1960s. Rodnick failed to consider the implications of the existence of a dedicated minority (whom he characterized as living in a world of illusion) who, while ranching and working for wages, steadfastly pursued their interest in and commitment to Assiniboine ceremonies and customs, regardless of the orientation of the majority or of Rodnick's mixed bloods. The contrasts in Assiniboine views in 1935 helped make possible the resurgence and perpetuation of Assiniboine religion and ritual in the generations to come.

An understanding of the contexts in which innovations have occurred and of how innovations have become culturally acceptable helps us put in better perspective the kinds of cultural revival to be found at Fort Belknap today. It helps us to see why Gros Ventre revivals have taken the form they have, with emphasis on the expression of the pursuit of prominence and primacy, and why attention to the pipes has such significance for Gros Ventre political and social life. This overview of change from 1778 to 1984 also provides historical perspective on the kinds of social conflicts and the sorts of contested meanings that exist between the old and the young and between Gros Ventres and Assiniboines today. As Chapters 2 and 3 explain, these groups have, in effect, experienced different sorts of pasts because, occupying different social vantage points, they have interpreted the past differently.

‹ 2 ›

The Generation Gap:
Interpreting Cultural Revival

When adult Gros Ventres of all ages talk about political, religious, or even family life at Fort Belknap, eventually they observe that there is a generation gap today. The young people at times understand the world and behave differently from their elders, and these differences sometimes make for tension and conflict. Despite such tensions, elders and youths regularly rely on each other and acknowledge their ties to each other in public (as in joint participation in giveaways or powwows) and in private. Many ritual and political symbols are emotionally compelling and meaningful to both elders and youths, though the generations may not interpret them in the same way. I found that, while many symbols are shared and social reciprocities are observed, meanings of symbols, as well as concepts about cultural identity and interpretations of Gros Ventre history, do vary according to age group.

I follow Karl Mannheim in my use of the term "generation": a group of coevals (or cohort), people born within a particular time span, whose shared experience significantly distinguishes them from contemporaries in other age groups. Thus a group "experiencing the same concrete historical problems may be said to be part of the same actual generation." Groups within the same generation that "work up the material of their common experiences in different specific ways constitute separate generation units." Gros Ventres on Fort Belknap today constitute what I am calling an elder generation and a youth generation, the latter comprised of two generation units, one I call the education clique and the other the militants.[1]

The Elder Generation

Persons born between 1895 and 1929 who are living as members of the Fort Belknap community (on or adjacent to the reservation in Harlem) number about 129. As members of a generation they possess shared experiences that significantly distinguish them from their deceased elders who were born in the late nineteenth century or earlier and also from Gros Ventres who were born after 1929. These elders were children or young adults when Gros Ventre ceremonial life was in full bloom. As children they attended pipe-bundle ceremonies and hand game rituals, observed their elders participating in sweat lodges, perhaps saw a medicine man cure a patient. They regularly attended house or tea dances, Christmas–New Year celebrations, and the Hays Fair, all of which were organized and participated in by their parents and grandparents. Most spoke the Gros Ventre language when they entered school, and although their parents encouraged them to speak English, other Gros Ventres addressed them by their Gros Ventre names, which they probably received from an elderly relative. They often interpreted for elderly Gros Ventres, who could not speak English fluently. Their concept of Gros Ventre cultural identity, particularly its ritual expression, was forged in these early childhood experiences. Sham battles, old men reciting war exploits, crow belt dances, horses packed with goods being given to visitors from other tribes, every household and each moiety contributing according to its means and abilities to Hays ritual life—this was Gros Ventre tradition to these children and young adults. But they were basically spectators—interested, enchanted, awe-struck spectators, but spectators just the same. If one of these children was chosen to serve on the dance committee, for example, his parents and other relatives did the actual work. Young adults occasionally served on a dance committee as helpers—"flunkies," as they put it. But their parents and grandparents forcefully impressed upon them that many of the Gros Ventres' ritual traditions were not to be their traditions in the future.[2]

Children of the early twentieth century were not allowed or encouraged to pursue an interest in native Gros Ventre religion or to take on major responsibilities in secular ritual life. Instead, they were urged to learn English and to acquire the educational, vocational, and domestic skills that would enable them to compete successfully with whites and to avoid exploitation and abuse as much as possible. One seventy-one-year-old woman remarked to me that her mother's mother would become angry if she spoke the Gros Ventre language: "She would say I had to compete with whites now—what good is speaking Indian?" Another elderly woman explained, "My dad told us kids that they had

142

to get an education—get A's—so they could get along well in the white man's world. He never taught us Indian things. We did get A's." Grandparents and parents in the early twentieth century were determined that Gros Ventres would "not take a back seat to anyone," recalled one sixty-six-year-old man. This meant learning to deal confidently and skillfully with the institutions of the wider society. As another elderly Gros Ventre man explained, "Young boys patterned themselves after others. Long ago young people liked to be warriors. I heard what a fierce warrior my grandfather was. When we realized we weren't going to live that life, I wanted to be an engineer. I admired the steam engineers that were here running the sawmill at Hays."

In the early twentieth century, old people were venerated: to have lived a long life they must have been blessed by the Supreme Being. They were given unqualified respect by well-brought-up young people. The advice and instructions of elderly people were not questioned. In fact, there were many behavioral prescriptions that young people and children felt keenly. One man recalls, "When I was young you never walked in front of an old fellow; you were trained that way." In short, when they were children, in the early twentieth century, the elder generation of today was expected to attend and enjoy Gros Ventre rituals yet they were not encouraged to perpetuate them.

By the time today's elders were adults, during and just after World War II, Hays society was experiencing economic and political pressures that resulted in change in Gros Ventre community life. As explained in Chapter 1, it became increasingly difficult for elderly people to continue their celebrations and rituals on the scale to which they were accustomed. Most families—including those with an elderly head of household—had subsisted by raising cattle and grain and/or by working in the lumber business centered in Hays. In the late 1930s, severe drought and a devastating forest fire destroyed the economic underpinnings of Hays ritual life. New federal policies precluded the possibility of rebuilding ranching operations. The individuals in today's elder generation were at this time attempting to raise their own children with inadequate resources. During and after the war—particularly during the 1950s—men and women in their twenties, thirties, and early forties left the reservation with the active encouragement of the federal government to obtain work elsewhere. Many sold their allotments of land. Those who remained gradually found it less and less practical or interesting to participate in dances and other such activities, especially as the elderly people who presided over them were dying year by year. Young people became more active in rodeoing than in Indian dancing. In the cities and towns, any Indian ritual life that was practiced (often none was) bore little resemblance to the ritual life of Hays. One elderly man says that in 1944 he "left the reservation and resolved never to look back." The elder generation is today proud of their accomplishments off the reservation. Many say that they never expected to return to the reservation; most never expected that their children would settle at Fort Belknap.[3]

In the early or mid-1960s or later, after living off the reservation anywhere from three to twenty years, many of the elder generation returned to Fort Belknap. Housing and other economic programs facilitated the resettlement process. Many elders obtained new housing at the agency or Hays or had older houses renovated. They faced both pressures and opportunities. Programs that stressed Indian culture, such as oral history projects, offered employment, recognition, and prestige. On the other hand, the generation of youths forcefully urged the revival of Gros Ventre ritual life, a revival that the elders—now in their sixties and seventies, for the most part—were unprepared or unwilling to lead, for reasons explored below.

The Youth Generation

Persons in the youth generation, born between 1930 and 1955, who now live on or adjacent to the reservation number about 297. As children they attended no Gros Ventre pipe-bundle ceremonies, hand games, sweats, curing ceremonies; they saw no sham battles and no crow belt ceremonies. A few, whose families lived in Hays, may have attended a Christmas dance, but the event would have been an attenuated version of the dances held in the 1930s and earlier. In the summer they attended rodeos rather than the Hays Fair. They did not speak Gros Ventre; many were not given a Gros Ventre name. In short, they had little understanding of Gros Ventre ritual tradition from firsthand experience. Many of those who had attended Indian dances had grown up at the agency, where the Assiniboines had a summer celebration well into the 1950s. Several attended boarding school rather than Harlem or Hays schools, or grew up off the reservation and had little contact with the Fort Belknap community except upon occasional visits.

This generation was profoundly affected by the War on Poverty and affirmative action programs of the 1960s and 1970s. These programs, as well as educational benefits available to veterans of Vietnam, enabled the youths to attend college or obtain employment in an era when Native American studies, Indian pride, and Indian rights were foci of the media, as well as of colleges and government agencies. In the late 1960s and 1970s they began to arrive at Fort Belknap from campuses

144

and cities to apply for jobs and housing. Youths became motivated or encouraged to be Indian, or were channeled into an interest in and commitment to being Indian in new ways. Within the generation, however, there were two groups with different orientations toward being Indian: the education clique and the militants. Probably at least three-fourths of the youth generation comprise the education clique.[4]

The Education Clique

The members of the education clique, on the whole, enhanced their concept of Indianness at colleges in Montana, where they joined students from other Montana reservations in enthusiastically developing Indian clubs, conferences, and powwows (intertribal dances). Colleges and universities aided such efforts in an attempt to respond to federal incentives for special programs for Native Americans and also to meet competition for Indian students from other campuses. In this context, too, political contacts were made with young Indians from outside the Fort Belknap area. Upon completion of their education, Gros Ventres who returned to Fort Belknap attained considerable success in supervisory jobs with various federally funded programs and, in some cases, in elections to the business council. They became actively involved in the dance committee and summer celebration (or powwow) at the agency. Their efforts at cultural revival centered on the Milk River Dance Committee, naming ceremonies, and memorial giveaways. Some began to attempt to participate in various kinds of native Indian religious rituals, but for the most part they concentrated on the secular rituals. They refer to themselves as the "educated" group.[5]

The Militants

The militants attended college or worked outside Montana. On city campuses they encountered a social protest movement (opposition to the war in Vietnam, the American Indian Movement) far more vocal and widespread than on Montana campuses. Many obtained jobs in urban poverty programs where confrontational tactics were important in attaining goals. The Indian community on urban campuses was smaller, far more multicultural, and less tied to reservation communities than was the case in the Montana schools. When these Gros Ventres returned to Fort Belknap, they competed with the education clique for jobs and for political positions. Their efforts at cultural revival have centered on the Chief Joseph Dance Committee and celebration (or powwow), which was established in 1974, and on participation in native Indian religion. Unlike individuals in the education clique, several of the leaders of the militants seek to acquire or purport to have acquired assistance from a spirit helper through a vision quest. The militants do not refer to themselves as "militants"; one suggested that "nonconformists" was appropriate, another "spiritual people."[6]

Many Gros Ventres born between 1930 and 1955, of course, did not attend college, but they have generally associated themselves with one or the other of these youth generation units in social and political activities.[7]

Interpretations of Culture Loss

Both the elder and youth generations agree that Gros Ventres have lost much of their culture. (Of course, in an anthropological sense, Gros Ventre culture has changed, not disappeared.) As to what has been lost and how and why it has been lost, however, they do not agree.

Both the elders and the youths agree that Gros Ventre ritual life, both religious and secular, had ended by the 1940s. And they agree that Gros Ventre political and social domination of Fort Belknap reservation ended several decades ago, as well. But, unlike youths, elders emphasize that the unity and cooperation of the Gros Ventre community (that is, Hays) also ended. The elders stress that this change represented as great a culture loss as the ritual that Hays unity made possible.

In explaining how it came about that Gros Ventre religious life ended, elders agree that *their* elders determined that the rituals would not be perpetuated—would not be learned by today's elders—and that this decision was supernaturally ordained. Elders' interpretations of the history of culture loss take the form of stories about people and events in the past. All of the stories have a common theme. One such story—this version told by a seventy-two-year-old woman—is about a powerful medicine man, Stiffarm, born in 1858, who at the turn of the century became a catechist and encouraged his people to become Catholics.

> Old Stiffarm, he was telling my mother, I was ironing, and he said—I guess they were playing and he was a little boy—this story. . . . He said they were playing way over the hill. You know how kids move all over when they are playing. . . . He happened to be left out there or something. The other kids went to the camps. By the time he come back there was no camps. They just left him. And he kept calling for his mother and nobody come, and he looked at the trail where they went and so he followed where the [tipi] poles [being dragged] left the mark. And he said, "It must have been about

146

the noon hour. I just really run. . . . It must have been noon hour, oh the sun was hot, and I was thirsty, and I was just arunning. They musta pulled out early because I couldn't catch up to them," he said. "And I was getting tired and here," he said, "the sun was just hot on me, and then, you know, the reflection of heat waves," he said. "I was getting kinda dizzy and I just ran and ran." Then, he said, "There was a little bank, . . . and the sun rays just hit that little bank. It wasn't a big bank. There," he says, "I seen a baby laying there. And I just stopped; I couldn't go any more. I just seen it laying there," he said. "It looked like it was in something." I don't remember what they call those rawhide basket-like . . . He says, . . . "This baby was there and I looked away and looked back and there's nothing. And after that, oh it was like I ate and had water, fresh water, and I caught up to the people." . . . So he said, "I didn't know what that meant, why it happened like that. I used to think about it all the time. So finally I got this medicine [power to cure]. . . ." And he said after they settled here he used to still doctor. I seen him doctor a couple of times. And he said, "They start gathering us, tell us to come and the priest would come and visit us and they tell us to come. . . ." And, he says, "First time we all went to the mission," and I guess it's the first Christmas they had there, maybe they went to church, but anyway he says, "When I seen the baby Jesus, that's what remind." He says, "No wonder that's why I seen that baby." It was just identical.[8]

To Gros Ventre elders, as a child Stiffarm clearly received a message from the supernatural—had a vision—and when he was an adult he understood the message: he should work on behalf of Christianity and encourage other Gros Ventres to do so.

Another story—this version told by a sixty-seven-year-old man—is about a man (born in 1881) who went up on a high butte to fast in order to obtain a spirit helper or supernatural assistance.

Eagle Child Butte—that's where all these Indians went whenever they wanted to make a vision quest. . . . I suppose . . . he was probably mixed up. He went to school at the mission and Indians were still trying to be Indians. He didn't go up to become a powerful medicine man. He just went up to really seek advice. And that's the advice he got. He got what he went up for. . . . It [the spirit] said after the priests came then there was no use for these so-called pipes or so-called Indian religion. . . . They [spirits] said we would have a different belief. . . . A different belief. . . . So they [he and other young Gros Ventres] didn't need the guidance that them people had years ago, the old Indians. That's the way he explained it to me.

Here a young man who had sought supernatural aid was instructed by spirit beings to devote himself, and encourage other Gros Ventres to devote themselves, to Christianity.

Another story commonly told by elders is that of the last time the

pipe bundles were opened. In one account, in 1936 the official Feathered Pipe keeper, Curly Head, held ceremonies with the pipe. Thereafter many elderly people died, thus thinning the ranks of ritual leaders, and a forest fire destroyed the livelihood of many Gros Ventres
when it burned away all the timber in the Little Rockies. Many people
thought Curly Head a reckless person, and assumed he had made
mistakes. The meaning of the story of the calamity of 1936 is clear:
religious ceremonies performed by people who are not completely
qualified to conduct them will result in disaster, in supernatural retribution. The Boy, who was never formally installed as keeper, was
considered unqualified to conduct rituals with the Flat Pipe, and the
stories about what happened after he opened the Flat Pipe all stress
that disaster resulted.

In speaking of pre–World War II Hays, elders today stress that tribal
unity and cooperation were the norm. Thus such celebrations as the
Christmas–New Year dance and Hays Fair were both expressive of and
made possible by the cooperation among community members. One
man, age sixty-four, explained the way things used to be and his sense
of loss thus: "In those days Indian [Gros Ventre] culture was helping
one another. Today people just help themselves." Another man, age
sixty-seven, similarly remarked, "People were different then. They
helped each other out. If someone was sick, everyone came and got his
hay cut. They were not jealous. They wished people well who were
doing good. They visited a lot." In the minds of elders today, the end of
Hays as a close-knit, cooperating community was as great a culture
loss as the end of ritual life. Elders account for the loss as a failure on
the part of the younger generation. One eighty-year-old woman commented, "These young people were not interested, so the old ways
[the dance committee and fair] were not passed on." Another, seventy-
one years old, remarked, "Younger people are greedy and seek to
profit personally." Elders attribute the young people's lack of interest
and individualistic orientation to the fact that they have married non–
Gros Ventres, especially métis. The loss of primacy is similarly attributed to intermarriage with Assiniboines and métis.

The youth generation interprets the history of culture loss differently than the elders. In youths' view, Gros Ventre rituals were abandoned because the elders were careless and irresponsible or too weak
to stand up to the harsh discipline at St. Paul's mission and other
boarding schools. One youth commented: "The mission put such fear
into people—of sin and hell, and associated Indian religion with the
devil—that this destroyed Indian tradition." Another youth remarked,
"The Gros Ventre elders didn't pass on Gros Ventre traditions to the
younger generation—they threw it away." And the comments of a

thirty-three-year-old man express quite overtly the youths' disappointment with elders:

> The old people were the ones that lost our culture for us. The old people were indoctrinated by the mission to not retain their culture. . . . The Catholic church took the competitive nature out of Gros Ventres so Hays is not the nucleus of Gros Ventre life today. Those in Hays gave up and let the Catholic church mold them. . . . Old people sit for hours and talk about the fair. How come it was not carried on? It was their responsibility and they didn't do it. . . . Elders in Hays don't have the correct interpretation of Gros Ventre culture and history; they may be old but what right do they have?

One youth, in discussing the end of the hand game ceremonies at Hays, explains that one Gros Ventre who had a hand game bundle was married to a devout Catholic, who objected to his having the bundle. The man decided that he also would be a staunch Catholic and gave his bundle to an Assiniboine (sometime in the 1940s or 1950s). "Four days later, he died." Another youth, in discussing the end of the Hays Fair, explained that the Feathered Pipe ceremony held then was participated in by "disbelievers"—"and the mountains burned." He does not attribute the disaster to mistakes made by the old men in charge of the ritual, but rather to the presence of Gros Ventres who had converted to Catholicism. The message of both stories is clear: the abandonment of Gros Ventre rituals brought supernatural retribution.

The elder and youth generations, then, interpret the history of culture loss quite differently. In the elders' view, sacred and even secular rituals ended ultimately because of supernatural intervention: the end of sacred ritual was ordained, and the end of secular ritual resulted from supernatural punishment for improper performance of rituals. In the youths' view, the end of ritual life was due to human failings and resulted in supernatural retribution. Elders and youths interpret the history of the 1970s and 1980s cultural revival differently, as well.

Interpretations of Cultural Revival

The 1970s saw repeated efforts, some more successful than others, to reintroduce ritual activity at Fort Belknap. Religious rituals, dance committee and powwow activity, and giveaway ceremonies to name and to honor individuals—all became frequent and elaborate. The elder and youth generations view the introduction and history of these ceremonies in quite different ways.

Religious Rituals

In the late 1970s and early 1980s attempts were made to revive ceremonies with the Flat Pipe. Moreover, several individuals went to the tops of buttes to fast in quest of a supernatural experience. Sweat lodges were erected and ceremonies were held inside. Elders' attitudes toward religious rituals were shaped by their experiences with *their* elders (medicine men and keepers), who did not instruct successors. Without such instruction, say the elders, religious rituals are dangerous to perform; in fact, supernatural punishment results. Youths, on the other hand, view Indian religion as central to Indian identity, and therefore Gros Ventre identity. They believe supernatural punishment results from failure to fulfill ritual responsibilities. To elders, the two pipe bundles are particularly sacred. They represent a past the elders are proud of, even in awe of, but at the same time the bundles' history suggests the danger inherent in performing sacred rituals without the proper training and qualifications. To youths, involvement with the pipe bundles is important as it symbolizes commitment to the revival of tradition, on the one hand, and rejection of white culture and repression, on the other hand.

The Boy, who had custody of the Flat Pipe in the late 1940s and 1950s, died in January 1957 and for nearly a year the pipe was left unattended in his cabin. By the time of Verne Dusenberry's visit in March 1958, Rufus Warrior—one of the knowledgeable elders, according to Dusenberry—had moved it, at The Boy's dying request, to his home to protect it. According to Dusenberry, the old men he spoke to felt that the powers of the Feathered Pipe were gone and that both pipes were no longer relevant to the concerns of Gros Ventre life. After Warrior died in 1967, his widow, Jeanette, assumed the responsibility for providing a safe place for the Flat Pipe. Iron Man's widow had watched over the Feathered Pipe for twenty years after her husband's death, and when she died, in 1979, it apparently remained alone in their house, and their son Joe "watched over" it.[9]

By the time I arrived at Fort Belknap in 1979, there was considerable talk among youths that the Flat Pipe should be or might be moved from Mrs. Warrior's house to the custody of a Gros Ventre man. Several willing candidates were mentioned. Two elders were sent to consult the Arapahoes in Wyoming (who have a Flat Pipe tradition and whose pipe bundle ceremonies were thriving). Their expenses were paid from the claim fund. In 1981 some youths organized another effort to involve Arapahoes. They obtained tribal funds—through majority vote of persons attending a tribal ("Treaty Committee") meeting on July 29—to pay the expenses of an Arapahoe delegation to come to Hays in

August and "clean and rewrap" the pipe. Before the youths' effort in 1981, both elders and youths expressed the feeling that something had to be done about the Flat Pipe, or even both pipes, because their neglect was the likely cause of misfortune in Hays. Yet the 1981 actions of the youths precipitated a major crisis, for elders and youths disagreed over what should be done about the pipes.

The elders' ideas apparently were greatly influenced by the old people who had spoken to Dusenberry in 1958. They seemed to have internalized the notion (although they did not explicitly verbalize it) that the pipe rituals are complex formulas that are both symbolic of creation and at the same time capable of affecting nature and humankind. These rituals can bring about order and good fortune; but if the formula is not carefully and exactly followed, disorder and disaster result. Elders had learned that ritual authority in pipe matters was won only by long and intense study and strong character. A person sacrificed time, a carefree life, and material goods to earn this ritual knowledge. Character was important, because anger and ill will adversely affected rituals' results.

Elders' feelings about the pipes—particularly the Flat Pipe, perhaps because it was viewed as the more powerful of the two bundles—are expressed in stories about past events that stress two themes. First, Gros Ventres (now deceased) who had the authority to perform pipe rituals proclaimed that the pipes were useless to subsequent generations. Second, persons who lack ritual authority yet involve themselves with the pipes bring about disastrous consequences. One frequently heard story concerns Horse Capture's decision to put the Flat Pipe away ("hang it up" on the wall and conduct no rituals).

One sixty-seven-year-old man, telling the story about Horse Capture, who was official keeper of the Flat Pipe until he died in 1924, explained, "Those elders [in the 1920s], they wanted them [the sacred pipe bundles] buried, because nobody. . . , see, they quit using them. . . . That old man Horse Capture and them, they said, 'They're done.' They just hung them up. Nobody used them."

Two stories about the Flat Pipe tell of the frightening or disastrous repercussions of the ritual participation of unqualified Gros Ventres: "When the woman danced with the Feathered Pipe" and "When the Flat Pipe bundle was opened." The following is a seventy-eight-year-old man's version of the first story, which tells of an event that reportedly took place in the first decade of the twentieth century:

> Lame Bull was supervising. That was the Feathered Pipe. He worked [supervised rituals of] both of them [the pipes]. . . . In 1912 they opened his pipe across from where I lived there on Peoples Creek, Hays. . . . I was

151

just little. . . . They put two tipis together; they called it a double tipi. In here they held the opening of the pipe. . . . After they opened the pipe [bundle] they took the pipe out and then they filled it with tobacco and they passed it around. . . . After they got done smoking then they danced with the pipe. This was a unique way of dancing—they held the pipe in front of them holding the bowl of the pipe with their left hand and on the right side the stem of the pipe, and they swayed with their body not moving the pipe. They never moved the pipe. . . . This woman, when they passed the pipe on to her—they had a way of handing that pipe—when they passed that pipe back they passed it, and whoever was holding it held this pipe at arm's length, and this other one just danced right into that pipe, and the other one moved back. This lady she started shaking that pipe around. She danced with it, jerked it back and forth with her arms. Boy! Lame Bull was one of them guys; I sure admired him. . . . He went over and had to take that pipe. Danced in there and took that pipe. And they stopped momentarily and then they started praying. Well, just about that time them tipis just about fell over. It was from shaking. Looked like the ground was moving! He started to pray then. He said, "Pity us. . . . We're trying to regroup these people here so they'll learn these pipe rituals and regulations. . . . Forgive these [younger] people; they never handled this pipe before."

Another story, which tells of an event that took place several years after the woman was said to have danced with the Feathered Pipe incorrectly and caused a tremor, concerns the opening of the Flat Pipe. According to this frequently related account, during the ceremony the fire in the pipe went out. The ritual was being conducted by a man who was not an official keeper (and thus not properly qualified). The fact that the pipe went out indicated that a mistake had been made. "He should have quit when it went out," one elder remarked to me. The man continued, however, and the next morning his son died—supernatural retribution, according to elders.

It is in the context of the elders' interpretation of the Flat Pipe's history that their feeling about the current attempt to revive its ceremonies can be understood. Elders oppose the youths' efforts to lead a revival of the ceremonies because they feel that the unqualified youths will make mistakes that will result in tragedy for all the people. And they feel that the youths do not comprehend the true meaning of pipe ritual and cannot or will not accept the necessary obligations. An eighty-eight-year-old woman remarked, "These young ones—modern Indians—don't respect it. . . . The younger ones, it is scary what they might do." In telling the story of how the Flat Pipe was once captured by the Gros Ventres' Assiniboine enemies (see Chapter 3), she concluded: "That tribe just kept getting sick and dying. It [the Flat Pipe] told the man who had it, 'Take me back and everything will be all right.' That will happen again if the [youths] take it." A sixty-seven-year-old man commented, "These young guys say, 'Give it to us; we will take care of it.' But the old people will never do it—they won't let them play with it. . . . We got a younger generation that want to be medicine men and Indians, and they want to get their hands on one of these pipes. So they say no—they'll be playing with them." In the same vein, a seventy-two-year-old woman remarked, "These young guys don't know anything about it. They shouldn't be allowed to fool with them." And a sixty-six-year-old woman insisted that the youths who initiated the effort to revive the pipe ritual "wanted that pipe to have ceremonies with it and put on a show." In her estimation, the youths' interest in the pipe was superficial, meant to demonstrate to themselves and others that they were "real Indians," not a wish to pray to the Supreme Being.

In August 1981 the delegation of Arapahoes invited by the young people arrived from Wyoming. The elders were upset, fearing that the youths would undertake a pipe ceremony under the direction of the Arapahoes. The youths did intend to get instruction from the Arapahoes so that they could subsequently perform ceremonies. On August 18, before such a ceremony could get under way, a group of female elders confronted the youths and the Arapahoes (who had been under the impression that elderly Gros Ventres wanted their help) and voiced their objections to the youths' plans. The Arapahoes returned to Wyoming, unwilling to proceed in view of the elders' feelings and the obvious conflict among the Gros Ventres over the pipe's status. The elders were pleased and relieved—pleased that they had defeated the youths, whom they considered disrespectful of their elders, and relieved to have averted a potential disaster. Elders were particularly gratified that some among them had influenced the Arapahoes by speaking to them in Gros Ventre (a dialect of Arapaho), thus demonstrating their command of Gros Ventre cultural tradition, in contrast to the youths, none of whom spoke Gros Ventre.

The youth generation takes a different view of the history of the pipes and the efforts to revive Flat Pipe ritual. A youth of forty-four years, telling of Horse Capture's "hanging up" of the Flat Pipe, said, "When that old man put it away, up on the wall, he said someday it will be taken down again." He (and other youths who tell similar accounts) is suggesting that the ritual authorities of the early twentieth century prophesied that the traditional Gros Ventre religion eventually would be revived. The prophecy is supernatural sanction for the cultural revival.

Many youths view the abortive effort to involve the Arapahoes in a Flat Pipe ceremony as an example of how elders unjustly impede their efforts. Others feel that the cause was a good one, but that the elders should have been approached more tactfully. One youth, typical of the individuals openly critical of elders, complained, "People want to get our Indian culture back but the powwow isn't enough. If you are for the powwow, eagle feathers, you should be for the pipe and Indian religion also. People who don't believe in it should stay out of it." Another, equally vocal youth, remarked, "Anyone here can change their religion; I did." In these youths' view, a person who does not participate in the revival of Indian religion is not really Indian and should not interfere in the efforts of youths to revive religious ceremonies. Moreover, to this youth and others, abandonment of Catholicism represents rejection of white cultural and social domination. The following comment by a youth is also revealing: "They don't use common sense—those bundles were given to us for a reason by the Creator to use. I don't fear them; I respect them." The concept that "using" traditional ritual objects is the major component of practicing Indian religion is widely shared among youths. This notion is at odds with the elders' understanding of the nature of the supernatural power associated with pipe ritual—motions, words, and, to some degree, thoughts were carefully learned and were as much a part of the ritual as the objects in the bundle. In fact, without them, use of the bundle objects is dangerous.

Even though the elders prevented Arapahoe involvement (and the instruction of youths), youths still view themselves as the leaders in Indian religion. One thirty-three-year-old man commented that, after all, the attempt to revive pipe ritual was led by youths and "if they hadn't done it, *nothing* would have been done." Thus he gave the credit to youths for a ceremony held late in 1981 and arranged and attended by elders. At that time an elder put a new cloth over the bundle and prayed for the well-being of the people.[10]

Elders take a dim view of several youths' efforts to fast for supernatural aid or for a spirit helper. They are playing at being medicine men, elders say, or showing off. A local newspaper's publication of a photo of a youth performing an Indian ceremony added fuel to these feelings. By allowing the photograph to be taken, elders say, he was trying to gain recognition from whites, to demonstrate Indianness to others. One woman, seventy-two years old, remarked that one had to be "called" to be a medicine man; "they don't just go around and want to be medicine men." The youths who fast on a high butte are "phonies" in the elders' eyes because they have borrowed extensively from other tribes, and have sought out medicine men of other tribes as mentors and instructors. Youths recently have participated in Sun Dances held by Arapahoes in Wyoming, by Crees at Rocky Boy, and by

Assiniboines at Fort Peck, and some participate in peyote (Native American Church) ceremonies on other reservations. One elder, eighty-eight years old, remarked, "Young people get things from here and there, add things, leave things out—that wasn't the way of old-timers; things had to be earned." One elder, a man sixty-three years old, expressed concern that if youths were able to learn sacred Gros Ventre rituals or parts of them (songs, for example), they might teach them to other tribes who would sacrilegiously "use them as social songs."[11]

Elders recall that the old people they knew advised against seeking medicine power (see Chapter 1). And some elders also worry that youths, who in their view lack the wisdom, character, and training to handle medicine power properly, might use any power received in order to do harm. One seventy-two-year-old elder worried, "It is rumored they are worshiping Satan"; others describe "bad" medicine and suspect some youths of seeking this power. The involvement of some militant youths in acts of violence on the reservation has done nothing to reassure the elders about their character.

Sweat lodges have been held at frequent intervals on the reservation in recent years. In this ceremony, water is poured over hot rocks inside a round enclosure; the resulting steam facilitates the ascension of prayers to the Supreme Being. One elder, a man sixty-three years old, observed, "They sweat every week. That was never an occurrence with Gros Ventres. They would sweat twice a year. Now it's any time somebody gets the urge. . . . The old men I remember did it for a reason." Another elder, a sixty-seven-year-old man, remarked, "These sweat things kind of got out of hand these days. [They used to have them on special, serious occasions], not every weekend." To these men, youths are trivializing the ceremony. One eighty-eight-year-old elder perceived the sweats as showing off because she saw an American flag being flown upside down during a sweat ceremony held by militant youths. The inverted flag also suggested to her that the ceremony was an effort by the American Indian Movement (AIM) to intimidate opponents. And as AIM symbols suggest violence to many people, their association with rituals reinforces the notion that youths may be seeking "bad" power.

Youths see the efforts to participate in Indian religion in a positive light. Many explain that the ceremonies *are* Gros Ventre tradition because, although instruction was received from other tribes, the things taught "originally" came from Gros Ventres. One thirty-three-year-old man explained that a youth who was now a medicine man did "learn it from a Chippewa-Cree, but this was once learned by him from a Gros Ventre and now returned to the Gros Ventres." He himself had

learned the sweat lodge ceremony from a Cree who learned it originally from a Gros Ventre. For youths, fasting on a butte is perceived as
central to Indian identity. Most youths express admiration for those
who have completed the rite: "[He] is the most holy man here now
because he fasted four days on Eagle Child Butte." Other youths feel
an urgent need to undertake the experience themselves, even if they
do not seek supernatural powers: "I plan to go and fast—not for
power—for peace or solitude. It is just something I want to do." This
man added that he had intended to fast in the summer of 1983 but
that he could not get time off from work.

The militants have a somewhat different orientation toward Indian
religion than the education clique. Militant youths *stress* the importance of becoming medicine men or practitioners of Indian religion.
They view youths who participate in secular Gros Ventre rituals but
who remain Catholic as not real Indians. Real Indians, in their view,
are spiritual people—a minority among youths—who try to follow the
old ways. One militant described the education clique thus: "Some
young people are trying too hard to live in the non-Indian society and
at the same time claim to be Indian. . . . They are modifying old ways
to fit today's fast pace." He describes those who do not fit his category
of "spiritual people" as "non-Indian-type Indians." Members of the
education clique are more likely to attend native religious functions
led by others than to pursue medicine power. Such youths may participate in rituals, such as fasting, without stressing the religious aspects of such activities, as was the case with the man who wanted to
fast for "peace or solitude." The youths of the education clique feel
they can be both Indian and Catholic. In fact, many express ambivalence about medicine power. One youth reportedly fasted for
medicine power and received a message that there was only bad medicine left to get—all of it non–Gros Ventre medicine. Some youths of
the education clique wonder, as one thirty-three-year-old man did, if
an elder was right when she reputedly said, "You don't speak Gros
Ventre so how can Gros Ventre power come to you? Whoever heard of
spirits speaking English?" Education clique youths also sometimes
suspect militant youths of using bad medicine to hurt those with
whom they are in competition.

The Dance Committee and the Powwow

Dances have been organized by various groups since the establishment of the reservation. Dance committees declined in importance in
mid-century; now they are important again. The Lodgepole community of Assiniboines had (and still has) a committee. The Hays Gros

Ventres had a committee but from the early 1960s until 1984 it was inactive. The Assiniboines who lived along the Milk River had their own committee, which they reorganized in the 1970s.

The revival of the Gros Ventre dance committee and the emergence of the powwow was spearheaded by youths (not elders) in the agency area. Views on the history of dance committee activity and the meaning of powwow symbolism vary. To Gros Ventre youths, the powwow and dance committee of today represent traditions perpetuated; to elders they are innovations. Elders associate Hays dance committee activity with Hays unity and cooperation—each person giving according to his means. Dances were largely intimate local affairs that expressed and reaffirmed Gros Ventre social organization. Elders also feel that the use of sacred symbols in the powwow is inappropriate. Youths view the powwow in the context of contemporary intertribal relations. To them a successful dance is one that attracts large numbers of people from other tribes. The several thousand dollars that such a celebration requires are often raised outside the Fort Belknap community as well as within it. Youths of the education clique focus their efforts on the Milk River powwow, the militants on the Chief Joseph celebration. To education clique youths, powwow symbols express their ideas about Gros Ventre prominence, primacy, and cultural tradition in general. Sacred symbols, too, are increasingly being incorporated into the powwow. Symbolism in the Chief Joseph powwow expresses the militants' ideas about native religion and their opposition to U.S. Indian policy. In order to place contemporary efforts at dance committee revival in context, I will briefly review the history of the Hays and the Milk River committees and the dance or celebration activity.

Hays Dance Committee, ca. 1902–1956   One autumn in the first decade of the twentieth century, the Gros Ventres in Hays got their logs in for the winter early and began to talk about having some kind of entertainment during Christmas week. They all decided to contribute logs to build a hall and to have a dance, with a Christmas tree and gifts for children. Those who took on the responsibility for organizing the people and collecting donations were young men—born between 1865 and 1886—and their wives. They relied on older men to participate as well; the older men were warriors and grass dancers, and could bring to the occasion ceremonies that the people particularly enjoyed. The log hall was round, with four large logs in the center to support the roof beams. Initially they built a fire in the center area; in later years they successively used candles, lamps, stoves, and heaters. The original floor was hard-packed dirt; later they built a plank floor.

The one door faced east. The Hays community was divided in half for the purposes of organizing people to contribute to the social events held in the hall. Those who lived north of the hall were called the Black Lodges, those to the south Mountain Crows. Inside the hall the Black Lodges sat on the north side and the Mountain Crows on the south. These two divisions had a friendly competition to see which could accumulate the most donations, recruit the most dancers, provide the best upkeep for their side of the hall, and so on. In short, they competed for a common goal—to provide a good celebration for the benefit of all the people.

Each New Year's Eve a new committee was picked by the old-timers, usually members of well-to-do families (sometimes children) but occasionally members of less well-to-do families who were prominent participants in the dances. The old people selected a men's chief and a women's chief. The men's chief then selected male helpers who helped him solicit and collect donations, gather firewood, and generally do men's work during the celebration. The women's chief selected female helpers who prepared the food for the dances. Behind the scenes, whether on the committee or not, were old people (born before 1865) who were viewed as the mainstay of the celebrations. The dancers and singers were from the age group born approximately between 1865 and 1894. Throughout the first two decades of the century these younger men were informally trained to become singers and dancers and were encouraged to participate and aid the dance or Christmas committee.[12]

The committee prepared a meal and invited Gros Ventres who had lost relatives during the year to a "mourners' feed" the night before the Christmas-week dances began. Old people might also provide a new outfit of clothes and recomb the hair of the surviving relatives to symbolize the end of the mourning period and their reentry into society. The committee also held house or tea dances at people's homes in the spring and fall to collect the money, food, and other items needed for the dance to be held during Christmas week. Before these dances the Black Lodges and Mountain Crows would pass out "bumming sticks" among their people. These were carved wooden sticks, sometimes painted, sometimes not, which obligated the recipients to bring something or donate in some way to the dance. Tea and refreshments were served at the house dances, and people danced to the accompaniment of a few hand drums and pledged donations to the Christmas-week celebration. More donations were obtained by the singing of families' "honor songs"—a person or family whose song was sung felt an obligation to donate. It was also the custom to confiscate people's property, with the understanding that they could redeem it by a donation. By such social pressures the committee and their elderly backers collected beeves, baked goods, coffee, and all they needed to feed those who attended the Christmas dances, including a few visitors from other reservations. Giveaways were organized by one moiety during the first three days of the week-long celebration, by the other moiety the next three days, and on the last day the two combined forces. They took turns sponsoring the tree and gifts for children in alternate years. The organizers saw to it that there was an announcer to preside and a man assigned to keep children quiet and young men in their assigned place by the door, where they could be eased out if they became rowdy.[13]

The old warrior cohort (born before 1865) was highly visible in the special ceremonies held during the Christmas dances. The most dramatic ceremony was the Grass Dance. One elder explained to me, "They felt this was special to a certain age group." Elders supervised the dance with its various regalia, helping and sanctioning younger people's efforts to dance with crow belts, whips, and so on. Two younger dancers, for example, were given permission to wear the belts

10. Grass Dance: two dancers performing the kettle dance (dog ritual), Fort Belknap Reservation, July 1906. After the puppy meat was speared, elderly warriors acted out their war exploits. The two dancers appear to be wearing crow belts and holding "forks" of somewhat different design than those in use earlier. Note the camps in the background. Courtesy of National Anthropological Archives, Smithsonian Institution, Washington, D.C. Photo by Sumner W. Matteson.

(bustles) of old dancers as they performed the long, elaborate dance—each stage of which had its own song—and speared pup from a kettle. When four of the old warriors had been given pup from the pot, they told their war stories. These old warriors were prominent participants throughout the celebration. One elder recalls, "They'd go through their acts and deeds and whatever they done when they were warriors. Then they'd have little sham battles in there—like if the Bloods come down then they'd tell a war story and then the Gros Ventres would tell a story." Such old warriors as Fork, who had a whip from the Grass Dance ritual of former times, taught younger men to dance with the whip in the early twentieth century. The whip came to be passed from one man to another, though not necessarily annually. The whip man could impel others to dance and generally enforce decisions of the dance organizers. As we saw in Chapter 1, the use of Grass Dance regalia necessitated generous distribution of property.

The Christmas celebration reaffirmed and reinforced Hays social order. Distinct male and female roles and age-group statuses were reflected in the dance activities. During the Grass Dance songs, only men danced—old men in full war bonnets and middle-aged men in roach headdresses. Women and children did not dance. Grass Dance songs were interspersed with owl, ringtail, and night dances, in which both men and women participated. The Boy (born in 1872) donated a drum to the committee, and it was taken care of by one of the singers for an indefinite time. By introducing and participating in the modification of Grass Dance features, the old warriors authorized and validated the innovations that the 1865–1894 cohort introduced and succeeded in making "traditions" in the early twentieth century.[14]

The Christmas-week dance, in fact the year-round activities of the dance committee, expressed Gros Ventre tribal identity, for almost all the participants were Gros Ventres and they viewed the events in large part as the perpetuation of old customs. The committee activity reaffirmed and encouraged unity and cooperation, while at the same time providing an outlet for the old pattern of competition through generous distribution, both by the moiety divisions and by the families who gave away property in honor of relatives during the dances. The New Year's Eve ceremony that marked the close of the week's dancing symbolized the themes of unity and identity. One elder explained that at midnight people lined up, some in a circle going one way, the rest in a circle going the other. When the announcer said, "Happy New Year!" "the drum blows were like an explosion." As they sang the New Year's song, individuals danced and shook hands with everyone in the opposing row. At times they leaned over and kissed a relative or friend. At the end of the two lines they doubled back. "It was a very impressive formation. They sang the song as long as the line was going. There were a lot of misty people. The feeling was that they lived to see another year." Afterward the committee served a meal to the crowd before everyone went home.

The old round hall eventually fell into ruin after a new, large square hall was built in Hays township in the mid-1930s by WPA workers, with the assistance of other Gros Ventre volunteers, and the dances began to be held there. After the mid-1930s the celebrations became smaller, less elaborate, and less well attended. By the 1940s the Black Lodge and Mountain Crow organization had ceased to function. Then in 1956 the square hall burned. In the late 1950s Hays, Lodgepole, and the river communities began to join forces in sponsoring dances, and the dances ceased to be regarded as exclusively Gros Ventre–sponsored celebrations.

Milk River Dance Committee, ca. 1902–1954   The Milk River dance committee had many of its origins in the Grass Dance, according to elderly Assiniboines today, for originally dances focused on Grass Dance ceremonies. Before the Assiniboines settled at Fort Belknap, the Grass or Crow Belt Dance was part of the ritual owned by the Crow (Raven) Society of the Sioux. The Raven Society had its origins in a dream or vision of a Sioux man, who organized the society and explained its ritual. It was a sacred society, for the man had the power to make raven-feather bustles out of bustles made of grass. The society members helped the needy, cured the sick, and kept order. When the Assiniboines lived near Cypress Hills, they made peace with these Sioux and bought from them the rights to and knowledge of the society and its rituals, including the elaborate dance. When the Assiniboines came to the Fort Belknap area in the 1870s, they had an active Raven Society. But gradually the members of the society died and their regalia, including crow belts or bustles, were buried with them. About 1900 or shortly thereafter the elders talked of reorganizing the society. An elderly Assiniboine explained to me how this was done: "They all agree and they make four of these belts. They eliminate some of the strict rules so that it was no longer sacred, but for entertainment. At this time they selected four men and gave them the right to wear crow belts and perform the dances of the society."

Shortly thereafter, the crow belt dancers and others appointed to perform or help organize the now secularized Grass Dances began to be referred to as a committee. During the dancing, belt wearers dramatized war exploits and served puppy meat to distinguished warriors and the dancers. The dance committee or Grass Dance Society in the early twentieth century had as many as seventeen positions—four feathered belt wearers, a fork man, two whip men, four chief singers, one or two announcers, and four women with war bonnets (the female war-bonnet wearers were added upon instructions received in a vision by an Assiniboine man).[15]

Later, in the 1920s or early 1930s, the committee became less directly associated with the Raven or Grass Dance Society. Some men, who had the right to use the belts or bustles, continued to wear crow belts during the complex ceremony, but the symbol of the American flag came to have as much or more importance at the dances. A man was appointed to "keep" or take charge of the flag, and he also supervised the committee's activities. By the 1940s, flagman had become the main office on the committee. Later, a woman—who was placed in charge of food preparation—was chosen as women's flag keeper (or flagwoman), "to make her on the same level" as the flagman. One Assiniboine elder noted that giving a flag to a woman committee member meant that "women got a chance to honor the flag." The introduction and later elaboration of the flag symbolism was probably an outgrowth of Assiniboine participation in World Wars I and II. The committee offices of announcer and whip man continued and the drumkeeper position was filled at times. The drumstick keeper (lead singer) replaced the four chief singers. And a secretary-treasurer (sometimes two positions rather than one) was added. In general, the number of offices decreased somewhat but the participation of the people may have increased. Dances were held during Christmas week and also for one day after the three-day Sun Dance ceremony in the summer. The food served at the dances was donated by the people— often after they had received a bumming stick—and collected by the whip men. The dance committee was supervised and encouraged by elderly Assiniboines. Young Assiniboines today point out that "they were so respected that everyone helped." Another added, "It was an honor." In those days the committee raised $200 or $300 and got promises of beef donations during house dances throughout the year. With the money they paid for food and heat and light.[16]

In 1952 the last Assiniboine Sun Dance, supervised by a few ritual authorities, was held at Milk River. After that year it was very difficult for the dance committee to attract crowds for the summer celebration, for the Sun Dance had been the main attraction. The Christmas-week celebration gradually became poorly attended, as well. By the 1960s, "just the powwow families [singers and enthusiastic dancers] went," according to one Assiniboine dancer. Interested families struggled to organize a summer dance, but few attended. These were "the years when everybody was low," as one Assiniboine put it. Then, in the 1970s, the cultural revival began, and by 1977 the summer dance had begun to draw large crowds, becoming more an intertribal than a local event. The number of committee positions increased to seventeen. And Gros Ventres began to serve on the committee regularly.[17]

For elderly Gros Ventres and Assiniboines the Hays and Milk River committees of the first half of the century are models of what a dance committee should be. These committees were successful because the community gave unanimous support to their activities with donations and enthusiastic participation. Gros Ventre youths were not active participants in these traditions. But they have heard stories about some aspects of the celebrations. This knowledge, however incomplete, is an important component of the present-day powwow.

The Milk River and Chief Joseph Powwows, 1974–1984   The revival of the Milk River dance committee began when the intertribal Indian Days dance became important at Fort Belknap. The Indian Days celebration or powwow is similar in content and organization to the other powwows held on weekends during the summer on reservations on the Northern Plains. People from the local community, as well as from great distances, camp on the powwow grounds, where giveaways are held in the daytime. Evenings begin with a "grand entry" parade of the

11. Raising the flag at the Milk River Powwow, July 1985. The flag bearer for the 1985 powwow, a veteran, begins the day's events by raising the flag. The flag is attended by another veteran, and the Assiniboine Flag Song is sung by the Gray Boys drum group. The powwow announcer, holding the microphone, is from another reservation; the others are Assiniboines. Photo courtesy of Harvey King.

163

12. At the concession stand, Chief Joseph Powwow, October 1985. The concession stand, where Indian fried bread, Indian tacos, sandwiches, soda, and coffee are sold, is one of the attractions of the powwow, particularly for children. The girl is wearing a "cloth dress" outfit—one of several contemporary styles of dress worn by female dancers. Photo courtesy of Harvey King.

local leaders and all the dancers who have entered dance contests. Veterans hoist the committee's American flag while singers perform the flag song. Then dancing, primarily to Grass Dance songs, which are used today in contest dancing, consumes the rest of the evening. There are contests for girls and boys and for "traditional" (slow) and "fancy" (fast) dancing for both men and women. A prize of as much as $2,000 is awarded for first place in men's fancy dancing. Fort Belknap dancers usually make up a minority of the contestants at the powwow, for renowned dancers of many tribes follow the powwow circuit, competing for prize money.[18]

The Fort Belknap powwow committee members, with the help of

their families, work together to raise money from the time they are selected by the retiring committee to the time the powwow concludes a year later. They hold bake sales and raffles almost weekly and collect donations in other ways to accumulate funds to be used for contest prizes, "rations" or groceries for campers, electricity, publicity, and payment to the drum groups and announcers. They solicit beef from non-Indian as well as Fort Belknap ranchers. Throughout the year they hold mourners' feeds for people whose relatives have died. The mourners' feed is a ceremony that reintegrates the bereaved into society and encourages them to participate in the upcoming powwow and other social events. Recently the committee members have staffed tribally operated bingo games and in return received a share of the profits for the powwow. In 1983 the Milk River committee raised close to $20,000. It is also the committee's responsibility to plan the program and attract the participants. The larger the crowd, the better.

Despite extensive cooperation among Gros Ventre elders, education clique youths, and militant youths in preparing for and putting on powwows, their views differ on the history and symbolism of the powwow at Fort Belknap today. There are three powwows: Milk River, Chief Joseph, and Education (for students, sponsored by the tribes' education office).[19] The Chief Joseph powwow is mainly the interest of the militant youths. The largest powwow is the Milk River celebration, and the Milk River committee is the one on which the education clique youths have primarily served since the mid-1970s, when a group of Assiniboines worked to involve more people in the celebration.

Many in the education clique see their recent participation in the Milk River committee activity as a revival of Gros Ventre primacy, one more Gros Ventre success in competing against other tribes by drawing crowds and raising prize money. Although Assiniboines view the powwow differently, to the Gros Ventre youths the Milk River powwow revival has been due largely to Gros Ventre participation. One youth commented, "In the 1960s the Assiniboines said the Milk River committee was theirs. Yeah, but who revived the cultural ways here? It was Gros Ventres. Nobody from other places was coming; we got them." Other Gros Ventres have pointed with pride to the respect that the powwow—particularly its management—has received from whites. Another youth stressed, "The most successful chiefs [flag men], best jobs, have been Gros Ventres. . . . All of the Milk River committee's new ideas, successes have come from Gros Ventres." The new ideas and successes he refers to include the following innovations, which were instituted in the late 1970s: a metal arbor, an eagle staff used prominently in the arbor, electric lights, bleachers, the distribution of bumming sticks, and the promotion of large monetary prizes for dance contests. One Gros Ventre committee member remarked, "I saw ways the powwow could be made more convenient for people; it was pitiful before. Now the has-beens are out and there has been a leadership change and more sophisticated younger people made the powwow take off." Gros Ventre youths point out that the eagle staff was made by a Gros Ventre for a Gros Ventre leader, who lends the staff to the committee. Before the metal arbor was built, each year the committee and other volunteers would bring poles and brush from the mountains and build a round arbor. The rectangular metal arbor was built in 1979 with funds from the Gros Ventre and the Assiniboine treaty committees. One youth remarked, "The arbor cost $65,000. Gros Ventres went out and got it, got it done, got it built." In 1980 a Gros Ventre suggested that an Assiniboine elder make a set of bumming sticks and that the committee hand them out to people before the celebration in

13. Grand entry, Milk River Powwow, July 1985: eagle staff and flags. As the spectators stand, a veteran carries the eagle staff at the head of the procession. It is fur-wrapped and decorated with eagle feathers. (The staff is similar in design to nineteenth-century men's warrior society regalia; it also compares with Running Fisher's staff in fig. 7). Two veterans follow with the American flag and the Fort Belknap flag. The Fort Belknap flag bears a seal in the shape of a nineteenth-century war shield, designed by an Assiniboine youth, George Shields, Jr., in 1969 and adopted by the business council as the official Fort Belknap seal in 1971. Members of the 1985 committee and their relatives are next in the procession. The grand entry opens the evening dance program. Photo courtesy of Harvey King.

14. George Shields with a bumming stick, 1985. Mr. Shields, an Assiniboine, has been involved in Assiniboine ceremonies all his life. Born in 1900, he served on numerous Assiniboine dance committees, and was a singer and dancer. In 1980, youths on the Milk River powwow committee asked him to make a set of bumming sticks that they could distribute throughout the community, a custom dispensed with several years earlier. This set of sticks—very similar to those in use in earlier times—served as an impetus for the distribution of bumming sticks in subsequent years. The stick he holds is about ten inches long, made of willow, with a ribbon and attached plume; the paper label bears a message asking the recipient of the stick to donate a particular item to the committee to help them fulfill their duties. Photo courtesy of Harvey King.

order to collect donations. Several education clique youths pointed to this as another example of Gros Ventre accomplishment. In 1982 the committee, whose flag man was Gros Ventre, introduced bingo on a grand scale—"big-bucks bingo," where several hundred dollars could be won. Even non-Indians came from surrounding towns to play, and more money was raised in a short time than earlier committees made by many bake sales and raffles. Youths cite the introduction of big-bucks bingo as another Gros Ventre accomplishment.

The youths of the education clique also stress that the Milk River powwow has provided an outlet for Gros Ventre attempts to achieve prominence and to make public displays of generosity. A few who have heard elders speak about Hays dances see the powwow activity as a continuation of the giveaway tradition associated with Hays before World War II. One man commented, "Gros Ventres knew how to put on a gathering—the fair, tea dances. People talked about how well we organized things. We have a lot to live up to as Gros Ventres." The effort to make the Milk River celebration as large as those on other reservations must be understood in this context. One youth remarked, "We knew we could have a powwow as big as others." These youths are ambitious: "Us Gros Ventres have to be something or somebody" or "show what we can do." The donation of the eagle staff is cited as an example of an individual's prominence. One youth, who had not yet served on the committee though he had been asked if he would be willing to serve, remarked, "I will have to be on it [to have high status in the community]," and he added that he would have to do something to improve the celebration, as well. When I inquired how the Milk River celebration differs from other powwows on the Northern Plains, youths commonly pointed out that the selection of the committee is done publicly during the evening activities in an elaborate ceremony. The incumbent committee members confer beforehand, then consult the prospective appointees to obtain their consent. Then at the dance, the committee members dance in the arbor while one man carrying the eagle staff picks people out of the crowd to serve on next year's committee. Then the old and new committee members have giveaways. People from Fort Belknap have observed that the Gros Ventre committee members take more time with giveaways and honor songs during this process than do the Assiniboines. In this way Gros Ventres call attention to the prominence of persons with committee positions.

Giveaways are particularly emphasized by the education clique youths as an expression of Gros Ventre culture. One youth remarked, "We are very pompous in ceremonies. Visitors appreciate this." He was referring to the custom of taking a considerable amount of time to hold a giveaway; Assiniboine giveaways, he implied, take less time. The quantity of goods given away, the practice of calling recipients one at a time and waiting until each collects his gift, the amount of talk surrounding each article or recipient—all affect the length of time a giveaway takes.

The eagle staff donated by a Gros Ventre man is characterized as more elaborate or ostentatious than those used on other reservations. As one youth explained, "Ours is really elaborate in construction compared to others because of his generosity in the number of feathers, each beaded, the staff wrapped in buffalo hide, medicine wheels of

15. Honor Dance for new (1986) committee members, Milk River Powwow, July 1985. On the last day of the powwow, the 1985 committee chose some of the 1986 committee members from the crowd; others were selected later. The 1986 men's flag bearer, women's flag bearer, drum keeper, secretary-treasurer, and whip man are dancing around the arena under the metal arbor, carrying gifts that were part of the series of giveaways held during the installation process. Note the child in the left foreground: children run uninhibited in and out of the arena and over the campground during the powwow. Behind the spectators are the camps. Photo courtesy of Harvey King.

quills, hair tassels. Other reservations' are simpler." The staff, then, symbolizes the importance of the ideal of prominence in Gros Ventre culture.

The education clique views the Milk River powwow as a perpetuation of Gros Ventre tradition, and also of Fort Belknap ritual tradition. In their discussion of powwow ritual, youths commonly mention the following features as ritual tradition at Fort Belknap: mourners' feeds, grand entry, hierarchy of committee positions, alternation of committee leadership between tribes, regalia associated with offices, the use of the eagle staff. One youth commented, "The flag man is familiar with traditions; everyone has had someone in their family on the committee so no one is ignorant about it." Others comment that they did not know all the traditions at first but that they learned from elders, specifically Assiniboine elders. Youths describe the mourners' feed as part of the Fort Belknap and Gros Ventre tradition. Several such feeds are held throughout the year before local dances in the fall, winter, or spring. In speaking of the tradition of the grand entry, youths point to the order in which individuals enter the arena. The person carrying the eagle staff enters, followed by persons walking side by side carrying the flags (United States, Canadian, and Fort Belknap), then the "royalty" (princesses and attendants) enter, followed by the men's traditional (slow) dancers (most of whom are contestants), then the remainder of the dancers (also mostly contestants), men preceding women and adults preceding children. Many youths also say that traditionally there is a hierarchy of committee offices. The highest is the men's flag bearer. The second highest is the secretary-treasurer, in the opinion of some, or the drumkeeper or the women's flag bearer, in the opinion of others. Many people cite as another tradition (for the last fifteen years) the alternation of the important offices between the two tribes and the equal division of offices between the tribes.

One tradition said to go back to the beginning of the century is the transfer of regalia, or objects associated with the various offices, when the offices are transferred. The men's flag bearer receives an American flag (and, according to some youths, a war bonnet); the women's flag

16. Grand entry, Milk River Powwow, July 1985: female dancers led by princesses. The Fort Belknap and other powwow princesses follow the male dancers (the dancer who carries the eagle staff has reached the far side of the arena). The princesses wear beaded crowns and cloth sashes that identify them by title. The fourth and fifth dancers from the left are carrying numbers, for they will be dance contestants. Photo courtesy of Harvey King.

bearer receives an American flag (and some say also a shawl). Many youths believe the men's flag owned by the committee (which now is not passed from one man to another—a new flag is given to the new officer) dates back to the early part of the century. According to youths, the whip men receive whips, the drumkeeper a drum; some add that the head cook receives a beaded spoon, the secretary-treasurer a feather, and the princess and other royalty beaded crowns. Many youths point out, however, that some of these original items have at times been lost and later replaced.

The eagle staff is used because "a leader is supposed to have one," in the words of one man. Another youth remarked typically, "This has always been with Indians. It is Fort Belknap's custom to have the chief or his representative carry the staff; the tribal chairman takes the place of the chief today." Most youths stress that the use of the eagle staff is a long-standing tradition at Fort Belknap, revived in the 1970s after being discarded in the late 1960s.

Assiniboines generally regard the grand entry, the new offices, and the eagle staff as recent innovations rather than traditions of the Milk River celebration. Staffs with eagle feathers and other objects were once carried by warriors—particularly members of certain warrior societies—to symbolize achievements in battle, but dance committee members in the early twentieth century did not carry them as a mark of committee office or as a symbol of tribe or community. To Gros Ventre education clique youths, however, perpetuating and strengthening these "traditions" is tremendously important. Since the late 1970s several committee positions have been added to provide for increased participation: in addition to the two flag bearers, the secretary-treasurer, drumkeeper, and two whip men, there have been added a head cook, two cultural advisers, four "coordinators" (basically cook's helpers), a princess, princess's attendant, junior princess, and junior princess's attendant. There are no fixed qualifications for these positions except that some are sex-specific. When the 1980 committee distributed bumming sticks, they put an article in the reservation newspaper explaining their purpose. By handing them out before each event to both the Gros Ventres and Assiniboines, they induced more people than usual to contribute. One committee member explained, "After it was explained to the people who got them, they knew what it was for and it made them part of the powwow." Many customs perceived as traditions are innovations that people accept in part because youths have been successful in presenting them as traditions.[20]

Finally, the education clique perceives aspects of the powwow as sacred. There is an ongoing attempt to make sacred some elements

171

that previously were sacred in a different context or were considered secular by the people at Fort Belknap. One youth said of the eagle staff, "It refurbishes one's *spiritual* awareness of what the celebration is about." Another commented that the staff traditionally was given to veterans or young men who fasted for visions. One youth stressed that the physical presence of the staff reminded the people that if they were asked to serve on the committee, they should not say no. In earlier times, when Gros Ventres accepted a pipe (which was a sacred symbol) from a petitioner, they risked supernatural retribution if they refused a request. For youths the staff serves the same purpose and, in the context of the powwow, has some of the same meaning as the pipe. Many people refer to the men's flag bearer as the "highest ceremonial position that exists now." The flags are not carried by women. Women (who are described as potentially harmful to some kinds of ritual during their menstrual periods) are forbidden to touch the flags or the eagle staff. Thus the flagwoman does not actually carry a flag. (In both Gros Ventre and Assiniboine culture, women were expected to avoid objects owned by men which were associated with supernatural power.) One youth described the drumkeeper as one who "coordinates sacred ceremonies and sings ceremonial songs in the sacred circle of the arbor." The spoon associated with the head cook's position was described by a young Gros Ventre announcer in 1983 as "the sacred spoon." One youth explained that the reason the traditional male dancers precede the other dancers in the grand entry is that "these are ceremonial people—lead singers, pipemen, bundle owners." One youth commented that the bumming sticks that are circulated today are given to people so they can "pray with" them and that the donations are made in this context. Other youths insist that "not anyone can make them"—an elder with the "right" to make the sticks must be called upon. Recently, before the powwow begins, the committee has been requesting a pipe ceremony—a man is asked to pray, using a (modern, individually owned) pipe, for good weather during the celebration. One youth said that the pipeman prayed to the "Thunderbird." Finally, a youth, discussing the giveaways held during the powwow, remarked that Fort Belknap was known for *"spiritual hospitality."*[21]

The militant youths primarily are supporters of and visible participants in the Chief Joseph's celebration, rather than the Milk River powwow. The Chief Joseph's celebration was started in 1974, when it was called Chief Joseph Veterans Memorial Committee. At the time, most people understood that the name Chief Joseph was selected because Joseph, as a well-known Nez Perce Indian warrior, was a symbol of the Indian veteran. The new powwow was initiated by a middle-aged Assiniboine man, who was responsible primarily for the concept and theme, and a Gros Ventre youth, who was responsible primarily for the organization and management of the event. The emphasis at first was on honoring deceased veterans from Fort Belknap. During the three-day event, which featured intertribal contest dancing, a roll call of the veterans' names was read. After two or three years, the emphasis and theme of the event changed from honoring veterans to honoring and memorializing the Nez Perce chief Joseph and his people (from Idaho), who were viewed as victims of the United States' mistreatment of Indians. The Nez Perce were defeated with heavy casualties in a battle with federal troops near Fort Belknap in 1877 (see map 2).[22]

The Gros Ventres who were initially involved with this celebration stress that their motive in helping to organize the powwow was to provide a vehicle for Gros Ventres who aspired to "do something" or "be somebody." One youth explained, "The [Milk] River Committee was all Assiniboines [before the late 1970s]. Why did us Gros Ventres have to sit on the side?" They also stress that the original idea for Chief Joseph's was a "revival of ceremonies honoring deceased veterans," that the ceremonies, such as the roll call and flag presentation to survivors, were older "cultural traditions" that had "died out."

When the emphasis of the powwow changed from honoring the veteran to honoring Chief Joseph and the Nez Perce, many of the youths initially involved became dissatisfied and turned to involvement with Milk River. Those who withdrew were members of the education clique; it is the militants who have stayed involved with the Chief Joseph powwow. They emphasize that the Assiniboine founder (whom they regard as an elder) had a vision experience that validated the change in emphasis of the Chief Joseph's committee: "He says he dreamed about these people—Nez Perce—that they said none of their people remembered them. That's why we started." The Chief Joseph powwow, like the Milk River powwow, is a symbolic vehicle for the youths' ideas about perpetuating Indian tradition and pursuing spiritual (sacred) things. One supporter remarked, "This [Chief Joseph's] is the only one [dance committee] I have anything to do with. On Chief Joseph's, what is important is the eagle staff, not the flag. . . . The grandfathers [supernatural spirits] and the Creator took away the roll call" and other veteran symbolism. Supernatural forces, he is suggesting, intervened in committee business to make the celebration more spiritual. Eagles pass between, or mediate, earth and sky. They symbolize the link between humans and the supernatural, and their feathers symbolically facilitate the transmission of prayers to the supernatural world above. Eagle feathers symbolize native religion.

Today the Chief Joseph's committee by and large tries to deemphasize the giveaway and contest elements of the powwow in order to avoid "materialism." One member maintained that the Milk River committee, which stresses giveaways and contests, "is nothing but a big show, everything for money. There is no tradition and culture in these powwows." By "tradition and culture" he means native religious ritual. Another remarked that prize money should not be given to individual dancers, but should be equally divided among all the dancers: "That is traditional, sharing." The Chief Joseph's committee members also deemphasize the perpetuation of "Fort Belknap tradition" and instead encourage a "spiritual" focus involving participation by "spiritual people" of other tribes. The Chief Joseph's committee also has fewer positions than the Milk River committee: chairman, secretary, treasurer, and the Assiniboine founder of the group, who serves with his wife as a cultural adviser. The cultural advisers select princesses, head dancers (an honorary position), pipemen (who pray at the celebration), and arena directors (who oversee and police the dance). The four pipemen (who may be from tribes other than the Fort Belknap Assiniboine and Gros Ventre) make "offerings" with their pipes to the Creator. Their rites are perceived as non-Christian.

The particular tone and style of the Chief Joseph's celebration are products of the involvement of the Nez Perce and of the urban experiences of the Gros Ventre and Assiniboine supporters of the committee. At the invitation of the committee, a large contingent of Nez Perce, including tribal leaders, attend the celebration and are the most active participants in ceremonies held at the site of Chief Joseph's battle with federal troops (about twenty miles from the Fort Belknap agency). The Nez Perce were fleeing to Canada to escape confinement on a reservation when they were attacked. Today Nez Perce participants in the Chief Joseph celebration place wreaths on markers that designate the spots where their relatives fell during the battle and offer honor songs and prayers for the deceased. The eagle staff used at the celebration was a gift from the Nez Perce to the Assiniboine founder of the powwow. The Gros Ventres who are particularly interested in the Chief Joseph celebration became emotionally involved with the tragedy of Joseph and his people, probably as a result of the media emphasis on Joseph, who was presented as a martyr of the Indian wars, along with Crazy Horse and other well-known leaders. Urban experiences in which ties were established with people of many tribes also have encouraged feelings of empathy with Nez Perce. One committee member explained that he considered one of the purposes of the celebration to be the strengthening of ties among all tribes, "to show the need for unity among all tribes": "We are all in this—we are all one. . . . We

174

have to throw out feelings of tribalism for the betterment of all Indians. That is the kind of theme it meant to me." One committee member, who recently returned to the reservation, noted that he became interested in the celebration because his Nez Perce friends in Seattle attended. The education clique youths are much less emotionally involved with Joseph because he was not a Gros Ventre or Assiniboine hero; they see no reason to honor him with a celebration when there are famous chiefs of the Fort Belknap tribes who could be honored. One education clique youth commented, "Chief Joseph asked the Gros Ventres for help but they turned him down as they had promised peace and had a pipe ceremony to sanction peace [with whites]. So they didn't help. How can we honor Chief Joseph then?" In other words, to honor Chief Joseph would be to reject Gros Ventre cultural (and religious) tradition.

The Chief Joseph's celebration differs from the Milk River powwow in one other important respect. Chief Joseph's celebration symbolizes Indian hostility to the United States and expresses a political militancy that is associated with urban-based Indian rights groups (such as AIM) in the early 1970s. One Gros Ventre youth remarked that the Chief Joseph committee appealed to him because he "heard of the shame of the Gros Ventres not helping and their informing on the Nez Perce" (a view of history not shared by most Gros Ventres). He is expressing a feeling that all Indians should have resisted the United States militarily. Another commented that symbols of the United States (U.S. flags, ceremonies for veterans) should not be part of an Indian celebration: "The people that killed the Nez Perce are the government that enslaved the people. That flag isn't an Indian flag so I can't honor it or the U.S. uniform."

Gros Ventre elders do not share the youths' enthusiasm for the Milk River and Chief Joseph's celebrations, both of which are held at the agency, although most elders do participate to some degree. Elders perceive the old Hays dances and the committee that organized them as Gros Ventre cultural tradition. They view the Milk River celebration as an Assiniboine event, as Assiniboine cultural tradition. Gros Ventres have a tradition of attending and, to some degree, of helping (with donations, and, rarely, by serving on the committee if their spouses are Assiniboines). But the celebration at Milk River is clearly perceived as Assiniboine. The Chief Joseph's celebration is regarded as foreign to Fort Belknap altogether, and associated with AIM. The involvement of Gros Ventre youths similarly is perceived as limited to AIM people. Despite their ambivalence, elders feel a strong moral obligation to donate time or resources to these committees if a relative is involved with the celebration. If asked to help, most feel reluctant to refuse—to do so would be considered antisocial or stingy. If they are asked but do not want to serve on a committee, they generally give a reasonable excuse (such as poor health) and offer to make a donation instead.

The specific customs that youths view as "tradition" Gros Ventre elders regard as "phony" or "showy" in comparison with the Hays celebrations, which in retrospect have come to stand for tradition even though they were largely innovative at the time. In their view, if something is not done as the old-timers used to do it, then it is not Gros Ventre tradition; it is phony. Elders remember the giveaway, for example, as a central part of the Christmas dances. But they resent the prominent position of youths in the giveaway ceremony today and frown upon its elaboration. One elder commented, "They try to outdo or see how much impression they can make by giving away a lot of things." The youths, he is suggesting, are concerned primarily with showing off, rather than with fulfilling social responsibilities, as the old-timers in Hays did when they held giveaways. Another elder remarked, "Giveaways never used to be so long; now it's boring." Another elder put it thus: "They go overboard on these giveaways." Another added, "They used to give away expensive things, like horses, beaded buckskin; now it's just blankets." And "My grandfather always said, 'Give away things that are worth giving away.'" Similarly, "They would give something away that came out of them [necessities, a sacrifice]. Today young people they don't know any better, they just buy a lot of things. It's quantity, not quality." Elders feel that it is easier today for a family to accumulate enough cash to buy several blankets than it was to have a giveaway in the years when they were growing up. The vocalization accompanying the giveaway also troubles elders because of both the time consumed and the element of self-praise involved: "Gros Ventres didn't brag about themselves—an elder would get up and talk about them." One man recalled that many giveaways were held while the dancing was going on—the announcer called out the event in a voice loud enough to be heard over the drumming and singing so that the dancing continued uninterrupted. Finally, elders insist that "when they had giveaways they gave to visitors or real old people because of their age," but "not to their relatives, like now; now they get it all turned around." Youths, who also recognize that property is often given to relatives, view the practice differently. As one said: "When we give to relations we reaffirm our blood lineages." He is pointing out that in an era when many people have non–Gros Ventre last names and when many have moved to the reservation only recently, public acknowledgment of Gros Ventre relatives, particularly elderly people, helps symbolize and affirm a person's identity as a Gros Ventre.

Elders acknowledge that mourners' feeds were a responsibility of the Hays dance committee but view the youths' efforts to perpetuate this custom as misguided. One elder expressed the commonly held opinion among elders that youths are involved in rituals in order to show off: rather than hold one mourners' feed a year, shortly before the Christmas celebration, "they have several feeds for the same mourners; they are getting carried away as usual."

Another reflected a widely held view that the dances today are commercialized: "Now these committees feed the mourners and expect them to donate—now it is just a way to raise money." Another elder said: "It used to be fun; now it is something like a rodeo—the best one wins here and goes on to the next place. Now it is all contests." Still another elder commented, "Then, it was for the simple joy of who's best. Now they can't scare up an owl dance [a noncontest dance]. Why the change? Big prize money. Contests are spoiling it. They dance for nothing but coins." These elders feel alienated from the contemporary powwow. By using images of "rodeo" and "dancing for coins," they suggest that the powwow encourages individualism rather than group unity, incorporates white values, and is too oriented to a white audience (although few whites actually attend).

For elders, the agency powwow does not symbolize Gros Ventre identity or unity. Elders stress that the use of three flags, the grand entry, and the eagle staff as a community or committee symbol are new aspects of the dance celebration, not traditions.

The youths' emphasis on sacred symbols in the powwow is particularly bothersome to elders. Elders feel that such attempts have trivialized and secularized ritual objects that once had religious significance for Gros Ventres. The eagle feather headdress or staff, for example, was used only by renowned warriors in the early twentieth century. Only elderly men could qualify to wear such regalia. One elder who danced as a youth recalled, "Old men wore [eagle feather] war bonnets; the middle-aged men wore porcupine roaches and bells. There were no women grass dancers [fancy dancers]." Today, all ages and both sexes wear eagle feathers on their costumes, and all grass dance. Another elder stressed, "You couldn't play around with eagle feathers like today—put them on everything." And another commented, "Now everyone has an eagle bonnet." Other elders point to the current custom of having four veterans dance (in a prescribed way) toward an eagle feather accidentally dropped by a dancer. One picks up the feather, tells about a dangerous experience he had in the service, and receives a gift. At the dances in Hays, one warrior would pick up *any* item dropped from a crow belt dancer. The warrior then would tell the story of something he did in battle and receive some form of payment from the dancer. Typical of elders' criticisms was this remark about the custom of picking up a feather: "Today they emphasize the feather more."

Naming Ceremonies

One of the rituals most frequently held today is the public bestowal of a Gros Ventre name on a child or an adult. This naming rite is a specialized form of the giveaway ceremony. Elders' and youths' views on the contemporary naming ceremony differ. To elders, the traditional Gros Ventre ceremony was the one that they saw as children and young adults. It was usually held in someone's home and reflected the cultural orientation of the old people living then. Youths today consider public naming to be traditionally Gros Ventre. The way they perform the ceremony reflects attitudes about Gros Ventre identity that have developed in the contemporary era.

At the time when the elders were born, most families gave a Gros Ventre name to their child at birth. Children received English names at baptism but were not called by those names until they entered school. Most babies were named privately and informally by a grandparent at home. A few boys—those from prominent families—were named at a public event. In the latter case, the family invited a noted warrior or medicine man to name the child, gave valuable presents to the namer, and sponsored a feed for those attending. At this formal ceremony the child was turned in each of the four directions to the accompaniment of prayers for his health and well-being. Or a family with the means might invite a group of elderly people to a feast and ask one elder to name the child there at home. But for most boys, and for virtually all girls, the naming was informal and did not involve gift giving on a large scale.

Among the twenty elders with whom I discussed their own naming ceremonies, four men had been named publicly. Three (born in 1895, 1906, and 1911) had prominent fathers who had the means to sponsor public gatherings and pay a warrior to name their sons; the family of the fourth elder (born in 1917), at the instigation of the child himself, paid for the name of a visiting Crow Indian he admired, and he was named by one of his elders during a Christmas dance at Hays in the early 1920s. Two of the women (born in 1896 and 1899) had grandfathers who were noted warriors and these men named their granddaughters at home when the girls were babies. The other fourteen elders—born between 1910 and 1924—were named at home, informally by women or by men who were not warriors. The boys were

178

named by a grandfather, or less frequently by another male relative. The girls were occasionally named by a grandfather or male relative, but usually by a grandmother. None of the elders had had any of their own children named publicly; in fact, some did not give their children Gros Ventre names at all, for by the time their children were born, many did not see the usefulness or relevance of a Gros Ventre name.[23]

All the elders stress that the person who gave a name had to have earned that name: "To name a child they invited a person that had distinguished himself in war against a traditional enemy. . . . The name was not [necessarily] from the family line but from a noted person." One elder's grandfather had named her after one of his war exploits: "He didn't just give me that name; he earned it." "Sometimes they invited a medicine man to do it," explained one man. A warrior generally gave a name that emanated from his war experience; a medicine man would give a name that came to him in a dream or vision.

The Gros Ventre name was socially significant, say the elders, because many old people could not speak English well, and so they communicated with children in the Gros Ventre language. And the name was significant in another sense. A warrior, in giving his name—or one of his names—that signified a daring exploit, was offering a prayer for the child's success in life. The success of the namer indicated to Gros Ventres that the namer had supernatural protection and thus the name might aid the child. Medicine men gave names that conveyed their prayer for a healthy, successful life for the child. (In fact, one elder noted that he had had his name changed by a medicine man in order to reverse a long history of illness.) An elder explained that "girls were named by a grandmother. That went according to traditional knowledge of the grandmother of people [deceased] she regarded as above average." In other words, the name given was symbolic of a prayer for a long, successful life. Gros Ventres believed that elderly people's prayers were likely to be answered.

To elders, naming ceremonies today are "showy" or "flashy" and not truly traditional. One elder commented, "Then there was not a big elaborate thing like today." Another remarked, "Now they make a big show of it." Today virtually every family holds a public ceremony to name a child of either sex, whereas in the past only genuinely prominent families that had wealth to distribute named a child in this fashion. To the elders, the fact that there are similarities between the naming practices of today and those of earlier times—that items are given away and the person receiving a name is turned in the four directions—is less important than the fact that the ceremony does not have the same meaning it once had to the participants. Especially

17. Gros Ventre naming ceremony, July 1983. This ceremony was held on land in Hays belonging to one of the members of the family that sponsored the event. Two children were named. A Gros Ventre youth (the little girl's mother's uncle) turns the child in each of four directions (facing south to start) as he prays for her good health and success in life. As the crowd watches, he announces the name chosen; then the drum group sings an honor song for the family of the girl. The drum group, the Hays Singers, is comprised of a Gros Ventre extended family and has been in existence for most of this century. After the naming ceremony, the family sponsoring the event had a feed and giveaway to honor the two little girls who received names, as well as the memory of a deceased relative. One of the tipis was given away to a guest, as well as blankets, quilts, dance shawls, and other items. Photo by Loretta Fowler.

important to elders is what they perceive as the loss of respect for elders—that youths sometimes give names and preside over the ceremonies as announcers.

One elder observed that probably youths were enthusiastic about public naming because then "everyone would know that the person had a Gros Ventre name." In a private naming, only "a few family members would know." Youths, he was suggesting, wanted Gros Ventre names "for show"—to signal Indian identity to others—and did not understand the true meaning of a Gros Ventre name. Another elder was annoyed during a naming ceremony when a youth publicly urged people to carry on or revive Gros Ventre cultural traditions. He explained: "People under thirty-five—what they tell about tradition is hogwash. For a person under thirty-five, a name is important because they want to be identified as an Indian who has a given name that sounds fancy, romantic."

Another elder recalled an incident that, from his point of view, exemplified the youths' lack of understanding of Gros Ventre naming tradition. A married couple wanted to name their two small children, but did not know the Gros Ventre language or how to choose a name. They apparently had no elderly relatives whom they could or would ask for assistance. They asked an elder if she knew any of the names of their deceased relatives. The elder recalled that two of their relatives (now deceased) had lived to be very old, and she told them their Gros Ventre names. The youths asked for the English translations of the names, and when they heard what the names meant—they referred to ordinary, rather mundane objects—they became upset and refused to use them. Eventually the elder allowed them to use two names from her own family which in English translation sounded more romantic.

Elders who witnessed public naming in their youth sometimes remark that the ceremony today is different from what they remember. One commented, "The last authentic public naming I saw was in 1931. Now I think they do it in a modern way. They don't adhere to the traditional way." Another explained, "Today naming is streamlined. They do away with a lot. Like in the old way of naming when you gave a horse away this old fellow came up and, after they gave sweetgrass and sage and pushed you in the four wind directions and told the history of the name, he receives the horse and shakes hands." Elders note that there is one elder living who was given the right to name publicly and that others who have named individuals are not entitled to the role: "Now it is anyone and everything!" exclaimed one elder. Some youths have asked elderly women to name children in public, for example. Elders insist that traditionally only men named in public.[24]

Elders often remark that there is no practical, meaningful use for a Gros Ventre name today. One elder noted that recently he named three of his grandchildren but then refused to name any more because "they don't use the names for anything today." No youths can communicate in the Gros Ventre language. But generally elders feel a moral obligation to help their younger relatives have naming ceremonies when requested to do so, whether they approve or not.

To youths, the naming ceremony is an extremely important symbol of identity. Youths point out that if they do not have a Gros Ventre name, they feel social pressure from their peers to acquire one. They note that some people with an Indian name claim to be "more Indian" than persons without one. A few youths have given their children the English translation of a Gros Ventre name as a legal name.

Youths view the public naming ceremony as an expression of Gros Ventre cultural identity particularly because it includes a giveaway, which offers an opportunity to pursue prominence. There is an announcer who presides, and an honor song is sung for the occasion. One youth commented, "Unlike Assiniboines, who are named at home, Gros Ventres have the full rite, a feast, public ceremony, giveaway. It imprints on your mind you have cultural responsibility. Assiniboines take it for granted that you can be given a name anytime, anywhere, by anybody. Not a Gros Ventre." (Of course, the statement represents this individual's opinion, not fact. In actuality, Assiniboines have their own naming ceremony, albeit one that is held at home.) The

18. A feed during a Gros Ventre naming ceremony, July 1983. Large quantities of food (including a steer) were prepared and served to the crowd by friends and relatives of the sponsoring family. The youth is passing food in a cardboard box to several elders. Guests are expected always to accept the food (this is said to be a Fort Belknap tradition). Food not eaten is taken home; thus the elderly woman has brought a large paper bag in which to take away food. Elders are often given special foods (internal organs, for example) not served to the crowd in general. Photo by Loretta Fowler.

youth's remark expresses the Gros Ventres' emphasis on primacy. The public naming ritual also is important to Gros Ventres who do not live on the reservation. They sponsor many public namings during the summer when they visit the reservation to attend the Milk River powwow.

A few youths impart a religious function to naming. One remarked, "When you make the journey across [die], when you travel on the journey, they [your dead relatives in the afterlife] only know you by your authentic tribal name, not your English name." A person without an Indian name, then, would not be able to join his tribesmen in the afterlife. Youths emphasize the necessity of a public, formal naming for all who wish to be recognized as culturally Gros Ventre—adults and children, males and females.

Youths regard any elder who is a full blood and well respected as qualified to name in public. The namer, say the youths, bestows the name of one of the relatives of the person being named. The name symbolizes the Gros Ventre cultural identity of the person named, for it establishes a link between him and his namesake, an old-timer from Hays. Several namings have been conducted by youths (who, not able to speak the Gros Ventre language, ask an elder how to pronounce the name to be given). One youth commented, "It's 1983 and people do what they want; there are no cultural structures to say it is right or wrong." He was expressing the view, common to many youths, that when youths must choose between the perpetuation of Gros Ventre identity and following customs that elders consider important, youths justifiably will choose to pursue Gros Ventre identity.

Memorial Giveaways

Today it is customary for Gros Ventres to have a feed and giveaway after the funeral of a family member. Then, one year later, the family has a memorial giveaway, and sometimes a feed as well. Some Gros Ventres recently have sponsored memorial giveaways for relatives who died years ago. Both elders and youths now have memorial giveaways and a giveaway and feed after the funeral of a relative.

But elders stress that in the days when they were children and young adults, Gros Ventre mortuary customs were different than they are today. One elder recollected:

Mourning started when the person died; there was silence, respect. They made their own casket, wore black. There was wailing, then others comforted, talked with them in a soft voice. Relatives stayed around home while others volunteered to dig the grave. Before I came on the scene they were put on cliffs or ledges. They were buried with valuables and clothes. There was a wake and a funeral mass and interment with wailing. Then the relatives were taken away from the grave by someone who would comfort. There was no public feed. They wouldn't go back home. When my [paternal] grandmother died, my grandfather and I did not go back to the house for six months. My mother took charge of the house. My grandmother's things were given away, some buried with her.

Another elder described the funeral customs of giving away the deceased's personal property thus: "If a person lost his wife he gave everything of hers away right there. The house was just cleaned out." In addition to these funeral rites, on Memorial Day Gros Ventres would gather at the St. Paul's Mission cemetery, where most Gros Ventres were buried. People would bring food to contribute to a community dinner; a prominent person would donate a beef to be cooked. The families would decorate the graves with flowers and a priest would say mass. Sometimes an individual might give away something in honor of a deceased relative on this occasion.

Today there is considerable social pressure to have memorial giveaways and feeds at funerals. Elders, therefore, frequently participate. They do stress, however, that the feed and giveaway of items purchased for the occasion and the memorial giveaway are not Gros Ventre traditions. These, they say, are innovations recently introduced by youths. One elder commented, "It is now a style, fad," implying that the customs were not "real" or meaningful (to her) as Gros Ventre rituals. Elders insist that the memorial giveaway is an Assiniboine custom that Gros Ventre youths adopted. Speaking about a recent trend to have several memorial giveaways for the same person, one elder remarked, "That isn't right; it keeps the spirit [of the deceased] around. In Rocky Boy [reservation] they do it every year. They [Gros Ventre youths] say they are doing it four years as Indians do things in fours! It is something they adopted." An elder explained her decision to help her daughter have a memorial giveaway for a dead child thus: "They never used to have these memorial giveaways—just gave away personal possessions of the deceased. Now people go into debt. They say they are proving to the people how much they loved the dead person. My daughter is having one. So I will help, but I don't believe in it."[25]

Many youths, on the other hand, refer to memorial giveaways as Gros Ventre cultural tradition revived. "It seems like a revival in the last twenty years after a lapse," as one youth said. Youths credit themselves with reviving this "tradition." Some express pride that Gros Ventres outdo other tribes in the lavish scale of their memorial giveaway. And youths speak proudly of the tremendous expense to which

Gros Ventres go to purchase items for the memorial giveaway. In short, the memorial giveaway serves as another occasion (like the naming ceremony or powwow committee member's giveaway) when Gros Ventres can attain prominence through public display of generosity. And youths feel social pressure to live up to the ideal of showing affection for kin through generosity: "It is hard to live here and not do it. People will think you didn't love your relation. You would be ostracized a little bit. That's why I did it for my dad." Gros Ventre youths also favorably compare these giveaways to those of the Assiniboines, an expression of their orientation to primacy at Fort Belknap. Youths also describe as Gros Ventre and Assiniboine—that is, Fort Belknap—tradition the custom of having men (some say veterans) pass out the food to the crowd at a feed. (The custom that guests must not refuse food is also described as a tradition; sometimes guests leave with several quart containers of meat, salad, beans, bread, soup, crackers, and cake.) As far as I can determine, Gros Ventre women served food to the crowd at the dances in Hays during the early twentieth century, although it is true that men served puppy meat to crow belt dancers, warriors, and black-dress wearers in the Grass Dance. Elders do not criticize the contemporary custom of veterans passing out food. They accept this and other ceremonies involving veterans at powwows (flag raising, for example), for honoring soldiers' bravery and respecting the memory of deceased relatives who were veterans is meaningful and important to elders and educated youths alike, although many militant youths are ambivalent about veteran symbolism.

Symbols of Identity and the Generation Gap: Origins and Social Implications

Since the mid-1970s there has been a surge of effort to "revive" rituals at Fort Belknap. Ritual elements from the cultural past of Gros Ventres or Assiniboines have been reintroduced, sometimes with changes in form or meaning. Sometimes "revival" has involved the introduction of innovations derived from a pan-Plains or intertribal milieu. Gros Ventre elders generally view the contemporary ritual activity as outside the Gros Ventre tradition. Education clique youths, on the other hand, see these rituals as traditional to the Gros Ventres and essential to the expression of Gros Ventre identity. In their ritual participation, militant youths, to a great extent, express their identity as Indians rather than Gros Ventres. Elders and youths, then, often interpret ritual symbolism differently. Their variant interpretations stem from their different life experiences.

185

The greatest source of conflict is the revival of religious rituals. When the elders were growing up, Gros Ventres with medicine power and with formal training in pipe-bundle and other rituals were still alive and using their ritual knowledge. In those days—from the turn of the century to the early 1930s—children were brought up to respect old people. Respect meant deference. Children were taught to put the interests of old people above their own and to comply immediately with the instructions of the elderly. This concept was explained to me thus: "Old people—right or wrong, they are right." Today's elders learned to view respect for old people as central to the meaning of Gros Ventre religion and social organization, for old age represented both supernatural blessing and ritual authority. Elderly, ritually knowledgeable Gros Ventre men were held in awe. Elders today tell many stories of the miraculous deeds of old-timers that they personally witnessed. For elders, then, Gros Ventre culture and Gros Ventre religion are rooted in respect for old people. Elders are proud of the respect they showed toward the old-timers. In their view it was respect for *their* elders' wishes that led them to avoid assuming positions of leadership in native Gros Ventre ritual life after the 1930s and to embrace Catholicism. They feel that their advanced years and their personal contacts with old-timers in earlier times entitle them to the respect of their juniors. As they see it, it is disrespectful of the youths not to accept elders' views on ritual authority. When youths disregard elders, the elders' self-esteem is threatened and their ideals are challenged.

Thus, in the view of elders, when these youths attempt to practice "Gros Ventre religion," they show obvious disrespect for elders. Their lack of respect indicates that their desire for cultural revival is sham. In the words of one elder, "Now things are backwards, young people are running things. It used to be the other way around." Another remarked, "Now they got it all turned around." The feeling that the youths' efforts at cultural revival are not sincere was expressed often during the crisis of the coming of the Arapahoes to rewrap the Flat Pipe. One elder stressed, "They just ignored us senior citizens. They soft-soaped us with a lot of 'We respect you old people' but they just ignored us." Moreover, the youths' proposal to remove the Flat Pipe from the home of an elder to that of a youth was a challenge to the status of all elders. Elders' perception of the youths' disrespect also underlies the elders' conviction that the youths' efforts are for show, to impress people, rather than sincere attempts to pray. The youths' disrespectful behavior contributes to the elders' perception of them as unqualified, lacking the necessary character, to become religious leaders or medicine men or to conduct Gros Ventre rituals.

Why would youths behave "disrespectfully" toward the elders, particularly youths pursuing Gros Ventre cultural identity? The life experiences of youths have differed significantly from those of elders; they do not view and were not taught to view age-group relations in the way that elders do. In fact, much of the behavior that elders consider disrespectful is not perceived in that way by youths. Many youths did not spend their childhood in the Hays community; even if they did live in Hays, the era of the old-timers had passed. There were no medicine men or keepers. Parents stressed the need to compete successfully with whites, and since parents felt that they themselves did not have the skills needed for successful competition in the 1970s (in college, for example), they encouraged youths toward independence and the kind of individualism and assertiveness they associated with whites. In short, the youths were not socialized to "respect" the aged, in the old sense of the word, or to hold them in awe.

Youths' understanding of how to be Indian (in religion, dance, politics, economics) was extended on campuses and in cities in a pan-Plains or intertribal social context in the late 1960s and 1970s. Their concept of identity was shaped by their contacts with other young Indians from areas outside of Fort Belknap and from mass media presentations of the "Plains Indian" which stressed vision quest experiences, martyrdom, and features of the mid-nineteenth-century Plains experience in general. Through contacts with young Indians from reservations other than Fort Belknap, youths were introduced to other tribes' ceremonies. Their realization that Gros Ventre elders could or would not teach them Indian ceremonies led to an ambivalence toward elders that at times approached antagonism. Youths had learned that Indian elders taught Indian tradition to young Indians. Gros Ventre elders did not do this; thus they were not behaving like elders. Despite the youths' familiarity with the pan-Plains ideal of respect for elders, they do not feel that elders today deserve deference in the sense that whatever elders do, "right or wrong, they are right." As one youth put it, "there are no more old people here. They are all gone." Elders, then, should be honored by gifts and invitations to ceremonies, but the youths feel that they themselves must provide leadership in cultural revival if Gros Ventre or Indian culture at Fort Belknap is to survive into the future.

The education clique and militant youths differ somewhat in their concepts of cultural identity, for they developed these concepts in different social contexts. The militant youths have a greater commitment to reviving native religion and to becoming medicine men, for they view native religion as an essential component of Indian identity. These youths obtained their education in urban areas outside Montana and did not have a chance to form close alliances with other youths from Fort Belknap or other Montana reservations. The social environment in which they experienced the wave of affirmative action hiring and Native American studies curriculum in the 1970s was multi-tribal and largely urban. Indian political action groups were dominated by sophisticated individuals skilled in urban politics. Militant youths' concept of Indian identity took form as they participated in protest groups that had an antigovernment focus and used confrontational tactics. One youth explained, "They therefore have a different, demanding approach." He attributed the militant group's aggression toward elders in the matter of rewrapping the Flat Pipe to the confrontational strategy that served them well in cities. For militant youths developing an awareness of their Indian identity in the 1970s, there were no "traditional" role models among the elderly, so they looked to media accounts of nineteenth-century Plains life and to the spiritual leaders of the protest groups whose rites were oriented toward a young, English-speaking, intertribal audience. These medicine men were often young. The press coverage of the ceremonies they performed furthered the group's goals.

Education clique youths, on the other hand, expanded their concept of cultural identity when they enrolled at one of the Montana campuses. The college peer group became a major source for ideas about Indian cultural identity in the 1970s. They visited their new friends on reservations where large powwows or other kinds of ceremonies were held, and there they developed ideas about Indian ritual. Exposure to the media's presentation of Indian identity as a nineteenth-century Plains identity did influence their interest in native religion, but their frequent and intimate contacts with youths from other Montana tribes and with Fort Belknap people revealed a wide range of Indian traditions, many of which originated in the twentieth century. The education clique give more credence to elders' opinions than militant youths do, and they show more interest in such activities as the hand game ritual, a ceremony important in Fort Belknap history but not part of the nineteenth-century Indian religion seen in the media. Education clique youths are particularly interested in perpetuating an identity that is distinctly Gros Ventre, or at least based on Fort Belknap tradition, rather than merely Indian identity. Their interpretations of ritual symbols and their concepts of identity are based on understandings derived from family oral tradition, from contacts with other Plains peoples at college and on visits to other Plains reservations, and from published and media accounts of Gros Ventres and other Plains peoples in the nineteenth century.

At college and on visits to powwows on other reservations, youths observed both old and young people participating in native religious rituals. Individually owned pipes and regalia could be obtained and mentors found among other tribes. They also became more familiar with the Gros Ventre pipe-bundle traditions through published works—their efforts led to the reprinting of Cooper's detailed study of the Flat and Feathered Pipes in 1975, and it was sold on the reservation. Photographs of late-nineteenth-century Plains Indians, as well as films and books about Indians produced in the late 1960s and 1970s and made available on campuses, portrayed Plains Indians with pipes and wearing eagle feather headdresses and carrying eagle staffs. Some Gros Ventre youths studied museum collections of Gros Ventre and Plains material culture. These representations influenced their ideas about the relationship between Indian identity and these kinds of sacred regalia. Ultimately the youths began to incorporate sacred symbols in powwows.

To education clique youths, Catholicism was not incompatible with prayers through pipe-bundle and other native rituals, for they observed Assiniboines at Fort Belknap and members of other Plains tribes participating in both native and Christian rituals. Moreover, in the 1970s Catholic priests had begun to participate in native rites or use native regalia. At Hays a priest fasted on a butte and incorporated a pipe in church ritual. On Rocky Boy reservation, fifty miles west of Fort Belknap, a priest vowed and completed the Sun Dance ritual. Catholic position on native rituals had changed from the time elders went to school at the mission. Native rituals were branded as heresy then. Today many priests view the rites as alternative ways to pray to the one God. This new position is difficult for elders to accept, but not for most youths. Education clique youths do not link Gros Ventre identity to the exclusive practice of native religion. The militant youths, however, tend to reject Christianity as symbolic of the oppressive policies of the United States and characterize Indian religion as fundamentally different, based on a different set of values.

To elders, the rituals that truly express Gros Ventre identity are the secular rituals of the past three decades of this century—the Hays Fair, the Christmas dance, the Memorial Day observance. These events were held in Hays and were made possible only by the cooperation of virtually all Gros Ventres. Even the people who lived in Dodson and the agency area came to Hays for these events. Dances were occasions when all Gros Ventres pooled what they had and worked together to put on a successful entertainment for each other. The dances helped to strengthen ties among Gros Ventres, ties that the old-timers taught were important. Elders' views on giveaways (in naming and funeral ritual, as well as on other occasions) took shape in the 1920s and

1930s, when Gros Ventres experienced particular economic hardship. It may be that these difficult conditions necessitated family giveaways on a smaller scale and the creation of institutions that encouraged the pooling of labor and resources. In any case, the comparative frequency of giveaways and the large quantity of goods given away today strike these elders as showing off. To elders, the giveaway also symbolized the fulfillment of the social responsibility of the well-off to provide for others. This was a year-round responsibility. It entailed taking firewood and meat to elderly and needy people in the Hays community, for example. The giveaways, presided over by old-timers, were considered a kind of sacrifice as well. Dances at the agency were associated with Assiniboines. To a great extent, elders perceive the old Hays dances and fairs to have been in competition with Assiniboine events at the agency. Thus for elders the powwow at the agency is not compelling as a symbol of Gros Ventre identity. It is for the education clique youths.

To educated youths, powwows and giveaways (in the powwow context or at namings or memorial ceremonies) are very important symbols of identity. The giveaway is particularly important to their identity as Gros Ventres. For those who have lived off the reservation for several years, it affords an opportunity to demonstrate publicly their kin ties to Gros Ventres on the reservation, both through the support of kin in accumulating property to distribute and in selection of kin as recipients. It is a way of recognizing, reaffirming, or claiming ties to people in the reservation community, kin or not. The powwows, with their emphasis on contest dancing, were held all over the Plains and on campuses in the late 1960s and 1970s. These celebrations were readily accessible to everyone. And youths' talents at fund raising for these costly events afforded them opportunities to exert leadership at Fort Belknap. There the powwows and the giveaways became arenas for the display of prominence and the pursuit of primacy—ideals many youths had heard about from older family members. And they were occasions for youths to affirm publicly their commitment to Gros Ventre and Fort Belknap tradition. The Milk River powwow offers education clique youths a way of expressing the ambition and competitiveness they were socialized for and does so in symbolic forms that also signify commitment to identity as a Gros Ventre and/or Fort Belknap Indian. Most youths obtained housing or jobs in the agency area and the agency powwow became the focus of their efforts.

For militant youths, the Milk River powwow and the giveaways are less compelling symbols of identity than Indian religion and the Chief Joseph powwow. To a great extent, these youths developed or elaborated on their concept of identity in an urban milieu dominated by media presentations of nineteenth-century Indian life, urban poverty programs, and intertribal protest groups that focused on influencing officials in Washington. These youths' experiences made them focus on issues of Indian poverty and discrimination. Materialism was associated with whites; "real" Indians were perceived as nonmaterialistic. Thus contest dancing conflicts with their view of Indian identity, and the Milk River powwow is less attractive to them than to the education clique. Chief Joseph is a compelling symbol for these youths, for in 1877 he and the Nez Perce attempted to flee U.S. jurisdiction rather than accept federal domination, and were massacred and martyred. (It is this episode of Joseph's life that receives emphasis in the ceremony, not his later years on the Nez Perce reservation.) The Chief Joseph celebration offers a way of expressing both the spiritual aspect of Indian identity and the social protest themes of the urban intertribal organizations of the 1970s.

In an urban context, the militant youths sought public recognition as Indians, not as Gros Ventres. And they did not want to be perceived as merely another disadvantaged minority, so visible symbols of Indian identity that would have meaning to non-Indians were important. Many let their hair grow and braided it, wore jewelry or items of clothing associated by the media with Indians (bandannas, bone chokers, Navajo silver), and incorporated religious rites (such as smoking a calumet pipe or using an eagle wing fan) in their demonstrations and meetings. In the reservation context, these symbols of Indian identity are still important to the militant youths. Acceptance of native religion, however they chose to define it, was essential to their transformation from a white to an Indian lifestyle, particularly after they returned to the reservation and obtained modern housing and managerial jobs. Rejection of Christianity was symbolic of their rejection of a white lifestyle. For many, the change in lifestyle marked a more fundamental personal transformation in which a former life of despair and destructive behavior was replaced by optimism and accomplishment. These individuals give the credit for their personal rebirth to native religion (the grandfathers, the spirits, the Creator).

For the education clique youths, on the other hand, the symbols of Indian identity are more firmly anchored in Fort Belknap, or at least in Montana, traditions. Living in Montana most or all of their lives, they were always regarded as Indians by white Montanans; there were no other significantly large minorities with whom they could be confused. Moreover, an Indian dialect of English, physical appearance, and Indian-sounding surnames further distinguished them from the general population in Montana. The education clique youths were drawn less by symbols of nineteenth-century Plains Indians (braids, for example) than by symbols of 1970s pan-Plains life, such as contemporary styles of beadwork (watchbands, key chains), forms of speech, and interest in hearing and learning powwow songs. In their view, the militants' emphasis on avoiding materialism makes them stress that "we are poor and downtrodden because that's how Indians should be"; this denial of the Gros Ventre ideal of prominence provokes the education clique to refute the militants' claim to be traditional. Education clique youths regard the militant youths' commitment to being traditional as excessive and anchored in the past rather than the present. They refer to militants as "nonreservation types." One education clique youth remarked, "These seventies superskins left here and were in urban areas. They learned about Indians from books. You can tell they weren't raised traditional." Also typical is the feeling that "AIM made a lot of people aware they were Indian who were halfway denying it before." The term "seventies superskins" embodies the notion that the militant youths wanted to be Indian only when it became fashionable or profitable to be one in the 1970s; "superskin" (a shortened form of superredskin) is derisive, suggesting that they go to ridiculous extremes to prove to themselves and others that they are Indian. Of course, the militant youths view the education clique in a reciprocally negative light: "non-Indian-type Indians."

The Milk River powwow and to a lesser extent the social dancing phase of the Chief Joseph celebration draw virtually all of the Fort Belknap residents. They come to visit, watch the crowd and the spectacle, listen to the singing, and support relatives who are participating as committee members or dancers. Despite disagreements among Gros Ventres (and among Gros Ventres and Assiniboines) over the meaning of specific ritual symbols or over what is traditional, most people at Fort Belknap contribute in some way to the success of the powwows and the naming and memorial giveaways. When a giveaway is held, a wide network of kinsmen work toward its success; in fact, such cooperation is an obligation of kinship.

Today English kinship terminology has replaced native Gros Ventre terms, but, to a considerable extent, behavior toward relatives reflects the kinship categorizations that formerly were expressed in native terminology. Gros Ventre kinship organization once was bilateral and generational, so that the term for sibling referred not only to siblings but to children of parents' siblings (cross- and parallel cousins) as well. Today the collateral relatives often are referred to as cousins and the lineal ones as brothers and sisters. But while liberal assistance continues to be expected of brothers and sisters, it is also expected of cousins. Ideally, requests are not refused, and such relatives feel obligated to help with the expenses of each other's giveaways and to give away property or money on behalf of such a relative if he or she is a powwow committee member. Persons classified as "grandparents" still include the siblings of one's parents' parents. These relatives feel an obligation to contribute to the best of their abilities to the giveaways of their "grandchildren." And, ideally, parents help their children and the children of their siblings, and vice versa. The extent to which particular individuals help each other, and the extent to which in-laws help each other, varies considerably. It is beyond the scope of this book to discuss all the factors that account for the variation. However, the wide kinship network that each individual has, given the cultural content of Gros Ventre kinship, draws large numbers of people into such community activities as the powwows and giveaways. Friends also may contribute to each other's giveaways.

Participation in a giveaway, especially if one is standing in the arena with other family members when property is given out, symbolizes membership in one of the extended families that comprise the Gros Ventre people. The symbolic head of the extended family is one of its elderly members. Standing beside the elder publicly links an individual to the Gros Ventre old-timers to whom the elder is related. This public demonstration is particularly important for individuals who have been living off the reservation and who want to announce or strengthen their Gros Ventre identity in the eyes of others. Participation in a giveaway also symbolizes one's generosity. Plains Indians, in their own eyes, are generous; whites are not. So Indian identity, too, is symbolized by participation in a giveaway.

Although the Milk River, Lodgepole, and Chief Joseph powwow committees (and the inactive Hays committee) have their own supporters, they do not work against each other's success. When revenue-sharing money became available from the federal government one year, for example, Milk River, Lodgepole, and Hays agreed to share funds with the newly formed Chief Joseph committee. It would be considered stingy and a violation of kinship obligations for an individual to support only the powwow that best expressed his or her concept of identity. Disagreements over powwow symbolism, then, do not isolate groups from one another; variant interpretations help shape the ongoing reorganization of Fort Belknap culture and society.

The generation gap at Fort Belknap can be understood only in the context of the late 1960s and 1970s, when new policies and programs emanating from Washington transformed reservation society. These new programs encouraged youths to attend college and to come to Fort Belknap and obtain jobs and modern housing. Many were encouraged to run for the business council. Youths developed or further stimulated their interest in native traditions and the struggle for Indian rights. It was the life experiences of the youths, then, so different from those of the elders, that enabled the transformation of Fort Belknap in the 1970s and 1980s. In the 1950s and 1960s, it was virtually impossible for most Gros Ventres to support themselves on the reservation. The reservation programs—such as they were—were administered by whites. Young people (today's elders) felt that there was no future for them at Fort Belknap. When the new federal policies and programs opened the door, today's youths stepped in and revitalized tribal government and attempted to revive cultural traditions or ritual life. Youths, with their experience in obtaining grants and administering programs on campus or in cities, were equipped to take advantage of the new opportunities. The elders had no such experience. On the other hand, the youths had been motivated and helped to acquire their skills and outlook by the elders, who had been committed to provide their children with higher education. Thus the elders' life experiences as parents or grandparents contributed to the transformation of Fort Belknap. Fort Belknap needed the skills of the youths. The youths had understandings and values that, on the one hand, set them apart from the elders, but, on the other hand, introduced a new flexibility and creativity into reservation society. When the youths began to serve on the business council, the council's leadership was revitalized. The people credited the council with the new activity and development. The perception that the council of the 1970s accomplished things was in stark contrast to the perception of the councils of the 1950s and 1960s, which did not have such dramatic, visible success.

Youths assumed these leadership positions with the support of the elders initially. Gradually, however, the youths who assumed leadership positions in political and economic affairs, as well as in ceremonial matters, became increasingly estranged from the elders. When budget cuts disadvantaged reservation residents, elders often placed the blame on young business councilmen. The new power and prestige of the council in the 1970s sometimes brought about intense competition among youths for council positions. The competition was often expressed as a struggle for power between the education clique and the militant youths. This struggle resulted in political paralysis one year, when the two sides had equal numbers of supporters on the council. After repeated voting, the council was still unable to elect officers because the vote was always tied. Finally, one side sued in tribal court to have a new election. The elders at Fort Belknap began to lose respect for the council and for the leadership ability of the youths. Moreover, as the agency area became the focal point for new economic activity, and most of the new houses were built there, elders in-

194

creasingly felt that Hays was disadvantaged. The proximity of Gros Ventre youths to Assiniboines at the agency further encouraged them to consult Assiniboines on cultural tradition and to revive the Milk River celebration. The youths' failure to defer to elders on such matters as the revival of religious ritual also helped alienate the generations.

While ritual revival has both brought about and given expression to conflict between elders and youths and between education clique and militant youths, it has also provided the means for the potential integration of the youths into the community, the validation of their leadership, and the eventual resolution of the conflict. The rituals build bridges between youths and elders to the extent that they activate kinship networks. Kinship ties involve obligations that elders find difficult to refuse. Through ritual participation youths are creating and extending networks of reciprocity among other youths. These networks bolster leadership positions. For the Gros Ventres still regard a leader as a "providing" man (or, to a lesser extent, woman). Through cultural or ritual revival youths provide not only property and food but also a heightened sense of activity, optimism, and progress. Elders temper and alter the cultural designs of youths, and in this way help give a particular form to the changing Gros Ventre culture. In so doing, both elders and youths express, perpetuate, and transform Gros Ventre cultural identity.

‹ 3 ›

Who Was Here First?
Gros Ventre and Assiniboine
Interpretations of History

The Gros Ventres and Assiniboines have shared the same territory, intermarried extensively, and borrowed ceremonies and customs from each other. But it is apparent to this observer that they have distinct cultural identities. Their cultural distinctiveness is in part a result of the fact that, although both tribes remember the same past, each has its own interpretations of past events and circumstances, and each group's interpretations contribute to its members' ideas about what kind of people they are. At Fort Belknap today, both Gros Ventres and Assiniboines frequently tell the story of how the two tribes came to settle on the Fort Belknap reservation. The Gros Ventre and Assiniboine versions of this story—which I call the "here first" story—differ, and each group's version works both to express and to shape its identity constructs. Folk histories orient social action, are used in the pursuit of political or economic ends, and encourage or retard particular kinds of changes.

In Chapter 1 we saw that the Fort Belknap tribes did not receive all the federal assistance, as inadequate as that was, to which they were entitled. The federal authorities openly compared the two tribes, and those comparisons affected policy and programs on the reservation. The negativism and competitiveness reflected in the "here first" stories were in great part fostered and encouraged by federal policies and their implementation. Furthermore, within this context, each tribe's perceptions of its relations with the other and its realization of each other's conflicting interpretations of history have shaped group identity and have given direction to the course of change at Fort Belknap.

The "Here First" Story: A Documentary Account

The question of occupancy of the Milk River valley is a complicated one. John Ewers addressed the problem, arguing convincingly that during the eighteenth and nineteenth centuries the Milk and Missouri river valleys were occupied by several groups. Alliances and the balance of power shifted several times, so that no one people had exclusive control or occupancy of the area.[1]

Before 1780 the Shoshones, Flatheads, Kutenais, Pend'Oreilles, and Crows controlled the valley of the upper Missouri and its tributaries, including the Milk. When a smallpox epidemic weakened the Shoshones and others, Blackfeet groups and their Gros Ventre allies who had acquired horses and firearms were able to dispossess the others of these lands. With the Piegans and Gros Ventres leading the way, the Shoshones were driven to the forty-ninth parallel (the Canadian border) by 1780 and by 1800 to the northern branches of the Missouri. By 1805 the Gros Ventres controlled the lower Milk area. With the help of the Blackfeet groups, they extended their control to the upper Missouri in the 1830s and 1840s, trading at American posts on that waterway (see map 2).

During the early nineteenth century the Assiniboines were between the Missouri and the Assiniboine rivers. One westernmost band (Big Devil's) habitually ranged as far west as the mouth of the Milk. Beginning in 1829 they traded at the mouth of the Yellowstone. Before that time they frequented more easterly posts. It is clear that the Assiniboines wintered north and east of the Milk, and usually only war parties came into Gros Ventre–Blackfeet territory. In 1838 the Assiniboines were greatly weakened by a smallpox epidemic and were reduced to about 400 tipis. Afterward they were unable to offer much challenge to the Gros Ventres. Edwin Denig, commenting on the Gros Ventre–Assiniboine wars, remarked in 1854, "Upon the whole the balance of damage has been decidedly against the Assiniboines."[2]

By 1851 the Assiniboines and Crows, on the eastern frontier of Gros Ventre country, were unable to penetrate beyond the Milk from the east or the mouth of the Musselshell on the south. But by 1853 the Gros Ventres were feuding with the Blackfeet groups and wanted to make peace with the Assiniboines. The Assiniboines particularly benefited from the peace as they received horses as gifts or in trade when they came to visit the Gros Ventres. Thus peace was made, and as a result, when the Gros Ventres and Blackfeet groups signed a peace treaty with the United States in 1855 and obtained recognition of their rights to certain territories in northern Montana (see map 3), the Gros Ventres agreed that their new friends the Assiniboines would hunt in their territory, in the lower Milk valley area as far as the Bear Paw Mountains and along the Missouri to the mouth of the Judith.[3]

The Gros Ventre friendship was apparently with the Canoer Mountain Village (Wah tó pah an da to, "those who propel boats") or Gens du Gauche division of the Upper Assiniboines (the westernmost group of Assiniboines). In 1855 Denig wrote that this Canoer Mountain Village group numbered 100 lodges (400 people) and that except when hunting, visiting, or trading in Gros Ventre territory, they normally ranged to Poplar River—farther west than the other Assiniboine divisions. Gauche, or Left Handed (also called Man Who Holds the Knife), was their headman until he died in 1843; then Whirlwind apparently became headman, at least by the 1850s. In 1855, at the time of the treaty, the Gros Ventres reportedly numbered 2,880. Both groups were entitled to annuity goods—the Assiniboines for fifteen years after their 1851 treaty and the Gros Ventres for ten years after their 1855 treaty. Federal agents distributed the goods on the Missouri throughout the late 1850s and 1860s, although goods did not always reach the tribes. The Gros Ventres' friendship with the Assiniboines was brittle, and when war broke out between the Gros Ventres and Blackfeet groups in 1861, the Gros Ventres began to shift southeast and ally themselves with the River or Northern Crows, trading at the mouth of the Musselshell rather than at Fort Benton. With hostile Blackfeet groups on the west and hostile Sioux on the east, the Gros Ventres could not control access to their country by themselves.[4]

About 1868 the Gros Ventres and Upper Assiniboines began to join forces against the Sioux in earnest. As the Crows gradually shifted to the southwest, the Gros Ventres and Assiniboines began to visit and intermarry regularly and to mount war parties against their common enemies. Neither group could have survived or continued to hunt in the lower Milk area without the help of the other. The Crows and Gros Ventres had suffered a major defeat at the hands of the Piegans in 1867 and probably lost many women and children. It may be that Gros Ventres began to intermarry with Assiniboines in greater than usual numbers during these years. According to their agent, an unspecified number of Gros Ventre men married 100 Assiniboine women in the summer of 1868. At this time, the Upper Assiniboine division called the Canoer Mountain Village was led by Long Hair, or Tonika, until his death in 1874. The agent reported that the Gros Ventres and Upper Assiniboines (no specific divisions were mentioned, but Long Hair's people must have been included) each totaled about 2,000 people in 1869. They apparently camped apart, but at least within a day or two of each other. In 1870 the agent reported sixty lodges of Assiniboines were camped with the main body of Gros Ventres—perhaps the relatives of the Gros Ventres' Assiniboine spouses or one or two bands of Canoer Mountain people; both seem possible interpretations. Both Gros Ventres and Assiniboines were issued supplies and received food and gifts from traders at the Fort Browning post on the Milk River. But after 1871 the ever-increasing numbers of Yankton and Santee Sioux in the area began to drive the Gros Ventres and Assiniboines westward into the Little Rockies and Bear Paws. An agency, Fort Belknap, was established farther west on the Milk, where they both received issues. By an act of Congress approved 15 April 1874, part of the Blackfeet–Gros Ventre territory described in the treaty of 1855 was set apart for the use and occupancy not only of the Blackfeet and the Gros Ventre tribes but also of the River Crows and "such other Indians as the President might from time to time locate thereon" (see map 3). This act served as subsequent justification for the government's enrollment of the Assiniboines at Fort Belknap agency.[5]

At Fort Belknap during the years 1873–1876 the agent issued supplies to both Gros Ventres and Assiniboines (including Upper Assiniboines from divisions other than Long Hair's). The Upper Assiniboines generally wintered on the Milk and frequented the agency more often and in larger numbers than the Gros Ventres, who generally wintered to the south on Clear and Beaver creeks. The agent reported that in 1874 there were 1,700 Upper Assiniboines in his vicinity and 960 Gros Ventres. The ranks of the Gros Ventres were reduced by smallpox in 1870, and several bands of Gros Ventres were apparently frequenting posts on the Missouri at this time. The Upper Assiniboines also received issues at the Lower Assiniboines' Fort Peck agency, at the mouth of the Milk. The Gros Ventres generally were far wealthier in horses than the Assiniboines, but during this time both the Gros Ventres and Assiniboines suffered periods of hunger and probably periods when one group shared food with the other. Both had periods of prosperity, particularly after a successful hunt, when they could sell many robes to the traders. In an effort to economize, the government closed the Fort Belknap agency in 1876 and ordered the Gros Ventres and Upper Assiniboines to go to Fort Peck for their goods. Many Upper Assiniboines complied; the Gros Ventres did not, for Fort Peck was in Sioux country. The closing of Fort Belknap produced considerable hardship for the Gros Ventres and their Assiniboine allies.[6]

In 1877 the United States Army was engaged in a conflict with the Nez Perce, who were moving toward the Bear Paws area in an effort to escape the troops by crossing the Canadian border. Several Assiniboine men were enlisted as scouts, including the chief headman of the Canoer Mountain Village Assiniboines at that time, Little Chief (who had been a band headman when Long Hair was chief headman). According to the recollections of Assiniboines and others living at that time, the Assiniboines understood that, in return for their aid, General Nelson Miles guaranteed the Assiniboines' subsistence and permanent occupancy of the Milk River valley area where they were living.[7]

In 1878 the government sent an agent to the reopened Fort Belknap agency. In 1879 Fort Assiniboine was established as a military post on the west side of the Bear Paws. Although annuities prescribed by treaty had expired for both tribes, at Fort Belknap the agent issued supplies to the Gros Ventres, and also to Upper Assiniboines who wintered on the Milk and frequented the agency regularly, although he continually asked the Indian Office whether or not he should issue to the Assiniboines. At Fort Assiniboine, both Gros Ventres and Assiniboines (and occasionally other tribes) were given assistance during hard times, apparently when the commander decided it was justified on humanitarian grounds or when it was expedient in order to prevent trouble between Indians and whites.[8]

During the 1870s the Gros Ventres and Assiniboines relied on each other, helped each other, and at times experienced conflicts that leaders worked determinedly to smooth over. On a particular occasion one group was probably more dependent on the other than at other times, and small bands or families of one tribe sometimes camped with a large group of the other. Each people, despite intermarriages with the other, had its own, distinct concept of group identity and a commitment to political and social autonomy. These distinctions still exist today.

The Expression of Identity Constructs in Folk History

Many of the stories that I have heard people at Fort Belknap tell about their past express identity constructs. The tribal characteristics emphasized vary with the story. The "here first" story appears to be the most widely known and most frequently told of the Gros Ventre and Assiniboine stories.

Gros Ventres

As I have discussed at length in Chapter 1, today when Gros Ventres characterize themselves they stress that they are a people who pursue success and in this way attain recognition for prominence from other Gros Ventres. Success is defined in terms of occupational or educational accomplishments and, to a certain extent, material well-being, for a prominent person must be able to take care of himself without depending on others. Recognition for prominence is achieved through generosity to others. Gros Ventres view themselves as exceedingly competitive, with whites as well as other Indians (and particularly with Assiniboines), and feel that in fair competition they should be able to best anyone. As they see it, their success is due in part to their assertive and tenacious as well as competitive nature. They also define themselves in terms of their custodial relationship to the two sacred pipe bundles, links between the Gros Ventres and the Creator. And finally, Gros Ventres view themselves as a people who have experienced reversals that were in large measure beyond their control, that were brought about by the Assiniboines, and that threaten the prosperity and proper order of things—namely, Gros Ventre primacy—at Fort Belknap.

The stories that Gros Ventres tell one another about their cultural history articulate these ideas about Gros Ventre identity. Aside from the "here first" story and tales of great deeds of warriors in preservation days, accounts of the generous deeds of old-timers are the most commonly told among the Gros Ventres. Individuals and groups (such as the moieties) are described as "good" in the context of their helping other individuals or the community at large. In telling how the Hays Fair was started by the old-timers, one elderly woman stressed that one man in particular

> made it big. Good man, that old fellow. He done it. God knows how he done it, but he *made* it, he made a big thing out of it. . . . Pretty soon they built the corrals and the buildings where they used to have the exhibits— that garden stuff, beef, pigs, chickens, beadwork, everything, just everything! Gee, those Gros Ventres were sure ambitious, and sure done things. They were self-supporting in them days. . . . They didn't get no kind of help. The government didn't help them with nothing. . . . Yeah, it sure was, that was great. Goodness, there was a lot of Gros Ventres in them days, and they'd have big camp.

She links the generosity of capable people with the strength and health of the Gros Ventre people—they were more numerous and unified when successful individuals donated to the community.[9]

Stories about the most respected business councilmen emphasize that they were self-made men who, in the words of one elderly man, "never did get any help . . . , any handouts . . . , what they got they· earned. So people used to draft them on the council." He says of these respected councilmen, old-timers all, "The reason why I say that them guys was real good is the humanitarian that they had, looking to their people; they really pitied their people." In the Gros Ventre view, one demonstrates that one is both successful and goodhearted (and deserving of high rank or social standing) by generously helping those less fortunate. In telling the life story of one respected old-timer councilman, one elderly man recalled, "He was a powerful man among the Gros Ventres. He had a lot of sway in there. He could sway them people any way he wanted to. They thought that much about him. He was one of the guys that went around, rode all over, anyone was having a difficulty, he was right there."

There is some variation in what individual Gros Ventres choose to emphasize when they tell the story of how the Gros Ventres and Assiniboines both came to settle at Fort Belknap. But storytellers all stress that the Gros Ventres were native to the Upper Milk River valley area and that only a very small group of Assiniboines subsequently were accepted into their territory. In these accounts, Gros Ventres were firmly ensconced and well off in horses and food and clothing, while the Assiniboines were poor and vulnerable and dependent on the Gros Ventres. The Gros Ventres are portrayed as generous to the Assiniboines and as a very successful people. Thus their primacy at Fort Belknap is well deserved. The stories fault Assiniboines both for being less successful than Gros Ventres and for being ungrateful, disloyal guests. The storytellers acknowledge that Gros Ventres eventually lost primacy in relation to the Assiniboines and fault Gros Ventre individuals as well as Assiniboines for the loss of primacy.

In one elderly woman's account many of these themes can be seen: "They [her Gros Ventre ancestors] said there was just a few of them [Assiniboines] come from Canada. And they said they were poor. They had dogs packing their pack. They come to this camp. They were so poor. Said the ladies just had half a buckskin for their gown and just like a slip they just had strings. And starving. . . . They came as far as Chinook. That's where they settled. . . . When they come there the Gros Ventres took pity on them. So I guess they finally settled over this way somewheres." In her story she is stressing that the Gros Ventres were native to the area while the Assiniboines were native to Canada. And the Gros Ventres in her account outnumbered the Assiniboines, so clearly they were firmly ensconced in the Milk valley area. She also stresses not only that the Assiniboines were in need of food ("starving") but that they lacked large herds of horses (for they had only dogs to carry their household goods) and fine clothes. By implication the Gros Ventres had many horses and better clothing. The Gros Ventres are portrayed not only as successful by the standards of prereservation days but also as generous, for they "took pity on" the Assiniboines and provided for them. The term "pity" also suggests an image of what supernaturals do when they give knowledge and power to humans during vision quests. The use of this term gives superordinate status to

Gros Ventres in relation to Assiniboines. Thus in this story the Gros Ventres deserve primacy over the Assiniboines at Fort Belknap.

These same themes are expressed in an elderly man's version:

> The way my grandfather told me, he said the Assiniboine tribe they were poor, had a small tribe. They must have got the heck knocked out of them someplace. It made them small, you know. The Gros Ventre tribe was big and they [Assiniboines] used to ask permission to camp close for protection, you know. They [Gros Ventres] said, "Sure, sure." The Gros Ventre were good to them. . . . From what I heard of what my grandfather said, there was only six families of the Assiniboines. A lot of them still in Canada. So that's how they got to be on Fort Belknap.

He emphasizes that the Gros Ventres not only outnumbered the Assiniboines but that they were stronger militarily, that the Assiniboines needed Gros Ventre protection to remain in the area. He points out the Gros Ventres' generosity: they were "good to" their visitors. By locating the main body of the Assiniboines in Canada, he challenges the notion that they were native to the Upper Milk area. His story continues:

> Them old-timers, they said that the Assiniboines were kinda, they didn't have no place, no place whatever. The Blackfeet must have been their enemy. They couldn't go to the white people. So there was a big Gros Ventre camp. And they thought, well they'll try that. Give it a try. And they did. There were only six families. They had their camps away from the, where the big Gros Ventre camp was. Six families ain't too much. Ain't very much. And finally, they noticed them. The Gros Ventres notice. These six camps were always someplace in the area. So they invited them in. Just a verbal, in them days there was no legal way anyway. I mean no legal adoption. They just kind of grew, kind of grew into the Gros Ventre tribe. . . . There were just six got in and they just kept getting in.

After reiterating that Assiniboines needed Gros Ventre protection, he stresses that Assiniboines settled at Fort Belknap without the *legal* right to do so. Legality of settlement became important in the twentieth century, during this man's youth, because of treaty claims and the allotment process. Gros Ventres have based their right to primacy on their 1855 treaty rights to north-central Montana. This narrator is asserting Gros Ventre primacy not only by virtue of their military superiority but also because Assiniboines could not claim treaty rights or "legal adoption."

Other elderly people's accounts embellish these themes. One woman described the arrival of the Assiniboines thus: "They were chased out of Canada by the Red Coats [British]. They crossed the Canadian line to be safe." Here this narrator is alluding to the fact that some Assiniboines joined with Crees and métis in revolting against the British during the Riel Rebellion. They were then considered outlaws by the Canadian government. She is indirectly contrasting the Gros Ventres (trusted allies of whites) with the Assiniboines, whom she portrays as renegades who entered the Milk valley to seek safe haven, rather than because this was their homeland. One man explained what his father had told him about the days when the father scouted for the U.S. Army. He patrolled the border, trying to keep tribes resident in Canada from crossing. He persuaded Assiniboines to stay in Canada by giving them presents, but later he saw that some of the presents (moccasins, for example) were being worn by Assiniboines in the Milk River camps. The father considered the Assiniboines' settlement in the Milk area to be not only a trespass but also evidence that Assiniboines abused Gros Ventre generosity. For in his view, the Assiniboines accepted gifts in return for not crossing the line, then, after they had the gifts, crossed the line anyway. An elderly woman gave this account of Gros Ventre generosity toward Assiniboines: "The old-timers said, 'It is winter; we can't send them away. Let them stay just for the winter.' But they stayed on and on." Again we see Gros Ventre generosity being exploited by the Assiniboines.

Another theme that emerges in these stories is that Gros Ventres had primacy over Assiniboines because that was how it was supposed to be. One woman said, "The Gros Ventres had this place [the reservation]. They were on top, should be on top." The Gros Ventres' success is viewed as in no small part a result of the supernatural assistance that came to them through their relations with the sacred pipe bundles. One elderly Gros Ventre man's account of a well-known story about Gros Ventre–Assiniboine relations makes this clear:

At one time I guess these Assiniboines were wondering why these Gros Ventres were so powerful in their battles and stuff. They were always fighting the Sioux and stuff and they had a pretty good survival rate, I guess. They were always, had plenty to eat. So the Assiniboines said, "Well, there's one thing we'll do—we'll sneak in there and steal their pipe and see if that's it." So they sneaked in there, and they did. They stole our [Flat] Pipe and kept it. Boy, I guess that winter was the hardest winter they ever had. Snow was deep and people were starving. And this one old lady that had this pipe . . . said this pipe spoke to her in a dream. Said, "You take me back to my people and you won't starve. They'll be meat here for you if you just take me back." So they had a big council there and they took this pipe [back]. They were sick and dying; they were having all kinds of bad things. So by golly, they made up a deal and tied the best horse to it that I suppose was in the best shape to travel. And they took this pipe back to the Gros Ventres, and, sure enough, it chinooked [warm winds came]. They [Assiniboines] sent the [hunting] party out . . . and there were some buffalo. And after that hands off the pipe. They didn't want nothing to do with it.

His account emphasizes that the success of the Gros Ventres was tied to their relationship with the pipe bundle; Assiniboines took the bundle out of envy. The Assiniboines' return of the pipe was, from the narrator's point of view, evidence that they recognized that the Gros Ventres had especially powerful rituals that were not accessible to the Assiniboines.

Another important theme that emerges in some accounts of how Assiniboines came to be at Fort Belknap is that a few Gros Ventres ("bullheaded" individualists in some stories) thoughtlessly married Assiniboine women, whose relatives then found it easier to "slip in." In one elderly man's story, "some of these Assiniboines would come in there and say, 'Well, I got a beautiful daughter but I ain't got no land.' 'Well, give her to me and I'll give you some land.' And this happened there and most of his wives, they were Assiniboines." After the first few Assiniboine families were taken in by the Gros Ventres, an elderly woman explained, "Gros Ventre men married them. And their relations kept coming." Another elderly woman told the story this way: "I blame _____ [a Gros Ventre man] for letting the Assiniboines in here. They used to not be around here. And they were poor. They didn't have horses like the Gros Ventres. They used big hounds. But he married some of them. He let them settle. They never found a paper on it, though." She is stressing that Gros Ventres, not Assiniboines, have treaty rights (a "paper") to Fort Belknap. This story of Gros Ventre individuals marrying Assiniboine women is often told in situations where Gros Ventres wish to criticize other Gros Ventres with Assiniboine ancestry; the stories are used to support an argument that Gros Ventre blood and Gros Ventre primacy were progressively weakened through intermarriage with Assiniboines.

Gros Ventre "here first" stories not only emphasize that the Gros Ventres were the first occupants of the Upper Milk River valley but also reaffirm their concept of themselves as a successful people who demonstrate their success to others through generosity and as a chosen people entrusted with special spiritual responsibilities (namely, the pipe bundles). The stories also cast the Assiniboines in a less favorable light by comparison, for they are portrayed as originally unsuccessful in Gros Ventre terms and as unable to compete with the Gros Ventres without duplicity. These accounts also express the value that Gros Ventres place on their primacy at Fort Belknap.

Assiniboines

When Assiniboines characterize themselves they stress that they are a people who "stick together" and "get along" with one another. They view themselves as directed by their old people, the wisest and most spiritual among them. Assiniboines portray themselves as a spiritual people who have continued to follow Indian religion and to perpetuate Indian ways despite perceived ridicule by others, including Gros Ventres. These traits are evidence of their moral worth as a people. Assiniboines contrast their history of getting along with each other and retaining Indian traditions with the Gros Ventres' history of fighting among themselves and rejecting Indian religion.

From the Assiniboine perspective, a good person is easygoing, obliging, and humble. Material generosity alone does not bring one the respect of others. One old man described the good person thus: "Easy person to talk to; anyone can say anything, ask favors, he'll always be glad to do it." An elderly woman stressed, "Helping people is our religion."

In the words of one young woman, "Assiniboines always stick together; they are unified." One middle-aged man typically denied the existence of bands or rivalry between kinship groups, insisting, "We are all one band." Their ability to get along with each other is contrasted with the Gros Ventre history of dissension. One elder, explaining how he suppressed dissent at an Assiniboine tribal meeting, said, "'Don't be like them,' I said, 'fighting among themselves, not getting anywhere.'" A young man, pointing to the Assiniboines' unwillingness to strike people from the tribal roll and their willingness to add people who were rejected by the Gros Ventres, explained, "Assiniboines they look at people and say, 'He's a member,' no matter what the blood degree is. He's an Indian because he can't be anything else. They [outside society] won't let him be." A young woman put it this way: "We Assiniboines don't say things about breeds [métis]. Gros Ventres put others down—Assiniboines and breeds—we never did that." In short, Gros Ventres are portrayed as less moral than Assiniboines, for, unlike Assiniboines, "the Gros Ventres don't take care of each other."

Gros Ventres are characterized as selfish: "Gros Ventres always want everything for themselves; they never want to be half and half." Yet Assiniboines note that they help Gros Ventres. One Assiniboine elder insisted that the Hays Fair was successful because Assiniboines helped: "That's how come the Hays Fair was what it was, 'cause they used to always help them. The whole one side was Assiniboine. And then their side. And over here was the River Assiniboine. . . . They always make it look like it was just done by themselves. It wasn't that way. The east side was always us [Lodgepole] over here." Thus, from the Assiniboine viewpoint, Gros Ventres lack humility.

One of the stories that elderly Assiniboines tell illustrates what can happen when people do not respect or get along with each other, the story of "how the agent was killed":

This [Assiniboine] man and his wife were having family problems and this lady she got mad and pouted and went back to her family, her mother and dad. So I guess she took his [mirror]—long ago the men really valued their stuff like a mirror because they used it to paint up with and comb their hair—and a hat. So I guess this man went over to·where his wife was. He told her, he said, "At least give me back my hat and my mirror. That's all I want. That's mine. Give it back to me." Here his father-in-law told him, "Well, you get out.... You're just like a dog." In other words, it's just like he would be a bastard. That's what it meant. So this man left but he was mad inside.... After that I guess he got his horse and everything and he stuck on a rifle and he went to where they was going for rations and here he caught up to his father-in-law.

The offended husband shot his father-in-law and, in shooting at the Indian police sent to arrest him, he also wounded Agent Simons, who later died. The story continues: "So that's when they punished all the men on the reservation. They cut their hair.... They said they were really pitiful. Some of them just wore scarves all the time.... Some of them got scared . . . ; even way late at night you could hear wagons [going south away from the river].... They ran away from the river [Milk River, where the shooting occurred and where most of the Assiniboines were living] and they came up here [Lodgepole]."

Assiniboines stress that it is important to be respectful to the elderly and to follow their direction. One woman asserted, "Assiniboines respect their elders; even if we don't agree, we say nothing. That's why we stick together." A young woman explained, "Assiniboine leadership is governed by age." Respect for the elderly is associated with the good, moral way of life, a way of life that is viewed as traditional. Elderly people symbolize traditional life. One woman explained why Assiniboines were successful in their undertakings:

They were always taught to respect the older people, and to respect each other.... They try to respect what the older people—their ideas, what they think because they think that they're wiser. They've lived their life and they know what things are.... Even if you don't like it, you don't say anything. You don't answer.... You think when you're going to say anything . . . and see if you have the right to say what you're going to say. You think before you say it. Don't just say anything that comes out of your mouth.... Maybe . . . that you're not that good to say something—talk about anyone.

Assiniboines emphasize that the ability to cooperate and the qualities of humility, patience, and caution set the Assiniboines apart from the Gros Ventres and account for much of the Assiniboines' success:

> Assiniboines sit back and watch the Gros Ventres. They know them to be a reactive people. Gros Ventres are confrontational. Assiniboines are not. . . . Assiniboines also opposed one-eighths but they sat back and waited. . . . They knew the Gros Ventres would act. They watched. They saw all the trouble caused and how bad the Gros Ventre social conflict, council and treaty committee conflict, looked to [congressmen]. So they accepted the one-eighths. Now they have two hundred more people. . . . The Assiniboines are crafty.

Assiniboines also feel good about themselves for holding on to traditional ways. One man stressed, "Assiniboines kept their culture. Gros Ventres did not." He was speaking of secular dances as well as religious ritual. A woman put it this way: "All through the years Assiniboines practiced these things. We did it quietly, without fanfare, not saying 'we did that. . . .' What we do comes from the heart, not to make the news." She was contrasting Assiniboines with Gros Ventres, for Assiniboines view Gros Ventres as a "showy" people who spend much time on *public* generosity.

The spiritual worth of Assiniboines, their identity as both a moral and a traditional people, is demonstrated, in the Assiniboine view, by the persistence of Assiniboine religion. Although a small minority of Assiniboines actually participate in hand games and spirit lodges or have spirit helpers, most point with pride and respect to the traditionalism of those that do. One elder explained, "We kept our ways—some didn't. That's our life. . . . The Gros Ventres never did care for their things. They just treated that hand game like a game. [Of course, this Assiniboine's viewpoint is not that of the Gros Ventres.] They would dance the owl dance and eat during it. But the Assiniboines take it seriously: it is sacred. . . . We Assiniboines—it was our life."

The stories that Assiniboine elders tell about their cultural history articulate and give supernatural sanction to these values. Questions about how contemporary customs began generally are answered by a story that tells of supernatural origin. The origin of the contemporary powwow is explained by one elder as follows: There was a man—a Sioux—who had a dream. "One day something appeared to him, some kind of a spirit, maybe in a dream." He had the same dream for four years and in the fourth year the spirit told him, "'The society of this religious dance has chosen you because you've taken good care of yourself and your people has respected you. . . . I know you got a child, I know you want to raise him to be respected,' this spirit said to this man. When the spirit mentioned that little boy this man got scared. . . . After that this man answered, 'Yes, I will, I will do it, what you told me.' " In other words, living a good life brings supernatural recognition. Once a spirit being makes contact, one must live a religious life; otherwise, there is the threat of supernatural sanction—that, for example, something might happen to one's child.

The man told the spirit that he would have to ask for help. The spirit replied, "That's good." The man told his wife, "I want you to cook some food, and I'm going to invite some four wise men, some older people's got spiritual powers, and I going to ask advice from them." When a person undertakes something important, he needs the help of others and the guidance of the elderly. Following the instructions given the man in his dream or vision, they made the regalia for the society dance (called the Raven or Grass Dance) and learned from him the songs and dances of the new society: "In those days people respect each other. Anybody request anything, should never say no. And of course this man was much respected by his people and his relatives." In the ceremony the man exhibited the ability to transform grass into raven feathers—this power was his gift from the spirit. The society also had social responsibilities: "Anyone lost a loved one, they get up food and they invite this man and they talk to him [comfort and encourage him]. . . . Or if somebody's mad, killing mad, . . . they talk to him, talk to him, and they calm down, and he quit his madness and lead a useful life again. . . . And there's somebody hard up on food, they go to these society people. . . . It's a society that they think about the people and trying to help their people." The story reaffirms values of sticking together and helping one another and finds supernatural sanctions for doing so. As the elder continued with the story he told how the Assiniboines conferred about purchasing this ceremony from the Sioux: "They all agree; they said, 'We try it, we gonna buy it.' " They achieved consensus, or stuck together.

Later, after the members of the Assiniboine society died, elders decided to revive the ceremony: "They talk about reorganize the society, and they all agreed." They prayed for the spirit's consent to "cut out all the rules, the strict rules that goes with this society because our people nowadays, young people, some they very mischievous. They gonna break the rules and we afraid if they break too many rules . . . it might cause us some kind of bad things to happen to us. . . . It be just for entertainment." And the old people selected men to carry on the ceremony. Here the narrator is justifying the directive role of elders, as sanctioned by the supernatural, and is noting that elders live up to their moral obligation when they help their less competent juniors.

210

Also, ritual innovations are validated by the decisions of elders who interceded with the spirit being who owned the society ceremony for permission to relax the rules. This secular dance was the forerunner of the modern powwow. Assiniboines also credit elders with the revival of the River powwow in the 1970s: "These old people were really interested and really tried hard."

The story of the origin of hand game bundles was explained similarly: "Our people they had some [bundles] somewhere made through visions" (a spirit being taught this ceremony to them). Hand game bundles had to be passed on to others on request: "If they ask you four times, you can't refuse them." But duplicates could be made. And innovations were sanctioned by supernatural signs. One bundle owner wanted to make a change in the ritual in accommodation to new conditions—"So I prayed and I got cloth offerings and I cooked up some food and I prayed"; that the new ceremony succeeded signaled supernatural approval. Individuals who were instructed in dreams to make or accept bundles and who refused to heed the call suffered supernatural retribution, according to Assiniboines. In one case, "He said he had had a dream three times, three times a person [spirit being] spoke to him telling him he had to make that bundle. The third time was the last warning. They had noticed he had been getting thinner and thinner." He was hesitating out of fear of ridicule by other Assiniboines who were embracing Catholicism, but he was prevailed upon by elders and "those who believed" to fulfill his duty. That bundle became "his life." Those who had a hand game bundle or other kinds of ritual responsibilities (such as knowledge of Sun Dance or Medicine Lodge ritual) and "put it away" also suffered retribution. Such a person literally "gave away his life."

In general, Assiniboines' stories cast historical events important to them as supernaturally ordained. The settlement at Lodgepole of a band of Assiniboines is explained, for example, as the result of a headman's dream: "He dreamed of a place that Assiniboines were to go and live. It was Lodgepole."

Assiniboine interpersonal relations reflect these ideals to a considerable extent. Public gatherings of Assiniboines, such as Treaty Committee meetings, are generally devoid of bitter dissension and, certainly, of criticism of elderly spokesmen. There are frequent community and family activities, particularly at Lodgepole, at which all interested Assiniboines generally are welcome. Much of Assiniboine ceremonial life is private. Most Assiniboine children are named at home, for example, rather than publicly. Many Assiniboine giveaways at the powwow are held not in the public arena but at the family camps. For Assiniboines, the private nature of their ceremonies reinforces their solidarity, their sense of togetherness. (Unlike the Gros Ventres, they say, they give things away to show respect and support for relatives and the community, not for personal aggrandizement.) When powwow offices are transferred, one elder explained, the accompanying giveaways on the part of the incumbent and the recipient are viewed as "gift exchange," not a demonstration of one's ability to make a large distribution. Young people generally do defer to elders. Assiniboine youths on the powwow committee credit elders, not themselves, with the committee's successes. And elders do not criticize these youths. Privately they may note with amusement (not disdain) that a mistake was made. But this comment by an elder is typical of the elders' official position: "Young people are running the powwow and doing a good job." Elders also are willing to sanction innovations of convenience. This accommodation is viewed as helping out, getting along, sticking together.

Among the Assiniboines, religious rituals have persisted—not in unchanged form, but they have persisted. For several years after the 1930s a core of dedicated "traditional families," a small minority among the Assiniboines, persisted in having hand games, seeking spirit helpers, singing the ceremonial songs, and continuing other forms of religious ritual (such as spirit lodges and the Sun Dance), sometimes through contacts with Fort Peck and Canadian Assiniboines and Rocky Boy Crees. Today these families generously open their religious activities to other Assiniboines, many of whom showed no interest previously but who now wish to participate. This acceptance is also a form of helping out, getting along, and sticking together, and it contributes to the perpetuation of traditional life. These rituals reaffirm the relationship of the participants with the supernatural and reinforce cooperation and goodwill among Assiniboines.

When Assiniboines tell the story of how they and the Gros Ventres came to settle on Fort Belknap reservation, individual versions vary slightly but some themes are consistent. Assiniboines stress that they, not the Gros Ventres, were native to the Upper Milk River valley area. They make some reference or allusion to the Assiniboines' relations with the United States Army. They emphasize that the Gros Ventres came to the Milk country "poor," and that Assiniboines—a "good" people—"pitied" them and shared their food with them. And the Gros Ventres are portrayed as morally inferior to the Assiniboines. In an elderly woman's version many of these themes are clear:

> They—the Assiniboines—were around Fort Assiniboine. And they lived around there, well, all over here, but they always wound up there because that's where they got their rations. There and then at Fort Benton.

212

And then sometimes someplace along the river here, then down to Wolf Point, then to Fort Union. . . . So that's where they were. And they said here where Havre is now . . . they said in one bend there they said there were just a lot of dry trees. They [the trees] were just white—that's the way they said in Indian—"just white with dry trees"—and here some Gros Ventres came.

In other words, Assiniboines dominated the area when a small number of Gros Ventres were allowed to camp on the Milk.

Her story continues this way:

They [the Gros Ventres] came from Canada. They came from way up north. They [her Assiniboine ancestors] said there was just a small group of them. They said that they [the Gros Ventres] would go to one, some tribe, and they would do something wrong. The way my mother-in-law used to always say—they say they sure must have been bad or crazy bunch because they'd do something and they'd get runned off. And they'd go to some other tribe of people and they'd get runned off. And that's how come they got clear over here and they camped among where them trees were—them dry trees.

The Gros Ventres were not native to the Milk River area, then, as the Assiniboines were. And the Assiniboines, with their greater numbers, controlled the area. The Gros Ventres were unable to get along with people, were of bad character, doing "something wrong" in relation to other people. The Assiniboines, on the other hand, or so it is implied, lived together peacefully helping and respecting one another. The story concludes thus: "Later they went over to Fort Assiniboine and that's when these Assiniboines shared their rations with them. . . . That's when they intermarried into the Assiniboine tribe, with that small group that came." She is emphasizing that the Assiniboines, a moral people, shared with the poor and weak Gros Ventres, even taking them as relatives. The story suggests that Assiniboines shared what they had because they were kind and obliging; there is no emphasis on their having wealth that obligated them to be generous, as in Gros Ventre stories of giving aid to Assiniboines.

In an elderly man's version, the "immorality" of the Gros Ventres is elaborated upon:

Assiniboines were roaming around this area. They were camped around Chinook. At that time Gros Ventres were west, by Browning. Then just thirteen Gros Ventre men came. They were outlaws, outcasts. They had no women. They asked for wives and got Assiniboine women. Later they were giving out rations at the agency at Chinook. These men came back. Assiniboines pitied them and shared rations with them. Others came. . . .

213

> They were outlaws, not sticking by their ways, when they came, so they never were able to get them back. . . . [Here he is referring to the contemporary situation in which Gros Ventre native religious ceremonies have not been revived.] And . . . the Gros Ventres just played with the [hand game]; they didn't pray.

He stresses that the Gros Ventres came as single men—men without family. Isolated individuals are poor by definition and morally suspect. Without women they cannot share or exchange food or participate in crucial social activities. To become social, moral men they depended on the Assiniboine women who married them and integrated them into family and group life. Assiniboines, then, are portrayed as generous, socially responsible, moral people. The narrator of the story characterizes the Gros Ventres as a people without commitment to values and standards of conduct, who do not "stick by their ways"; a people who are irreverent, disrespectful of spiritual life, for in his view they "played with" their ceremonies—that is, secularized them—instead of perpetuating them as sacred rites. The Assiniboines, in contrast, it is implied, retained their commitment to a spiritual life. The story also asserts that Assiniboines were well ensconced in the Fort Belknap area, whereas Gros Ventres were not. And the suggestion that only Assiniboines were entitled to rations from the federal government undermines the Gros Ventre claim to primacy through treaty right.

Another elderly man emphasizes the Assiniboines' ties with the United States Army:

> The Assiniboine people they put them up here west from present-day Harlem, Chinook . . . ; that's why they establish Fort Belknap Agency. That's why Fort Belknap Agency started. The Assiniboines they put them there. At the same time, the United States Cavalry they stationed at Fort Assiniboine. . . . Gros Ventres and Assiniboines, they live together at Chinook at that time and after they [Assiniboines] moved why naturally Gros Ventres have to come. Assiniboine chiefs at that time they live at Chinook. Gros Ventre chiefs come there and they want to share the commodities what United States government provide for Assiniboines. Rations. . . . So Assiniboines they agreed to share with Gros Ventres.

He is emphasizing that the Assiniboines are a moral people, a generous people, who shared with the less well-off Gros Ventres. In this story, the Assiniboines also are recognized by the federal government as first occupants of the Milk River valley and as important potential allies of the army. In Assiniboine folk history there is an account of how Assiniboine elders promised to help General Miles in his battle against Chief Joseph's Nez Perce near present-day Chinook in 1877; in return, the general promised them the right to occupy the Milk River area. The Gros Ventres, it is said, did not help Miles because they were not in the area. This is the incident indirectly referred to in the above story. These stories of the agreement with Miles reaffirm the Assiniboines' respect for old people and are testimony to the wisdom of following the elders, for Assiniboines did remain in the Milk River area.

These stories reaffirm the Assiniboines' concept of their cultural identity and their views on Gros Ventre identity. The stories portray the Assiniboines as the first occupants of the Upper Milk valley and as generous helpers of the difficult Gros Ventres. The Gros Ventres are presented as obstacles to the creation of a harmonious, prosperous society at Fort Belknap.

In the Gros Ventres' and Assiniboines' "here first" stories, different or conflicting interpretations of the same events evolved out of their different cultural and social vantage points. For example, Gros Ventres interpret the marriages of Gros Ventres and Assiniboines as acts of generosity by the Gros Ventre wife takers, who then supported their new in-laws. Assiniboines interpret the marriages as acts of generosity by the Assiniboine wife givers, who integrated their outcast in-laws into society. Narrators in both tribes stress that Gros Ventre men married Assiniboine women, although there were in actuality marriages between Assiniboine men and Gros Ventre women. Gros Ventres interpret the marriages as symbolic of their greater wealth and ability and of their primacy at Fort Belknap, for the groom pays brideprice in horses. And the Assiniboines interpret the marriages as symbolic of their greater nurturing behavior toward kin, for the bride brings food and moccasins to the groom. As discussed in Chapter 1, the Gros Ventres' role in trade was enhanced by their ownership of many horses and they emphasized generous distribution of material wealth in the validation of status. The horse-poor Assiniboines relied more on employment with agents, traders, and the military; thus they emphasized ties with the army more than the Gros Ventres did in validating their status.

The theme of each tribe's "here first" story is superiority over (and negative evaluation of) the other tribe. Thus the Assiniboines' stories ignore their receipt of horses from Gros Ventres and the history of alliance and joint defense. Similarly, the Gros Ventres ignore the alliance and the fact that, apparently with Gros Ventre consent, negotiations for the 1887 cession of lands included Assiniboines. Both the Assiniboines and the Gros Ventres stress their occupancy of the area north of the Bear Paws—the site of the present-day reservation—despite the fact that they both ranged over a wider area than that. Both tend to deemphasize or ignore the fact that each borrowed ceremonies from the other (the Gros Ventres purchased the Grass Dance

215

from the Assiniboines, for example, and the Assiniboines obtained the hand game ceremony from the Gros Ventres). The emotions—positive and negative—evoked by the stories figure in relations between the tribes.

Folk History in Social Relations

Narrators ignore, emphasize, and reinterpret the histories they have learned, so that the stories change over time as they are made relevant to new audiences. The stories, made appropriate to new circumstances, influence people to behave in particular, sometimes new ways.

When I was at Fort Belknap, the Gros Ventres used the "here first" story to mobilize support for political goals, specifically to persuade a majority of Gros Ventres to change the tribal membership rolls. The Gros Ventres related the story often in visits with other Gros Ventres. The Gros Ventre version of the story played on Gros Ventre people's emotions so that they were moved to vote against the enrollment (or the recognition of the previous enrollment) of individuals with mixed Assiniboine–Gros Ventre ancestry. Rejection of persons with more Assiniboine than Gros Ventre blood symbolically affirmed the Gros Ventres' primacy at Fort Belknap. Their action also brought a measure of hope that, since they had been able to mobilize a majority of the Gros Ventres to oppose the federal government's efforts to prevent the expulsion of individuals from the existing tribal roll, the Gros Ventres might be able to make political gains. One possible gain would have been to obtain the government's acknowledgment of their right to a hearing on the legitimacy of the Little Rockies cession.

The "here first" narrative was the story most frequently told when I inquired about reservation history during 1979–1984. At this time the Gros Ventres were experiencing considerable discord because of tension between older and some younger, well-educated reservation residents. The youths were eager to revive Gros Ventre customs and ceremonies; the older Gros Ventres were resentful of what they thought was the young people's implied disapproval or criticism of them. The young Gros Ventres grew increasingly frustrated because they thought that, unlike the Gros Ventres, Assiniboines had an active ritual life centering on native ceremonies. In this context, the Gros Ventres' perception of their loss of primacy in relation to the Assiniboines received new impetus. As we shall see, these circumstances—which aggravated Gros Ventre resentment toward Assiniboines—also help to account for the change in the way the Assiniboines are presented in the "here first" story today as opposed to the 1920s and 1930s versions.

When the Assiniboines were holding tribal meetings to discuss the enrollment of the individuals of mixed Assiniboine–Gros Ventre ancestry whom the Gros Ventres had removed from their tribal roll, elderly leaders persuaded them to accept the persons rejected by the Gros Ventres by stressing, through the vehicle of the "here first" story, the importance of getting along with one another and sticking together and by holding up the bickering Gros Ventres as an example of what could happen if they were "selfish" and divisive. They appealed to the Assiniboines' view of themselves as a people morally and spiritually superior to the Gros Ventres. In voting to accept the individuals, the Assiniboines also strengthened their political position on the reservation because many of the newly enrolled "Assiniboines" or their relatives were disposed to work on behalf of Assiniboine interests.

The "here first" stories told in the 1920s and 1930s differed in some key respects from the stories told in the 1980s. To a considerable extent the differences reflect the different political goals of the narrators in the three eras. The contrasts also reflect the different social contexts and relations in which the narrators' versions appear.

Several versions of the "here first" story were recorded in the 1920s, for this period was a time of great political conflict over the nature of Gros Ventre and Assiniboine relations. The Gros Ventres were struggling to gain more authority in agency affairs, trying to wrest control over reservation resources from the whites who had mismanaged and misappropriated those resources for more than forty years. They were struggling also to win the federal government's acknowledgment of their unjust treatment and compensation for the injustice. The Assiniboines, too, were engaged in a struggle with the government. They wanted greater economic assistance and sought to prevent the Gros Ventres from gaining political control that would endanger Assiniboine status on the reservation. The struggle between Indians and whites shaped the two tribes' relations with each other during this period. The Gros Ventres' pursuit of primacy was given new impetus, for the establishment of an Enrollment Commission of 1921 (composed of one Gros Ventre, one Assiniboine, and the superintendent) to determine who would receive allotments offered an opportunity for Gros Ventres to control the criteria for allotment and thereby attain greater self-determination and demonstrate primacy in relation to the Assiniboines. Apparently the Gros Ventre member of the commission dominated the proceedings, for seventy-six individuals who were living among the Assiniboines were rejected for the allotment roll. Forty-three were Northern or Canadian Assiniboines, who were not members of Little Chief's Upper Assiniboines in the early 1870s; the others were Sioux, Crees, French-Chippewas, and Lower Assiniboines. The "here first" stories recorded in 1921 and 1922 reflect this sociopolitical context.[10]

This 1922 version from a fifty-year-old Gros Ventre is typical of the stories transcribed during the enrollment controversy. In the story, as in the versions of the 1980s, the Gros Ventres are presented as initially dominant over the Assiniboines numerically and in terms of wealth. The Assiniboines are described as traveling with dogs and as benefiting from Gros Ventre generosity. And the Gros Ventres, not the Assiniboines, are shown to be entitled to government rations. Thus the theme of Gros Ventre primacy is given support throughout. Note this excerpt:

> When I was five years old [1877] the Gros Ventres were camped on Two Creeks [north and south fork of Milk River] near where Chinook, Montana, is now. When we were camped on Two Creeks, old Fort Belknap was located where Chinook is now. . . . At this time there were some Assiniboines camped there also. When the time came, the day set for the Gros Ventres to be at the agency to receive these rations, the Assiniboines got ready to go also; they were camped with the Gros Ventres at the time, so they got ready and hooked up their dogs to go to the agency. . . . This agent told them, the Assiniboines, that these rations belonged to the Gros Ventres. Then he told the Gros Ventres that if they wanted to they could give some to these Assiniboines as it seemed that they were hungry and needed grub. The Gros Ventre chiefs met in council and talked it over among themselves. . . . The Gros Ventres then went to the agent and told him that they had agreed among themselves to give them half of the rations. . . . After the rations were issued the agent told the Gros Ventre chiefs that within a few days he was going to make an annuity issue, clothes, blankets. . . . They [the Gros Ventre chiefs] agreed that the Assiniboines were needy and had to have this stuff, so they decided to give them part of the annuity issue.[11]

But this version, and others recorded during 1921–22, differ in a few respects from the contemporary ones. The above narrative begins, "When I was a boy the Gros Ventres used to move around all over this country here and when we moved to the lower country we met these Assiniboines every once in a while." There is no claim of exclusive occupancy of northern Montana. And an essential element of the remainder of the story is the identification of the "original Assiniboines," whom the Gros Ventres accepted as valued allies and with whom they agreed to share reservation resources. These original Assiniboines are contrasted with the "Canadian Indians," renegades and refugees who surreptitiously slipped into the reservation from the late 1870s to the early twentieth century. Thus, as the story continues, the Gros Ventre chiefs said,

> "We are at war with the Sioux tribe and ought to take the Assiniboines in to help fight the Sioux and be a part of the Gros Ventre tribe and to keep them with them in the tribe." They decided to take them into the tribe and told the agent so. . . . When the Assiniboines were taken into the tribe there were about thirty or forty lodges of them. . . . Whenever the Gros Ventres moved to the agency to get rations the Assiniboines were always there waiting for rations. At that time whenever I saw the Assiniboine camp there would be more lodges. It seemed that since we took in the thirty or forty lodges all the Assiniboine-speaking Indians would come into the tribe and draw rations just the same as the other Assiniboines did. Soon after the original Assiniboines were taken into the tribe they seemed to increase so fast that there were more Assiniboine lodges than Gros Ventre. . . . A few years after, they had a big fight in Canada— the Northern Assiniboine, Red River half-breeds [métis] and other Indians against the Canadian government. Soon after we heard of this fight we heard that some of the Assiniboines had run away from the fight and came to this reservation and were in the Assiniboine camp. . . . On ration days when I went to the agency with my father I saw strange Assiniboines among the original Assiniboines and I knew that they were strangers. After these Assiniboines came from Canada we heard that they were drawing rations. It was supposed that only the original Assiniboines were to draw rations but the Canadian Assiniboines were drawing rations also.[12]

The stories do not explain why, if the Gros Ventres were much more numerous than the forty lodges of Assiniboines originally taken into the tribe, the rations and goods were equally divided between the two tribes, as the narrator describes. In the 1920s, however, the policy of the Gros Ventre business council was to try to give each tribe an approximately equal share of reservation resources, regardless of population size.

One other important theme in the remainder of the narrative is that the Gros Ventres were deceived and betrayed by the federal government, which allowed the trespass. Thus, as the story continues, the Gros Ventre chief went to the agent to object to the Canadian Assiniboines' living on Fort Belknap and drawing rations: "They are not a part of the original Assiniboines that we took into the tribe." The agent responded that the Assiniboines whom the Gros Ventres had accepted into their tribe had "recommended that I issue rations to the Canadian Assiniboines, that if we ran them off they would starve to death. . . ." "The agent said that there would be allotments made to us, . . . that a roll of all the rightful Indians who belonged here would be made, and that all the Canadian Assiniboines would be rejected when the roll was made. We just kept them here in order to keep them from starving to death." The narrator thus sought to persuade the government to support the decision of the Enrollment Commission. The fact that the Assiniboines were challenging the Enrollment Commission's findings threatened Gros Ventre primacy: "Now the Assiniboines are trying to run everything on the reservation, to get ahead of the Gros Ventres, trying to get these people admitted on the rolls. The Gros Ventres understand that if any adoptions are to be made, it is up to the Gros Ventres to make the adoptions. . . . I am not kicking against the original Assiniboines that were taken into the tribe but object to them taking any other Assiniboines into their tribe without the permission of the Gros Ventres."[13]

The Assiniboines' "here first" story in 1921 and 1922 had many of the same elements as the story they told in the 1980s:

> We Assiniboine Indians got here in this part the country, more than sixty years [ago]. And . . . we have first right in this reservation. . . . We come from west . . . ; we was going west by Milk River. . . . And we move up to Chinook. . . . Before this we seeing few families of Gros Ventre Indians come to our chief and prayed wish to stay with us Indians. So the Assiniboine chief take them as adopt. They stayed with us eversince. . . . Adjutant come and asking the Indian chiefs [to] lease some of they land to government so they can build a fort for a guard the Indians. The adjutant tell us that enemy Nez Perces will come fight us Assiniboine Indians. And they did come and fight us but we save ourself and our country, too. But the Gros Ventre Indians that was with us before this they left us and going back south. But after the fight was over, then [the Gros Ventres] got back again and prayed the chief. Our chief let them be with us. So then adopt the Gros Ventre Indians.

This story, like the 1980s version, stresses that the Gros Ventres were vulnerable and dependent on the kindness of the Assiniboines: the Gros Ventres "prayed to" the Assiniboines, whom they recognized as stronger and more numerous than themselves. In another account, an elderly man emphasized, "Forty-five years ago was the time of the Nez Perce war in September 1877. There wasn't enough Gros Ventres to adopt the Assiniboines. There were more Assiniboines than Gros Ventres." The assistance that the Assiniboines gave General Miles against the Nez Perce in 1877 was emphasized as evidence that the Assiniboines had earned a place at Fort Belknap through service to the United States Army. Another narrator also stressed that the Assiniboines' aid to the army gave them legal or "treaty" rights at Fort Belknap and that the Gros Ventres' claim was suspect: "They say they own this reservation. If they do why they deserted the Assiniboine tribe and their government troops when the Nez Perce Indians coming into the Milk River region . . . ? They violated their treaties but the Assiniboine tribe uphold their treaties with the government of the United States."[14]

Unlike today's Assiniboines, however, those of the 1920s portrayed themselves as occupying or controlling the Milk River valley before the Gros Ventres; they did not present themselves as native occupants: the first narrator quoted above puts the Assiniboines in control in the valley about 1860. Another aspect of the Assiniboine "here first" story that was specific to the 1920s (the time of the allotment crisis) was the stress on the acceptance of the Northern Assiniboines, the "Canadian bunch" of Assiniboines, as indicative of the Assiniboines' moral superiority. In some versions, the acceptance of and assistance to these northern people is justified on the grounds that they are kin and therefore must be fed, be incorporated into society. One elderly Assiniboine put it this way: "The Assiniboine Indians referred to as Northern Assiniboines were recognized on the reservation the same as other Assiniboine Indians, that they were one people, and that the Gros Ventres should remember the advice given them by their dead ancestors and try and get along peacefully with the Assiniboines." Gros Ventre objections to the northern bands are characterized as "only for selfishness." Another man explained that the Assiniboines at Fort Belknap clearly "adopted" the "Canadian bunch"; otherwise, they would not have been issued rations. Another said that the Gros Ventres were trying to "separate us from our own relatives . . . [but] they are our own tribe, our own relatives. Their grandparents are our own grandparents. Therefore they have equal rights with us on the Fort Belknap reservation." The Assiniboine narrators tried to present the Gros Ventres as unreasonable, difficult people and characterized the Assiniboines as cooperative and eager to follow the government's lead.[15]

The Gros Ventre "here first" stories recorded in 1936, when both tribes' claims against the government for treaty violations were being settled, show a hardening in the Gros Ventre attitude toward both Assiniboines and the federal government. Their attitude was fostered by the government's disregard of the Enrollment Commission's findings and by its failure to live up to the promises made when the Gros Ventres accepted the Indian Reorganization Act in 1934. The BIA had guaranteed that each tribe could manage *its own* affairs and, to a considerable extent, could make its own decisions without federal interference. The earlier Assiniboine victory in the enrollment issue was a blow to the Gros Ventres' image of themselves, to their pursuit of primacy. In 1936, when Gros Ventres were trying to persuade the government to live up to its promises of political autonomy in relation to the Assiniboines, *all* the Assiniboines are portrayed as trespassers in the "here first" story—gone is the category of "original Assiniboine":

> Our people have always told us that the Fort Belknap reservation was exclusively ours. They got that country by conquest. They drove the Snakes out of that country, probably before the Revolutionary days. Now, from that time on until the treaty of October 17, 1855, the Gros Ventres defended that territory. They were part of the Blackfeet Nation. The Piegans, Bloods, and Gros Ventres were part of the Blackfeet Nation. Under the treaty of October 17, 1855, a specified territory was set aside for the use of the Gros Ventres for their absolute control. They understood that land to be their exclusive territory. . . . They did not consent in the first place to have other Indians placed on that territory. . . . In the next place, the Gros Ventres as a tribe are in the Blackfeet Nation [the only groups with treaty rights to the Milk River valley area] and never adopted the Assiniboines.

In 1936 a Gros Ventre spokesman argued to officials that the Gros Ventres wanted "to be paid for the land that the Assiniboines have been allotted." The story stresses the Gros Ventres' right to exclusive control of Fort Belknap by reason of their military control: "They got that country by conquest. They drove the Snakes out of that country." And the 1855 treaty, a legal document made at a time when the Gros Ventres were formidable enough to have been courted by the government and to have perceived themselves as having self-determination, is emphasized. The narrator stresses that there was no legal, documented "adoption" of Assiniboines by Gros Ventres. Gros Ventre leaders insisted to officials at this time, "We find in the records of the Court of Claims that the Assiniboines just moved across north of the Missouri River without any formal orders. . . . The Assiniboines had their treaty in 1851 prior to the treaty of 1855. Why didn't they assert their rights before?"[16]

The Assiniboines, desperate at this time to complete "economic rehabilitation" under the provisions of the IRA, were alarmed by government threats that if the tribes did not form a joint government, the economic development program would be jeopardized. They attempted to thwart the Gros Ventres' efforts to secure a separate tribal government by countering Gros Ventre claims of control of the north-central Montana area with their own. An Assiniboine spokesman told officials, "We have always lived in that country. We always fought other tribes off when they tried to come on that land." This elder's story is typical:

> As far as being in that territory, we have been there a long time before the treaties were made. We were there far before the Gros Ventres. They came

from Canada into our country. The Assiniboines had a larger population and they occupied more property at that time. We went through three [smallpox epidemics] that reduced the Assiniboine nation. After that we didn't cover as big a territory as we used to occupy so that made it look like we never had no right there. We fought all the neighboring tribes before the treaties were made. The Assiniboines were noted warriors. . . . It should be remembered that we have been there a long time before the treaties were made.

Thus he claims native occupancy. The narrators also stressed that through intermarriage the Gros Ventres and Assiniboines were one family. For example, an elder asserted during his version of the "here first" story, "There are many Gros Ventre men married to Assiniboine women. There are half Assiniboine and half Gros Ventre on that reservation. These Gros Ventres' children are half Assiniboine and half Gros Ventre." In this way he sought to counter Gros Ventre efforts to achieve political autonomy in relation to the Assiniboines. And Assiniboine spokesmen also denied that the Gros Ventres and Assiniboines had ever had problems getting along with one another. One man remarked, "We have always gotten along with the Gros Ventres fine until this claim was awarded them. Some of the statements made indicate that they have been bucking the Assiniboines and have been protesting them being on the reservation. I never heard nothing about it." Another stressed how Assiniboines had aided the ungrateful Gros Ventres:

I am very much surprised to hear our friends make all this protest talk against the Assiniboines. It all happened one hundred years ago. We have been protecting our friends, the Gros Ventres, in wars with different tribes. We know the Gros Ventres for a long time and we always made friends with them. . . . If these protests were made then . . . there would be no Gros Ventres left in that part of the country because the Assiniboine population is greater than that of the Gros Ventre. I am not trying to make anybody feel bad at this time, but I am telling the truth.[17]

Thus in the 1930s (as in the 1920s) Assiniboines portrayed Gros Ventres as difficult to get along with, as unreasonable.

By the 1970s and 1980s the Gros Ventre and Assiniboine attitudes toward each other had hardened in response to conflict over the claim payment and the ritual revival. Assiniboines who in the 1920s and 1930s had talked about Gros Ventre families settling among them now spoke of Gros Ventre men arriving alone. Gros Ventres who mentioned "original" Assiniboines in the 1980s asserted that there were only a few families; in the 1920s the number mentioned was about five times greater. The feeling that the federal government had betrayed them

223

was less in evidence among Gros Ventres in the 1980s than in the 1920s and 1930s; in the contemporary era the emphasis was on how the Assiniboines had abused the Gros Ventres' friendship and trust. And both groups' 1980s versions definitely assert native occupancy, as they had begun to do in the 1930s.

Identity and the Multitribal Context

Gros Ventres and Assiniboines share some general conceptualizations and values. There are some broad understandings—for example, about social relations, the supernatural, and the reservation experience itself—that members of both tribes have in common. And there is a complex of social institutions that articulate these understandings and in which they all participate in some fashion or to some degree. Yet the subtleties of these common understandings point to tribal variation. The variations are specialized versions of similar but not identical concepts and value orientations. The variation is due in part to differences in the two peoples' cultural heritage and historical relationships. But Gros Ventre and Assiniboine cultural identities have taken form in a multitribal community. And the fact of a jointly experienced history also has affected group identities and the ways they changed.

Gros Ventres and Assiniboines share the ideal of generosity and institutions for its expression, and they have some common understandings about how humans can obtain supernatural aid and about how to deal with the dominant white society. This is to be expected, for they have a common heritage of a big-game hunting/pastoral economy and some associated features, similar kinds of experiences dealing with the incursions of whites into their territory, and similar kinds of opportunities and limitations as a result of reservation settlement.

When they were equestrian hunters, for example, generosity was a cultural ideal shared by both tribes before and after contact with whites. It was an integral part of the ethos of both. For their hunting way of life, sharing and gift giving had practical implications and was associated with leadership roles. Such generosity was institutionalized and its importance symbolized in a ritual context. Most ceremonies involved the presentation of food and gifts from one family or group to others. These rituals took distinctive forms for Gros Ventres and Assiniboines; yet there were occasions when one tribe—or a segment of one—would act as host to the other in a jointly attended ceremony. The coming of whites necessitated the formation of more regular alliances between bands or tribes; gift exchange of one sort or another was a means to initiate and maintain alliances. Generosity of wealthy or influential men—those successful in trade or in dealings with the army, for example—had special emphasis in this era, particularly in the context of intermediary chieftainship. Traders, for example, gave gifts to prominent Gros Ventre men and Assiniboine headmen alike.[18] On the reservation, generosity and sharing had new importance as a strategy for survival in an era when resources were more limited and access to them was controlled by federal officials. Giveaway ceremonies worked to a degree to level economic differentials. Today, as well, individuals of both tribes subscribe to the idea that accumulating property to be given away in honor of a relative is a good thing. And Indians stress that they accumulate material possessions not to "hoard" them (as whites do) but rather to bestow them on others. The characteristic of generosity serves for Gros Ventres and Assiniboines alike to highlight the Indian's moral superiority to whites. This remark by a Gros Ventre elder in 1983 expresses the sentiments of members of both tribes:

> The Indian's a generous person really. He'll give you anything he's got. They [Gros Ventres] liked doing that. I mean, it was something that I think all Indians like; that's why I every once in a while get to talking to people on the outside and always tease them about putting their money away. The Indian's the only one person I know that keeps money in circulation. So if you're going to have [say] anything about a recession, don't blame it on the Indians, because it ain't the Indians that's a doing it. It's you fellows doing it by hiding your money all the time. The Indian he keeps it a rolling.

Similarly, both peoples shared certain ideas about relations with the supernatural: humans could obtain aid from supernatural sources through intense, sincere thought. Rituals that worked on this principle (such as the Sun Dance) were common to both tribes. When humans petitioned the supernatural, they strove to provoke pity in the supernatural; thus they suffered in a variety of ways during the course of particular rituals. Concepts about the nature of thought—that it can cause things to happen—fuel contemporary belief in "bad medicine" as an explanation for misfortune and illness. Moreover, power attained from supernatural sources was a form of property. It could be transferred, but the transfer had to be legitimate.[19]

Both peoples have experienced the effects of being Indian in a world dominated by whites and both have made their way in the physical, socioeconomic, and political confines of a reservation community. Accommodation rather than overt resistance was the strategy both groups initially adopted, for neither had experienced all-out war with

225

the United States Army, and in fact had been aided against their enemies by the army. Thus whites appeared to offer opportunities as much as or more than impediments or problems. The specific nature of Gros Ventre and Assiniboine strategies in their attempts to reach accommodation with whites varied, but both were "friendly Indians" in the context of nineteenth-century Indian–white politics on the Northern Plains. The constraints of reservation life affected both tribes. With resources controlled by white administrators, for example, both Gros Ventres and Assiniboines expected their leaders to secure food and property for them by appearing to cooperate with whites. The general outlines of reservation politics, then, are common to both tribes.

On another level, the Gros Ventres and the Assiniboines have their own ways of working out these common understandings—the cultural ideal of generosity, ideas about access to supernatural assistance, and accommodation as a way of coping with encapsulation within a dominant society, to name but a few—in the social arena. Thus, while similar concepts about the world may or may not be socially articulated through the same symbolic forms, an analysis of the symbols' meanings nonetheless reveals variation in these views. Variation is due in part to differences in cultural heritage and in part to the fact that the two tribes have jointly occupied the reservation, aware of each other's views and affected by each other's actions.

Take, for example, the ideal of generosity. Today this ideal is symbolically expressed in the context of public giveaway ceremonies that are part of several kinds of rituals in which both Gros Ventres and Assiniboines participate. One of the most important of these rituals is the Milk River powwow held each summer. Individuals from both tribes fill the roles of doners, recipients, singers, witnesses, and sometimes announcers (when there are two announcers) during any particular ceremony. Yet the giveaway means (and has meant in the past) something different to the Gros Ventre participants and observers than to the Assiniboines. To the Gros Ventres, public giving away provides a means to attain others' acceptance of high social status and also acknowledgment that a person is "somebody," is successful, in, for example, competing in the society at large. Assiniboines emphasize that the giveaway primarily is testimony to one's nurturance of and bonds with kin. Thus the quantity of property given is more important for the Gros Ventres than for the Assiniboines. And giving away in the public arena is especially important to Gros Ventres; Assiniboines just as often hold giveaways privately in camp (in the family headquarters). When Assiniboines give to other Assiniboines (all of whom are described as kin in some contexts), such generosity strengthens the bonds of kinship between doner and recipient. A Gros Ventre doner, to a great extent, views the distribution of his goods as testimony to his success.[20]

The Gros Ventres' commitment to attaining social standing through generous distribution is in part a result of a long tradition that (as discussed in Chapter 1) began upon their acquisition of large horse herds. The Assiniboines, much less affluent in horses, probably put more emphasis on generalized sharing and on extending their social networks. On the reservation, several Gros Ventre men were apparently wealthy in stock; those Assiniboines who had large herds were by and large women married to whites or, later, their descendants. Gros Ventres continued their commitment to the pursuit of prominence through generous distribution and, as a whole, were more prosperous than the Assiniboines. The Assiniboines also had frequent visits from Assiniboines in Canada and at Fort Peck reservation in eastern Montana; the burden of sharing with these visitors may have undermined their ability to accumulate stock and other property. The Gros Ventres, then, were able to view themselves as socially superior and materially better off than the Assiniboines, and they prided themselves on carrying off larger celebrations (which included numerous giveaways) than the Assiniboines. The differences in giveaway tradition reflect the Gros Ventres' pursuit of primacy at Fort Belknap—their behavior as prominent men in relation to needy Assiniboines—and the Assiniboines' effort to cope with economic problems by generalized sharing and to counter Gros Ventre primacy by alliances with other groups.

There are contrasts in the way that Gros Ventres and Assiniboines view relations with the supernatural. Intense and sincere thought, or prayer, is facilitated by and sometimes dependent on the guidance of a qualified person. This dependence on an authority is emphasized more among the Gros Ventres, who have a clearly recalled age-grade tradition associated with degrees of ritual authority and a tradition of a priesthood in charge of tribal medicine bundles and other ceremonies. Among the Assiniboines, there was and is little that an individual who dreams or otherwise receives a personal message from the supernatural lacks authority to do. Moreover, the transfer of power is obligatory among Assiniboines if a proper request (involving a gift or payment) is made: the moral obligation to help others is strong in the realm of religious prerogatives, just as in economic and social spheres. But Gros Ventres view transfer of the right to pray—in certain ways (with a pipe, a hand game bundle, and so on), at least—as legitimate only when it is earned through some proper form of apprenticeship. And a request alone does not automatically guarantee one's acceptance as an apprentice. As has been discussed in Chapter 2, it has been Assiniboines who have responded to Gros Ventre youths' requests for instruction and leadership in ritual revitalization, for Assiniboine elders do not feel bound, as Gros Ventres do, to do things exactly as their ancestral ritual authorities did. Whereas Gros Ventres often attribute illness to mistakes resulting from inadequate apprenticeship, Assiniboines generally attribute illness to failure to pursue wholeheartedly the powers and responsibilities gained.

And the two tribes have experienced Catholicism differently. Gros Ventres are generally more strongly committed and committed in far larger numbers than Assiniboines. Elderly Gros Ventres, for example, unlike Assiniboines, generally are uncomfortable about participating in both Indian religion and Catholicism, for the two faiths differ in their ritual symbolism and associated priestly knowledge. The church services at Hays are well attended, and virtually every Gros Ventre family is represented. In contrast, an average of about twelve people attend mass on Sunday at Lodgepole. Gros Ventres have resisted Catholic officials' attempts to include Indian symbols and, initially, lay participation in the rites, for in their view such innovations have not been earned and violate ritual formulas. The Assiniboines, on the other hand, have embraced such changes, for in their view any changes can be authorized by lay innovators as well as by the Catholic priests.

To some extent, the Gros Ventre commitment to Catholicism was given impetus by the establishment of St. Paul's Mission in the heart of the Gros Ventre community. But, in addition to this fact and the obvious contrast between Gros Ventre and Assiniboine religious heritage, these differences are due to intertribal relationships and perceptions of those relationships. The Gros Ventres' strategy of civilization developed in the context of their pursuit of primacy in relation to Assiniboines; their claims of civilization were reinforced by conversion. The Assiniboines were pursuing a strategy of compliance which depended in part on convincing the federal officials that they were in need of assistance. Native religion, at least in modified form (a Sun Dance without self-torture, for example), was not necessarily an impediment to this strategy. As discussed below, the divergent strategies developed in the context of competitive relations between the two tribes. Each tried to counter the strategy of the other—the Gros Ventres tried to present the Assiniboines as backward and the Assiniboines attempted to portray the Gros Ventres as uncooperative.

In their past relations with government officials, both tribes have presented themselves as accommodating. But the Gros Ventres have stressed to officials and have behaved in such a way as to signify to themselves as well that they are progressive, fully capable of managing their community by themselves and of competing with whites on white terms if given a fair chance. Progress was associated both with the pursuit of prominence and with primacy in relation to others, particularly the Assiniboines. In politics today, higher education is a more potent symbol of leadership ability for Gros Ventres than for Assiniboines. Assiniboines have conveyed the impression to officials that they want to accept policies and programs initiated by the government, to cooperate. While virtually all Gros Ventre councilmen have been described as "progressive" in Indian Office correspondence, some traditional Assiniboine men (leaders in native religion) have always been elected to the council. One agent remarked that many Assiniboines viewed their council as "a sacred affair." In point of fact, after the turn of the century, Indian agents did not hold the Assiniboines to the same standards of civilization as the Gros Ventres. In short, Assiniboines have been skilled at eliciting the protection of officials, thus undermining Gros Ventre efforts at primacy.[21]

The different tribal strategies come through clearly in the speeches at the cession council of 1895, as well as in business council meetings throughout the twentieth century. At the 1895 council, when federal officials tried to buy from the tribes an area on the reservation where there was gold, the Assiniboine leader Little Chief remarked to federal officials, "You see me stand here, weak, and I can not dig that mine, but your race can." Gros Ventres disagreed; they wanted to mine the gold themselves. Assiniboines presented themselves to some degree as dependent on the federal government: "I am a poor man, and, when you come here and support me for a few more years, I am glad of it," said one man. Spokesmen stressed their history of cooperation. One remarked, "When the Great Father has anything to say to me, I always say yes; when you advise anything hard to me I always say yes." And they emphasized that, in return, they expected assistance: "The Great Spirit has directed my living. . . . I am dependent on the Great Father also. Those two have owned me so far. . . . When I am in need of anything I want to go up to the agent and ask him for it, and I would like to see him give it to me." The Assiniboines also chastised the Gros Ventres for their independent stance in comparing them unfavorably to themselves and their cooperative attitude:

> These young men here are all wearing the government clothes; they should take them off of them and then they would have nothing but their breechcloths to go home in. . . . You see me here a poor man. I have got

the same kind of clothes, and when I run out I go in the warehouse and ask for them. . . . I wonder how those Gros Ventres would live if they couldn't get anything from the warehouse here. . . . I wonder how these young men would like to starve.[22]

In the 1930s, when the tribes were considering the IRA, the Gros Ventre leaders were particularly interested in gaining political power. The Assiniboine leaders stressed their need for more economic aid from the federal government. The Gros Ventres presented the Assiniboines as a people who held them back; the Assiniboines brought out the uncooperative attitude of the Gros Ventres toward the government's policy of preventing separate tribal governments. In this way, each tribe tried to influence federal officials to accept its view of how the IRA should be implemented at Fort Belknap.

The Gros Ventres' strategy was in some ways a product of the kinds of relations they had had with other tribes before reservation settlement. More wealthy, they considered themselves superior to Assiniboines, Crees, and métis. But on the reservation, Assiniboines not only began to increase in numbers so that they dominated the cession council of 1895 and the allotment council of 1922; they also took in métis families as "relations." The presence of the métis was particularly galling to the proud Gros Ventres, for whites considered the métis more civilized than the Gros Ventres. The Gros Ventres' struggle to achieve respect from federal officials and to attain greater control over reservation affairs by appearing progressive was further stimulated by the relationship between the métis and Assiniboines, co-occupants of Fort Belknap. The Assiniboines, with far fewer horses than the Gros Ventres, were at a disadvantage even after they settled on the reservation, for horses were a major source of income. In political relations, Assiniboines had more difficulty impressing officials with their progressive bent because they chose many elderly headmen at a time when Gros Ventres were seating younger bilingual men on the business council. And perhaps the elderly headmen were more in awe of whites than the younger, educated councilmen. The Assiniboines also noted that on humanitarian grounds officials consistently rejected Gros Ventre demands to have particular Canadian or Lower Assiniboines evicted from Fort Belknap during the late nineteenth and early twentieth centuries. The obvious rewards of their emphasis on their dependence, coupled with their economic disadvantage in relation to the Gros Ventres, stimulated the Assiniboines' cooperative and less progressive strategy.

The competition between these two tribes, reflected in contrasts between the giveaway, religious, and political traditions of each people and in their "here first" stories, can be understood only in the context of the multitribal community. Gros Ventres' and Assiniboines' close proximity intensified competitive relations, or the opportunity for competition, that existed before reservation settlement. Both tribes recognized the potential problems of joint occupancy. After the intertribal wars were on the wane and the Gros Ventres and Assiniboines were in the process of settling in to a reservation life, each stressed the need for political autonomy. Both wanted separate areas of settlement, the Gros Ventres on the upper Milk (in Little Rockies and Bear Paw country) and the Assiniboines to the east in lower Milk country. At a meeting with a Senate committee in 1883, Running Fisher, speaking for the other Gros Ventre chiefs present, said, "My country does not belong to the Assiniboines, it belongs to me. I want to have the Assiniboines with me, but I want to mark out my own lands." Little Chief, speaking for Assiniboine chiefs, agreed that it would be better to settle apart and was comfortable with settling in the lower Milk country: "If the Gros Ventres are dissatisfied with us we would like a reservation down the Missouri River, with the Lower Assiniboines, from Medicine Crow, near Medicine Lodge, Big Bend Milk River, east or southeast to the Missouri River. We would like a reservation by ourselves." After the committee pressed them, the Assiniboines agreed that they would accept one agency and one reservation for both tribes: "The Gros Ventres could settle on the upper end and they would take the lower end and open up farms," the committee reported. According to Little Chief, "If the Gros Ventres would be satisfied we would just as soon have our reservation on the lower part of Milk River, below the Little Rocky Mountains, and joining the Lower Assiniboines and Yanktons. . . . We will go anywhere the government wants, but we want equal rights on the reservation with the other Indians." But the federal government, intent on confining Indian groups to as small an area as possible, insisted subsequently on a jointly occupied Fort Belknap reservation.[23]

The two tribes were encouraged to be competitors because they shared limited resources on the reservation and did not receive all the federal assistance to which they were entitled because of graft and mismanagement at the agency. And of equal importance, they were openly and individually compared with each other by federal authorities and by whites in general. The Gros Ventres' and the Assiniboines' self-images were shaped to some degree not merely by what whites said about them but by how whites characterized and evaluated them in relation to each other. What whites thought of them could, of course, influence the kinds of economic programs and political opportunities offered by the government. Thus the intense competition at Fort Belknap stimulated the Gros Ventres' commitment to progress and primacy and the Assiniboines' to compliance and to incorporation of people from bands other than the Canoer Mountain and of non-Assiniboines into a "Fort Belknap Assiniboine" tribe. Both of these developments date from the time of joint reservation settlement.

Each tribe faced the challenges and coped with the crises precipitated by contact with whites and with encapsulation in the wider, dominant society in its own characteristic way. Some strategies were more effective than others. It was particularly stressful for each tribe to have to evaluate its success in adapting against the successes of the other tribe. What seemed like a reasonable and wise choice at a particular point in time often appeared less so in the context of the other tribe's choices. The creative adaptations of one tribe had the potential of undermining or augmenting the self-confidence and challenging or reaffirming the assumptions and interpretations of the other. I suggest that this kind of stress has contributed to a tendency to define group identity, at least in part, by negative characterizations of the other group. A tradition of intermarriage between the Gros Ventres and Assiniboines has contributed to the ways they have characterized each other, as well. With a sector of the Fort Belknap population having relatives in both tribes and participating in both societies, the perpetuation of distinct group identities was more difficult. I suggest that the Gros Ventres and Assiniboines pursued distinctive identities in part by sharpening and emphasizing moral contrasts and intensifying negative evaluations of each other.

The two tribes' conflicting historical accounts of their settlement on Fort Belknap are, on the one hand, a way for each tribe to claim and pursue a competitive edge. On the other hand, they are a way of ordering and coping with the inevitable comparisons that the members of each tribe draw between themselves and the other tribe. Finally, the stories express and help perpetuate each tribe's sense of its own, distinct cultural identity where there are no firm boundaries between Gros Ventre and Assiniboine social organization and where federal officials and others have denied these two peoples separate cultural and political identities.

Conclusions

In many respects Gros Ventres have been culturally distinct from other peoples over the past two centuries. But theirs has not been a cultural continuity made solely of "persistence," or resistance to change. It also has come from people's interpretation and reinterpretation of new conditions and relationships in an effort to make changes meaningful and acceptable. The Gros Ventres at Fort Belknap do not share one public set of understandings, orientations, and goals, nor do they take a universally accepted view of past events, circumstances, and personalities. Their interpretations of the past and present differ and conflict, as do their behaviors. The exchange and mutual adjustment of their different perspectives help shape the nature of change at Fort Belknap. A focus on these complexities helps us to see things about this society that we would not see if we were to take it for granted that culture is shared or if we were to ignore variation by constructing a composite Gros Ventre culture or a pan-Indian Fort Belknap identity. Culture (uniform or not) and social forces are interdependent; it is by examining this interdependence through time that we come to understand the nature and direction of change at Fort Belknap and of change among the Gros Ventres. In studying Fort Belknap history, I used a multifaceted approach—one that combined ethnohistory, cohort analysis, and folk history—which reveals how the past influences the lives of people today and how their interpretations of the past influence contemporary culture and society. This multifaceted approach brings to light the dynamics of Fort Belknap life, suggests the need to reexamine such concepts as acculturation,

233

factionalism, and pan-Indianism, and contributes to a better understanding of contemporary Plains Indian societies in general.

Cultural and Historical Complexities

The student of Fort Belknap culture and history, or of the Gros Ventres, is impressed first and foremost by the remarkable degree to which each tribe has maintained its cultural identity. The cultural distinctiveness of the Fort Belknap peoples is particularly startling given the literature on them and the statements of the people themselves on first meeting. Such sources encourage the observer to find culture loss or assimilation or cultural merging. While in some ways the Fort Belknap peoples behave much like whites, their interpretations of those behaviors differ from their white neighbors'. Linked to the Gros Ventres' ideas about their identity are concepts about the supernatural, success, leadership, and relations with other Indians and with whites which differ from those of the Assiniboines. On one level there is a "Fort Belknap culture" to the extent that there are some broad-based understandings—for example, about social relations, the supernatural, and the reservation experience itself—which virtually all Indian members of Fort Belknap society share. Certain ritual symbolism is meaningful and important to Gros Ventres and Assiniboines alike. And there is a complex of social institutions that articulate these understandings and in which they all participate in some fashion or to some degree. Yet, on another level, the subtleties of these commonly held cultural understandings are worked out somewhat differently by various groups of people in the community. For people view the world from different cultural and social vantage points. Gros Ventre age groups' understandings often are not only not broadly shared but in fact in direct conflict. Some variations are specialized versions of the same general value orientations and a broadly shared ethos.

Both Gros Ventre elders and youths, and Assiniboines as well, recognize the possibility that fasting for medicine power may result in communication between human and supernatural beings and that humans may obtain supernatural aid in this way. Youths view non–Gros Ventre Indians as appropriate authorities from whom to learn how to acquire and use power obtained in a fast or how to pray in a sweat. Elders view such authorities as false. But, unlike Assiniboines, both groups recognize the need for apprenticeship to authorities.

All Gros Ventres attend the powwows and participate in them to varying degrees. Powwows are occasions for the affirmation of pride in community and Indian identity, and they are occasions for symbolic

234

statements about one's place within a kin network, as well as for meeting obligations to kin. But the powwow also has come to symbolize different things to elders and youths. For example, the powwow and associated giveaway are for education clique youths a vehicle for demonstrating Gros Ventre primacy. Militant youths see the powwow as a vehicle for the expression of hostility toward the United States. For elders, the powwows at the agency do not express Gros Ventre identity; these ceremonies articulate for elders the importance of kinship obligations, yet at the same time are understood as examples of the youths' estrangement from their elders. The Grass Dance symbolism of the Milk River powwow expresses Gros Ventre identity for youths, just as it did for the elders when they attended dances in Hays in the early twentieth century. (The same symbols—the offices and regalia of whip men and drumkeeper, for example—express Assiniboine cultural identity to Assiniboines, as they did earlier in the century.) Today elders and youths interpret the gift giving that accompanies the transfer of these offices as the fulfillment of obligations of leadership. Elders and youths view the arena direction duties (to keep the arena clear of spectators during contests, for example) as appropriate for the whip man because of their familiarity with Grass Dance tradition. Yet the Grass Dance symbolism, while to a degree it mobilizes support for the powwow among both elders and youths, is subject to various interpretations. Elders associate the regalia used in the Milk River powwow with Assiniboine culture. Many youths interpret some of this Grass Dance symbolism as an expression of Gros Ventre culture and also (unlike elders) as evidence of their commitment to and the relevance of Indian religion in their lives today.

The ideal of primacy, that Gros Ventres are and should be more successful and influential at Fort Belknap than Assiniboines, is shared by Gros Ventre elders and youths. But for elders the ideal is expressed in political struggles over enrollment and claim money. For youths the ideal is also expressed in powwow committee activity.

Gros Ventres see their business councilmen in large part as intermediaries between the federal government and themselves. Higher education symbolizes to elders and youths alike that a person is well equipped to pursue Gros Ventre political goals. Individuals who stand for election to the council attempt to woo constituents by promising to aid them by attaining better services, benefits, or justice from the federal government. None would seek to terminate the federal government's role as trustee for the tribes, but self-determination is important—they feel that Gros Ventres (or Fort Belknap tribes) should make and implement policy in their own community. Some Gros Ventre youths who have attended college try to appeal to voters by presenting themselves as "traditional people," who wear clothing that symbolizes nineteenth-century Indian identity, pursue the life of a medicine man, and confront whites with overt hostility when necessary (as did Indian warriors in the wars of the last century). But to elders, these militant youths go against the grain of Gros Ventre political philosophy, for their actions symbolize to others that they reject the progressive strategy pursued by prominent Gros Ventre leaders of the past. For youths today, progress means increased demand for self-determination, and many (the militant youths particularly) express militancy in the pursuit of these goals by wearing clothing and performing in ceremonies that signify to others a traditional identity.

Both Gros Ventres and Assiniboines place high value on generously helping kinsmen and both define kin bilaterally and use generational terminology to some degree. But Assiniboines differ from Gros Ventres in applying the category "kinsmen" to a more wide-reaching group. Kinship for them is a symbol that mobilizes people to cooperate and extend hospitality and aid across band divisions and reservation boundaries. In general, Assiniboines appear to have wider networks of kin than Gros Ventres. And, as has been explored in Chapter 3, broadly shared understandings of generosity, religion, and political strategies for dealings with whites have Gros Ventre and Assiniboine variants.[1]

Gros Ventres and Assiniboines, old and young, undertake joint ventures and together transact the day-to-day business of making a living, conducting rituals, and mobilizing community support for various joint projects and positions on the reservation. To a considerable extent, however, these activities are understood differently by various groups. Cultural variation works not only to bring conflicts into focus but also to stimulate individual and group flexibility, maneuverability, and creative reformulations and thus to influence the nature and direction of change. Thus, if we are to grasp the dynamics of Fort Belknap society, it is particularly important to explore contested meanings.

The people at Fort Belknap must continually adjust and reformulate their notions of what is and what ought to be in order to cope with the variant perceptions and responses and the social complexity of their community. All are aware of the wide range of viewpoints, strategies, and choices of those around them. The realization of these potentialities stimulates individual and group creativity. Recently two elderly Gros Ventre women have named children at public gatherings. They have responded to pressure from youths to take a prominent role in ritual. Yet, at the same time, they have acknowledged the validity of the elders' view that traditionally only men gave names at large public gatherings, for they have named people only at family-hosted events, and not in the powwow arena during the large intertribal powwow. Despite their perceived and stated differences, Assiniboines and Gros Ventres may opt in some situations to accept each other's political views and methods. Gros Ventre individuals sometimes seek help from Assiniboine councilmen, whom they perceive as particularly responsive to people in distress. And Assiniboine individuals who want the assistance of an assertive advocate in, for example, conflicts with BIA officials may ask a Gros Ventre councilman to intercede, for Gros Ventres are viewed as particularly aggressive and tenacious. Certainly the extreme fluctuations in policy and program implementation that characterize federal administration of reservations make flexibility and creativity particularly useful.

Awareness of different and contested meanings stimulates innovations that for some people may serve to resolve perceived discrepancies and incongruities and to encourage creativity. Many Gros Ventre youths were motivated to become active in powwows at the agency because they valued such ceremonies; and they were committed to Gros Ventre primacy, yet at the same time realized that Assiniboines dominated powwow activity. To validate primacy, they began to compete with Assiniboines in a new way and, in so doing, altered the form and content of powwow ritual at Fort Belknap. And elders were faced with the problem of how to assert their authority in religious rituals in the face of the youths' challenge. Their decision to attend a public ceremony in which one elder placed cloth over the pipe bundle and all prayed for the tribe's welfare—the first such gathering in at least twenty years—was an attempt to reconcile their views with the youths'. They did not try to recreate the old pipe-bundle rituals, but acted toward the bundle with respect and reverence. The ceremony was potentially the beginning of a new tradition. Comments that tribal identity or culture has been lost—even though people also allude to Gros Ventre and Assiniboine ways of doing things—is at times an inducement to innovation. Tribal leaders' remarks that there are no longer two distinct tribes serve to recruit support across tribal lines; at other times, councilmen appeal for a tribal vote.

Variant interpretations promote the tribes' competitive orientation toward one another, and the competitiveness encourages innovations. As we have seen, Gros Ventres and Assiniboines by and large shared the same reservation conditions and were jointly administered, yet the two groups viewed these conditions differently and developed divergent strategies in relations with federal officials over the years. The start of a powwow at Hays in 1984 (with a grand entry, contests, and other features not present in the dances held in earlier years) was precipitated by a feeling among many Gros Ventres (particularly el-

237

ders) that Hays was the proper location for a Gros Ventre celebration, rather than the agency area, where Assiniboines had a long history of holding dances. Moreover, many perceived Gros Ventre traditional dances as differing in key respects from those of the Assiniboines (in the number and kinds of committee positions, for example). This celebration was the first successful modern powwow held at Hays. The powwow may have set the stage for future friendly competition between the agency and Hays powwow committees to see which group could attract the largest crowd or organize the best dance generally. Moreover, Gros Ventres have designed bumming sticks for the Hays powwow which differ dramatically from those designed by an Assiniboine for use in connection with the Milk River powwow. The Hays sticks are larger and more elaborate than those at the agency (just as the eagle staff designed by a Gros Ventre is more elaborate than those used in other reservations' powwows). And these new Hays sticks look different than those used by the Gros Ventres in the early part of the century. The new design reflects the Gros Ventres' interest in developing symbols of Gros Ventre identity that express Gros Ventre values, distinguish the tribes, and present the Gros Ventres to advantage in relation to the Assiniboines.

Gros Ventre life today has been profoundly influenced by the interplay of different ideas and approaches. Gros Ventre ritual emphasizes secular rites; powwow activity and naming and memorial giveaways far outnumber ceremonies characterized by Gros Ventres as "Indian religion." The gap between the views of elders and youths accounts for the secular emphasis; elders have effectively hampered attempts to revive Gros Ventre religion. Elders' views also influenced the development of powwow symbolism, for the youths, unable to obtain instructions and enthusiastic support from elders, adopted many symbols from the Assiniboines' dance committee tradition. Thus Grass Dance symbolism—particularly powwow commitee offices and regalia borrowed from the Raven Society—is noticeably more prevalent at Fort Belknap than on many other reservations. These symbols are compelling for Gros Ventre youths, but often they mean something different to them than they do to Assiniboines. Symbols are shared but interpreted differently, and they motivate different kinds of behavior in Gros Ventre elders and youths and Assiniboines. The effort to introduce sacred symbols (pipeman, eagle staff) into the powwow also was encouraged by Gros Ventre elders' resistance to the revival of religious rites. And the origin and character of the Chief Joseph celebration reflects the different views of Indian identity held by Gros Ventre generation units, as well as the Gros Ventres' commitment to primacy (for originally this powwow was in large part organized to compete with the Assiniboines' Milk River powwow) and the Assiniboine beliefs about dreams.

Politics at Fort Belknap is distinguished by the leaders' successful efforts to take over the management of reservation programs formerly run by whites and by the business councilmen's youthfulness. Elders, given their experiences and orientations in the 1940s and 1950s, were intent on pushing their children (and grandchildren, in some cases) to obtain higher education. It is largely to their efforts that the high percentage of Gros Ventre youths with college training can be attributed. And they conveyed to the youths the Gros Ventre tradition of the pursuit of self-determination. The youths' interest in serving on the council (and in returning to the reservation when they could have obtained jobs elsewhere) and the goals they pursued were stimulated by their college experiences as well as by encouragement from elders. The youths' political roles and their political goals, then, were a product of both the experiences and perceptions of elders and youths. Moreover, the elders' second thoughts about the youths' service on the business council and the resultant controversy over the councilmen's role at Fort Belknap came about because the two groups held different views on leadership. To elders, salaries and per diem payments that were large by Fort Belknap standards suggested that youths helped themselves instead of others, the antithesis of legitimate prominent status. To youths, the financial consideration was appropriate to the professions for which they were trained and which were essential to the successful pursuit of self-determination in the 1970s.

The perspective that the militant youths brought to Fort Belknap politics challenged and affected the views of other groups, and the working out of these conflicts shaped contemporary political culture. The militants returned to Fort Belknap with an interest in pursuing treaty claims and righting other wrongs done the tribe. They became active in the treaty committee activities and brought to this cause the confrontational strategies they had seen effectively employed in urban and national contexts. Although other Gros Ventre groups were appalled by such tactics, they, like the militants, were committed to pursuing primacy, and the confrontational approach became an aspect of the claim payment issue and contributed not only to bitterness but also to the hardening of the Gros Ventre position toward those with Assiniboine and French-Chippewa ancestry. (Here the value placed by the militants on intertribal cooperation took a back seat to their insistence on tribal "sovereignty," for the federal government opposed the Gros Ventres' efforts to prevent some members of the community from receiving Gros Ventre claim money.) The divergence between Gros Ventre and Assiniboine ideas on tribal enrollment was in large part a reaction to the Gros Ventres' efforts to come to terms with the different perspectives of the militants and the elders and educated clique youths.

The competitive component of symbols of identity serves to foster a sense of cultural distinctiveness. To be culturally distinct is important to Native American people today. In their encounters with other people from different reservations or Indian communities during the 1960s and 1970s, youths were confronted with the problem of defining and comparing their own identity with that of others. As one youth told me, "When the new Indian awareness came, it wasn't enough just to realize you were Indian; it was *what kind of Indian* [that was important]." Studies of the Plains powwow have emphasized the powwow's role in establishing bonds between tribes and in the creation of an Indian rather than a tribal identity for Native Americans. (See, for example, Samuel Corrigan's study of the powwow on the Canadian Plains and James Howard's work on powwows in Oklahoma.) Such studies describe the powwow as a type of revitalization movement that has developed as a response to the pressures of encapsulation in Euro-American society and that fosters Indian unity as a replacement for tribal unity. To the people of Fort Belknap the powwow does symbolize their Indianness, the bond they have with other Native Americans and their shared experiences as a disadvantaged, exploited minority. In addition, the unique features of the Milk River powwow may serve to distinguish this reservation from others culturally. But because its symbols also have different meanings for various groups on the reservation, the powwow ritual also is a way for people to speak to each other about how to be Gros Ventre or Assiniboine, old or young. In the pursuit of a distinct cultural identity that can change with the times, contested meanings are of particular relevance. This disagreement works to challenge ideas about tradition and helps validate experimentation with new interpretations and new symbols. Through the experimentation going on in contemporary ritual life, the people of Fort Belknap are working out a new system of roles and statuses and developing criteria for assigning people to those tasks and positions that are appropriate for a new set of social and historical circumstances.[2]

Different and conflicting folk histories at Fort Belknap contribute to cultural distinctiveness. What particularly strikes the outsider about Fort Belknap is the extent and intensity of disagreement about the interpretation of history. An analysis of how folk histories operate socially shows that folk histories are symbolic vehicles, used not only to express cultural identity but also to validate innovation and competition. Thus the "here first" story was frequently told during the debate over the distribution of claim money. Historical traditions or folk histories have received particular emphasis in Fort Belknap culture, for contested histories figure importantly in politics and ritual innovation.

An exploration of variant interpretations of culture and history held by Gros Ventre elders and youths and by Assiniboines at Fort Belknap tells us more about how and why Gros Ventre culture and society are changing than a composite picture could convey. For on what basis would one group's interpretation of a past event or of ritual symbolism prevail over another? In actuality, all the different and conflicting interpretations have influenced the transformation of Fort Belknap and of Gros Ventre life. These insights into Gros Ventre cultural dynamics would not have been possible without a consideration of Assiniboine culture and society and the ways in which Gros Ventres and Assiniboines influence each other. For example, the Assiniboines' acceptance of innovation based on dreams and their ideal that elders meet the requests of youths helped make possible the ritual changes introduced by Gros Ventre youths. And what it means to be an elder today cannot be understood apart from what it means to be a youth, and vice versa. The conflicts at Fort Belknap do not impede overall political and ritual cooperation. Conflicts are not primarily about access to resources and power; to a large extent they are about how to make sense of the world and the Fort Belknap people's place in it. They are about what being Gros Ventre means today, how Gros Ventres should behave toward each other and others, and what kinds of changes are consistent with Gros Ventre culture. Conflicts help articulate these various perspectives and provide the impetus for their resolution or accommodation and for innovation. Over time, then, changes are accepted and interpreted as cultural continuities. As time passes, the generation born after 1955 will form new ideas about culture and history and introduce them into Fort Belknap life.

A realization of how different interpretations come into play helps us to reevaluate descriptions of cultural merging, particularly as expressed in the concept of pan-Indianism. In their studies of powwows, some scholars concluded that when such things as language, costume adornment, and songs no longer distinguish tribal groups, tribal cultural identity gives way to pan-Indian identity (a blend of several Plains cultures). But we have seen that what appears the same to an outside observer—dance regalia or events during Gros Ventre and Assiniboine giveaways, for example—may be interpreted quite differently by Gros Ventres and Assiniboines. Powwow symbols can serve as symbols of Indianness at one level and as symbols of tribal identity at another.

Moreover, borrowed customs may be interpreted as tradition and eventually become integral parts of ceremonies. In large part, cultural continuity hinges not on lack of change but on people's interpretations of change.

An approach that views culture and social forces as interdependent is essential for understanding both long-term and short-term change. We find at Fort Belknap that ideas about relations with whites (as well as other peoples) had as great an impact on the kinds of transformations there as have the policies and programs initiated by white officials. Ecological and economic conditions influenced the opportunities and limitations experienced by the people at Fort Belknap, but their interpretations of those opportunities and limitations also have shaped the strategies they employed and the choices they made. The people of Fort Belknap were not simply acted upon by their neighbors and administrators or by their environment in general as they changed; they helped select and shape changes. Gros Ventre cultural identity was not and is not anchored in a particular set of ceremonial forms or a pattern of structural alignments that order the behavior of groups and individuals. Rather, it emanates from interpretations that make changes meaningful and acceptable and enable the Gros Ventres to try to shape their own history.

We have seen that the meaning of Gros Ventre identity changed through successive eras. An ethos in which prominence and tenacity were important, the association of Gros Ventre well-being with the pipe bundles, and commitment to moiety or intragroup competition were constant features of Gros Ventre life since the trade era. The ways in which prominence and tenacity were expressed—stock raising, fairs, college education, for example—were influenced by the circumstances in which Gros Ventres found themselves. Men's moieties were transformed into two residence-based organizations by Gros Ventres who wanted to perpetuate their ceremonial life and social organization in the twentieth century, when the men's moieties were no longer feasible. The Gros Ventre communities at the agency and Hays may be attempting to reorganize powwow activity along the moiety principle now that economic conditions on the reservation have given them the means to do so. The pipes have always been associated with Gros Ventre cultural identity, but the perception of their role in Gros Ventre life and the Gros Ventres' behavior toward the bundles changed as the generations experienced reservation conditions differently. Native religious ceremonies were opposed by missionaries (who controlled needed resources) and seemed to the Gros Ventres to impede their efforts to influence reservation affairs at the turn of the century, partic-

242

ularly because other "Christian" Indian groups were characterized by whites as more civilized than the Gros Ventres. It was at this point that ritual life began to emphasize secular activity and Christianity began to take the place of native sacred rituals. At the same time the presence of Assiniboines and French-Chippewas on the reservation also was seen as impeding Gros Ventre goals, and it was then that a commitment to primacy began to be expressed in political and ritual contexts. Hostility toward whites never figured as importantly at Fort Belknap as on many other reservations; the attitude toward whites who married Gros Ventre women and toward their descendants was not one of resentment. These people were viewed as helpmates in the quest for prominence and primacy. And they did not compete politically with the prominent Gros Ventre men, who were viewed as competent to hold business council offices; only when leaders from Hays asked their help on delegations did they become involved before World War II. Thus, generally they have not been categorized as "mixed-bloods," as less Gros Ventre than those without known white ancestry. Instead, marriage to Assiniboines and French-Chippewas came to undermine one's identity as Gros Ventre. These features of life at Fort Belknap are all products of particular social and historical circumstances in interplay with the Gros Ventres' changing cultural orientations.

Attention to what change meant to the Gros Ventres and/or Assiniboines enables a much-needed revision of existing interpretations of Fort Belknap history. The works of the historians Edward Barry and Michael Foley offer interpretations based on analysis of many of the same documents consulted in the present study, although I relied on a wider range of sources, some of which are not the sort normally used by historians (for example, field notes of anthropologists, museum collections). Barry presents the Gros Ventres as a people whose way of life changed from Indian to white during the nineteenth and twentieth centuries. Barry relied on an acculturation model to explain the nature and direction of change among the Gros Ventres, and, in fact, in Fort Belknap society as a whole. He contrasts Gros Ventres and Assiniboines basically in terms of degrees of acculturation. To Barry, stock raising, fairs, and desire for allotment and self-determination are indicative of the loss of native culture. Barry interprets the social forms of Fort Belknap life through his own cultural screen: "The Fort Belknap people found themselves with an obsolete value system." In Barry's view, the Gros Ventres and Assiniboines have "retained only vestiges of their earlier heritage and developed a culture reflecting that of local settlers, missionaries, and Indian Service employees. . . . Adaptation to nineteenth-century ideas of individualism, self-reliance, desire for educa-

243

tion and private property neared completion in the 1920s." Gros Ventre or Assiniboine culture, in his view, was the way of life that preceded reservation settlement.[3]

Foley uses essentially the same documentary sources as Barry did, but argues that the Gros Ventres' and Assiniboines' history—the way life has changed at Fort Belknap—is explained not by acculturation but by exploitation and abuse. In Foley's view the Gros Ventres and Assiniboines are virtually culturally indistinguishable. As Indians, they were all helpless victims of white exploitation. According to him, economic conditions (more specifically political economy) predetermined Indian behavior. No acknowledgment of Gros Ventre or Assiniboine creativity, maneuverability, or adaptability is made. In the Gros Ventre case, for example, he does not recognize prominent men as a cultural category—all alike are viewed as impoverished. Ceremonial life, patterns of reciprocal or redistributive exchange, contrasts between Gros Ventre and Assiniboine strategies are irrelevant to Foley, who, in his effort to document the federal mismanagement and general corruption at Fort Belknap, rejects the idea that its people had cultural and social systems through which they were able to influence their circumstances of encapsulation in the wider American society.[4]

We can better understand the ongoing transformation of Fort Belknap if we examine the relationship between past and present by the use of several different methods. A careful study of documentary sources combined with the insights gained from fieldwork enables us to see trends, strategies, and processes over a long time span—in the case of the Gros Ventres, over two hundred years. We can examine the sources of change, how the Gros Ventres' choices and limitations are influenced by their and the Assiniboines' interactions with whites and with each other or by other social forces. We can trace their own ideas about what they experienced. But to trace the ways in which the "Gros Ventre people" have changed is, in some ways, limiting. We need to look also at the varying ways in which people who occupy different conceptual and social vantage points experience and interpret the past. One useful means of doing so is cohort analysis.

Cohort analysis—based on both ethnohistory and fieldwork—refines the abstractions, the common-denominator approach. And it gives new and additional insights into how and why a particular way of life changes—insights overlooked or obscured by the study of "a people." I have argued that the nature and direction of change at Fort Belknap are due in large part to contrasts in the generations' interpretations of culture and history and to their efforts to act upon, resolve, or ignore contested meanings. To focus on one cohort or on only what is common to all cohorts would distort cultural dynamics at

Fort Belknap. Cohort analysis demonstrates the usefulness of going beyond the identification of new ideas or social forms that are introduced (directly or indirectly by white administrators, for example) to consider how innovations are received by and affect different cohorts.

The generation gap is not a mere clash of interests but rather a result of contested meanings that emanate from different life experiences, from experiencing historical events and circumstances differently. Thus, for youths, "revival" of "traditions" or "traditional" symbols—in large part innovations, not revivals—validates ritual change in a contemporary social context. Elders reject many of the changes and the meanings youths attribute to them. The contrast in interpretations has affected relations between these cohorts and has contributed to the youths' acquisition of greater authority in reservation society, for the rituals they instigate and dominate have important political and social repercussions. The preeminence of college-educated youths in politics and government has influenced the commitment to tribalism at Fort Belknap (that is, the replacement of white administrators with Gros Ventre and Assiniboine ones in the management of the reservation) and to a growing emphasis on national networking (on communication with Indian leaders in other tribal governments and BIA positions throughout the region and country). The preeminence of the youth cohort in ritual life and recognition of the social context in which this cohort developed its awareness of Indian identity account for the nature of much ritual symbolism today. And the War on Poverty programs affected cohorts differently and influenced their political participation at Fort Belknap. Thus changes and their effects result not merely from white contacts or experiences in the wider American society but also from the cohorts' perceptions of the reality and the potentiality of their world and their struggles to realize those potentialities and shape that reality to their own visions.

Finally, comparison of folk histories and their use over time to express cultural orientations and motivate behavior can bring to light sources and directions of change not revealed by the ethnohistorical research and can expand our perspective on cohorts. Contrasts in the folk histories and the ways these contrasts figure in social relations show how the Gros Ventres' and Assiniboines' ideas about and behavior toward each other influence their strategies and choices and how their ideas and behavior are influenced by comparisons made of them by others. Exploration of these kinds of mutual influences is particularly revealing in multitribal communities, such as Fort Belknap. Incorporation of the notion of blood into the definition of cultural identity, for example, is a recent innovation that can be more clearly understood through analysis of the "here first" stories and their social uses.

Intertribal relations, particularly in a multitribal community, are quite as important as Indian–white relations in providing a context for change. As I have shown, competitive orientations influenced the meanings Gros Ventres and Assiniboines attributed to events. The Gros Ventre tendency to blame reversals on Assiniboine faults and to minimize white responsibility is a case in point. Each people creates and uses contested meanings in their folk histories to maintain self-esteem in the competitive context. Leaders in each group used the symbols of folk history to motivate others politically, economically, and ritually. Each tribe is integral to the other's sense of group identity and to the other's conception of goals and possibilities. Yet the borrowings (of rituals, for example) and mutual dependence are denied in folk history as self-esteem is affirmed and goals are pursued. The conflict between Gros Ventres and Assiniboines is not merely a clash of interests but a struggle over what kind of Indians Fort Belknap people are and will be; it is a struggle over the meaning of Indian in the contemporary world. That struggle is better understood by attention to the relation between culture change and folk histories.

Overt social conflict and contested meanings are far more obvious and more significant at Fort Belknap than at Wind River reservation, which the Gros Ventres' "relatives," the Arapahoes, share with another tribe, the Shoshones. I turn now to consider the Gros Ventre case in the light of what we know of other Plains Indian communities. In making these observations, some of which are rather tentative, I hope to suggest directions for future research and to stimulate new studies.

Plains Indians in Comparative Perspective

In comparing Northern Arapahoes and Gros Ventres over time we can see that despite common cultural origins they differed in a number of respects. In particular, they made different kinds of political adaptations to encapsulation in the wider American society. Their variant political patterns and strategies are due in large part to the different social environments in which each tribe lived in the postcontact period. The circumstances encountered by the Gros Ventres and the options available to them on the Northwest Plains in Montana differed in some important ways from those of the Northern Arapahoes on the Central Plains, in Wyoming and Colorado.[5]

Both tribes had an age-set/age-grade tradition that influenced political adaptation, but this tradition developed in two different directions. The tribes' regional experiences may explain some of the contrasts. Furs and robes were transported overland in the Central Plains in the early nineteenth century, and thus traders dealt in smaller volumes there than on the Northwestern Plains, where they relied on Missouri River steamboats for transport. The buffalo rapidly diminished in the Central Plains, so by mid-century there were even fewer opportunities for Arapahoe individuals to develop trade relations that would have promoted wealth differentials. War with whites and white settlement of the area in the 1860s and 1870s cut into the size of Arapahoe horse herds and leveled wealth differentials to a great extent. These factors that minimized a young man's chance to attain rank through manipulation of property helped elderly priests maintain control of the age-grade system. Only one age set occupied each of the four age grades at any one time. There were four age sets and the members of each owed respect and cooperation to sets senior and junior to them. Supernatural sanctions underlay the novice–instructor or grandson–grandfather bond. These factors promoted cooperation and unity among all men and resulted in less emphasis on competition and "besting" than among the Gros Ventres.[6]

On the Northwest Plains, trading companies continued to purchase robes and pelts well into the 1870s, even though the volume of trade gradually declined. Individual Gros Ventres established partnerships with these traders, and these links helped them to attract followers or avoid camp life for long periods of time. Throughout the century, the Gros Ventres were beset by formidable enemies and no territory was secure to them for very long. These factors may have helped make a moiety organization central to the Gros Ventres' age-set/age-grade system. The several age sets that made up each age grade not only competed with each other but were organized into competing moieties. The moiety system linked alternate generations and channeled competition between adjacent generations into ritualized, socially constructive forms. The need for particularly aggressive warrior societies may have been a factor in the emergence of the moiety competition. The competition between moieties over the display of generosity may have helped level differentials, as well, but wealth continued to be associated with rank. Moreover, the devastating effects of warfare and the division of the tribe into many small bands that apparently were separated for years at a time probably weakened the theocratic component of the age-grade system, for it was increasingly difficult to hold large tribal gatherings and bring together all the elderly men of the highest grade who would have had to preside over the rituals. By the late nineteenth century the Gros Ventres, unlike the Arapahoes, did not have a group of elderly ritual authorities who directed the entire ceremonial hierarchy.[7]

At this time the Arapahoes still had a political organization that integrated bands and cross-cut kin groups through the age-grade ceremonial hierarchy, which was directed or validated by their priests. The Gros Ventres relied on the organization of age sets into moieties to integrate bands and cross-cut kin groups. In both cases, the age-group system promoted cooperation within and between age groups.

As I have argued elsewhere, the Arapahoe age-set/age-grade tradition facilitated the mobilization of consensus and the legitimation of intermediary leadership after Indian–white contact, even in the reservation context. Cooperation between men (and their wives) was facilitated by obligations of age-set members toward one another and sacred obligations between junior sets and the elder sets that gave them ritual instruction. Cooperation was encouraged by supernatural sanction and the priests' authority. Throughout the twentieth century religious ritual has buttressed new forms of political organization and remained central to Arapahoe identity. In the Gros Ventre case, the moiety competition of age sets, not religion, served to unite age groups, and the moiety system directed rivalry toward group ends even though supernatural sanctions were less in evidence. Native religious rituals were not essential to the men's moiety organization or to the later residence-based moieties. And the Gros Ventres' strategy of pursuing civilization was better served by church attendance than by participation in the sacred lodges. Gros Ventre unity and leadership were finally undermined in the 1940s when out-migration, economic decline, and other problems fragmented the Gros Ventre community at Hays and dismantled the moiety system.[8]

The Gros Ventre case strengthens the argument that an age-group tradition helps legitimize centralized tribal government and intermediary leadership. For the Gros Ventres, like the Arapahoes, had an elected business council that was able to mobilize consensus and retain legitimate authority—until the problems of the 1940s and 1950s. Ungraded societies for which we have studies (Teton Sioux, primarily) have a history of deep political divisions and widespread rejection of a centralized government and of intermediary leadership. The Assiniboine case presents a problem, however: even though the Assiniboines lacked an age-grade system, they show no evidence of these difficulties. They accepted intermediary leadership and, at least in crises for which we have documentation, were able to reach consensus and unify behind intermediaries. Bands have not developed animosities that obstruct political consensus, and there is an emphasis on band cooperation in ritual contexts. A resolution of the puzzle of the Fort Belknap Assiniboines' political history is beyond the scope of this work, but an answer may lie partly in the perpetuation of an early-nineteenth-century ethos that encouraged cooperation between bands, for such cooperation was integral to their pedestrian hunting-gathering life. Unlike the Arapahoes and Gros Ventres, the Assiniboines were a horse-poor society. Wealth differentials were less in evidence and authority was more diffused. Perhaps the Assiniboines would not have welcomed pan-tribal institutions (age sets and age grades, for example) for political integration because they were not so deeply involved in the equestrian lifestyle.[9]

Indian strategies and choices in Indian–white relations were also shaped by regionalism. The pattern of relations between Indians and whites affected and was affected by the internal politics of Indian societies. The Arapahoes were "hostiles" in the 1860s and 1870s, the Gros Ventres "friendlies." Conditions on the Central Plains—voluminous emigrant traffic through Wyoming, extermination of the buffalo, numerous attacks by whites on Indians, the settlement of Colorado—propelled the Arapahoes and other groups in this area (Cheyennes and Teton Sioux) into military resistance in an effort to hold what was left of their hunting territory. No whites settled among the Arapahoes; by 1878, when the Northern Arapahoes settled at Wind River, Arapahoe women who had married or been living with white men either returned alone to the tribe or lived apart with their men.[10]

The Gros Ventres, on the other hand, saw their relations with whites as a chance for greater individual prominence and successful competition with other tribes. The Gros Ventres engaged in no battles with whites after the 1830s and suffered no massacres by them. Their hunting territory was not invaded by white settlers or emigrants, for the traffic and settlement lay farther south, particularly to the southwest, in Piegan country. Similarly, other tribes of the Northwest—some bands of Bloods and Siksikas, the Piegans, the Upper Assiniboines, the Crows—were not engaged with whites in very extensive hostilities, if any at all. Rather, they saw their relations with whites as primarily advantageous in their struggle with other Indians, especially when Teton and Yankton Sioux began pushing into Montana to hunt buffalo in the late 1860s. Gros Ventres continued to be heavily involved in trade with whites throughout the 1870s. Several white men were married to Gros Ventre women, and they settled among the Gros Ventres and aided their in-laws. The conditions of contact were considerably different in the Central and Northwestern Plains, and this factor affected the tribes' strategies in their dealings with whites as well as in their internal political affairs.

About the time the Arapahoes settled at Wind River in 1878, they were presenting themselves as former hostiles who now were willing to be friendly with whites. They often gave the appearance of civilization or progress but in fact worked to impede cultural repression, particularly of their ceremonial organization, by disguising their activities so that the agent interpreted them as civilized. While Arapahoes unified behind seemingly progressive leaders in order to influence officials, they saw whites as basically impediments to the good life and as exploitive of Indians. The Gros Ventres, on the other hand, enthusiastically pursued activities that whites defined as examples of civilization and progress, not to dissuade whites from interfering with their ritual life and not because they were replacing their values with those of whites, but to compete successfully with whites and others in order to attain their own cultural ideals of prominence and primacy.

Deeply ingrained political conflict and rejection of intermediary leaders and centralized government may be due in part to a commitment to a hostile strategy, as well as (or instead of, in the case of the Assiniboines) a tradition of ungraded age-group relations. Hostility—that is, refusal or reluctance to cooperate with federal officials—characterized the politics of reservations where hostiles did not, like Arapahoes, make the transition to friendly status. Federal officials also described peoples that fought other tribes or fought among each other as uncivilized, even if these same peoples ceased to fight with whites. Hostility or feuding among bands also was characteristic of peoples classified as hostiles. Murder was rare among reservation Arapahoes, Gros Ventres, and Assiniboines—all friendlies. It was common among Teton Sioux groups, for whom violence was often an effective political tactic.[11]

The comparison of the meaning of progress to Arapahoes and to Gros Ventres points to a recurrent problem in the literature on North American Indians. The use of culture-laden terms, such as "progress," to describe activities that have quite different meanings to various peoples distorts our understanding of change. In the case of the Gros Ventres, a misunderstanding of actions described as progressive by observers and of Gros Ventre statements about being progressive had led writers to conclude that Gros Ventres were attempting or experiencing a transition from Indian to white identity, which I have shown has not been the case.

And, finally, the Gros Ventre strategy of progress needs to be considered in the light of the histories of other groups that have impressed federal officials as progressive. Have these groups fared better in terms of treatment from the federal government than those described as traditional or backward? Studies of non-Plains people, such as the Menominees and the Cherokees, have shown that success at adapting to the wider American society, particularly economic success, often provokes a negative response from neighboring whites. Federal agents are encouraged to institute measures to suppress Indian competition with whites. Whites did view Gros Ventre (and Assiniboine) stockmen as competitors and, although I cannot document it, may have exerted pressure on officials to restrain the Indians' progress. The dourine eradication campaign, for example, was applied only to the Indians' stock, not to the stock of whites, who used the same range. And local mining entrepreneurs certainly viewed Indians as competitors in the 1890s. Moreover, the federal government did not exert any special effort, financial or otherwise, on behalf of the exemplary Gros Ventres. And corruption and exploitation appear to have been particularly excessive at Fort Belknap—one agent was actually prosecuted, a rare occurrence in matters of Indian Office corruption. It may be that the opportunity for graft was increased by the Gros Ventres' agricultural accomplishments: agents had more funds to purchase crops and stock from them to meet agency needs, and therefore more opportunity to make fraudulent purchases. It was easier for agents to profit from fraudulent transactions with Indian agriculturalists than to attempt fraud with non-Indians.[12]

I return now to the issue of conflicting interpretations of history at Fort Belknap. The generation gap is pronounced at Fort Belknap, but not at Wind River. The Gros Ventres and Arapahoes both experienced the implementation of termination policy in the 1950s and both were affected in major ways by the War on Poverty and the Native American pride movement. In the 1940s and 1950s the Gros Ventres suffered the withdrawal of economic rehabilitation programs and the undermining of their business council by lack of federal support. On their own, the Gros Ventres had no mineral resources to generate income, reinvigorate the business council, and infuse people with confidence. As we have seen, termination policy undermined community unity, as well. The Arapahoes, on the other hand, had some oil wells paying royalties, but the BIA withheld the money. The business council successfully persuaded Congress to give them control of the royalties. Thereafter, the council made regular per capita payments to all members of the tribe. Thus the council achieved tremendous prestige and solidified its position as provider for its constituents. Arapahoes generally did not move away from the reservation to find work, as Gros Ventres felt forced to do. Much of their per capita income was channeled into the fulfillment of ritual responsibilities. These differences set the stage for the differential effects of the War on Poverty programs in these societies. Job programs and other services were instituted on both reservations. Young Arapahoes took less advantage of the educational opportunities and continued to find the source of their cultural identity in Wind River tradition, even if they did attend college off the reservation. Many attended a local community college whose founding was aided in some part by the potential of Indian enrollment and the indirect benefits from Indian per capita payments, which bolstered the local economy. War on Poverty programs relieved unemployment at Wind River but did not hire many off-reservation Arapahoes. The emphasis on Native American pride reinforced the authority of Arapahoe elders, who, in contrast to their Gros Ventre counterparts, had not relocated after World War II and had been trained as ritual leaders in earlier years. At Fort Belknap, the War on Poverty era resulted in new people and new ideas.

All Indian communities have seen far-reaching changes because of the processes set in motion by War on Poverty programs and the Native American pride movement. But we have yet to work out how the urban, off-reservation experiences of Indians or the intertribal contacts they made have affected particular Native American communities, particularly rural, reservation ones. And we have not looked at contrasts in the reception of new people and new ideas among different segments of the same reservation population—tribe versus tribe, clan versus clan, male versus female, for example. There are reports that the Native American pride movement—or the "Indian boom," as one of the Fort Belknap people put it—has improved the status and expanded the roles of the elderly in a few societies outside the Plains. But the question needs to be explored further, for in the case of the Gros Ventres, the status and role of elders may actually have declined.[13]

The perception among members of a multitribal community that the tribes do not get along is commonly reported by ethnologists. Arapahoes and Shoshones, Gros Ventres and Assiniboines say this about themselves at times. However, Gros Ventres and Arapahoes perceived and dealt differently with their multitribal situation. Wind River is a multitribal community, and Arapahoes and Shoshones are antagonistic. Their folk histories sometimes reflect divergent interpretations of the same events. But Gros Ventre and Assiniboine interpretations are not only competitive and different, they incorporate in a central way characterizations of each other, and the events that figure in folk history are by and large jointly experienced ones. Unlike the situation at Fort Belknap, Arapahoe and Shoshone social systems are for the most part separate. Until the 1980s they did not intermarry, and they have separate business councils with separate budgets. They also have no tradition of being allies in prereservation days. The Gros Ventres and Assiniboines were more interdependent than the Wind River tribes; their struggle to remain culturally distinct yet allied has colored the themes and interpretations in their respective folk histories, as well as their relations with each other. It is not enough merely to note antagonisms in a joint community; we need to look for the sources of conflicts and how precisely conflicts affect society and culture.

Much of the literature on contemporary Native Americans tends to oversimplify, overgeneralize, and stereotype. Such labels as "pan-Indianism" versus "tribalism," "revitalization" or "revival," and "the new activism" are used without careful consideration of the fact that these processes mean different things and take different forms in different social contexts, within as well as between societies. Moreover, changes come not only from interaction with the dominant, non-Indian society but also from the pressure and influence exerted by Native Americans on each other. The various segments of particular societies encounter the same ideas, behaviors, and events past and present; yet they may perceive and work them out in the social arena in quite different ways. We can uncover the particular historical, cultural, and social circumstances that make for such differences by confronting and exploring the contested meanings that make up American Indian life today.

Abbreviations

BCIM	Bureau of Catholic Indian Missions Records, Marquette University, Milwaukee, Wisconsin
BYU	Beinecke Rare Book and Manuscript Library, Yale University, New Haven, Connecticut
CF	Fort Belknap Agency, Central Files, 1907–39, RG 75, National Archives, Washington, D.C.
CU	Regina Flannery Herzfeld, Field notes, Department of Anthropology, Catholic University of America, Washington, D.C.
FRC	Fort Belknap Records, RG 75, Federal Archives and Records Center, Seattle, Washington
HBC	Hudson's Bay Company Archives, Provincial Archives of Manitoba, Winnipeg, Canada
IIR	Reports of Inspection of the Field Jurisdictions of the Office of Indian Affairs, 1873–1900, RG 75 and 48, National Archives, Washington, D.C.
LR	Letters Received by the Office of Indian Affairs, 1881–1907, RG 75, National Archives, Washington, D.C.
LR-MS	Letters Received by the Office of Indian Affairs, 1824–81, Montana Superintendency, M234, National Archives, Washington, D.C.
MIHS	Missouri Historical Society, St. Louis, Missouri
MOHS	Montana Historical Society, Helena
MSU	Special Collections, Montana State University, Bozeman
OP	Oregon Province Archives of the Society of Jesus, Gonzaga University, Spokane, Washington
SNR	Superintendents' Annual Narrative and Statistical Reports from Fort Belknap Agency, 1907–38, RG 75, National Archives, Washington, D.C.

Notes

Introduction

1. On the northern and central Plains (in Montana, Wyoming, and western North and South Dakota) there are thirteen reservations. Six are occupied by more than one tribe: Fort Belknap (Gros Ventre, Assiniboine), Wind River (Arapahoe, Shoshone), Rocky Boy (Cree, French-Chippewa), Fort Peck (Assiniboine, Yanktonais Sioux, Hunkpapa Teton Sioux), Fort Berthold (Mandan, Hidatsa, Arikara), Standing Rock (Hunkpapa Teton Sioux, Blackfeet Teton Sioux, Yankton Sioux, Yanktonais Sioux). Five have more than one formerly autonomous tribal division: Pine Ridge (Oglala Teton Sioux, Upper Brule Teton Sioux), Rosebud (Oglala Teton Sioux, Upper Brule Teton Sioux), Blackfeet (Piegan, Blood, Siksika), Cheyenne River (Minneconjous Teton Sioux, Blackfeet Teton Sioux, Two Kettles Teton Sioux, Sans Arcs Teton Sioux), Crow (Mountain and River Crow). Only two reservations are occupied by one tribal group, Lower Brule and Northern Cheyenne. On the southern Plains in western Oklahoma, all the Plains Indian nonreservation communities are multitribal. (For the many multitribal reserves in Canada, see Douglas R. Parks, Margot Liberty, and Andrea Ferenci, "Peoples of the Plains," pp. 288–89.)
2. In *Lakota of the Rosebud: A Contemporary Ethnography*, Elizabeth S. Grobsmith makes this observation about the Brule Sioux on Rosebud reservation (p. 44).
3. One of the earliest ethnographic studies of a contemporary (post–World War II) Plains community was Gordon Macgregor's *Warriors without Weapons: A Study of the Society and Personality Development of the Pine Ridge Sioux*. Although there were cultural and social differences among communities and age groups at Pine Ridge, Macgregor chose to produce a description of "Sioux culture" or "the Pine Ridge Dakota" based on the "sum total" characteristics, not a picture of any one individual or group or of the majority (p. 184). Studies that use an acculturation model to describe variation generally begin with a composite traditional culture as a standard against which to measure change. Grobsmith's (*Lakota*) "Brule," whether "traditional" or "assimilated," actually are descendants of three peoples with somewhat different histories, who

257

were generally autonomous before reservation settlement. In *Modern Black-feet: Montanans on a Reservation*, Malcolm McFee identifies Indian- and white-oriented groups, but the ancestors of these people were from three distinct Indian groups with separate histories.

4. In *The Fort Belknap Assiniboine of Montana*, David Rodnick describes Assini-boine culture and the way it changed without considering the effect of these people's relations with their neighbors, the Gros Ventres. The shortcomings of his approach are discussed in chap. 1. William K. Powers' model of Oglala culture in *Oglala Religion* is that of the "traditionals" or "full-bloods." He views their thinking as uninfluenced by other Oglalas on Pine Ridge reserva-tion. However, Alice B. Kehoe's study, "The Dakotas in Saskatchewan," pp. 163, 170–71, avoids focusing on only one group; she discusses how relations between Dakota Sioux and Cree peoples on the same reservation influenced the identity constructs of each group. And see Loretta Fowler, *Arapahoe Pol-itics, 1851–1978: Symbols in Crises of Authority*, for a discussion of how Shoshones and Arapahoes influence each other politically. See also Edward P. Dozier's work *Hano: A Tewa Indian Community in Arizona*, which considered how Hopis' and Tewas' joint occupancy of the same village influenced the way each changed. Two studies consider the mutual influence of Indians and non-Indians: Niels Winther Braroe, *Indian and White: Self-Image and Interac-tion in a Canadian Plains Community*, and Karen I. Blu, *The Lumbee Problem: The Making of an American Indian People* (on the interactions of whites, blacks, and Lumbees).

5. The acculturation model is the most common way of accounting for diversity. Among studies of this kind are McFee, *Modern Blackfeet*; Fred Voget, "Crow Sociocultural Groups"; Robert A. White, "The Lower-Class 'Culture of Excite-ment' among the Contemporary Sioux"; Grobsmith, *Lakota*. In *Lakota*, the most recent of these studies, Grobsmith argues that variation among Rosebud communities or villages is to be understood in terms of degrees of assimila-tion, but she departs from many acculturation studies by noting that "it is difficult to say that one [community] is more 'Indian' than the other," for all the various communities' histories have unfolded in the reservation context (p. 37). Just what defines Indianness in the Rosebud context, however, is not explored. On some reservations, such as Pine Ridge, the native categories "full-blood" and "mixed-blood" or "half-breed" do exist. By and large, eth-nographers have not incorporated the native perspective into or differentiated it from the acculturation models they construct. Acculturation studies gener-ally do not focus on native criteria of identity; rather, arbitrary or ethnocentric criteria are used (see Robert E. Daniels, "Cultural Identities among the Oglala Sioux").

In "Indians and the Metropolis," Joseph G. Jorgensen also has criticized the acculturation model, arguing that contemporary Indian lifestyles are due not to their degree of acculturation but to their full integration into the United States political economy as an exploited population (p. 84). See also Richard O. Clemmer, "Truth, Duty, and the Revitalization of Anthropologists: A New Perspective on Culture Change and Resistance," and Raymond J. DeMallie, "American Indian Kinship Systems: The Dakota," pp. 235–36.

6. For examples of the factionalism approach, see Katherine Weist, "The North-ern Cheyennes: Diversity in a Loosely Structured Society"; Raymond J. De-Mallie, "Pine Ridge Economy: Cultural and Historical Perspective."

7. For example, Edward M. Bruner, in "Mandan," describes the Mandans and Hidatsas on Fort Berthold reservation as culturally "merged." And Susan R.

Sharrock identifies a Cree-Assiniboine "hybrid" or fused ethnic unit, distinct from either the Cree or the Assiniboine ethnic unit, in nineteenth-century western Canada ("Crees, Cree-Assiniboines, and Assiniboines: Interethnic Social Organization on the Far Northern Plains," pp. 103, 111–13).

8. In addition to the approaches that stress culture loss, persistence, and the effects of powerlessness, a Marxist or "conflict model" of history has been used by John H. Moore ("Cheyenne Political History, 1820–1894"). This model has not yet been applied to Cheyenne history after the turn of the century, however. In Moore's view, new economic and political conditions provoked conflicts between interest groups—soldier societies' and council chiefs' followers (agnatic and matrilineal/matrilocal components of social structure)— and this conflict accounts for contrasting versions of Cheyenne narratives as well as a major change in Cheyenne social organization in the mid-nineteenth century. In my view, the assertion of economic and political interest does not account adequately for all the kinds and processes of change in Gros Ventre society today.

9. The pioneer acculturation studies, which do not deal with post-1950s society, were included in Ralph Linton, *Acculturation in Seven American Indian Tribes,* and Edward H. Spicer, *Perspectives in American Indian Culture Change.* See also Charles S. Brant, *Jim Whitewolf: The Life of a Kiowa Apache Indian.* Probably the majority of publications on Plains history do not consider events of the recent past, an indication that in many authors' view, traditional or "real" Indian culture has disappeared. See Raymond J. DeMallie, "Sioux Ethnohistory: A Methodological Critique."

10. Two authors who focus on persistence are Peter J. Powell, *Sweet Medicine: The Continuing Role of the Sacred Arrows, the Sun Dance, and the Sacred Buffalo Hat in Northern Cheyenne History,* and Powers, *Oglala Religion.* Powers, for example, argues that Oglalas have retained cultural identity because their system of religious beliefs "has persisted for more than 250 years" and that "the boundaries of Oglala ethnicity are synonymous with the boundaries of religious belief." Religious beliefs are expressed in several rituals that were held in the days of early contact and are still held today. Oglalas (that is, "traditional" Oglalas) have "religious values" distinct from Euro-Americans because they have adapted "intrusive" Euro-American elements to their own value system instead of adopting the value system of Euro-Americans (pp. xiv, xv, 124). But Powers' view of the Oglalas' cultural change overlooks the extent to which they have adopted or developed new ideas or values that are not those of Euro-Americans. Oglalas are distinguished from Euro-Americans not only by religious beliefs but also by beliefs about decision-making and sharing, for example, which are perfectly compatible with wholehearted belief in Christianity and which have evolved in social environments very different from those of precontact times. Moreover, Powers concludes that "mixed-bloods" are not as culturally Oglala as those who practice native religion exclusively; yet other studies show that beliefs and behavior of mixed-bloods as well as those of traditionals are in many ways distinct from those of Euro-Americans. It also is the case that rituals that have persisted have new meanings for the Oglalas today; individual motives for participation in the Sun Dance no longer center exclusively on a quest for power but include the desire for recognition as an Indian and the desire to recover from alcoholism (Beatrice Medicine, "Indian Women and the Renaissance of Traditional Religion").

11. In *The Forgotten Sioux,* Ernest L. Schusky studies the history of federal ad-

ministration of Lower Brule reservation but does not include the Brules' perspective on these events and relationships or their strategies in dealing with whites. The implication is that the Brule are passive recipients of programs. Joseph G. Jorgensen's *Sun Dance Religion: Power for the Powerless* argues that the origin and persistence of the modern Wind River Shoshone Sun Dance is a response to deprivation produced by metropolis–satellite political economy and associated racism. He stresses that the Sun Dance provides the only means for Shoshones (and Utes) to achieve status and self-esteem and that because of discrimination and deprivation they are politically apathetic and disgruntled. By focusing on "apathy" due to powerlessness, Jorgensen ignores the fact that Wind River Shoshones seek and attain status and self-esteem in political as well as ritual contexts and that their political participation is greater than that of non-Indians. Historian Richard White's work *The Roots of Dependency: Subsistence, Environment, and Social Change among the Choctaws, Pawnees, and Navajos* also views the history of the Pawnees (and other groups) up to the 1870s as a gradual loss of culture and of decline attributable to their incorporation into a global capitalist system.

12. Clifford Geertz, *The Social History of an Indonesian Town*, pp. 12, 202, and *The Interpretation of Cultures*, pp. 7, 12, 17, 18, 144, 361.

13. Geertz, *Social History*, pp. 5, 203, 207. Two works that take this perspective on Native American history are Loretta Fowler, *Arapahoe Politics*, and Blu, *Lumbee Problem*.

14. Geertz, *Interpretation of Cultures*, pp. 367, 405, 407.

15. Mildred Mott Wedel and Raymond J. DeMallie, "The Ethnohistorical Approach in Plains Area Studies," pp. 110, 116. Wedel reminds us that the value of documents for the interpretation of history depends on their credibility, the history of the document itself, the basis of the author's expertise, and the potential for bias. See also William C. Sturtevant, "Anthropology, History, and Ethnohistory," on the use of written sources and the use of ethnography ("upstreaming") to criticize and reinterpret documentary sources (pp. 456–59). Anthropologists have sometimes been justly criticized for their uncritical use of documents. On the other hand, historians who use the ethnohistorical method often misuse or uncritically use anthropological theory in their work.

16. Sturtevant, "Anthropology, History, and Ethnohistory," pp. 462–63. On method in folk history, see Jan Vansina, *Oral Tradition: A Study in Historical Methodology*; R. M. Carmack, "Ethnohistory: A Review of Its Development, Definitions, Methods, and Aims"; David C. Pitt, *Using Historical Sources in Anthropology and Sociology*, pp. 54–56. Fred Eggan addresses the problem of how to identify actual events in oral traditions ("From History to Myth: A Hopi Example"). In *Hano* Dozier explores how stories and beliefs about the past are directives for proper Tewa behavior and affect Tewa–Hopi relations (pp. 19, 24, 26). Laura Bohannan, in "A Genealogical Charter," discusses how social relationships influence the way in which genealogies change and how genealogy validates political relationships among the Tiv (pp. 311–15). See also Charles Hudson, "Folk History and Ethnohistory," pp. 58–62. More recently Edward M. Bruner and others explore how narratives both shape and reshape societies and their individual members and, at the same time, comment on the social world ("Introduction: The Opening Up of Anthropology," pp. 3, 5; Keith H. Basso, "'Stalking with Stories': Names, Places, and Moral Narratives among the Western Apache"). I know of no study of a Native American community that employs cohort analysis. Renato Rosaldo uses this method in historical reconstruction; he does not explore how different cultural perspec-

tives of cohorts work to change a society's culture and social organization (*Ilongot Headhunting, 1883–1974: A Study in Society and History*).

17. The transcriptions of Gros Ventre words follow Allan Taylor's system except that for θ I use O, for open *o* I use *a*, for wedged *c* I use *c*, and for the value of *ts* with aspiration I use *ch*. I thank Dr. Taylor for checking the accuracy of my transcriptions.

There are two explanations of the origin of the name Gros Ventre. One explanation is that the sign for Gut People (Atsíínaa, in Blackfoot) was misinterpreted by the French as Big Stomach (see Hugh Lennox Scott, "The Early History and Names of the Arapaho"). The other is that the sign for Waterfall People was similarly misinterpreted (Allan R. Taylor, "The Many Names of the White Clay People"). Today the Gros Ventres refer to themselves as "Gros Ventre," pronounced *grow vaunt*. There are two spellings of the tribal name Arapaho—the Northern division uses Arapahoe; the Southern, Arapaho.

18. *Siouan and Caddoan Linguistics* (March 1980), pp. 10–14; Raymond DeMallie, personal communication.

19. "The Fort Belknap Reservation Area—Its Resources and Development Potential," Missouri River Basin Investigations Project Report no. 198, Billings, Mont., 1972, pp. 3, 44, MSU; office files, Bureau of Indian Affairs and Tribal Office, Fort Belknap, Mont.

20. Population figures throughout this chapter are from office files, Bureau of Indian Affairs, Fort Belknap, Mont.

21. The métis on Fort Belknap are "non-wards" of the federal government, as they are not enrolled on a reservation and are not federally recognized as Indians. Other métis, such as those on Rocky Boy reservation, are enrolled. See Verne Dusenberry, "Waiting for a Day That Never Comes: The Dispossessed Métis of Montana."

22. "Fort Belknap Reservation Area," pp. 2, 13–14, 18, 80, MSU; office files, Bureau of Indian Affairs, Fort Belknap, Mont. According to the Census of Population, 1980, vol. 1, chap. B, pt. 28, Montana, U.S. Department of Commerce, pp. 7, 58–59, the population of Harlem is 1,023 (Indians, 319); Chinook, 1,660; Malta, 2,367; Havre, 12,121.

23. Census of Population, 1980, vol. 1, chap. C, pp. 40, 263; office files, Bureau of Indian Affairs, Fort Belknap, Mont.

24. Office files, Tribal Office, Fort Belknap, Mont.

25. Office files, Tribal Office and Bureau of Indian Affairs, Fort Belknap, Mont.

1. Ways of Being Gros Ventre, 1778–1984

1. Edward E. Barry, "The Fort Belknap Indian Reservation: The First One Hundred Years, 1855–1955," and Michael F. Foley, "An Historical Analysis of the Administration of the Fort Belknap Indian Reservation by the United States," both in Special Collections, MSU; David Rodnick, *The Fort Belknap Assiniboine of Montana: A Study in Culture Change*.

2. For a history of trade in the country occupied by the Gros Ventres, see Arthur J. Ray, *Indians in the Fur Trade: Their Role as Trappers, Hunters, and Middlemen in the Lands Southwest of Hudson Bay, 1660–1870*, and John C. Ewers, *The Blackfeet: Raiders on the Northwestern Plains*, pp. 19–71.

3. John C. Ewers, *The Horse in Blackfoot Indian Culture*, pp. 18, 212, 305, 308, 310, 312, 314–16, 319, 334, 338. See also Oscar Lewis, *The Effects of White Contact upon Blackfoot Culture: With Special Reference to the Role of the Fur Trade*, pp. 55–56, 59.

4. John M. Cooper, *The Gros Ventres of Montana*, pt. 2, *Religion and Ritual*, ed. Regina Flannery, p. 68. The dates of birth of Cooper and Flannery's informants ranged from 1854 to 1875.
5. Ibid., pp. 1–9, 33–172, 365–67. A better translation of the Gros Ventre term for "Supreme Being" is "He Who Rules All by the Power of Thought."
6. Ibid., pp. 36–38, 44–46, 53–54, 68.
7. Ibid., p. 179.
8. Ibid., pp. 173–242; Regina Flannery, *The Gros Ventres of Montana*, pt. 1, *Social Life*, pp. 36–40; A. L. Kroeber, *Ethnology of the Gros Ventre*, pp. 227–60. (On the order of the grades, see Kroeber, p. 260, and on supernatural aid for war, see Edward S. Curtis, *The North American Indian*, 5:114, 117.) The wives of the novices in the second through the fifth grades also obtained supernatural aid when they participated in some phases of the rituals.
9. Flannery, *Gros Ventres*, pp. 36–43, 101–3.
10. Edmonton House Journal, 25 May 1800, B60a/5, and "Journal of Occurrences, Bow River Expedition," 1822–23, B34a/4, both in HBC. The Blackfeet groups also had an age-group system, but it lacked the extensive, underlying supernatural sanctions of the Gros Ventres'. Penalties for nonconformity were substantially higher for Gros Ventres. The Blackfeet age-group system lacked the "ceremonial grandfather" feature, for example; there was no group of elder and elderly men occupying the highest ceremonial positions who could induce cooperation among their juniors (see Frank Henderson Stewart, *Fundamentals of Age-Group Systems*, pp. 323–25).
11. Alexander Philip Maximilian, *Travels in the Interior of North America, 1832–34*, ed. Reuben Gold Thwaites, 23: 70, 72–73, 135, 165–66; Cooper, *Gros Ventres*, p. 52.
12. Nicolas Point, *Wilderness Kingdom: Indian Life in the Rocky Mountains, 1840–1847*, trans. Joseph P. Donnelly, pp. 102, 106, 110, 131, 199, 210. Cooper was told that in the early nineteenth century the Gros Ventres had other sacred pipe bundles (such as the Beaver Pipe) that were not as important or powerful as the Flat and Feathered pipes (ibid., p. 166).
13. F. V. Hayden, *Contributions to the Ethnography and Philology of the Indian Tribes of the Missouri Valley*, p. 340; *Report to the Commissioner of Indian Affairs*, 1864, p. 296; Lemuel Burke, "Diary, 1877," SC 500, MOHS.
14. Robert H. Lowie theorized that the Gros Ventres (and the Arapahos and Blackfeet groups, the other nomadic Plains peoples that had age-group systems) acquired their age-set/age-grade organization and its associated symbols from the Mandan or Hidatsa horticultural villagers (*Plains Indian Age Societies: Historical and Comparative Summary*, pp. 948, 951). There is no documentary evidence to support Lowie's conclusion, but Arapahos and Gros Ventres could have visited and traded with the Mandans and Hidatsas before the late eighteenth century. Lowie assumes that the horticultural villagers would have been more likely than the nomadic hunters to develop this kind of complex, elaborate system. But we do not know when the Mandan and Hidatsa acquired or originated their age-group systems. Madeline Lattman Ritter recently argued that the Plains Indians developed or borrowed their age-group systems because they faced frequent warring and wanted to integrate the males of local groups whose size and composition fluctuated throughout the year or had sizable numbers of men living away from a permanent settlement (Ritter, "The Conditions Favoring Age-Set Organization," *Journal of Anthropological Research* 36 [1980]: 87–104). However, several other village and nomadic peoples who had the same characteristics did not develop an age-

group system. Ritter's approach does not consider the historical and social contexts that must have had a bearing on the development of age grades. At this point we can only speculate about why, how, and when the Gros Ventres and others organized their age-set/age-grade systems.

15. My view of the effect of trade relations on Gros Ventre society contrasts with Oscar Lewis's. Lewis argues that "tribes which had little contact with each other met at trading posts with the result of much borrowing and spreading of culture elements." He concludes that age-grade societies were borrowed by nomads from the villagers while they all congregated at the American Fur Company posts in the 1820s. In his view, the nomads borrowed the age-grade system because it was a "mechanism for expressing and channelizing the vertical mobility which came with an increase in wealth" in trade goods. But Lewis ignores the fact that intertribal visiting and trading certainly antedated the establishment of posts, even antedated the first visit of a Canadian trader in the villages of the Mandan and Hidatsa (see Bruner, "Mandan," pp. 197, 199–200). Moreover, as I have pointed out, trade goods merely supplemented horses in property transfers during ceremonies. Lewis also suggests that pipe bundles and their purchase also developed when the nomadic groups visited the traders' posts (Lewis, *Effects of White Contact*, pp. 40–42, 45–46, 60–61). See Cooper, *Gros Ventres*, p. 33, on hereditary keepership.

16. David Thompson, *David Thompson's Narrative, 1784–1812*, ed. Richard Glover, p. 235 (see also Ray, *Indians in the Fur Trade*, pp. 138–41); Hudson House Journal, 12 August and 14 July 1782 and 1 March 1783, B87a/5-6, HBC.

17. "Peter Fidler's Journals," 22 January 1793, E3/2, HBC. References to gift-giving practices and treatment of Gros Ventre "chiefs" appear throughout the journals of the traders of Hudson's Bay Company who operated in the region. See, for example, Hudson House Journal, 2 May 1786, B87a/8; Manchester House Journal, 15 February 1788 and 6 March 1792, B121a/2, 7; Edmonton House Journal, 9–10 January 1800, B60a/5; Chesterfield House Journal, 1 October 1801 and 22 February 1802, B34a/3—all in HBC.

18. J. Kipp to K. McKenzie, 5 September 1834, Box 33, Chouteau Collection, MIHS; George Nidever, *The Life and Adventures of George Nidever*, ed. William Henry Ellison, p. 27; Maximilian, *Travels in the Interior*, 23:71–72, 74, 125–27; Point, *Wilderness Kingdom*, pp. 102, 110, 182, 210.

19. Daniel W. Harmon, *A Journal of Voyages and Travels in the Interior of North America*, ed. Daniel Haskel, p. 291; Chesterfield House Report, 1822–23, B34e/1, HBC; Point, *Wilderness Kingdom*, pp. 15, 124, 262 (actually, the majority fell somewhere in between rich and poor); *Report to Commissioner*, 1856, p. 76. And see Ewers, *The Horse*, p. 31.

20. Flannery, *Gros Ventres*, pp. 29, 70, 73–75, 82; Regina Flannery Herzfeld, field notes, 24 August 1940, CU (these field notes are the transcripts, originally taken in shorthand, of Flannery's conversations and interviews with Gros Ventres through bilingual interpreters during her 1940, 1945, and 1948 research on Fort Belknap reservation); Cooper, *Gros Ventres*, pp. 231–32. Some husbands did not share their profits or favored one wife over another, Flannery learned; these were not considered "good" men.

21. Flannery, *Gros Ventres*, pp. 41–42, 82–86; Herzfeld, field notes, 13 August 1940, CU; Cooper, *Gros Ventres*, pp. 37, 64, 122.

22. Alexander Henry and David Thompson, *New Light on the Early History of the Greater Northwest: The Manuscript Journals of Alexander Henry and of David Thompson*, ed. Elliott Coues, 2: 728–30; Edmonton House Journal, 16 December 1796, B60a/2, HBC.

23. Maximilian, *Travels in the Interior*, 23: 125–26, 166; Kipp to K. McKenzie, 5 September 1834, Box 33, Chouteau Collection, MIHS; Point, *Wilderness Kingdom*, pp. 102, 110, 210; "Fort Benton Journal, 1854–56," 14 January and 4 March 1856, pp. 59 and 65 and passim, pp. 1–99, *Contributions to the Historical Society of Montana* 10 (1940).

24. "Fidler Journal," 28 December 1792, E3/2, HBC. References to gun trade and repair appear throughout the Hudson's Bay Company journals.

25. Manchester House Journal, 31 January 1791, 121a/6, HBC; Duncan M'Gillivray, *The Journal of Duncan M'Gillivray of the North West Company at Fort George on the Saskatchewan, 1794–5*, ed. Arthur S. Morton, p. 50; Chesterfield House Journal, 6 October 1800 and 1 March 1801, B34a/1-2, HBC; "Journal of Occurrences," 28 October 1822, B34a/4, HBC; Point, *Wilderness Kingdom*, pp. 210, 212.

26. Hazard Stevens, *The Life of Isaac Ingalls Stevens by His Son Hazard Stevens*, 1:355–56, 2:114; "Edwin A. C. Hatch Diary," 20 September 1856, SC 810, MOHS; *Report to the Commissioner*, 1857, pp. 120–21; Fort Belknap Journal, 11 November 1873, 2 and 13 January 1874, SC 251, MOHS. See also James Stuart, "Fort Browning, Montana Territory: The Private Memoranda and Record of Current Events, 1871–73," 1 November 1871 and 8, 12, 30 March 1872, Coe Collection, BYU. For the Treaty of 1855, see United States, *Statutes at Large*, 11 (17 October 1855): 657.

27. Ewers, *The Horse*, pp. 20–27, 316, 318–20, 338–39. Note also that Flannery's informants stressed that the gift of a horse brought considerably more prestige than gifts of trade goods: "The importance of various transactions could be gauged by whether or not a horse were included, other things such as fancy clothing, ornaments, guns, etc. being mentioned as 'thrown in'" (*Gros Ventres*, p. 78).

28. Matthew Cocking, "An Adventurer from Hudson Bay: Journal of Matthew Cocking, from York Factory to the Blackfeet Country, 1772–73," ed. Lawrence J. Burpee, pp. 108–12 (6–7, 16–19, 22 October, 4 November, and 1, 4, 14–15 December, 1772); "Cumberland House Journal, 1775–76," 2 July 1776, vol. 14, p. 67, in *Cumberland House Journals and Inland Journal, 1775–82*, ed. E. E. Rich and A. M. Johnson. On Gros Ventre–Assiniboine relations before 1777 see also Ray, *Indians in the Fur Trade*, pp. 21–23; James Isham, *James Isham's Observations on Hudsons Bay, 1743*, ed. E. E. Rich, pp. 113–15, 310–11, 314. Isham states that in the 1740s the Crees and Assiniboines were at war with the "Earchethinues" and raided them for horses and that the Crees traded with them.

29. "Cumberland House Journal, 1776–77," 24 January and 30 June, 1777, 15:112, 168, in *Cumberland House Journals*, ed. Rich and Johnson (entries showing numbers and arrival dates of Gros Ventres also appear throughout the "Hudson House Journals" for 1779–80, 1780–81, and 1781–82, in ibid.); Hudson House Journal, 25 December 1785, B87a/8, and Manchester House Journal, 26 April and 1 May 1788, B121a/2, both in HBC; M'Gillivray, *Journal*, 12 March 1795, p. 62. Descriptions of trade and the expulsion of the Gros Ventres from the vicinity of South Branch appear in South Branch journals (see William Tomison to William Walker, 26 December 1787 and 24 July 1788, B205a/2–3, HBC), and references to the Gros Ventres' being discouraged from even approaching Manchester House appear in that house's journal, 12 May 1790 (B121a/4), HBC. Population estimates for 1780 are Gros Ventres, 3,000; Blackfeet groups, 15,000; Assiniboines, 10,000 (Douglas H. Ubelaker, "The Sources and Methodology for Mooney's Estimates of North American Indian Popula-

tions," in *The Native Population of the Americas in 1492*, ed. William M. De-
nevan, pp. 270–71); and western Crees, 2,200–6,800 (Ray, *Indians in the Fur
Trade*, p. 105). According to James Bradley, Culbertson estimated in 1835 Gros
Ventres, 500 tipis; Blackfeet groups, 1,550 tipis; Assiniboines, 1,000 tipis; Crows,
720 tipis ("Bradley Manuscript," *Contributions to the Historical Society of
Montana* 8 [1917]: 153). Isaac Stevens in 1855 reported Gros Ventres, 2,970;
Blackfeet groups, 8,530 (Stevens, *Life of Isaac Stevens*, 2:505), and Hayden
estimated about 4,000 Crees (*Contributions*, pp. 236–37).

30. W. Tomison to J. Bird, 25 October 1793 and Bird to Tomison, 8 November 1793,
South Branch Journal, B205a/8, HBC; M'Gillivray, *Journal*, 29 August 1794 (pp.
13–16) and 12 March 1795 (p. 63); Buckingham House Journal, 22 October 1793
and 5 February 1794, B24a/2, HBC. See also Edmonton House Journal, 16
December 1796, B60a/2, HBC.

31. Henry, *New Light*, 2:530–31.

32. Harmon, *Journal*, 10 June 1801 (pp. 51–52), and see 26 July 1803 (p. 77); Chester-
field House Journal, 29 October 1801 (M'Gillivray noted that L'Homme de
Callumet led the attack on South Branch House and was shot [*Journal*, 29
August 1794, pp. 13–14]), 21 and 22 February 1802, 3 and 8 March 1802, B34a/3;
Edmonton House Journal, 24 and 25 May 1800, 4 February 1808, B60a/5, 7;
"Journal of Occurrences," 15 and 24 October 1822, 2 March 1823, B34a/4—all in
HBC; Thompson, *Narrative*, p. 311; Henry, *New Light*, 2:719–20.

33. Chesterfield House Journal, 1 December 1800, B34a/2, HBC; Henry, *New Light*,
2:531, 734–35.

34. Henry, *New Light*, 2:531 (1809), 734 (1811), 656–57, 660 (entries for 22, 27, 31
October, 5 November 1810).

35. J. Bird to J. McNab, 23 December 1806, in Edmonton House Journal, B60a/6;
Chesterfield House Report, 1822–23, B34e/1; "Journal of Occurrences," 6
November 1822, 34a/4—all in HBC; Henry, *New Light*, 2:531. Mention of Gros
Ventre visits to the posts occur in Henry, *New Light*, 2:657 (1810); Edmonton
House Reports, 1822–23 and 1823–24, B60e/5–6; "Journal of Occurrences,"
1822–23, passim, B34a/4; Rocky Mountain House Journal, 1828–29, passim,
B184a/1—all in HBC.

36. Meriwether Lewis and William Clark, *Original Journals of the Lewis and Clark
Expedition, 1804–1806*, ed. Reuben Gold Thwaites, 6:101, 106; P. J. De Smet,
Western Missions and Missionaries: A Series of Letters, p. 256; James Stuart,
"Fort Browning," 22 June 1872, Coe Collection, BYU. "Staetan" probably repre-
sents the traders' efforts to write the Southern Cheyenne word for the Gros
Ventre, *hestohetan* (Rodolphe Petter, *English–Cheyenne Dictionary*, p. 582).
(Hayden also recorded this term, His-tu-í-ta-ni-o, in *Contributions*, p. 290.)
Petter notes that the Cheyenne term is a form of the Arapaho word for Gros
Ventre, *hitunena* (begging man). Lewis and Clark's information on the tribes
that they did not come in contact with (for example, the Gros Ventre and
Arapaho) is problematic, for we do not know their source for tribal names and
descriptions. But bands of Gros Ventres were observed in the company of the
Arapahoes by Fidler and others throughout the early nineteenth century and,
according to Pierre-Antoine Tabeau, in 1804 the Caninanbiches and Squi-
hitanes spoke the same language and together roamed between the Yellowstone and Platte Rivers (*Tabeau's Narrative of Loisel's Expedition to the Upper
Missouri*, pp. 154–55). More than forty tipis of Gros Ventres probably left the
Saskatchewan area; Lewis and Clark may have underestimated the Staetans'
numbers or perhaps there are other bands yet to be identified in the records
left by traders and travelers.

37. "Fidler Journal," 15 August and 20 September 1800, E3/2, and Chesterfield House Journal, 17 February, 27 September, 3 October, 7 November 1801, and 15 January and 1 February 1802, B34a/2–3, both in HBC; Henry, *New Light*, 2:720. They reportedly lost 180 horses to the cold and 288 to raiders.

38. M'Gillivray, *Journal*, 22 September and 5 November 1794 and 9 April 1795, pp. 27, 39, 69; Chesterfield House Journal, 31 October and 22 December 1801 and 15 April 1802, B34a/3, HBC; François Larocque, *Journal of Larocque from the Assiniboine to the Yellowstone, 1805*, ed. L. J. Burpee, p. 44. On the Gros Ventres' sojourn with the Arapahoes and their return to Montana in 1832, see W. P. Clark, *The Indian Sign Language*, p. 198; Hayden, *Contributions*, pp. 341–42; Nidever, *Life and Adventures*, p. 26.

39. Thompson, *Narrative*, p. 311; Henry, *New Light*, 2:720; J. Rowand to George Simpson, 8 January 1830, George Simpson Inward Correspondence, 1830–44, 3M57 (and see Bow Fort Journal, 17 November 1833, B21a/1); "Journal of Occurrences," 15 October, 19 November, 4 December 1822, B34a/4—all in HBC. Attacks on Americans are mentioned in Henry, *New Light*, 2:735; Edmonton House Report 1824–25, B60e/8, and J. Rowand to G. Simpson, 8 January 1830, 3M57, George Simpson Inward Correspondence, 1830–44, both in HBC.

40. Ramsay Crooks to Pierre Chouteau, 17 February 1833, and W. M. Astor to Pierre Chouteau, 17 April 1833, Box 29, Chouteau Collection, MIHS; Maximilian, *Travels in the Interior*, 23:62, 71, 75, 112; De Smet, *Western Missions*, p. 254. On the American Fur Company's encouragement of the robe trade, see J. Hamilton to A. Culbertson, 5 May 1835, Box 31, Chouteau Collection, MIHS.

41. Nidever, *Life and Adventures*, pp. 26–27; Maximilian, *Travels in the Interior*, 23:73, 126; Bradley, "Affairs at Fort Benton from 1831 to 1869," *Contributions to the Historical Society of Montana* 3 (1900): 230, 232.

42. Edwin Thompson Denig, *Five Indian Tribes of the Upper Missouri—Sioux, Arickaras, Assiniboines, Crees, Crows*, ed. John C. Ewers, p. 77; Bradley, "Affairs," p. 219.

43. Bradley, "Affairs," p. 273; Kroeber, *Ethnology*, pp. 197–98.

44. Denig, *Five Indian Tribes*, pp. 80, 91–93, 96, 199; *Report to the Commissioner*, 1870, p. 200; "Fort Belknap Journal, 1873–75," passim, SC 251, MOHS; W. Fanton to E. Smith, 5 February 1874, LR-MS.

45. Henry Reed Report, 14 January 1863, and William Dale Report, 15 November 1864, Indian Agent Reports, SC 897, MOHS; Bradley, "Manuscript," pp. 313–14; Charles Larpenteur, *Forty Years a Fur Trader on the Upper Missouri: The Personal Narrative of Charles Larpenteur, 1833–1872*, ed. Elliott Coues 2:335; *Report to Commissioner*, 1862, p. 179; 1863, p. 165; 1869, pp. 299–300; 1870, pp. 198, 200. On smallpox among the Gros Ventres in 1869, see Peter Koch, "Life at Muscleshell in 1869 and 1870," *Contributions to the Historical Society of Montana* 2 (1896):296–97; A. S. Reed to Alfred Sully, 9 November 1869, "General Correspondence—Fort Benton Post," 1867–74, SC 933, MOHS. On the Crows' visits to the Milk River agency, see A. J. Simmons to F. Walker, 9 January and 8 May 1873, and T. Mitchell to E. Smith, 5 July 1876, LR-MS (M234, R495, 505).

46. L. B. Palladino, *Indian and White in the Northwest: A History of Catholicity in Montana, 1831 to 1891*, p. 195; *Report to Commissioner*, 1860, p. 83, and 1855–74, passim. See John C. Ewers, "Ethnological Report on the Blackfeet and Gros Ventre Tribes of Indians," in *Blackfeet Indians*, p. 109, on Gros Ventre territory and its distance from White settlements, and James Bradley, "Affairs at Fort Benton," p. 274, on the Gros Ventres' lack of need for provisions.

47. Bradley, "Manuscript," p. 153, and "Affairs at Fort Benton," p. 226; Hazard,

Life, 2:505; *Report to Commissioner*, 1865, p. 511; 1867, p. 256; 1870, pp. 190, 200; 1874, p. 264.

48. Henry wrote that the Bloods were reputed to be as hostile to traders in the early 1800s as the Gros Ventres, but they were "not so brave" as the Gros Ventres (*New Light*, 2:733, 736). Point commented to De Smet that the Gros Ventres were more "courageous" than the other northern Plains peoples he knew (De Smet, *Western Missions*, pp. 254, 256). Flannery, *Gros Ventres*, pp. 103–4.

49. Flannery, *Gros Ventres*, pp. 89–90.

50. Kroeber, *Ethnology*, pp. 233–34, 268.

51. Cooper, *Gros Ventres*, p. 65; Herzfeld, field notes, 20 July 1945, CU.

52. See Foley, "Historical Analysis," pp. 34–231, and Barry, "Fort Belknap," pp. 39–109, for more detail about reservation conditions in the late nineteenth century.

53. Cooper, *Gros Ventres*, pp. 34–36, 102, 117–20, 122, 131, 148, 152–55, 158, 160; Herzfeld, field notes, 13, 14, and 31 August 1940 and 8 July 1948, CU.

54. F. Eberschweiler to J. Stephan, 30 June and 16 July 1888, BCIM; Feusi to Commissioner of Indian Affairs, 20 September 1891, File 35265-1891, LR; Charles Mackin, "As You Please—Autobiography," pp. 49–50, and W. P. Campbell to I. A. Standing, 6 June 1890, St. Paul's Mission Records, both in OP.

55. On the age-group system see Cooper, *Gros Ventres*, p. 174 (Fly and Old Men's dances were held after reservation settlement but people of any age apparently entered); Kroeber, *Ethnology*, p. 233. On the abandonment of the Sun Dance, see *Report to Commissioner*, 1885, p. 131; 1886, p. 182. The Gros Ventres told Flannery in 1940 that their Sacrifice Lodge was abandoned while other tribes' were not because theirs was the most difficult to go through (Cooper, *Gros Ventres*, p. 196, and Herzfeld, field notes, 31 August 1940 and 14 July 1948, CU).

56. Lincoln to Commissioner of Indian Affairs, 6 February 1884, Box 17, FRC. On abortive attempts to unify, see Eberschweiler to J. Cataldo, 24 May 1886, St. Paul's Mission Records, OP, and Eberschweiler to Stephens, 15 March 1888, BCIM.

57. Kroeber, *Ethnology*, pp. 235–39; Flannery, *Gros Ventres*, pp. 38, 41–42; R. Belt to Commissioner of Indian Affairs, 20 August 1892, File 31098-1892, LR. The Wolfmen purchased the Grass Dance from the Assiniboines about 1875 and adopted it as a replacement for their moiety dance, the Wolf Dance.

58. Cooper, *Gros Ventres*, pp. 264–68; Herzfeld, field notes, 3 August 1940, CU. For example, Bull Lodge, who used "bad medicine," was described in 1879 by Agent Lincoln as "a kind of renegade Gros Ventre who stays most of the time with the Crows" (Lincoln to Commissioner of Indian Affairs, 1 December 1879, Box 29, FRC). See also *The Seven Visions of Bull Lodge*, ed. George Horse Capture, a romanticized account of Bull Lodge's life. A man with medicine power could be a keeper, but he was obligated not to use his power to harm others.

59. On intertribal visits, see E. Fields to Commissioner of Indian Affairs, 22 October 1887, Box 17; J. Kelley to J. Clark, 13 February 1894, Box 54; L. Hays to Indian Agent, Shoshone Agency, 14 May 1898, Box 55; M. Bridgeman to J. Sample, 6 February 1901, and Bridgeman to Indian Agent, Shoshone Agency, 26 January and 12 August 1901, Box 56—all in FRC. On the Ghost Dance among the Gros Ventres see Simons to Commissioner of Indian Affairs, 5 December 1890, File 38204-1890, LR; Cooper, *Gros Ventres*, pp. 252–56.

60. On the hand game among the Gros Ventres, see Cooper, *Gros Ventres*, p. 256; Herzfeld, field notes, 14, 19, 28 August 1940, CU; Rodnick, *Fort Belknap Assiniboine*, p. 11. See Alexander Lesser, *The Pawnee Ghost Dance Hand Game: Ghost Dance Revival and Ethnic Identity*, for a general discussion of the hand game as a revitalization movement and the diffusion of the ceremony through the Plains.

61. Cooper, *Gros Ventres*, p. 257.

62. Lincoln to Commander of Fort Benton, 14 November 1878, Box 31; Lincoln to Commissioner of Indian Affairs, 21 April 1879, Box 46; and Lincoln to J. Keine, 11 December 1883, Box 54—all in FRC. See Ewers, *Blackfeet*, pp. 255–58, on the whisky trade.

63. Proceedings of Councils of the Commissioners Appointed to Negotiate with the Fort Belknap Indians, pp. 7, 11, in U.S. Congress, Senate, Letter from the Secretary of the Interior, Transmitting an Agreement Made and Concluded October 9, 1895, S.D. 117, vol. 4, 54th Cong., 1st sess.

64. G. Sanders, 25 June 1887, G. E. Sanders Papers, Glenbow Museum, Calgary, Canada; Lincoln to Keine, 11 December 1883, Box 54, FRC; Herzfeld, field notes, 20 July 1945 and 8 July 1948, CU; W. Allen to L. Hays, 28 and 31 July 1896, and Flathead to Allen, 22 December 1896, Box 49, FRC.

65. Between 1878 and 1882 the hunts generally were successful and the robe trade was good, although rations were relied on in the winter months (see Lincoln to Commissioner of Indian Affairs, 7 October and 9 December 1878, 3 September 1879, 1 October 1882, Box 29, and 2 January 1882, Box 17—all in FRC; Thomas O'Hanlon to Thomas Powers, 18 October, 8 November, 30 December 1881, 1 October 1882, Box 103, T. C. Powers Papers, MOHS; Secretary of Interior to Commissioner of Indian Affairs, 1 July 1882, File 12017-1882, LR. In fall 1881, Agent Lincoln reported to the Commissioner that the Gros Ventres had many robes: "They feel rich" (4 February 1882, Box 17, FRC). In 1883, however, although some game, especially small game, was obtained during parts of the year, it was no longer possible to subsist on buffalo or profit from the robe trade. Agent Lincoln noted that the game was "practically exhausted" (Lincoln to Commissioner of Indian Affairs, 21 July 1883, File 13947-1883, LR). Trader Thomas O'Hanlon wrote, "The Indians are hungry and there is no game and no trade" (O'Hanlon to Power and Bro., 23 October 1883, Box 104, T. C. Powers Papers, MOHS). Inspector C. H. Howard observed that the "Indians don't have hides to sell now to buy supplies" (5 November 1883, Report no. 4706, IIR). By 1884 the primary means of subsistence for most of the year was agency rations. Lincoln wrote the Commissioner, "It is a pretty sudden change from having plenty of buffalo robes to trade last winter, to having none this winter" (3 January 1884, Box 17, FRC). Trader O'Hanlon noted that the Gros Ventres who traded brought him the furs of small animals, and that they were especially good at trapping beaver (O'Hanlon to Powers and Bro., 19 November 1885, Box 104, T. C. Powers Papers, MOHS).

66. On the Indian Police, see *Report to Commissioner*, 1882, p. 106; 1884, p. 115; 1887, pp. 141–42; Lincoln to Commissioner of Indian Affairs, 1 May 1882, Box 29, and 1 January and 5 November 1883, Box 17—all in FRC; C. H. Howard, 5 November 1883, Report no. 4706, IIR. On the plowing of land for chiefs, see Lincoln to Commissioner of Indian Affairs, 13 October 1883, Box 17; Fields to Commissioner of Indian Affairs, 7 June 1888, Box 17, and 20 December 1888, Box 18—all in FRC; *Report to Commissioner*, 1888, p. 160. On the issue of hides, see Lincoln to Commissioner of Indian Affairs, 8 September 1884; Fields to Commissioner of Indian Affairs, 27 April 1887 and 4 August 1887—all in Box

17, FRC. On purchases, see Lincoln to Commissioner of Indian Affairs, 5 April 1886, Box 17, and Fields to Commissioner of Indian Affairs, 20 December 1888, Box 18, both in FRC; Eberschweiler to Cataldo, 28 July 1885, Box 1, St. Paul's Mission Records, OP. On the issue of cattle, see *Report to Commissioner*, 1885, p. 131; 1887, p. 142; 1888, p. 161; Fields to Commissioner of Indian Affairs, 4 August 1888, Box 17, FRC; Eberschweiler to Stephan, 25 January 1887, Box 23, BCIM; Reduction of Indian Reservations (January 9, 1888), p. 5, H.E.D. 63, 50th Cong., 1st sess., and Letter from the Secretary of the Interior, Transmitting an Agreement Made and Concluded October 9, 1895, p. 3, S.D. 117, 54th Cong., 1st sess. On Gros Ventre demands for cattle, see Fields to Commissioner of Indian Affairs, 22 August 1887, Box 17, and Proceedings of Indian Council, 20 September 1888, Box 31, both in FRC; Eberschweiler to Cataldo, 24 May 1886, St. Paul's Mission Records, OP; Proceedings of Councils of the Commissioners Appointed to Negotiate with the Fort Belknap Indians, 5–9 October 1895, passim in Letter from the Secretary of the Interior, ibid.

67. On Running Fisher's and other Gros Ventres' scouting, see Lincoln to Commissioner of Indian Affairs, 3 September 1881, Box 17, FRC; O'Hanlon to Powers and Bro., 12 December 1881, Box 103, T. C. Powers Papers, MOHS. On Running Fisher's relations with the agent, see Minutes of Council in C. Dickson to Commissioner of Indian Affairs, 27 February 1886, File 7335-1886, LR. On the 1894 delegation, see Proceedings of Council with Gros Ventre and Assiniboine Delegation, 16 November 1894, File 48739-1894, LR.

68. On Sleeping Bear, see Lincoln to E. Otis, 25 November 1885, Box 54; Lincoln to Commissioner of Indian Affairs, 7 December 1885 and 15 February and 2 March 1886, Box 17; W. Logan to Commissioner of Indian Affairs, 4 August 1907, Box 21—all in FRC; *Report to Commissioner*, 1896, p. 191.

69. "Indian Book," 1895, St. Paul's Mission Records, and Mackin, "As You Please— Autobiography," both in OP; Mary Amadeus to J. Kelley, 16 March 1895, Box 49; Eberschweiler to Simons, 18 October 1889, Box 47; J. Kelley to J. Clark, 20 January 1894, Box 54—all in FRC.

70. See Edward Moale to Lincoln, 22 August 1879, Box 31, and Fields to Commissioner of Indian Affairs, 2 August 1887, Box 17, both in FRC; Fields to Commissioner of Indian Affairs, 25 May 1889, File 14268-1889, LR; P. McCormick, 9 July 1895, Report 5355, IIR. Of course, whites married to Gros Ventres also were able to take advantage of their situation, grazing stock under their wives' names so that they avoided grazing fees, obtaining rations and other Indian supplies, and so on.

71. See Ewers, *The Horse*, pp. 21, 30.

72. O'Hanlon to Powers and Bro., 12 December 1881, Box 103, T. C. Powers Papers, MOHS; Kroeber, *Ethnology*, p. 180; Regina Flannery, "The Dearly-Loved Child among the Gros Ventres of Montana," *Primitive Man* 14 (1941): 33–37. On tea dances, see Herzfeld, field notes, 6 August 1940, CU; *Report to Commissioner*, 1885, p. 131; and Report on Indians Taxed and Indians Not Taxed in the United States at the Eleventh Census, 1890, p. 368, House of Representatives Miscellaneous Document no. 340, vol. 50, pt. 15, 52nd Cong., 1st sess. Also see Rodnick, *Fort Belknap Assiniboine*, p. 8 (he reports that the Assiniboine received the tea dance, in which dancers pretended to be drunk, from the Blackfeet before reservation settlement and revived and changed it in 1891).

73. Herzfeld, field notes, 27 July 1945, CU.

74. M. A. Thomas, 17 October 1885, Report 5169, and Walter Graves, 3 September 1898, Report 5502, both in IIR.

75. J. Brooke to Lincoln, 28 July 1878, Box 31; Lincoln to E. Hayt, 6 October and 13

August 1878, Box 29; Lincoln to Commissioner of Indian Affairs, 9 January 1882, Box 17; Lincoln to Commissioner of Indian Affairs, 26 December 1878, Box 29; N. Miles to Lincoln, 4 August 1879, Box 31; Lincoln to Hayt, 1 June 1879, Box 29; Lincoln to Commissioner of Indian Affairs, 10 December 1881, Box 17; Lincoln to Commissioner of Indian Affairs, 5 February 1883, Box 17—all in FRC; *Report to Commissioner*, 1880, p. 115; 1879, p. 98; 1882, p. 105; Lincoln to Commissioner of Indian Affairs, 9 January 1882, File 1303-1882, LR; Eberschweiler to Stephan, 25 January 1887, Box 23, BCIM.

76. Lincoln to Commissioner of Indian Affairs, 13 October 1883, Box 17, FRC. By the act of April 15, 1874, Congress had reduced the boundaries of the Blackfeet Reservation without the tribes' consent (United States, *Statutes at Large*, vol. 18, p. 28).

77. Minutes of Council Meeting, 24 February 1886, File 7335-1886, LR; Eberschweiler to Cataldo, 24 May 1886, Box 1, St. Paul's Mission Records, OP; Reduction of Indian Reservations: Message from the President of the United States, H.E.D. 63, vol. 25, 9 January 1888, 50th Cong., 1st sess., pp. 21–23.

78. Secretary of War to Secretary of Interior, 11 July 1887, File 18124-1887, LR; Report of Meeting between Bloods, Gros Ventres, Assiniboines, 9 June 1887, G. E. Sanders Papers, Glenbow Museum, Calgary; Eberschweiler to Cataldo, 28 July 1885, Box 1, St. Paul's Mission Records, OP.

79. Eberschweiler to Cataldo, 24 May 1886, Box 1, St. Paul's Mission Records, OP; Report of the Subcommittee of the Special Committee of the United States Senate, Appointed to Visit the Indian Tribes in Northern Montana, 7 March 1884, S.R. 283, 48th Cong., 1st sess., p. 236.

80. Lincoln to Hayt, 13 August 1878, Box 29; Fields to Commissioner of Indian Affairs, 8 August 1888, Box 17; Gros Ventre Chiefs to Lincoln, 18 October 1878, Box 46 (and Lincoln to Hayt, 18 October 1878, Box 29)—all in FRC; Report of the Subcommittee of the U.S. Senate, 7 March 1884, p. 247. On the entry of Crees and French-Chippewas and Northern Assiniboines, see Lincoln to Commissioner of Indian Affairs, 16 October 1882, File 19517-1882, LR; Lincoln to Commissioner of Indian Affairs, 16 September 1885, Box 17, and Allen to Hays, 7 August 1897, Box 49, both in FRC; Cataldo to Bureau of Catholic Indian Missions, 11 June 1891, BCIM (at St. Paul's Mission, the French-Chippewa students in the 1890s are all listed as "Assiniboine Half Breeds" or "Mixed Assiniboine" [School Attendance Records 1891, File 3, Box 5, St. Paul's Mission Records, OP]); and see Allen to Hays, 10 June 1896, Box 49, FRC; Report on Indians Taxed, 1890, p. 365. On the Gros Ventres' civilized image, see *Report to Commissioner*, 1881, p. 119; 1882, p. 105; Lincoln to Commissioner of Indian Affairs, 8 February 1885, Box 17, FRC; Eberschweiler to Cataldo, 1 April 1886, Box 1, St. Paul's Mission Records, OP. The Gros Ventres also worked to enroll other Gros Ventres who had been living on the Northern Arapahoe and the Crow reservations.

81. *Report to Commissioner*, 1884, p. 114; 1886, p. 182; 1896, p. 188; W. Junkin, 27 July 1889, Report 4654, and C. Duncan, 26 August 1896, Report 5850, both in IIR; Eberschweiler to W. McAnaney, 25 February 1893, Box 48; M. Bridgeman to J. Sample and W. Allen, 1 August 1900, Box 32; Fields to Commissioner of Indian Affairs, 18 June 1889, Box 18; McAnaney to Commissioner of Indian Affairs, 13 April and 12 May 1893, Box 18—all in FRC; Herzfeld, field notes, 9 August 1940, CU.

82. Proceedings in Letter from the Secretary of the Interior, Transmitting an Agreement Made and Concluded October 9, 1895, with the Indians of the Fort Belknap Reservation, S.D. 117, 54th Cong., 1st sess., p. 14; Rodnick, *Fort Belknap Assiniboine*, p. 118.

83. See Foley, "Historical Analysis," pp. 196–231.

84. See ibid., pp. 232–423, and Barry, "Fort Belknap," pp. 110–243.

85. John Carter, "Notes on the History, Social and Ceremonial Organization of the Gros Ventres of the Prairie, 1909," American Museum of Natural History, New York; Logan to Commissioner of Indian Affairs, 30 June 1909, Box 21, FRC; Herzfeld, field notes, 13 and 30 August 1940, 10 July 1945, and 8 July 1948, CU.

86. Herzfeld, field notes, 13, 15, 30–31 August 1940, CU; Carter, "Notes."

87. Herzfeld, field notes, 19 July 1945, CU; Regina Flannery, "The Changing Form and Functions of the Gros Ventre Grass Dance," *Primitive Man* 20, no. 3 (1947): 42, 50, 61.

88. Flannery, "Changing Form and Functions," pp. 65–66; Fowler, field interviews, personal possession.

89. Logan to Commissioner of Indian Affairs, 19 December 1904, Box 20; Tribal Council Proceedings, 29 January 1904, Box 447, and 7 October 1909, Box 32—all in FRC. Bridgeman was convicted of fraud and sent to prison (an extraordinary event, for dishonest agents usually were simply transferred); Hays committed suicide before he could be indicted.

90. Commissioner of Indian Affairs to Secretary of Interior, 12 December 1907, File 70749-1907, LR; Logan to Commissioner of Indian Affairs, 19 December 1904, Box 20, and 15 December 1908, Box 21, both in FRC; Sleeping Bear et al. to McNichols, 27 January 1907, File 154-21040-1908, CF.

91. Powderface to Logan, 13 December 1909, and Powderface to Miller, 12 February 1914, both in Box 91; W. Granger to F. E. Farrell, 12 January 1910, File CO-CR, Box 78—all in FRC.

92. Fowler, field interviews.

93. Miller to Commissioner of Indian Affairs, 23 February 1911, Box 21; Miller to Business Council, 13 October 1911, Box 68; Martin to Commissioner of Indian Affairs, 19 July 1915, Box 23; Marshall to Commissioner of Indian Affairs, 8 and 29 August 1921, Box 27; E. B. Meritt to Buckman et al., 14 August 1914, Box 95—all in FRC; Martin, 1915, p. 27; Symons, 1919, p. 30; Marshall, 1921, p. 24—all in SNR; Petition from Gros Ventre and Assiniboine Chiefs, 30 May 1901, File 30166-1901, LR.

94. Logan to Commissioner of Indian Affairs, 21 July 1909, Box 21; Farrell to Logan, 1909, and "Lame Bull Estate," 1 September 1909, Box 87; Curly Head to Miller, 8 June 1911, Box 77; Munro to Commissioner of Indian Affairs, 22 July 1918, Box 26—all in FRC; Carter, "Notes." Bushy Head killed his wife because she committed adultery (Herzfeld, field notes, 24 August 1940, CU).

95. Logan to Commissioner of Indian Affairs, 21 July 1909 and 1 May 1910, Box 21; Paul Plumage to Miller, 24 December 1910, and Henry Dwarf to Miller, 19 December 1910, Box 87; The Boy to Farrell, 26 January 1910, Box 75; Report of Rufus Warrior, Spring 1912, Box 95—all in FRC; Flannery, field notes, 11 and 19 July 1945, CU.

96. Logan to Commissioner of Indian Affairs, 29 October 1902, Box 20, and Symons to Commissioner of Indian Affairs, 4 December 1919, Box 26, both in FRC; Logan, 1910, p. 1, SNR.

97. James Snow et al. to Miller, 25 March 1914, Box 76, and R. Warrior to Miller, 21 October 1913, Box 22, both in FRC.

98. Munro to Commissioner of Indian Affairs, 12 January 1918, Box 25, and Cato Sells to Buckman et al., 22 June 1914, Box 85, both in FRC; B. Feusi to W. Ketcham, 24 April 1917, BCIM.

99. J. Marshall, 1924, pp. 20–21, SNR; Herzfeld, field notes, 13 August 1940 and 22 July 1948, CU; Fowler, field interviews.

100. Flannery, "Changing Form and Functions," pp. 51–52, 64–67; Herzfeld, field

notes, 12 July 1945, CU. Flannery notes that women had more wealth in this era because the federal government insisted that wives and daughters would inherit equally with males.

101. Flannery, "Changing Form and Functions," pp. 50–68; Herzfeld, field notes, 11–13 July 1945, CU.
102. M. T. Spooner to C. Tieback, 26 December 1902, Box 52; Logan to Commissioner of Indian Affairs, 9 March 1906, Box 20; Farrell to Logan, 3 January 1909, Letters Rec'd. F, Box 81; J. Matt et al. to Miller, 15 January 1911, Box 83; Frog to Agent, 12 February 1912, Box 81; W. D. Cochran to Miller, 12 March 1913, Box 78—all in FRC; Post to Ketcham, 4 December 1913 and 2 January 1914, BCIM.
103. A Gros Ventre, John Sanborn, mentions Gros Ventre attendance at the Crow fair in 1910 (Sanborn to Miller, 9 August 1910, Box 94, FRC). Fred W. Voget notes that Black Lodge is a district on the Crow reservation; Mountain Crow is a band or division among the Crow (*The Shoshoni-Crow Sun Dance*, pp. 278, 319).
104. Logan to Commissioner of Indian Affairs, 9 March 1906, Box 20; The Boy to Logan, 4 September 1909, Box 75; Miller to Commissioner of Indian Affairs, 22 July 1912, Box 22—all in FRC; Logan to Commissioner of Indian Affairs, 12 November 1906, File 100975-1906, LR; Miller, 1911, p. 12, SNR; Herzfeld, field notes, 20 August 1940, CU.
105. Miller to Commissioner of Indian Affairs, 10 February 1913, Box 22, and C. Rastall to G. Dutro, 20 September 1916, Box 39, both in FRC; Fowler, field interviews.
106. For description of Hays Fair activities, see *Chinook Opinion* (for example, 11 August 1921, 23 August 1923), *Phillips County News*, 13 August 1925, and *Harlem News*, 16 August 1935.
107. Fowler, field interviews.
108. "Letters Received," 1923, File R, Box 92, FRC. Fair committeemen are mentioned in newspaper accounts of the fair.
109. Minutes of council meeting, 6 October 1931, pp. 10–11, File 133, Box 34, FRC; Sleeping Bear et al. to McNichols, 27 January 1907, File 154-21040-1908, CF; Logan, 1910, p. 12, and Marshall, 20 July 1921, p. 11, both in SNR.
110. Logan to Merrill Gates, 6 December 1902, Irregularly Shaped Papers 87, Land Division, Records of the Bureau of Indian Affairs, RG 75, National Archives, Washington, D.C.; Miller, 3 September 1914, p. 19, and Martin, 20 July 1915, p. 27, both in SNR; Martin to Commissioner of Indian Affairs, 13 April 1915, Box 23; Martin to Frances Densmore, 11 October 1915, Box 36; Rastall to Commissioner of Indian Affairs, 21 February 1917, Box 25; Rastall to F. Reilly, 29 June 1916, Box 38; Munro to Commissioner of Indian Affairs, 16 and 29 July 1918, Box 26; Sells to Buckman et al., 21 August 1918, Box 44—all in FRC; Charles Lusk to E. Boll, 11 June 1915, BCIM.
111. Miller to L. J. Bauman, 23 February 1911, Box 68, and F. Baker to Commissioner of Indian Affairs, 13 March 1912, Box 22, both in FRC.
112. Winters v. United States, 6 January 1908, U.S. Reports, Supreme Court, 207:340; Logan to Commissioner of Indian Affairs, 10 December 1905, File 23566-1906, and W. A. Clark to Commissioner of Indian Affairs, 25 January 1906, File 8230-1906, both in LR; Logan to Commissioner of Indian Affairs, 29 April 1906 and 4 March 1907, Box 20; Buckman to Logan, 17 December 1909, Box 75—all in FRC; Feusi to Ketcham, 14 January 1920, BCIM.
113. 35th Annual Report of Indian Rights Association, 1917, p. 44, and 37th Annual Report of Indian Rights Association, 1919, p. 48, both at Historical Society of Pennsylvania, Philadelphia.

114. C. F. Hauke to G. Cochran, 21 May 1913, File 313-67110-1913; Report of the Enrollment Commission, 30 November 1921, and A. Moccasin to Secretary of Interior, 27 March 1923, File 053-100334, pt. 1, 1921—all in CF; United States, *Statutes at Large* 41 (3 March 1921): 1355.

115. C. Burke to Secretary of Interior, 19 June 1922, File 053-100334, pt. 1, 1921, and petition of 24 July 1923, in Gros Ventre Councilmen to Commissioner of Indian Affairs, 5 March 1924, File 053-22711-1924, both in CF; Marshall to Commissioner of Indian Affairs, 29 September 1922, Box 27, and Minutes of General Meeting of Fort Belknap Indians, 29 August 1922, File 063, Box 120, both in FRC.

116. Gros Ventre Councilmen to Commissioner of Indian Affairs, 5 March 1924, File 053-22711-1924, and Buckman et al. to Secretary of Interior, 10 July 1922, File 053-100334, pt. 1, 1921, both in CF.

117. Buckman et al. to Commissioner of Indian Affairs, 30 December 1913, Box 85; Miller to Commissioner of Indian Affairs, 19 April 1913, Box 22; Marshall to Commissioner of Indian Affairs, 21 December 1926, Box 28—all in FRC; Blackfeet et al. v. U.S., Court of Claims Reports 81 (April 8, 1935): 101 (for disposition of judgment money, see U.S., *Statutes at Large* (20 June 1936), 49:1569); Minutes of Tribal Council, 3 July 1922, Tribal Office, Fort Belknap, Mont.; office files, Bureau of Indian Affairs, Fort Belknap; Rodnick, Fort Belknap Assiniboine, p. 71.

118. Logan to Commissioner of Indian Affairs, 9 March 1906, Box 20, FRC; *Phillips County News*, 13 August 1925, 17 July and 28 August 1930, 9 August 1934.

119. Miller, 1911, p. 12, and Rastall, 1917, p. 12, both in SNR; *Chinook Opinion*, 23 August 1923; *Phillips County News*, 13 August 1925; Sumner W. Matteson, "The Fourth of July Celebration at Fort Belknap," pp. 94, 96.

120. J. Piet to Ketcham, 25 February 1908; H. Post to Ketcham, 5 September and 8 November 1912—all in BCIM; Herzfeld, field notes, 31 August 1940, CU; Fowler, field interviews; Cooper, *Gros Ventres*, p. 270.

121. Plains Congress Minutes, 5 March 1934, File 066-4894-1934, pt. 2AA, Records Concerning the Wheeler-Howard Act, 1933–37, RG 75, Records of the Bureau of Indian Affairs, National Archives, Washington, D.C.; Tribal Delegation to Plains Congress, File 066, Box 122, FRC; F. Cohen to Shotwell, 8 January 1934; Earl Wooldridge to Commissioner of Indian Affairs, 24 September 1934; J. W. Elliott to Commissioner of Indian Affairs, 9 October 1934—all in File 308.1-308.3, Box 189, FRC; Elliott to Election Judges, 26 October 1934; Elliott to Commissioner of Indian Affairs, 27 October 1934; Record of Indian Reorganization Act Vote, Indian Reorganization Act Correspondence 1935—all in File 308.3, Box 189, FRC.

122. John Collier to Elliott, 21 May 1935; F. Cohen to Collier, 16 June 1935; W. Zimmerman to Fort Belknap Council, 17 August 1935—all in Indian Reorganization Act Correspondence, 1935–36, File 308.3, Box 189, FRC; W. Bolen to Commissioner of Indian Affairs, 15 January 1934; Collier to Elliott, 5 July 1935; and S. Tretheway to Elliott, 12 July 1935—all in File 066, Box 122, FRC; Lists of Voters, 5 October 1935; Election Board to Commissioner of Indian Affairs, 20 October 1935; Proposed Constitution of Fort Belknap Indian Community (ca. 1935)—all in File 308.3, Box 189, FRC; Annual Statistical Report, 1933, File 051, Box 112, FRC.

123. Commissioner of Indian Affairs to Delegation of 1936, 15 June 1936, File 056-10991-1936, and Transcript of Conference with Fort Belknap Delegates, 28 November 1936, p. 9, File 066-9581-1936, both in CF; Report of Fort Belknap Delegation, 14 April 1936, File 066, Box 122, FRC; Gros Ventre Council to

Secretary of Interior, 10 July 1936, and Zimmerman to Elliott, 10 August 1936, both in Indian Reorganization Act Correspondence, 1936, File 308.3, Box 189, FRC; Census, 1934, Indian Census Rolls, 1888–1940, Records of Bureau of Indian Affairs, RG 75, National Archives, Washington, D.C.; L. W. Shotwell, 1933, SNR. There was a total of 166 Gros Ventre-Assiniboines on the reservation; the total population was 967.

124. Minutes of Council Meeting, 23 February 1937, 064, Box 120, FRC; F. Cohen to Commissioner of Indian Affairs, 25 June 1937, File 066-9581-1936, CF; R. King to Commissioner of Indian Affairs, 23 April 1937; Hagerty to Boyd, 13 April 1937; Assiniboine Tribal Council to Will Rogers, 19 April 1937; Boyd to Commissioner of Indian Affairs, 26 April 1937; Zimmerman to Boyd, 3 May 1937; Council Resolution, 15 June 1937—all in Indian Reorganization Act Correspondence, 1937, File 308.3, Box 189, FRC.

125. *Harlem News,* 3 July 1936 and 24 June 1938; *Phillips County News,* 20 August 1936; Herzfeld, field notes, 13 and 15 August 1940 and 8 July and 2 August 1948, CU. In 1936 a Sun Dance was held at Hays, directed and sponsored by a French-Chippewa from another reservation. Some Gros Ventres today cite Gros Ventre participation in the rite as an additional cause of that year's disasters.

126. J. W. Wellington, taped interview, Summer 1974; Superintendent's Report 1952, Box 8, Wellington Collection, MSU.

127. See Foley, "Historical Analysis," pp. 424–40; Barry, "Fort Belknap," pp. 244–66; Rodnick, *Fort Belknap Assiniboine,* p. 81.

128. Statistical Report, 1951, Box 2; Superintendent's Report, 1952, p. 12, Box 8; Brief on the Fort Belknap Reservation, 1956, Gros Ventre file, Box 8—all in Wellington Collection, MSU; Wellington to House of Representatives, Questionnaire on Tribal Organization, 19 June 1953, p. 12, File 100, Box 127, FRC; Minutes of Fort Belknap Community Council, 18 October 1951, 20 October 1954, 23 April 1956, 6 May 1957, and 11 March 1958—all in Tribal Office, Fort Belknap, Mont.

129. Minutes of Fort Belknap Community Council, 22 July 1955, 2 September 1955, 9 January 1956—all in Tribal Office, Fort Belknap, Mont.; *Harlem News,* 20 June 1958; Brief on the Fort Belknap Reservation, 1956, Gros Ventre file, Box 8, Wellington Collection, MSU.

130. Ten Year Program, 1955–56, Box 2, Wellington Collection, MSU; Minutes of Fort Belknap Community Council, 23 June 1954, Tribal Office, Fort Belknap, Mont.; Wellington to House of Representatives, Questionnaire on Tribal Organization, 19 June 1953, p. 12, File 100, Box 127, FRC; office files, Bureau of Indian Affairs, Fort Belknap.

131. Superintendent's Statistical Report, 1951, Gros Ventre file, Box 8, Wellington Collection, MSU; Data for Superintendent's Statistical Report, 1952, File 051, Box 113, FRC.

132. Minutes of Hays District Community Meeting, 7 February 1943, Box 121, FRC.

133. Rodnick, *Fort Belknap Assiniboine,* p. 120; Brief on the Fort Belknap Reservation, 1956, Gros Ventre file, Box 8, Wellington Collection, MSU.

134. Fowler, field interview, 14 August 1981.

135. Minutes of Fort Belknap Community Council, 4 February 1952 and 10 January 1956, Tribal Office, Fort Belknap, Mont.

136. Minutes of Fort Belknap Community Council, 1 May 1939, File 064 (and see 18 November 1938, File 064, Box 120); Al Chandler to Clark, 24 October 1945, File 064; Charles Heacock to Joe Jennings, 10 April 1942, File 064—all in Box 121,

FRC; Minutes of Fort Belknap Community Council, 15 July 1955 and 7 May 1957, Tribal Office, Fort Belknap, Mont.

137. John Herrick to R. Warrior, 18 March 1939, File 064; Resolutions 1938 (no. 186), File 064, both in Box 120, FRC; Herzfeld, field notes, 14 July 1948, CU; Minutes of Fort Belknap Community Council, 16 May 1946 and passim 1946–56, Tribal Office, Fort Belknap, Mont. Discussion of the claim appears in Minutes of Fort Belknap Community Council, 19 January 1951 and 19 January 1952, Tribal Office, and in the Blackfeet files, Wilkinson, Cragun & Barker, 1957–1963, Washington, D.C. See also Blackfeet et al. v. U.S., Indian Claims Commission Cases, 18 (March 31, 1967): 241, 289. The court decided that the Assiniboine (and Fort Peck Sioux) would share in the award, but affirmed that until 1888 the Blackfeet confederacy had exclusive title to the lands in question. The Blackfeet and Gros Ventre received 100 percent of the amount due for the lands Congress appropriated; the Assiniboine and Fort Peck Sioux got half of the same amount.

138. Correspondence on Resolutions by Tribal Council, 1943, File 064.2, Box 122, FRC; Minutes of Fort Belknap Community Council, 2 July, 3 and 10 August 1953, Tribal Office, Fort Belknap, Mont.; File on 1964 referendum, Office of the Bureau of Indian Affairs, Fort Belknap, Mont.

139. Herzfeld, field notes, 12 July 1948, CU; Rodnick, *Fort Belknap Assiniboine*, p. 109; Minutes of Hays District Committee, 17 January 1942, Box 121, FRC.

140. Minutes of Fort Belknap Community Council, 7 January 1946; 9 January 1956, Tribal Office, Fort Belknap, Mont.

141. Minutes of Fort Belknap Community Council, 1 September 1954 and 7 January 1958, both in Tribal Office, Fort Belknap, Mont. Discussion of the claim appears in Minutes of Fort Belknap Community Council, 19 January 1952 and 1 April 1957, Tribal Office, Fort Belknap; Blackfeet Files, Gros Ventre Correspondence, Wilkinson, Cragun & Barker, Washington, D.C.

142. Minutes of Fort Belknap Community Council, 8 February 1952 (and see 13 May 1955), Tribal Office, Fort Belknap, Mont.

143. Minutes of Fort Belknap Community Council, 5 August 1957 and 8 April 1958, Tribal Office, Fort Belknap, Mont.; *Harlem News*, 20 June 1958.

144. "Fort Belknap Rehabilitation Program 1942," pp. 11 and 24, Gros Ventre file, Box 8, Wellington Collection, MSU; Rodnick, *Fort Belknap Assiniboine*, p. 67; Minutes of Fort Belknap Community Council, 3 September 1958 and 6 December 1954, both in Tribal Office, Fort Belknap, Mont.

145. Minutes of Fort Belknap Community Council, 10 May 1951, Tribal Office, Fort Belknap, Mont.

146. L. W. Shotwell, 1933, SNR; "Fort Belknap Rehabilitation Program 1942," p. 10, Box 8, Wellington Collection, MSU; Clark to Mrs. Waverly Kuhnhenn, 22 March 1945, File 064, Box 121, FRC; Rodnick, *Fort Belknap Assiniboine*, p. 67; Herzfeld, field notes, 13 July 1945, CU. On participation with the Assiniboines, see *Harlem News*, 1 July 1960. On assistance from the tribal government, see Minutes of Fort Belknap Community Council, 28 March 1942, File 064, Box 121, FRC; 1 February 1954; 7 February, 7 March, 6 June, 3 October, 5 December 1955; 13 November and 11 December 1956; 5 February, 1 March, 1 April 1957, and 3 February 1958—all in Tribal Office, Fort Belknap, Mont.

147. Herzfeld, field notes, 2 August 1940, 11 July 1945, and 15 July 1948, CU; Fred Gone statement, Box 14, Wellington Collection, MSU; Rodnick, *Fort Belknap Assiniboine*, pp. 123–24; Clark to Margaret Reynolds, 2 October 1946, File 072, Box 126, FRC.

148. Herzfeld, field notes, 13 August 1940 and 10 and 14 July 1945, CU; Minutes of Fort Belknap Community Council, 4 February 1946, Tribal Office, Fort Belknap, Mont.; J. H. Myers to Clark, 19 June 1946, Box 14, Wellington Collection, MSU.

149. Herzfeld, field notes, 20 July 1948, CU; "Flat Pipe Opened" and "Feathered Pipe Ceremony," both in Box 14, and Photographs of Flat Pipe Bundle Opening, 1951, Box 12, Wellington Collection, MSU (Wellington commented that at the Feathered Pipe ceremony of the summer of 1952 [Flannery's photographs are dated 1951] the pipe "was thought to be a substitute"); Minutes of Fort Belknap Community Council, 13 November 1956 and 10 May 1951, Tribal Office, Fort Belknap, Mont.

150. "Opening of Gros Ventre Sacred Flat Pipe Bundle," Box 14, Wellington Collection, MSU; Herzfeld, field notes, 10 and 19 July 1945 and 20 July 1948, CU.

151. Minutes of Fort Belknap Community Council, 13 November 1956, Tribal Office, Fort Belknap, Mont.

152. Verne Dusenberry, "The Significance of the Sacred Pipes to the Gros Ventre of Montana," *Ethnos* 26 (1961): 26–27; interview by Homer Loucks with Julia Schultz and Peter Long Horse, 21 April 1961, Oral History 76, MOHS.

153. Minutes of Fort Belknap Community Council, 23 June 1958, Tribal Office, Fort Belknap, Mont.; file on 1958 referendum, Bureau of Indian Affairs, Billings, Mont. (the referendum results were approved by the secretary of interior 19 January 1959).

154. Herzfeld, field notes, 13 July 1945, CU.

155. Theodore W. Taylor, *American Indian Policy*, pp. 3–4, 19, 69–70; Robert M. Kvasnicka and Herman J. Viola, *The Commissioners of Indian Affairs, 1824–1977*, pp. 312, 315–20, 327, 329, 334, 343.

156. Statements of Gros Ventres are taken from my field notes and taped field interviews, 1979–1985.

157. *Camp Crier*, 25 June 1971; Leonard Haxby to John Cragun, 6 March 1968, Gros Ventre Correspondence, vol. 2, Blackfeet files, Wilkinson, Cragun & Barker, Washington, D.C.

158. U.S. Department of Commerce, *Census of Population*, 1980, vol. 1, chap. C, pt. 28, Montana, p. 262; office files, Tribal Office, Fort Belknap, Mont.

159. Fred W. Voget, "Adaptation and Cultural Persistence among the Crow Indians of Montana," p. 172.

160. Labor Force Reports, office files, Bureau of Indian Affairs, Fort Belknap, Mont.

161. *Camp Crier*, 19 February 1971.

162. Community Action Program Application, 1966, office files, Bureau of Indian Affairs, Fort Belknap, Mont.

163. Based on Tribal Roll, 1984, office files, Bureau of Indian Affairs, Fort Belknap, Mont.

164. *Camp Crier*, 25 June 1971 and 17 November 1972; Tribal Roll, 1984, office files, Bureau of Indian Affairs, Fort Belknap, Mont. On the disposition of the claim funds, see U.S., *Statutes at Large*, 86:64 (18 March 1972) and 1171 (25 October 1972); 96:2035 (3 January 1983); and Mona Bell Azure et al. v. Morton, 14 May 1975, *Federal Reporter*, 2d ser., 514:897. Despite the tribe's wishes, in 1983 Congress decided that Gros Ventres with one-fourth combined Gros Ventre and Assiniboine blood and at least one-eighth Gros Ventre blood would be paid if they were not on the Assiniboine roll.

165. Barry, "First One Hundred Years," pp. 66, 89, 97.

166. Ibid., pp. 143, 149.

167. Ibid., pp. 54, 76, 78, 93, 111, 143.

168. Ibid., pp. 84, 167–69, 181–82 (my italics).
169. Foley, "Historical Analysis," pp. 152, 208, 403; Proceedings, pp. 14, 19, in Letter from the Secretary of the Interior, Transmitting an Agreement Made and Concluded October 9, 1895, S.D. 117, 54th Cong., 1st sess.
170. Rodnick, *Fort Belknap Assiniboine*, "Preface," pp. 6, 8, 20, 71, 72, 88–90, 94, 125.

2. The Generation Gap: Interpreting Cultural Revival

1. Karl Mannheim, "The Problem of Generations," p. 304. See also Norman B. Ryder, "The Cohort as a Concept in the Study of Social Change," and Alan B. Spitzer, "The Historical Problem of Generations."
2. Almost all individuals in this cohort were born between 1901 and 1929. Of the 129 elders living on or near the reservation in 1984 (100 live elsewhere), only 10 were born before 1901. My understanding of the elder cohort is drawn from repeated recorded conversations with ten men and eleven women in this group during 1979–1985 and less frequent discussions with ten others. Their years of birth ranged from 1895 to 1929; most were born between 1906 and 1918. I found no differences between males' and females' interpretations of the stories, nor were there significant differences between Hays, Dodson, and the agency.
3. The economic problems of the 1930s are discussed in chap. 1. The reader can also consult Loretta Fowler, "Political Middlemen and the Headman Tradition among the Twentieth-Century Gros Ventres of Fort Belknap Reservation," for a more detailed discussion of the 1937–1964 era. Only one World War II veteran that I know of went to college on the GI Bill.
4. My understanding of the youth cohort is drawn from recorded interviews and several informal conversations with each of thirteen men and women in this group. I also had less frequent conversations with nine other men and women of this cohort. In addition to the 297 youths on or near the reservation in 1984, 494 live elsewhere. There were no significant differences between the interpretations of males and females. The terms "education clique" and "militants," used to describe the generation units, are somewhat problematic, for they can imply a negative characterization. The militants often describe the other unit as a "clique" or as the "educated faction" (even though most of the militants themselves have college educations). The education clique often refers to the other unit as "militants" or "AIMs." Each group also at times refers to the other by the name of the group's leader; however, I have avoided using personal names in my discussion. In my use of the terms, my intent is rather to point to the education clique's college campus activities and to the militants' more confrontational approach to political relations and to their view of themselves as nonconformists or purists. By these terms I intend no negative characterization of either generation unit.
5. One of the most influential of the campus organizations was the Kyi-Yo Club at the University of Montana in Missoula. The club organizes an annual pow-wow and various other activities for Indians. Many Gros Ventre youths were officers and members in this organization. See *Montana Kaimin*, vols. 72–76.
6. For background on the American Indian Movement, see Velma S. Salabiye and James R. Young, "American Indian Leaders and Leadership of the Twentieth Century: A Bibliographic Essay," p. 75. A few education clique youths had some involvement with AIM protest activities when they were in college, but their participation was short-lived.
7. There is also a small number of Creeventre youths, some of whom associate

Notes

with the education clique; some are not involved in the youths' activities. There are no Creeventre elders. The Creeventre youths probably have their own interpretations of Gros Ventre history; I did not pursue this possibility systematically.

8. All of the elders' narratives were recorded between 1981 and 1984.

9. Verne Dusenberry, "The Significance of the Sacred Pipes to the Gros Ventre of Montana," pp. 23, 26–27.

10. The elder who placed the offering is particularly respected by elders because he has a college degree.

11. Actually, of course, borrowing among tribes was common in prereservation days.

12. The cohort born between 1825 and 1864 had subsisted by the hunt most of their lives. They had been greatly involved in intertribal warfare, and the religious ceremonies of the age-graded series and the sacred pipe bundles were an integral part of their daily lives. Many were medicine men. By the early twentieth century this group was attempting to transmit their knowledge and values to their children or grandchildren. They brought to the twentieth-century celebrations segments of nineteenth-century rituals, such as reciting war coups, that only they had earned the right to perform. And by their participation and encouragement they validated innovations of the younger cohort born between 1865 and 1894.

   The cohort born between 1865 and 1894 was greatly influenced by the elder 1825–1864 cohort. They were born too late to have participated in communal buffalo hunts, war parties, or Sacrifice Lodge and other religious ceremonies of the age-graded series, but they attempted to adhere to the elders' values while at the same time transforming these value orientations to fit contemporary circumstances. They viewed the protection of the pipes as a sacred duty, even if performance of pipe rituals was not possible. These individuals sought and attained ritual status as singers and dancers in a secular context; thus they earned the right to make innovations and to lead in secular ritual life.

   For their help in reconstructing the history of the Hays Dance Committee I especially thank John Capture, George Chandler, Dorrance Horseman Black Wolf, Ruby Jones, Andrew and Teresa Lame Bull, Gordon Lodge, Elmer Main, Estelle Mount, Bertha Snow, and Jeanette Warrior. I also am grateful to Selena Ditmare, Jenny Gray, Gilbert Horn, Harvey King, Harris Rock, George Shields, and Ron Speakthunder for their help in reconstructing the history of the Milk River Dance Committee. If there are any errors, they are my responsibility.

13. The tradition of using sticks to symbolize property that was to be donated apparently goes back at least to the early nineteenth century. Daniel Harmon noted that Indians in the Saskatchewan area brought food to a gathering if they received a stick of wood (*Journal*, p. 313). Flannery recorded accounts of people of this era who witnessed prominent men presenting sticks to individuals as a pledge of gifts to come. In the twentieth century, the sticks were presented by a committee to potential doners. Often the decoration of the stick signaled what the recipient was expected to bring. In the 1980s the Milk River powwow committee has at times even attached typed labels to the sticks specifying the desired goods.

14. The reader can consult William K. Powers, "Contemporary Oglala Music and Dance: Pan-Indianism versus Pan-Tetonism," for descriptions of the types of songs and dances that were common on the Plains in the early twentieth century and that are common today. Basically, the Grass Dance or war dance

278

and the songs associated with it derived from a mid-nineteenth-century ceremonial complex that spread from tribe to tribe throughout the Plains (see
James H. Howard, "Notes on the Dakota Grass Dance"). Today there are
variations of the dance (some traditional or straight, some fancy), which is
free-style and allows for a great deal of individual creativity in the steps and
body movements. In the early twentieth century, only men participated in the
Grass Dance; today women and children also take part at Fort Belknap and
elsewhere on the Plains. The owl dance (also known as the rabbit dance or the
two-step) is a partner dance in which "men and women clasp hands in
skater's position and shuffle forward" (Powers, "Contemporary Oglala Music,"
p. 275). The ringtail dance is basically a round dance, performed in a circle,
with dancers moving clockwise in a sidestepping movement. The night dance
is a partner dance in which, through comic antics, partners attempt to make
each other laugh.

15. See David Rodnick, *The Fort Belknap Assiniboine of Montana*, pp. 123–24;
Robert Lowie, *The Assiniboine*, pp. 66–70.
16. The flag tradition was apparently incorporated in the Assiniboine dance celebration and committee regalia by Standing Bear. The flag was presented to
him by federal officials: "A Commissioners came here on the reservation from
Washington D.C. and renew the treaty of peace of 1851 made at Fort Laramie.
These Indians sworn allegiance to the United States flag to protect persevere
[sic] peace, wealth, happiness and life of all the United States peoples. The
same flag was presented to Standing Bear" (A. Moccasin to Secretary of Interior, 27 March 1922, in file 053-100334, pt. 1-1921, CF).
17. In 1952 the Sun Dance was directed by the elderly First Chief (J. W. Wellington
Collection, Box 14, MSU).
18. For a description and history of the powwow on the Plains and a discussion
of a pan-Indian tradition in the Plains powwow, see Powers, "Contemporary
Oglala Music" and "Plains Indian Music and Dance"; Samuel W. Corrigan,
"The Plains Indian Powwow: Cultural Integration in Manitoba and Saskatchewan."
19. The Education Powwow, held in the spring, is sponsored by the tribal education office. Tribal members on and off the reservation who are college students or former students are invited to attend, and some are selected as head
dancers. Students of high school age and younger also are encouraged to
participate, and invitations are sent to other reservations in Montana.
20. Women's positions are secretary-treasurer, head cook, princess, and princess
attendant; and one of the cultural advisers is female. Both men and women
can be coordinators.
21. The man who remarked that the staff reminded people not to refuse to
participate may have heard about or read about the Gros Ventre custom of
presenting a pipe to a person when a request was made. A pipe thrust into the
hands of an individual obligated him to grant the request of the bearer of the
pipe, on pain of supernatural sanction. Of course, women do handle the flags
of their male relatives, just as they danced with war trophies of their male
relatives in prereservation days.
22. Gros Ventre stories of Chief Joseph's battle with the army express two themes.
First, the Gros Ventres did what they could to help Nez Perce who were in
need of food and clothing. Second, the Gros Ventres promised not to fight
with the army; therefore, they had a sacred obligation not to intervene to help
the Nez Perce militarily. A story is also told about some emissaries from the
Nez Perce who were killed by Gros Ventres who mistook them for enemies.

23. One elder, I later learned, was named at a dance in the late 1920s; her prominent father asked The Boy to name her.
24. The elder is considered to have authorization to name others because he was instructed in this ceremony by The Boy. I could not determine to my satisfaction what qualified The Boy to name publicly, for he was not a warrior or a medicine man. As an elderly man, he was considered an authority on Gros Ventre culture and instructed Cooper and Flannery, and sometimes nuns from the mission, in Gros Ventre traditions. During this time in his life he gave Indian names to several white people at dances. Most Gros Ventres remember him as the last elder to name publicly.
25. The Assiniboine memorial feast was held a year after the death of a relative. Food left at the grave for the spirit of the deceased symbolically released it from the domain of the living. People in attendance partook of the food and received gifts from the relatives of the deceased person.

3. Who Was Here First? Gros Ventre and Assiniboine Interpretations of History

1. John C. Ewers, "Ethnological Report on the Blackfeet and Gros Ventre Tribes of Indians," p. 2.
2. Ibid., pp. 28–30, 34–35, 37–38, 51, 56, 58, 63, 65, 69–71; Edwin Thompson Denig, *Five Indian Tribes of the Upper Missouri: Sioux, Arickaras, Assiniboines, Crees, Crows*, pp. 68–69, 71–73, 77, 80, 89, 91.
3. Ewers, "Ethnological Report," pp. 81–84, 89, 91, 98, 103–6; Denig, *Five Indian Tribes*, pp. 63–64, 91–92. See the 1855 treaty in U.S., *Statutes at Large*, 11:657.
4. Denig, *Five Indian Tribes*, pp. 79–81; Ewers, "Ethnological Report," pp. 89, 138–41.
5. *Report to the Commissioner of Indian Affairs*, 1867, p. 256; 1869, pp. 289–92, 299–300; 1870, pp. 200–201; A. Sully to Commissioner of Indian Affairs, 18 and 26 February 1870, LR-MS; James Stuart, "Fort Browning, Montana: The Private Memoranda and Record of Current Events, 1871–73," entries for October 1871, March, May, and November 1872, William Robertson Coe Collection, BYU; U.S., *Statutes at Large*, vol. 18, pt. 3, p. 28. The Indian agent indicated that Long Hair was also called Whirlwind, but I am unable to determine if the Whirlwind of the 1870s is the same man as the Whirlwind who Denig reported was head chief in the 1850s (see *Report to the Commissioner*, 1870, p. 200). On 12 March 1872 L. Burnett informed the adjutant general that 500 horse-poor Upper Assiniboines (60 tipis) ranged the same country as their well-mounted Gros Ventre friends (Letters Sent, Fort Benton, Records of the U.S. Army Continental Commands, 1821–1920, RG 393, National Archives).
6. "Fort Belknap Journal, 1873–75," entries for November 1873, January through April 1874, and February 1875, SC 251, MOHS; A. J. Simmons to F. Walker, 9 January 1873, LR-MS; *Report to the Commissioner*, 1874, p. 50; T. S. Kutlaw to Ast. Adj. Gen., 6 August 1875, "General Correspondence—Fort Benton Post," SC 933, MOHS; W. Fanton to E. Smith, 7 November 1873 and 3 February 1876, LR-MS. Fanton reported that the Gros Ventres had many more horses than the Assiniboines and that they objected to the Upper Assiniboines' hospitality to Red Stone's Canoe band of Lower Assiniboines (Fanton to Smith, 5 February 1874, LR-MS). Fanton also stated that when the "hostile" Sioux were near, the Gros Ventres and Assiniboines "joined camps" (Fanton to Smith, 1 September 1875, LR-MS). *Report to the Commissioner*, 1876, p. 93; 1877, p. 137; T. Mitchell to Smith, 5 July 1876, LR-MS. Mitchell wrote that the Gros Ventres were unwill-

ing to go to Fort Peck for fear that the more numerous Sioux there would seize their property. He stated that nineteen lodges of Assiniboines who were intermarried with the Gros Ventres delayed going to Fort Peck despite his insistence (Mitchell to Smith, 7 September 1876, LR-MS).

7. See the Assiniboine narrations in Box 14, J. Wellington Collection, MSU; Statement of William Bent in Miller to Commissioner of Indian Affairs, 10 March 1911, Box 21, FRC.

8. *Report to the Commissioner*, 1878, p. xliv; W. Lincoln to G. Ilges, 16 October 1878, Box 31; Lincoln to Commissioner of Indian Affairs, 7 October 1878, and Lincoln to E. Hayt, 3 July 1878, both in Box 29—all in FRC. Lincoln reported that 600 Upper Assiniboines were permanently allied with 1,000 Gros Ventres.

9. The narratives throughout this chapter are from my tape-recorded field interviews, unless otherwise indicated.

10. For the history of the enrollment process, see File 053-100334, pt. 1-2-1921, CF.

11. Statement of The Boy to General H. Scott, ca. 1922, Blackfeet files, Wilkinson, Cragun, & Barker, Washington, D.C. See also Minutes of the General Meeting of the Fort Belknap Indians, 29 August 1922, 063 Tribal Enrollment, Box 120, FRC.

12. Ibid.

13. Ibid.

14. Testimony of Speakthunder on Rattling Day, Dancing Dog, and August Moccasin to Secretary of Interior, 27 March 1922, and Boy Chief to Commissioner of Indian Affairs, 15 December 1921—all in File 053-100334, pt. 1-1921, CF; Minutes of the General Meeting of the Fort Belknap Indians, 29 August 1922, p. 4, 063 Tribal Enrollment, Box 120, FRC.

15. Ibid.

16. Transcript of Conference between Assiniboine and Gros Ventre Delegation, Tribal Attorneys and Representatives of Indian Office in Washington, 28 November 1936, pp. 1–2, 5–6, in File 066-9511-1936, CF.

17. Ibid.

18. See Loretta Fowler, *Arapahoe Politics, 1851–1978: Symbols in Crises of Authority*, for a more extensive discussion of intermediary leadership.

19. For more detail on Gros Ventre and Assiniboine concepts about the supernatural, the reader can consult John Cooper, *The Gros Ventres of Montana:* pt. 2, *Religion and Ritual*, and Robert Lowie, *The Assiniboine*.

20. The literature on giveaways focuses on the social functions, not the symbolic associations in Plains ceremonies (see Alice B. Kehoe, "The Giveaway Ceremony of Blackfoot and Plains Cree"; Katherine Weist, "Giving Away: The Ceremonial Distribution of Goods among the Northern Cheyenne of Southeastern Montana"; Elizabeth S. Grobsmith, "The Lakhota Giveaway: A System of Social Reciprocity"). Mary Jane Schneider, "Economic Aspects of Mandan/Hidatsa Giveaways," also views the giveaway as primarily an "ethnic boundary," since there are variations in form and content from reservation to reservation (p. 49).

21. H. Miller to Commissioner of Indian Affairs, 2 February 1914, Box 46, FRC.

22. Letter from the Secretary of the Interior, Transmitting an Agreement Made and Concluded October 9, 1895, with the Indians of the Fort Belknap Reservation (12 February 1895), pp. 8, 9, 16, 17, S.D. 117, vol. 4, 54th Cong., 1st sess.

23. Report of the Subcommittee of the Special Committee of the United States Senate, Appointed to Visit the Indian Tribes in Northern Montana (7 March 1884), S.R. 283, 48th Cong., 1st sess., pp. 247–48. The interpreters chosen at the September 19, 1883, conference were William Bent for the Assiniboines and Jack Brown for the Gros Ventres.

Notes

Conclusions

1. See David Rodnick, "Political Structure and Status among the Assiniboine Indians."
2. Samuel W. Corrigan, "The Plains Indian Powwow: Cultural Integration in Manitoba and Saskatchewan," pp. 256, 268, 270–71; James H. Howard, "Pan-Indian Culture of Oklahoma," pp. 215–20.
3. Edward E. Barry, "The Fort Belknap Indian Reservation: The First One Hundred Years, 1855–1955," MSU. Barry's and Foley's manuscripts were prepared for the tribes' litigation efforts beginning in the 1960s.
4. Michael F. Foley, "An Historical Analysis of the Administration of the Fort Belknap Indian Reservation by the United.States," MSU.
5. John C. Ewers considered whether the Northwest Plains area was distinct from the rest of the Plains by virtue of culture traits and argued that it was not ("Was There a Northwestern Plains Sub-Culture? An Ethnographical Appraisal"). Others have discussed the cultural variation between the Prairie or Eastern Plains and the rest of the Plains in terms of ecological factors (see Waldo R. Wedel, *Prehistoric Man on the Great Plains;* Fred Eggan, *The American Indian: Perspectives for the Study of Social Change,* pp. 45–77). Preston Holder has discussed ways in which the cultural ecology of the Prairie and Great Plains areas influenced the course of their postcontact histories (*The Hoe and the Horse on the Plains: A Study of Cultural Development among North American Indians*). No work has yet been done comparing the Southern Plains and other areas.
6. A definitive discussion of the origins and variation of the age-group systems is not possible given the lack of documentary sources on Arapahoes and Gros Ventres in the eighteenth century. The reader can consult Loretta Fowler, "'Look at My Hair, It Is Gray,'" for more detail on these age-set/age-grade systems.
7. On the moiety system as an aspect of age grading, see Frank Henderson Stewart, *Fundamentals of Age-Group Systems,* p. 322.
8. Fowler, *Arapahoe Politics, 1851–1978.*
9. Ibid., pp. 298–99.
10. S. Douglas Youngkin discusses a case where different bands, some with a hostile and some a friendly strategy, were placed on the same reservation, and considers the repercussions of these strategies on social relations between tribes and between Indian and white ("'Hostile and Friendly': The 'Pygmalion Effect' at Cheyenne River Agency, 1873–77").
11. Personal communication, Raymond DeMallie.
12. For the Menominee case, see Nancy O. Lurie, "Menominee Termination: From Reservation to Colonization."
13. See Pamela Amoss, "Coast Salish Elders." But, as was the case with the Gros Ventres, Gerry C. Williams reports that among nonreservation Indians of Oklahoma renewed interest in traditional culture was stressful for the elderly, who were not very knowledgable about traditions ("Warriors No More: A Study of the American Indian Elderly").

References

Archival and Unpublished Sources

Billings, Montana

Office of the Bureau of Indian Affairs, office files.

Bozeman, Montana

Montana State University, Special Collections:
  Edward E. Barry. "The Fort Belknap Indian Reservation: The First One Hundred Years, 1885–1955." 1973.
  Michael F. Foley. "An Historical Analysis of the Administration of the Fort Belknap Indian Reservation by the United States." 1975.
  "The Fort Belknap Reservation Area—Its Resources and Development Potential." Missouri River Basin Investigations Project, Report 198. Billings, 1972.
  Interview with J. W. Wellington, Summer 1974.
  J. W. Wellington Collection.

Calgary, Canada

Glenbow Museum, G. E. Sanders Papers.

Fort Belknap, Montana

Bureau of Indian Affairs, office files.
Tribal Office:
  Minutes of Fort Belknap Community Council.
  Minutes of Tribal Council.

Helena, Montana

Montana Historical Society:
  Lemuel Burke, Diary, 1877 (SC 500).
  Edwin A. C. Hatch Diary, 1856 (SC 810).

283

References

Fort Belknap Journal, 1873–1875 (SC 251).
General Correspondence—Fort Benton Post, 1867–1874 (SC 933).
Indian Agent Reports, 1861–1871 (SC 897).
Interview by Homer Loucks with Julia Schultz and Peter Long Horse, 21 April 1961 (Oral History 76).
T. C. Powers Papers, 1867–1951 (MS 55).

Milwaukee, Wisconsin

Marquette University, Bureau of Catholic Indian Missions Records.

New Haven, Connecticut

Beinecke Rare Book and Manuscript Library, Yale University, William Robertson Coe Collection: James Stuart, "Fort Browning, Montana Territory: The Private Memoranda and Record of Current Events, 1871–73."

New York, New York

American Museum of Natural History, Anthropology Department: John Carter, "Notes on the History, Social and Ceremonial Organization of the Gros Ventres of the Prairie, 1909."

Philadelphia, Pennsylvania

Historical Society of Pennsylvania, Annual Reports of the Indian Rights Association.

St. Louis, Missouri

Missouri Historical Society, Chouteau Collection, 1752–1890.

Seattle, Washington

Federal Archives and Records Center, Fort Belknap Records, 1877–1958, 604 boxes, Record Group 75.

Spokane, Washington

Gonzaga University, Oregon Province Archives of the Society of Jesus: Charles Mackin, "As You Please—Autobiography," ca. 1891.
St. Paul's Mission, Montana, Records.

Washington, D.C.

Catholic University of America, Department of Anthropology: Regina Flannery Herzfeld, field notes (personal possession).
National Archives:
  Records of the Bureau of Indian Affairs, Record Group 75:
    Central Files, 1907–1939, Fort Belknap Agency.
    Indian Census Rolls, 1888–1940.
    Irregularly Shaped Papers, Land Division.
    Letters Received by the Office of Indian Affairs, 1824–1881, Montana Superintendency.
    Letters Received by the Office of Indian Affairs, 1881–1907.
    Records Concerning the Wheeler-Howard Act, 1933–1937.

Superintendents' Annual Narrative and Statistical Reports from Fort Belknap Agency, 1907–1938.

Records of the Office of the Secretary of the Interior, Record Group 48, and Records of the Bureau of Indian Affairs, Record Group 75.

Reports of Inspection of the Field Jurisdictions of the Office of Indian Affairs, 1873–1900, Fort Belknap Agency.

Records of the U.S. Army Continental Commands, 1821–1920, Record Group 393.

Wilkinson, Cragun & Barker Law Offices, Blackfeet files.

Winnipeg, Canada

Provincial Archives of Manitoba, Hudson's Bay Company Archives:
Bow Fort Journal, 1833–34 (B 21a).
Buckingham House Journals, 1792–1799, 6 vols. (B 24a).
Chesterfield House Journals, 1800–1802, 1822–23, 3 vols. (B 34a).
Chesterfield House Reports, 1822–23, 2 vols. (B 34e).
Edmonton House Journals, 1795–1800, 1806–08, 7 vols. (B 60a).
Edmonton House Reports, 1815–1824, 6 vols. (B 60e).
Peter Fidler's Journals, 1790–1809, 5 vols. (E 3).
George Simpson Inward Correspondence, 1830–1844.
Hudson House Journals, 1778–1787, 9 vols. (B 87a).
Journal of Occurrences, Bow River Expedition, 1822–23, 1 vol. (B 34a/4).
Manchester House Journals, 1786–1793, 8 vols. (B 121a).
Rocky Mountain House Journals, 1828–1831, 5 vols. (B 184a).
South Branch Journals, 1786–1794, 8 vols. (B 205a).

Federal Documents

Federal Reporter, 2d series.
Indian Claims Commission Cases.
Reports to the Commissioner of Indian Affairs, 1846–1906.
Statutes at Large.
U.S. Congress, House. *Reduction of Indian Reservations: Message from the President of the United States* (9 January 1888). House Executive Document 63, vol. 25, 50th Cong., 1st sess.
_____. *Report on Indians Taxed and Indians Not Taxed in the United States at the Eleventh Census: 1890.* House Misc. Document 340, vol. 50, pt. 15, 52d Cong., 1st sess.
U.S. Congress, Senate. Letter from the Secretary of the Interior, Transmitting an Agreement Made and Concluded October 9, 1895, with the Indians of the Fort Belknap Reservation (12 February 1896). Senate Document 117, vol. 4, 54th Cong., 1st sess.
_____. Report of the Subcommittee of the Special Committee of the United States Senate, Appointed to Visit the Indian Tribes in Northern Montana, 7 March 1884. Senate Report 283, 48th Cong., 1st sess.
U.S. Court of Claims. *Blackfeet v. United States,* 81, 101 (1935).
U.S. Department of Commerce, Bureau of the Census. *Census of Population, 1980,* pt. 28, Montana.

References

Newspapers

Camp Crier, Tribal Office, Fort Belknap, Montana.
Chinook Opinion, Chinook, Montana.
Harlem News, Harlem, Montana.
Montana Kaimin, University of Montana, Missoula.
Phillips County News, Malta, Montana.

Books and Articles

Amoss, Pamela T. "Coast Salish Elders." In *Other Ways of Growing Old*, ed. Pamela T. Amoss and Stevan Harrell. Stanford: Stanford University Press, 1981.

Basso, Keith H. " 'Stalking with Stories': Names, Places, and Moral Narratives among the Western Apache." In *Text, Play, and Story: The Construction and Reconstruction of Self and Society*, ed. Edward M. Bruner. 1983 Proceedings of the American Ethnological Society. Washington, D.C., 1984.

Blu, Karen I. *The Lumbee Problem: The Making of an American Indian People*. New York: Cambridge University Press, 1980.

Bohannan, Laura. "A Genealogical Charter." *Africa* 22 (1952): 301–15.

Bradley, James. "Affairs at Fort Benton from 1831 to 1869." *Contributions to the Historical Society of Montana* 3 (1900): 201–87.

———. "Bradley Manuscript." *Contributions to the Historical Society of Montana* 8 (1917): 105–250; 9 (1923): 226–351.

Brant, Charles S., ed. *Jim Whitewolf: The Life of a Kiowa Apache Indian*. New York: Dover, 1969.

Braroe, Niels Winther. *Indian and White: Self-Image and Interaction in a Canadian Plains Community*. Stanford: Stanford University Press, 1975.

Bruner, Edward M. "Introduction: The Opening Up of Anthropology." In *Text, Play, and Story: The Construction and Reconstruction of Self and Society*, ed. Edward M. Bruner. 1983 Proceedings of the American Ethnological Society. Washington, D.C., 1984.

———. "Mandan." In *Perspectives in American Indian Culture Change*, ed. Edward H. Spicer. Chicago: University of Chicago Press, 1961.

Carmack, Robert M. "Ethnohistory: A Review of Its Development, Definitions, Methods, and Aims." In *Annual Review of Anthropology*. Palo Alto: Annual Reviews, 1972.

Clark, W. P. *The Indian Sign Language*. Philadelphia: L. R. Hamersly, 1885.

Clemmer, Richard O. "Truth, Duty, and the Revitalization of Anthropologists: A New Perspective on Culture Change and Resistance." In *Reinventing Anthropology*, ed. Dell Hymes. New York: Vintage, 1969.

Cocking, Matthew. "An Adventurer from Hudson Bay: Journal of Matthew Cocking, from York Factory to the Blackfeet Country, 1772–73." Ed. Lawrence J. Burpee. *Transactions of the Royal Society of Canada*, 3d ser., 2 (1908): 89–121.

Cooper, John M. *The Gros Ventres of Montana*, pt. 2, *Religion and Ritual*. Ed. Regina Flannery. Washington, D.C.: Catholic University of America Press, 1957.

Corrigan, Samuel W. "The Plains Indian Powwow: Cultural Integration in Manitoba and Saskatchewan." *Anthropologica* 12 (1970): 253–77.

Curtis, Edward S. *The North American Indian.* Ed. Frederick Webb Hodge. 20 vols. Cambridge: Cambridge University Press, 1907–30.

Daniels, Robert E. "Cultural Identities among the Oglala Sioux." In *The Modern Sioux,* ed. Ethel Nurge. Lincoln: University of Nebraska Press, 1970.

DeMallie, Raymond J. "American Indian Kinship Systems: The Dakota." In *Currents in Anthropology: Essays in Honor of Sol Tax,* ed. Robert Hinshaw. The Hague: Mouton, 1979.

———. "Pine Ridge Economy: Cultural and Historical Perspective." In *American Indian Economic Development,* ed. Sam Stanley. The Hague: Mouton, 1978.

———. "Sioux Ethnohistory: A Methodological Critique." *Journal of Ethnic Studies* 4 (1976): 77–83.

Denig, Edwin Thompson. *Five Indian Tribes of the Upper Missouri: Sioux, Arickaras, Assiniboines, Crees, Crows.* Ed. John C. Ewers. Norman: University of Oklahoma Press, 1961.

De Smet, P. J. *Western Missions and Missionaries: A Series of Letters.* New York: James B. Kirker, 1863.

Dozier, Edward P. *Hano: A Tewa Indian Community in Arizona.* New York: Holt, Rinehart & Winston, 1966.

Dusenberry, Verne. "The Significance of the Sacred Pipes to the Gros Ventre of Montana." *Ethnos* 26 (1961): 12–29.

———. "Waiting for a Day That Never Comes: The Dispossessed Métis of Montana." In *The New Peoples: Being and Becoming Métis in North America,* ed. Jacqueline Peterson and Jennifer S. H. Brown. Lincoln: University of Nebraska Press, 1985.

Eggan, Fred. *The American Indian: Perspectives for the Study of Social Change.* Chicago: Aldine, 1966.

———, ed. "From History to Myth: A Hopi Example." In *Essays in Social Anthropology and Ethnology.* University of Chicago Studies in Anthropology Series in Social, Cultural, and Linguistic Anthropology 1. Chicago: Department of Anthropology, University of Chicago, 1975.

Ewers, John C. *The Blackfeet: Raiders on the Northwestern Plains.* Norman: University of Oklahoma Press, 1958.

———. "Ethnological Report on the Blackfeet and Gros Ventre Tribes of Indians." In *Blackfeet Indians.* American Indian Ethnohistory Series, ed. David Agee Horr. New York: Garland, 1974.

———. *The Horse in Blackfoot Indian Culture.* Bureau of American Ethnology Bulletin 159. Washington, D.C.: Smithsonian Institution, 1955.

———. "Was There a Northwestern Plains Sub-culture? An Ethnographical Appraisal." *Plains Anthropologist* 12 (1967): 167–74.

Flannery, Regina. "The Changing Form and Functions of the Gros Ventre Grass Dance." *Primitive Man* 20 (1947): 39–70.

———. "The Dearly-Loved Child among the Gros Ventres of Montana." *Primitive Man* 14 (1941): 33–37.

———. *The Gros Ventres of Montana,* pt. I, *Social Life.* Washington, D.C.: Catholic University of America Press, 1953.

"Fort Benton Journal, 1854–56." *Contributions to the Historical Society of Montana* 10 (1940): 1–99.

Fowler, Loretta. *Arapahoe Politics, 1851–1978: Symbols in Crises of Authority.* Lincoln: University of Nebraska Press, 1982.

References

_____. "'Look at My Hair, It Is Gray': Age Grading, Ritual Authority, and Political Change among the Northern Arapahoe and Gros Ventre." In *Plains Indian Studies: A Collection of Essays in Honor of John C. Ewers and Waldo R. Wedel*, ed. Douglas H. Ubelaker and Herman J. Viola. Smithsonian Contributions to Anthropology 30. Washington, D.C.: Smithsonian Institution, 1982.

_____. "Political Middlemen and the Headman Tradition among the Twentieth-Century Gros Ventres of Fort Belknap Reservation." *Journal of the West* 23 (1984): 54–63.

Geertz, Clifford. *The Interpretation of Cultures*. New York: Basic Books, 1973.

_____. *The Social History of an Indonesian Town*. Cambridge, Mass.: M.I.T. Press, 1965.

Grobsmith, Elizabeth S. "The Lakhota Giveaway: A System of Social Reciprocity." *Plains Anthropologist* 24 (1979): 123–31.

_____. *Lakota of the Rosebud: A Contemporary Ethnograpy*. New York: Holt, Rinehart & Winston, 1981.

Harmon, Daniel W. *A Journal of Voyages and Travels in the Interior of North America*. Ed. Daniel Haskel. New York: Allerton, 1922.

Hayden, F. V. *Contributions to the Ethnography and Philology of the Indian Tribes of the Missouri Valley*. Philadelphia: C. Sherman, 1862.

Henry, Alexander, and David Thompson. *New Light on the Early History of the Greater Northwest: The Manuscript Journals of Alexander Henry and of David Thompson, 1799–1814*. Ed. Elliott Coues. 3 vols. New York: Francis P. Harper, 1897.

Holder, Preston. *The Hoe and the Horse on the Plains: A Study of Cultural Development among North American Indians*. Lincoln: University of Nebraska Press, 1970.

Horse Capture, George, ed. *The Seven Visions of Bull Lodge*. Ann Arbor: Bear Claw Press, 1980.

Howard, James H. "Notes on the Dakota Grass Dance." *Southwestern Journal of Anthropology* 7 (1951): 82–85.

_____. "Pan-Indian Culture of Oklahoma." *Scientific Monthly* 81 (1955): 215–20.

Hudson, Charles. "Folk History and Ethnohistory." *Ethnohistory* 13 (1966): 52–70.

Isham, James. *James Isham's Observations on Hudsons Bay, 1743, and Notes and Observations on a Book Entitled a Voyage to Hudsons Bay in the Dobbs Galley, 1749*. Ed. E. E. Rich. Toronto: Champlain Society, 1949.

Jorgensen, Joseph G. "Indians and the Metropolis." In *The American Indian in Urban Society*, ed. Jack O. Waddell and O. Michael Watson. Boston: Little, Brown, 1971.

_____. *The Sun Dance Religion: Power for the Powerless*. Chicago: University of Chicago Press, 1972.

Kehoe, Alice B. "The Dakotas in Saskatchewan." In *The Modern Sioux*, ed. Ethel Nurge. Lincoln: University of Nebraska Press, 1970.

_____. "The Giveaway Ceremony of Blackfoot and Plains Cree." *Plains Anthropologist* 25 (1980): 17–26.

Koch, Peter. "Life at Muscleshell in 1869 and 1870." *Contributions to the Historical Society of Montana* 2 (1896): 292–303.

Kroeber, A. L. *Ethnology of the Gros Ventre*. American Museum of Natural History Anthropological Papers 1 (1908).

Kvasnicka, Robert M., and Herman J. Viola, eds. *The Commissioners of Indian Affairs, 1824–1977*. Lincoln: University of Nebraska Press, 1979.

Larocque, François. *Journal of Larocque from the Assiniboine to the Yellowstone, 1805.* Ed. L. J. Burpee. Canadian National Archives Publication 3 (1910).

Larpenteur, Charles. *Forty Years a Fur Trader on the Upper Missouri: The Personal Narrative of Charles Larpenteur, 1833–1872.* Ed. Elliott Coues. 2 vols. New York: Francis P. Harper, 1898.

Lesser, Alexander. *The Pawnee Ghost Dance Hand Game: Ghost Dance Revival and Ethnic Identity.* 1933. Rpt. Madison: University of Wisconsin Press, 1978.

Lewis, Meriwether, and William Clark. *Original Journals of the Lewis and Clark Expedition, 1804–1806.* Ed. Reuben Gold Thwaites. 8 vols. New York: Dodd, Mead, 1904–5.

Lewis, Oscar. *The Effects of White Contact upon Blackfoot Culture: With Special Reference to the Role of the Fur Trade.* American Ethnological Society Monograph 6 (1942).

Linton, Ralph, ed. *Acculturation in Seven American Indian Tribes.* New York: Appleton-Century, 1940.

Lowie, Robert H. *The Assiniboine.* American Museum of Natural History Paper 4 (1909).

―――. *Plains Indian Age Societies: Historical and Comparative Summary.* American Museum of Natural History Paper 11 (1916).

Lurie, Nancy O. "Menominee Termination: From Reservation to Colonization." *Human Organization* 21 (1972): 257–70.

McFee, Malcolm. *Modern Blackfeet: Montanans on a Reservation.* New York: Holt, Rinehart & Winston, 1972.

M'Gillivray, Duncan. *The Journal of Duncan M'Gillivray of the North West Company at Fort George on the Saskatchewan, 1794–5.* Ed. Arthur S. Morton. Toronto: Macmillan, 1929.

Macgregor, Gordon. *Warriors without Weapons: A Study of the Society and Personality Development of the Pine Ridge Sioux.* Chicago: University of Chicago Press, 1946.

Mannheim, Karl. "The Problem of Generations." In *Essays on the Sociology of Knowledge,* ed. Paul Kecskemeti. New York: Oxford University Press, 1952.

Matteson, Sumner W. "The Fourth of July Celebration at Fort Belknap." *Pacific Monthly* 16 (1906): 92–102.

Maximilian, Alexander Philip. *Travels in the Interior of North America, 1832–34.* Ed. Reuben Gold Thwaites. Early Western Travels, 1748–1846, vols. 22–24. Cleveland: Arthur H. Clark, 1906.

Medicine, Beatrice. "Indian Women and the Renaissance of Traditional Religion." In *Sioux Indian Religion: Tradition and Innovation,* ed. Raymond J. DeMallie and Douglas R. Parks. Norman: University of Oklahoma Press, 1987.

Moore, John H. "Cheyenne Political History, 1820–1894." *Ethnohistory* 21 (1974): 329–59.

Nidever, George. *The Life and Adventures of George Nidever.* Ed. William Henry Ellison. Berkeley: University of California Press, 1937.

Palladino, L. B. *Indian and White in the Northwest: A History of Catholicity in Montana, 1831 to 1891.* Lancaster, Pa.: Wickersham, 1922.

Parks, Douglas R., Margot Liberty, and Andrea Ferenci. "Peoples of the Plains." In *Anthropology on the Great Plains,* ed. W. Raymond Wood and Margot Liberty. Lincoln: University of Nebraska Press, 1980.

Petter, Rodolphe. *English-Cheyenne Dictionary.* Kettle Falls, Wash., 1915.

References

Pitt, David C. *Using Historical Sources in Anthropology and Sociology*. New York: Holt, Rinehart & Winston, 1972.

Point, Nicolas. *Wilderness Kingdom: Indian Life in the Rocky Mountains, 1840–1847*. Trans. Joseph P. Donnelly. New York: Holt, Rinehart & Winston, 1967.

Powell, Peter J. *Sweet Medicine: The Continuing Role of the Sacred Arrows, the Sun Dance, and the Sacred Buffalo Hat in Northern Cheyenne History*. 2 vols. Norman: University of Oklahoma Press, 1969.

Powers, William K. "Contemporary Oglala Music and Dance: Pan-Indianism versus Pan-Tetonism." In *The Modern Sioux: Social Systems and Reservation Culture*, ed. Ethel Nurge. Lincoln: University of Nebraska Press, 1970.

———. *Oglala Religion*. Lincoln: University of Nebraska Press, 1977.

———. "Plains Indian Music and Dance." In *Anthropology on the Great Plains*, ed. W. Raymond Wood and Margot Liberty. Lincoln: University of Nebraska Press, 1980.

Ray, Arthur J. *Indians in the Fur Trade: Their Role as Trappers, Hunters, and Middlemen in the Lands Southwest of Hudson Bay, 1660–1870*. Toronto: University of Toronto Press, 1974.

Rich, E. E., and A. M. Johnson, eds. *Cumberland House Journals and Inland Journal, 1775–1779 and 1775–82*. Hudson Bay Record Society Publications 14, 15 (1951–52).

Ritter, Madeline Lattman. "The Conditions Favoring Age-Set Organization." *Journal of Anthropological Research* 36 (1980): 87–104.

Rodnick, David. *The Fort Belknap Assiniboine of Montana: A Study in Culture Change*. 1938. Rpt. New York: AMS, 1978.

———. "Political Structure and Status among the Assiniboine Indians." *American Anthropologist* 39 (1937): 408–16.

Rosaldo, Renato. *Ilongot Headhunting, 1883–1974: A Study in Society and History*. Stanford: Stanford University Press, 1980.

Ryder, Norman B. "The Cohort as a Concept in the Study of Social Change." *American Sociological Review* 30 (1965): 843–61.

Salabiye, Velma S., and James R. Young. "American Indian Leaders and Leadership of the Twentieth Century: A Bibliographic Essay." *Journal of the West* 23 (1984): 70–76.

Schneider, Mary Jane. "Economic Aspects of Mandan/Hidatsa Giveaways." *Plains Anthropologist* 26 (1981): 43–50.

Schusky, Ernest L. *The Forgotten Sioux: An Ethnohistory of the Lower Brule Reservation*. Chicago: Nelson-Hall, 1975.

Scott, Hugh Lennox. "The Early History and Names of the Arapaho." *American Anthropologist* 9 (1907): 545–60.

Sharrock, Susan R. "Crees, Cree-Assiniboines, and Assiniboines: Interethnic Social Organization on the Far Northern Plains." *Ethnohistory* 21 (1974): 95–122.

Siouan and Caddoan Linguistics. March 1980.

Spicer, Edward H., ed. *Perspectives in American Indian Culture Change*. Chicago: University of Chicago Press, 1961.

Spitzer, Alan B. "The Historical Problem of Generations." *American Historical Review* 78 (1973): 1353–85.

Stevens, Hazard. *The Life of Isaac Ingalls Stevens by His Son Hazard Stevens*. 2 vols. Boston: Houghton Mifflin, 1900.

Stewart, Frank Henderson. *Fundamentals of Age-Group Systems.* New York: Academic Press, 1977.

Sturtevant, William C. "Anthropology, History, and Ethnohistory." In *Introduction to Cultural Anthropology: Essays in the Scope and Methods of the Science of Man,* ed. James A. Clifton. Boston: Houghton Mifflin, 1968.

Tabeau, Pierre-Antoine. *Tabeau's Narrative of Loisel's Expedition to the Upper Missouri.* Ed. Annie Heloise Abel. Norman: University of Oklahoma Press, 1939.

Taylor, Allan R. "The Many Names of the White Clay People." *International Journal of American Linguistics* 49 (1983): 429–34.

Taylor, Theodore W. *American Indian Policy.* Mount Airy, Md.: Lomond, 1983.

Thompson, David. *David Thompson's Narrative, 1784–1812.* Ed. Richard Glover. Toronto: Champlain Society, 1962.

Ubelaker, Douglas H. "The Sources and Methodology for Mooney's Estimates of North American Indian Populations." In *The Native Population of the Americas in 1492,* ed. William M. Denevan. Madison: University of Wisconsin Press, 1976.

Vansina, Jan. *Oral Tradition: A Study in Historical Methodology.* Chicago: Aldine, 1965.

Voget, Fred W. "Adaptation and Cultural Persistence among the Crow Indians of Montana." In *Political Organization of Native North Americans,* ed. Ernest L. Schusky. Washington, D.C.: University Press of America, 1980.

――――. "Crow Sociocultural Groups." In *Acculturation in the Americas: Proceedings and Selected Papers of the XXIX International Congress of Americanists,* ed. Sol Tax. Chicago: University of Chicago Press, 1952.

――――. *The Shoshoni-Crow Sun Dance.* Norman: University of Oklahoma Press, 1984.

Wedel, Mildred Mott, and Raymond J. DeMallie. "The Ethnohistorical Approach in Plains Area Studies." In *Anthropology on the Great Plains,* ed. W. Raymond Wood and Margot Liberty. Lincoln: University of Nebraska Press, 1980.

Wedel, Waldo R. *Prehistoric Man on the Great Plains.* Norman: University of Oklahoma Press, 1961.

Weist, Katherine. "Giving Away: The Ceremonial Distribution of Goods among the Northern Cheyenne of Southeastern Montana." *Plains Anthropologist* 18 (1973): 97–103.

――――. "The Northern Cheyennes: Diversity in a Loosely Structured Society." Ph.D. dissertation, University of California, Berkeley, 1969.

White, Richard. *The Roots of Dependency: Subsistence, Environment, and Social Change among the Choctaws, Pawnees, and Navajos.* Lincoln: University of Nebraska Press, 1983.

White, Robert A. "The Lower-Class 'Culture of Excitement' among the Contemporary Sioux." In *The Modern Sioux: Social Systems and Reservation Culture,* ed. Ethel Nurge. Lincoln: University of Nebraska Press, 1970.

Williams, Gerry C. "Warriors No More: A Study of the American Indian Elderly." In *Aging in Culture and Society,* ed. Christine L. Fry. New York: Bergin, 1980.

Youngkin, S. Douglas. " 'Hostile and Friendly': The 'Pygmalion Effect' at Cheyenne River Agency, 1873–77." *South Dakota History* 7 (1977): 402–21.

Index

Acculturation model, 4–9, 257–58n3, 258n5, 259n9; applied to Fort Belknap, 2, 5–6, 8, 22, 136, 139–40, 234, 243–44

Act of April 15, 1874, 200, 270n76

Aged, status of, 26, 28–29, 33, 37, 43, 74, 78, 82, 90–91, 143, 176–78, 186–87, 193, 282n13

Age grades, 28–30, 54, 56–58, 60, 132, 227, 262–63nn 8, 10, 14–15, 267n55

Age group relations: Assiniboine, 162, 207–12, 215, 217, 241; Gros Ventre, 78–80, 82, 83, 100, 102–3, 107–10, 113, 123, 160, 179, 239, 252. See also Generation gap

Age group system, 13, 21, 28–34, 51–52, 56, 60–61, 246–48, 282n6. See also Aged, status of; Age grades; Age sets; Moieties

Age sets, 29–30, 33, 56, 60

Agriculture, 17, 62–63, 67, 83, 100, 102–4, 124, 136–38

Akaskin, 43

Allotment, 72–74, 83, 90–91, 93, 100, 106, 128, 133, 137–39, 230

Allotment Act of 1921, 91, 101, 108

American Fur Company, 31, 35, 47, 263n15, 266n40

American Indian Movement, 145, 155, 175, 192, 277n6

Annuities, 40, 49, 199, 201, 218

Arapahoe Indians, 13, 45–48, 52, 58–59, 88, 120, 150–51, 153–54, 186, 246–52, 257n1, 258n4, 261n17, 262n14, 265n36, 266n38, 270n80

Archithinue Indians, 41–42, 44–45, 264n28. See also Blackfeet Indian groups; Gros Ventre Indians, names of

Arikara Indians, 257n1

Assimilation. See Acculturation model; Federal government, Indian policy of

Assiniboine Indians, 13, 24, 34–35, 41–42, 48–51, 53–54, 62, 64 (fig.), 65–66, 70–71, 80, 90–94, 96–98, 102–5, 109, 120–24, 126–30, 132–33, 135–40, 149, 156–57, 161–62, 165–66, 168–69, 171–74, 182, 184–85, 189–90, 198, 200–201, 203–6, 217, 222, 229–231, 243, 248–50, 257n1, 258n4, 259n7, 264n28, 267n57, 269n72, 275n137, 279n16, 280nn5–6, 281n8; attitude toward Gros Ventres, 207–9, 212–15, 220–23; bands of, 198–200, 207, 248; Catholicism of, 211, 228; Cree relations with, 13, 24, 41; language used by, 12–13; Lodgepole community of, 208, 211, 228; Lower division of, 67, 70, 139, 155, 200, 212, 218, 231, 280n6; Milk River community of, 14, 127, 161, 208; Northern division of, 70, 91–93, 139, 212, 218–21, 227, 230; religion of, 161, 173, 209–12, 214, 225, 227–28, 234, 239, 241, 280n25, 281n19; Upper division of, 48–49, 70, 92, 139, 199–201, 218–20, 249, 280nn5–6, 281n8. See also Age group relations: Assiniboine; Cultural identity: Assiniboine; Folk history, Assiniboine; Giveaway: Assiniboine; Gros Ventre–Assiniboine relations; Kinship: Assiniboine; Marriage: Assiniboine-

293

Index

Epidemics: measles, 51, 56; smallpox, 34–35, 43, 46, 51, 198, 200, 223, 266n45

Ethnohistorical method, 11–12, 136–39, 260n15

Ethos, Gros Ventre, 21–22, 27, 36–38, 51–52, 55, 72, 99, 131–34, 140. *See also* Competition; Fierceness; Primacy; Prominence

Ewers, John, 26, 40, 198, 282n5

Factionalism approach, 4, 6, 258n6

Fall Indians, 261n17

Fanton, W., 49, 51, 280n6

Feathered Pipe, 27–28, 33–34, 37, 55–56, 59, 65, 75–76, 97–98, 110–13, 123, 134–35, 140, 142, 144, 147–53, 186, 189, 202, 206, 242, 262n12, 263n15, 276n149, 278n12. *See also* Pipe symbolism

Federal government, Indian policy of, 2, 23, 52–54, 61, 66–67, 71–74, 85, 87, 90, 92–105, 107–8, 143, 197, 202, 216–17, 219–26, 228–32, 237, 242; and civilization, 2, 11, 52–54, 62, 132; and detribalization, 98, 104–5; and relocation, 98–99; and termination, 98–100, 103, 107, 251; and trust responsibility, 17–18, 53–54, 71–73, 79–80, 84–85, 89, 91, 100, 138, 231, 235, 251, 271n89

Feed (feast), 185

Feusi, B., 85

Fidler, Peter, 35, 39, 43–44, 46, 265n36

Fields, Edwin, 62

Fierceness, 22, 26–27, 29–30, 34, 41–52, 54–55, 67, 84, 90, 97, 106, 117–19, 132, 134, 143, 187, 202, 242, 267n48. *See also* Primacy; Self-determination

Firearms, 38–39, 42–44, 47–48, 62–63

First Chief, 279n17

Flag: American, 35, 38, 48, 162, 170–73, 175, 279nn16, 21; Fort Belknap, 166, 170

Flag man. *See* Dance committee; Milk River: modern

Flannery, Regina, 27, 36–38, 51–52, 59, 66, 74–76, 78, 84–86, 97–98, 110–11

Flathead Indians, 32, 68, 198

Flat Pipe, 27–28, 33–34, 37, 54–57, 59, 65, 75–76, 97–98, 110–13, 122–23, 134–35, 140, 142, 144, 147–48, 150–51, 153–54, 186, 188–89, 202, 205–6, 237, 242, 262n12, 263n15, 278n10, 278n12. *See also* Pipe symbolism

Fleming, Darrell, 108

Fly Lodge, 29, 56, 267n55

Foley, Michael, 22, 136, 138–39, 244, 282n3

Folk history, 12, 19, 197, 216, 240–41,

Folk history (*cont.*)
245–46, 252, 260n16; Assiniboine, 201, 208–17, 220, 222–24, 230–32, 252; Gros Ventre, 97, 118–19, 127, 135, 140–41, 146–49, 151–53, 165, 175, 188, 190, 201–6, 215, 217–24, 230–32, 252, 279n22

Fools Dance, 94

Forest fire (Little Rockies), 97–98, 148–49, 274n125

Fork, 160

Fork keeper. *See* Grass Dance

Fort Alexander, 39

Fort Alexandria, 43

Fort Assiniboine, 54, 56, 61–63, 67, 201, 212–14, 220

Fort Augustus, 44

Fort Belknap Agency, 49–51, 53, 200–201, 203, 214, 218

Fort Belknap Community Council, 17–18, 96–97, 99, 101–9, 112–13, 115–18, 120–22, 124–25, 127, 133–35, 138

Fort Belknap reservation, 13–18, 53, 67–68, 257n1. *See also* Cultural identity: Fort Belknap; Population: Fort Belknap

Fort Belknap trading post, 33

Fort Benton, 38–39, 49–50, 199, 212

Fort Berthold reservation, 257n1, 258n7, 281n20

Fort Browning, 45, 200

Fort Lewis, 31, 48

Fort McKenzie, 48

Fort Peck Agency, 200, 212–13, 227, 280n6

Fort Peck reservation, 91, 139, 155, 257n1, 275n137

Fort Piegan, 47

Fort Shaw School, 84

Fort Union, 213

Fort Vermilion, 43, 45

Fourth of July celebration, 75, 76 (*fig.*)

Fowler, Loretta, 258n4, 260n13

French-Chippewa Indians, 14, 16, 23, 70, 73, 91–92, 94–95, 97–98, 104, 108, 114, 121–22, 126–28, 130, 133, 135, 139, 148, 205, 207, 218–19, 230, 239, 243, 257n1, 261n21, 270n80, 274n125

Friendly strategy, 226, 282n10

Frog, 87

Full blood category, 125–27, 183

Gauche, 48; band of, 199

Geertz, Clifford, 9–10

General, The, 31, 35

Generation: definition of, 19, 141; born 1825–64, 146, 155, 158–60, 278n12; born 1865–94, 142, 146, 151, 155, 158, 160, 278n12. *See also* Elder generation; Youth generation

Library of Congress Cataloging-in-Publication Data

Fowler, Loretta, 1944–
    Shared symbols, contested meanings.

    Includes index.
    1. Atsina Indians—History. 2. Atsina Indians—Social
life and customs. 3. Assiniboine Indians—History.
4. Assiniboine Indians—Social life and customs.
5. Indians of North America—Great Plains—History.
6. Indians of North America—Great Plains—Social life
and customs. I. Title.
E99.A87F69   978′.00497   86–47976
ISBN 0–8014–1878–X (alk. paper)
ISBN 0–8014–9450–8 (pbk. : alk. paper)

www.ingramcontent.com/pod-product-compliance
Lightning Source LLC
Chambersburg PA
CBHW030640270326
41929CB00007B/150